THE SCOPE OF ANTHROPOLOGY

Methodology and History in Anthropology

General Editor: David Parkin, Fellow of All Souls College, Oxford

Just as anthropology has had a significant influence on many other disciplines in recent years, so too have its methods been challenged by new intellectual and technical developments. This series is designed to offer a forum for debate on the interrelationship between anthropology and other academic fields but also on the challenge that new intellectual and technological developments pose to anthropological methods, and the role of anthropological thought in a general history of concepts.

THE SCOPE OF ANTHROPOLOGY

Maurice Godelier's Work in Context

Edited by
Laurent Dousset and Serge Tcherkézoff

berghahn
NEW YORK · OXFORD
www.berghahnbooks.com

First published in 2012 by

Berghahn Books
www.berghahnbooks.com

Library of Congress Cataloging-in-Publication Data
The scope of anthropology : Maurice Godelier's Work in Context / edited by
Laurent Dousset and Serge Tcherkézoff. -- 1st ed.
    p. cm. -- (Methodology and history in anthropology v.23)
    Includes bibliographical references and index.
    ISBN 978-0-85745-331-0 (hardcover : alk. paper) -- ISBN 978-1-78238-
532-5 (paperback: alk. paper) – ISBN 978-0-85745-332-7 (ebook)
    1. Ethnology--Philosophy. 2. Ethnology--Methodology. 3. Ethnology--
Melanesia. 4. Big man (Melanesia) 5. Godelier, Maurice. I. Dousset, Laurent.
II. Tcherkézoff, Serge.
    GN345.S39 2012
    306.01--dc23

                                                            2011037635

British Library Cataloguing in Publication Data
A catalogue record for this book is available from the British Library

Printed on acid-free paper

ISBN: 978-0-85745-331-0 hardback
ISBN: 978-1-78238-532-5 paperback
ISBN: 978-0-85745-332-7 ebook

CONTENTS

LIST OF FIGURES AND TABLES

Figures

Tables

INTRODUCTION

Laurent Dousset and Serge Tcherkézoff

'From initiation rituals in Papua New Guinea to the Twin Towers': this is how Maurice Godelier (2008b) summarizes the anthropological project and its remit, the scope of anthropology. Hegel's declaration that 'nothing that is human is foreign to me' is both apt and applied in practice, simultaneously tracing the purpose of a scientific programme and the curves of a personal trajectory. More than a simple assertion that the human being is a social animal, Maurice Godelier's work is guided by the precept that the human being has to actively produce society in order to live. It is a condition of existence. The intellectual path of a man who has taught several generations of anthropologists evinces both the broad ambitions of anthropology as a science of universal significance and a view of social reality as a tangible and, in principle, an intelligible set of facts. The practice of the social sciences reveals a constant dialectic between ethnography and theory, the particular and the general, the local and the global, the diversity of facts and their unification in anthropological analysis. The relentless intellectual movement between the acknowledgement of the particularistic nature of the local and the general scientific project it advances is a constant feature of Maurice Godelier's corpus. Such a project is feasible only if knowledge is progressively accumulated, if the theoretical apparatus is part of a developing paradigmatic choice, if schools of thought and their epistemological frameworks are non-dogmatic. Students of Maurice Godelier have heard him say, on many occasions, that one needs to be capable of using the ideas and concepts that generate understanding, irrespective of any loyalty towards a particular intellectual guide. The above is and has been Maurice Godelier's approach ever since he began to practice anthropology: Godelier in a nutshell, so to speak. As he is one of the most prominent and influential French anthropologists, both in and outside France, the present volume was written with two objectives in mind: to pay tribute to a scholar for whom the social sciences in general and anthropology in particular have a purpose and follow a rationale, and to demonstrate, according to Godelier's own premises, that through the diversity of approaches, fields and domains, the scope of anthropology is concerned with the intelligibility of social forms and transformations.

Godelier was born on 28 February 1934 in Cambrai, northern France; his modest family background hardly provided the conditions necessary for him to become, as a young man, the assistant of the historian Fernand Braudel at the Ecole Pratique des Hautes Etudes, and later the assistant of Claude Lévi-Strauss at the Collège de France. A few contingencies, as he himself calls them, contributed to his intellectual emancipation. Having been spotted as a brilliant pupil, he gained entrance to the local catholic school which his parents could not have afforded without the priests' help.

Two events that occurred during his school years seem to have marked his later life and work. First, his encounter with a Polish priest which opened his mind to contemporary art – in particular surrealism and cubism – and to the way it reconfigures or restructures recognizable elements into a different phenomenology; and, secondly, that with a young communist who gave him the confidential address of a bookshop in Paris that sold Marxist books. These events were crucial since, as we will see in the following chapters, while Maurice Godelier applied materialist theory to his anthropological work, he also promulgated a form of Marxism that was not mainstream, one in which the structural transformations of systems became central, and in which structuralism and Marxism coexist as combined methods of investigation.

Indeed, he became friends with Michel Foucault, whose lectures on psychiatry he was following, but turned his back on the kind of materialism that Foucault and others, such as Louis Althusser, were developing at the time and which proclaimed the death of the subject. Similar reasons distanced him from Louis Dumont in later years, at least the Louis Dumont of *Homo hierachicus* (1967). Dumont sometimes opposed too sharply individualistic societies to holistic societies, while for Godelier the individualistic attitude in Western society is precisely what constitutes its holistic character.

Rather, he turned his interest towards scholars who were analysing concrete historical and social facts in a structural way, but integrating the materialist approach when addressing the social transformations of these structural systems. They included, among others, Jean-Pierre Vernant (e.g. 1962), a historian and anthropologist specializing in ancient Greece and developing a structuralist approach to Greek mythology and society; Jacques Gernet (e.g. 1972), whose work on Chinese civilization had been groundbreaking; or Paul Garelli (e.g. 1969), a scholar of Assyrian history. As Descola, Hamel and Lemonnier explain (1999: 8), through the analysis of the principles of causality, Godelier endeavoured to graft a physiological structure onto Lévi-Straussian structural morphology. The analytical separation between infrastructure and superstructure is not systematically reflected in a distinction of social institutions but, in many societies, coexists in one and the same social institution, such as kinship, in which functions or causalities are embedded and overlap. Godelier particularly crystallized this approach in his two volumes of *Horizon, trajets marxistes en anthropologie*, originally published in 1973, and his *L'idéel et le matériel*, published in 1984.

The theoretical and methodological framework that he had developed was applied to the study of the Baruya people of Papua New Guinea where he did several years of fieldwork. Although he was later celebrated for his work among the Baruya, thus creating favourable conditions for opening up French anthropology to Anglophone colleagues, as at the time Papua New Guinea was a field dominated by British and American anthropologists, the choice of Papua New Guinea was not made without some hesitation.

Indeed, while he was Lévi-Strauss's assistant, he first spent a year in Mali where, under the auspices of UNESCO, his project was to analyse the impact of a controlled state economy on village economy. Godelier soon realized that there was a ministry for economic planning in Mali, but that there was no economic plan. His project became, as he terms it, a project without a subject, and he used the time in Mali to read and work on the literature of economic anthropology, which resulted in 1965 in the publication in the journal *L'Homme* of his first major article, nearly sixty pages long: *Objet et méthodes de l'anthropologie économique*. Before 1965, he had written a few papers on economic anthropology (see the bibliography at the end of the volume), a field largely neglected in French universities and research centres, where studies on kinship and religion had dominated the scene since Lévi-Strauss's *Structures élémentaires de la parenté* (1947). This paper, however, would mark him as an anthropologist with a particular approach, and strengthen a new field in French anthropology: the study of non-Western economic systems. As the title of his article indicates, there is only one object of study in economic anthropology, but there are multiple and complementary methods. The very first paragraph provides insights into what has become the objective of several years, if not decades, of Godelier's work:

> L'anthropologie économique a pour objet l'analyse théorique comparée des différents systèmes économiques réels et possibles. Pour élaborer

cette théorie, elle tire sa matière des informations concrètes fournies
par l'historien et l'ethnologue sur le fonctionnement et l'évolution des
sociétés qu'ils étudient. A côté de l''économie politique' vouée, semble-t-
il, à l'étude des sociétés industrielles modernes, marchandes ou planifiées,
l'anthropologie économique se veut en quelque sorte comme 1''extension'
de l'économie politique aux sociétés abandonnées de l'économiste. ... Ainsi
par son projet, l'anthropologie économique prend à sa charge l'élaboration
d'une théorie générale des diverses formes sociales de l'activité économique
de l'homme car l'analyse comparée devrait nécessairement déboucher un
jour sur des connaissances anthropologiques générales (1965: 32).[1]

Going against the materialist mainstream and political economy of
the time, Godelier concludes in this paper that there is no absolute
economic rationality. Rationality itself is a social and historical
concept. Similarly, there is no rationality that can be phrased in
economic terms alone. In fact, the notion of rationality is very close
to the analysis of the foundations of the structures of social life and
the causalities of these structures' transformations. Hence, if there is
rationality, it is not vested in the individual or the nature of the human
being, but lies within the conscious and unconscious aspects of social
relationships (also see Godelier 1966).

Therefore – and contrary to the dogmatic Marxist approaches
that others had promulgated – the idea of a linear evolution in which
societies and their economic systems evolve in mechanical ways
from one step to the next had to be abandoned, even from a Marxist
perspective: evolution is, if anything, multi-linear. The economic
anthropology that Godelier proposed was thus quite distinct from what
might have been expected from a Marxist point of view: economic
systems are embedded in other social structures such as kinship,
politics or religion; infrastructure and superstructure coexist in the
same social institution; rationality is not an absolute concept, nor is
it a human characteristic; it is the expression of social relationships.
In other words, there is no purely economic domain in social life;
there are only methods that crystallize the economic domain in an
analytically comprehensive way.

It was only after the publication of this article that he prepared
his fieldwork in Papua New Guinea, fieldwork that later became
the grounds for intense exchanges between Francophone and
Anglophone anthropologists. It was Lévi-Strauss who suggested that
Maurice Godelier should work in Papua New Guinea rather than in
Latin America which, following Alfred Metraux's advice, had been his
original intention. Because of the research already undertaken in this
region of the world by Anglophone anthropologists, Maurice Godelier
soon encountered Edmund Leach, Jack Goody, Andrew and Marilyn
Strathern and others, and engaged with a whole new network of

scholars. With the move away from Africanist or Latin American studies, where he could have easily evolved without becoming involved with British and American anthropology, he was soon part of exchanges of ideas and theories that went beyond the French context.

His work among the Baruya was groundbreaking, and his monograph *La production des Grands Hommes* (1982b) still remains one of his favourite works. In his previous publications, he suggested methodological and theoretical approaches to the analysis of the relationship between ideology and political economy in classless societies. 'With the publication of *La Production des Grands Hommes* this anthropology shows its full strength' in the study of an actual classless society, Alexander Alland writes in a review (1983).

In the light of Godelier's innovative multi-methodological and multilevel approach to socio-economic systems, in which infrastructure and superstructure are embedded in identical social institutions and structures within classless societies, Philippe Descola, Jacques Hamel and Pierre Lemonnier published a tribute in an important volume in 1999, unfortunately only available in French: *La production du social: Autour de Maurice Godelier.* This is a collection of papers originally presented at a conference held in Cerisy-la-Salle in 1996. The volume tackled important issues arising from Godelier's work: discussions of Marxist approaches to the social fact and to evolution (Godelier 1973); illustrations and analyses of the relationships between the *idéel* (sometimes translated as the 'mental') and the material (Godelier 1984); the consideration of Godelier's contributions to Papua New Guinea ethnography (Godelier 1982a); the analysis of his work on the uses and conceptions of the human body, sexuality or gender (Godelier and Panoff 1998); and his contributions in the domain of psychoanalysis and ethno-psychoanalysis (Godelier and Hassoun 1996).

The present volume attempts to go beyond *La production du social* in the form of a contribution to the question Maurice Godelier addresses in his latest book, *Au fondement des sociétés humaines: Ce que nous apprend l'anthropologie* (2007), and which inspired its title: what is the scope of anthropology? Literally translated, the title suggests a reinvigoration of the social sciences in a contemporary setting: 'the foundations of human societies: what we can learn from anthropology'. 'It is evidently not on nuclear physics nor molecular biology nor the neurosciences that one can rely to understand the opposition that has dominated Islam for centuries, that between Sunnites and Shiites', Godelier (2007: 222) writes in his conclusion. 'Only the social sciences can achieve this task' (idem). Anthropology has the scope to engage with the world, past and present, as it is, and with all its diverse social and cultural forms and their transformations. It can 'analyse and understand the conditions of appearance and of disappearance of the various ways of organizing life in society, of the various ways of thinking and acting, which are the roots of the diversity of the known forms of individual and collective identities' (idem). Godelier thus goes back to his own origins, albeit more explicitly: societies are systems and have structures that undergo transformations that only the historical and anthropological sciences can explain. More than ever before, the answers produced by anthropology as a collective enterprise are relevant in understanding the contemporary world.

In this sense, Maurice Godelier's programme is resoundingly positive and this volume will illustrate that we believe he has made the right choice. The social sciences are able to communicate about the world as it appears: nothing that is human is foreign. They are able to understand particular phenomena while providing explanations that transcend the local lens. 'My position is clear', he writes in the introduction, 'the crisis of anthropology and of the social sciences, far from announcing, by way of deconstructions, their disappearance, or more simply their dissolution into the soft forms of "cultural studies", is in fact a necessary passage to achieving a reconstruction at a level of rigour and critical vigilance that did not exist in the preceding steps of their development' (2007: 10). The present volume shows that the richness and diversity of anthropological fields of investigation are not synonyms for confusion or for a total incapacity to make any kind of generalization. It demonstrates that, despite the particularity of individual questions asked and specific phenomena studied, anthropology is an organized, collective and productive enterprise. Let us now turn to more detailed considerations.

The Enigma of the Gift (1999), first published in French in 1996, is an important step in Maurice Godelier's more recent trajectory. While he had already been combining materialist and structuralist approaches in his previous work, in this book he elaborates a significant theoretical shift which enables clarifications of local ethnographic structures and practices, while simultaneously crystallizing what appear to be general features of the social order and its reproduction. This shift, epitomized by the *Enigma of the Gift*, is a central focus for many chapters in the present volume. Maurice Godelier's work displays a continuity with respect to the centrality of the material aspects of social reproduction. *L'Idéel et le Matériel* (1984) had already foreshadowed what would become a major theoretical contribution to our understanding of the concept of society and its reproduction in time and space. But *The Enigma of the Gift* and the two volumes published thereafter – (*Metamorphoses de la parenté* in 2004 and *Au fondement des sociétés humaines* in 2007) – can and should be considered as marking a new era in his anthropological thinking. It marks a move from the analysis of the means of production, be they material or immaterial, to that of the symbolic and imaginary orders that control and reproduce these means. The politico-religious domain constitutes the centrality of social structure since, as Maurice Godelier has advocated for years, it is not sufficient that institutions of control and domination exist. It is also necessary that people who are dominated and controlled accept these institutions.

The *Enigma of the Gift* reconsidered a problem that had occupied anthropology from its early days, most visibly in the work of Marcel Mauss: the structure and nature of exchange as constitutive of the social order, and the attributes of the things that are exchanged as constitutive of the social individual. The domain of exchange as a systemic practice offers two important epistemological points of entry into the social order. First, it is organized by accepted and shared systems of values and codes of practices and as such is one of the most visible aspects of social reproduction. However, it also ties persons organically to things (and things to persons) and to other persons, bridging in an overt manner the erroneous dichotomy between the collective and the individual and between persons and things. Marcel Mauss observed how people or parts thereof remain in the things that are exchanged (or given). Marilyn Strathern's theorization of the partible person or the dividual explicitly elaborates this insight (e.g. Strathern 1988, Mosko 1992).

The second epistemological opportunity afforded by a focus on exchange is the potential to combine structuralist and materialist approaches. While the objects exchanged are evidently the consequences of a particular type of organization of the means of production, and while the social and material values that underpin exchange provide for the organization of these means, exchange is also, from a structural point of view, the elementary condition for the substantiation of the social: in the exchange of people in marriage, of goods and of words. Whether one adopts a materialist or a structuralist approach, exchange reveals itself as more than a mere social practice. It is constitutive, a precondition, of the capacity of the social to reproduce itself in time and space. In the light of these epistemological opportunities it is no surprise that, through the *Enigma of the Gift*, Maurice Godelier reopens the question of exchange in general, and of a specific type of exchange, the gift, in particular. This is no surprise either when we consider how earlier in his career, he had already distinguished himself from other French Marxists, such as Althusser, through the combination and conjunction of Marxist and structuralist concepts and approaches, as Jonathan Friedman explains in his chapter of this volume.

After Marcel Mauss (1923–24), Claude Lévi-Strauss (1950), Annette Weiner (1992) and many others, Maurice Godelier thus re-examines the question of the gift and of exchange in general and observes two main characteristics. First, he notes the existence of non-competitive forms of gifts and counter-gifts that seem to challenge the central idea according to which material exchanges seem to be structured. The general expectation of the equivalence of values, between the things given and those returned, is confounded. His second major observation is that certain things, in particular those considered active in the religious domain, are not given. Maurice Godelier thus conceives a new typology of objects in particular and of exchange in general. First, there are objects that are alienable and alienated as merchandise; second objects that are given and thus alienated but which remain in part inalienable since some parts of the giver remain embedded in the thing given; and, finally, objects that may not be given nor sold, but that need to be kept. This is the case with sacred objects or, as in Western societies, to use Godelier's own example, the constitution of democratic regimes. Following Annette Weiner (1992), Godelier highlights how the tendency to give is inseparable from the tendency to keep. The drive to give structures the social field, while the drive to keep is a condition for the reproduction of the social order.

What is significant in the reproduction of this order is the centrality of the inalienable and its structuring capacity, as Polly Wiessner shows in her chapter in this volume. Two of Godelier's major propositions must be combined to understand the theoretical consequences of the centrality of the inalienable. First of all is the necessity for humans to fabricate structured societies in order to live. It is a condition for existence. Secondly, there is a need to elaborate fixed points, what Wiessner calls 'centres', around which the reproduction of structured societies takes place. The inalienable, what can neither be given nor exchanged but which needs to be kept and transmitted, constitute these fixed points, these 'centres' of the most sacred. The transmission of the inalienable is embedded in ritual practices and is the scope of religion as such. We are here, as already foreshadowed, witnessing a considerable transition in the thinking of Maurice Godelier: a transition from a stress on infrastructure in its material and immaterial aspects as the engine of social structure, towards an approach in which the political and the religious constitute the foundation of the fabric of social life and structure. This important shift was to be refined by Godelier in his *Metamorphoses de la parenté* and *Au fondement des sociétés humaines*, as we will see below.

In the first two chapters of this volume, Joel Robbins and John Barker both further this analysis of the inalienable, of what can only be transmitted. The former highlights the notion of 'culturally enjoined secrecy' or 'secrecy as a value' while the latter focuses on the 'conjuncture of structures'. Robbins accentuates the equivalence that Godelier proposes between the inalienable, the sacred and the 'centre', by adding the 'secret', as an intimate part of the reproduction of the social order. Godelier had previously underlined the importance of the secret-sacred relationship, particularly when analysing masculine ritual initiations among the Baruya of Papua New Guinea (see also Herdt 1999). Robbins goes further, suggesting that the secret is necessary 'in order to keep the world going' in the eyes of Urapmin people.

In his chapter, Robbins demonstrates how Urapmin language ideology reinscribes the model of society as being constituted of three levels of structural exchange as Lévi-Strauss proposed; of goods, women and words. However, he then subverts this articulation of elementary structures by drawing on Godelier's work on the crucial role of the act of keeping in the construction and reproduction of society.

Joel Robbins thus broadens the domain of analysis of the *Enigma of the Gift* and includes the study of 'language as ideology', one of the topics which structuralism, even though it was on its programme, largely neglected. 'A language ideology is a society's set of ideas about what language is and how communication works', Robbins explains, and, putting it in Godelier's terms, suggests that through the study of language ideology it is possible to analyse the exchange of words as constituted in a given society's imaginary. Indeed, according to Godelier, the sacred conceals something from the collective and individual consciousness, it is opaque, secret and hence withheld from the general system of exchange and giving. Robbins draws a structural analogy to Godelier's relationship between things that are given and those that are kept within the domain of language ideology. He makes two general observations. First, Westerners are determined to give intentions away but keen to keep as many material goods as they can for themselves. Second, Urapmin people, on the other hand, are determined to keep their thoughts to themselves, but give away most of the goods that come to their hands. The importance of secrecy in the Melanesian world can hence be interpreted in terms of broader understandings of exchange. When it comes to the exchange of words, Urapmin people stress what is not given, what is not spoken or muted almost exclusively, thus highlighting the value of withholding words in verbal exchange.

While Joel Robbins, through his analysis of Urapmin language ideology, reinforces the proposition that the inalienable is central in social reproduction, Polly Wiessner and John Barker confirm this rather through a negative proof: the social consequences encountered when the inalienable – centres and fixed points, the sacred and secret – is in danger of being significantly transformed or even destroyed. They depict two divergent consequences when the inalienable is endangered, in particular through Christianization and modernization. Polly Wiessner depicts semantic and symbolic transformations engendering displacements and even dilution of the centre among the Enga of the Papua New Guinea Highlands. John Barker, on the other hand, observes among the Maisin of Papua New Guinea a 'conjuncture of structures', a concept proposed by Sahlins (1985). Linking the centrality of exchange to another important aspect of Godelier's work – the delineation of political systems centred on great men (Godelier 1986) – Barker traces the historical and cultural roots of contemporary 'great men' leaders amongst the Maisin through the analysis of the relationship between inalienable objects and the imaginary.

Indeed, when the Maisin speak of 'tradition', they are referring precisely to exchanges and the values that underlie them, drawing an implied contrast with European stinginess and individualism (similarly to what Joel Robbins in his chapter discerns as the difference between the intention of giving and actual giving). The Maisin's perception of what they consider as the inalienable (and thus not give-able) part of their culture is rather explicit. Indeed, tradition marks items that lie outside the range of ordinary exchange and includes stories and non-discursive objects called *kikiki* that John Barker translates as 'heritage'. This chapter investigates, precisely, how contact with the Western world caused potential transformations in the identification of these non-exchangeable and thus culturally central elements.

The pre-contact Maisin had a system close to that of great men systems, 'based on distinct spheres of difference rather than based upon a common measure'. While we will reconsider the definition of the great men type of leadership, in particular through Margaret Jolly's and Mark Mosko's chapters, let us for the moment simply mention that John Barker reports the two most prominent leaders as being the peace chiefs and the war chiefs. The Maisin also had two types of ranked clans, the Kawo and the Sabu. Their relationship was asymmetrical. The Sabu were 'lower' and had to show respect to the 'higher' ranked Kawo who, on the other hand, had to look after and provide advice to the Sabu. The distinction between these two types of clans also determined the type of leader a man might become. The opportunity for a man to become a leader, however, also largely rested on his ability and on circumstances, a feature which is also central to the argument of Mark Mosko's chapter on the Mekeo. Many leaders in fact came from the 'lower' Sabu clans. The apparent contradiction between the hierarchy of clans and the capacity for members of the lower clans to become leaders is explained by John Barker by the strong preference for restricted and balanced exchanges, for example in the preference for sibling exchange in marriage, which thus reorganized individual and political agencies among the two clans.

An important question thus arises about the continuity of this structural organization based on asymmetrical and symmetrical exchange apropos inalienable verbal and non-verbal objects when the Maisin experienced Christianization and broader contact with the Western world. Polly Wiessner describes a story of destruction for the Enga. John Barker, however, observes among the Maisin the encounter of two systems which are mutually intelligible. He does not perceive Christianity as a continuation of the existing Maisin systems, nor does he describe a story of destruction or of systemic resistance. He rather speaks of a 'conjuncture of structures'.

The Maisin have experienced a gradual conversion by a rather tolerant mission. Missionaries brought the '*giu*', Christian knowledge as conveyed in worship services, sermons and the Bible. In return, converts listened respectfully to the missionaries and the teachers. In other words, there is a structural analogy in the relationship between Kawo and Sabu clans around *kikiki*, the inalienable objects, and between missionaries and converts around '*giu*', the inalienable centre of Christian religion. Drawing both from Godelier's insights on exchange systems and the inalienable, and from analyses of great men systems, John Barker confirms that the transition to competitive types of leaders, such as big men and nascent capitalists, is by no means automatic. The underlying principle seems to remain unaltered and intelligible: 'a hierarchical exchange partnership defined by inalienable objects that promised a transcendence of obligation and a "heaven" of equality', to quote Barker (this volume).

The situation of the Enga, though also in Papua New Guinea, is different in many respects. Like Joel Robbins and John Barker, Polly Wiessner situates the core cultural features in the inalienable. However, Wiessner tells us a story of destruction, asking what happens to marriage and alliance, descent, cooperation and exchange when the inalienable is dismantled. Following Annette Weiner, Godelier (2005) proposed that no society can survive over time if there are no fixed points, the inalienable. He underlined the importance of religion and politics rather than of alliance and descent in structuring society, a point to which he returned in his *Métamorphoses de la parenté*. There, one of his important conclusions was that nowhere are a woman and a man sufficient to create a new human being since everywhere religious, spiritual or imaginary forces are necessary for individual and social reproduction. Kinship is thus subject to religious and political imaginaries that pervade the social body and enable the reproduction and transmission of the inalienable.

Considering such conclusions, Polly Wiessner asks what happens when the centre, the inalienable, the sacred (and the secret in Joel Robbins' view) does not hold. In Enga society, as elsewhere, the inalienable is definitely gendered. Men have inalienable rights through birth to clan membership, rights to land and affiliation with their maternal kin. Unlike the Baruya studied by Godelier, 'power was acquired by managing wealth and not by handling sacred objects or administering secret spells and rites' (this volume). On the other hand, women's inalienable inherited rights were few and were limited to support from maternal kin. However, women had considerable rights and powers in accepting or rejecting a potential bride, since they had to be asked for their consent. An important point in understanding how Christianization had such a destructive effect on the inalienable of Enga society is thus its relationship to gender. It was a relationship dominated by separation, in which, as Wiessner explains, the ideology highlighted public roles for men and private roles for women (but see Margaret Jolly's chapter in this volume, and Strathern 1988). The basis for this distinction and strong separation rested on the fear of contamination by menstrual blood and other feminine influences that would inhibit the physical and mental maturation of men.

The first pillar of Enga society, as Wiessner explains, was dismantled when a clan's sacred ancestral stones and objects were destroyed or relegated to cultural shows. The second pillar, gender segregation, was dissolved when missions downplayed the power of menstrual blood and boys and girls started interacting on a regular and daily basis (see Meggitt 1989). The third pillar was destroyed between 1960 and 2008, when activities that united male clan members diminished, thus eroding the clan structure. The destruction or displacement of inalienable objects, the end of gender segregation and the unity of male clan members were, according to Wiessner, the three principal steps in decentring the inalienable and prohibiting the reproduction of the group as an entity sharing inherited values.

The breaking down of these three pillars is particularly visible in Wiessner's analysis of marriage practices and patterns. There was a considerable decline in arranged marriages which were connected to the structuring of the clans and access to land and an increase in people's own choices of marriage partners. More than forty per cent of women explain that they had been courting, fell in love, and decided to marry with or without parental consent. In only ten per cent of the cases did parents and relatives arrange marriages and their daughters comply. Wiessner also observes a considerable increase in divorces. Both are associated with the weakening of the father-son relationship, as sons are increasingly seeking land from their maternal uncles rather than from their paternal clans. Over the next decades, the author believes, these new associations to land – due to the weakening of father-son relationship, which is itself a consequence of new marriage choices and increased divorces – will induce a shift from a strong patrilineal and patrilocal society to a cognatic one. When fixed points are fragmented, uncertainty arises. For the present, it is only maternal kinship that remains stable and inalienable.

Several issues arise from these analyses. The first is the centrality of the inalienable in structuring the coherence of social formations and reproduction. These are objects or verbal forms that cannot be given, but can only be transmitted. They constitute the pillars of society and are in many, if not all, cases sacred, and often simultaneously secret. Christianization and Westernization have produced several types of reactions. In some, as in Barker's example of the Maisin, the local context allowed for a structural transposition of the foreign imaginary into local patterns of exchange and hierarchy. In other cases, as seen in Wiessner's discussion of the Enga, Westernization has, through transformations in the inalienable itself, created dramatic social change. Other concerns have been revealed as central to the reproduction and the transmission of the inalienable, concerns prevalent in both Godelier's Baruya ethnography and his broader Pacific anthropology: rank or hierarchy, gender and secrecy.

Godelier has repeatedly underlined how gender inequalities among the Baruya were linked to a system of social hierarchy (among men) and expressed through rituals of secrecy, of gendered separations and the transmission of the inalienable, reproducing a culture of men in sacred and secret activities and places. Among the Baruya, male domination is the most visible and fundamental basis for social organization and cultural reality (Godelier 1982b). Moreover, social reproduction is here intimately linked to sexual and homosexual activities and their control. As Gilbert Herdt explains in his chapter, Godelier identified the role of men's houses as pivotal in understanding the development of sex roles and the male psyche in particular. The male domination of the social and the human body, Herdt (1999) observed for the Sambia, was implied in the material aspects of production, but more importantly in ritual activities, and in particular those rituals that inscribe a gender onto the body. According to Sambia mythology, originary human bodies were hermaphroditic and it was only repeated rituals of insemination that endowed bodies with their masculine or feminine form. Social hierarchy or domination, the construction of gender and sex and the transmission of the inalienable are thus inseparably connected.

Herdt also notes, however, that the role of sex in the creative production of culture and social reality has been less understood, even though sexology studies have considerably improved in methodology and epistemology due to the influence of anthropology which is well suited to 'conceptualize these total systems of meanings, knowledge and practices' in which sexual practices are embedded (Herdt, this volume). What is still lacking is a constructive and interdisciplinary dialogue between the social sciences and the other ('natural') sciences with respect to a global understanding of the role of sex in social structure and practice.

Indeed, Herdt distinguishes two pivotal epochs in the history of sexology studies which he calls the 'before' and 'after' the Cascais conference of 1993. Here he tries to bridge the gap between the approaches of natural sciences interested in universal features of individual sexual behaviour and practice, and the social sciences which concentrated on the cultural aspects of such patterns. By default in the early days, sexologists treated sexuality as part of nature, but not as natural, since they were typically interested in the abnormal. They understood abnormal sexuality as a disease phenomenon located in individual, rather than social bodies. After the Cascais conference, however, there has been increasing research on sexual culture and life ways, addressing both the cultural and individual dimensions of the sexual.

In *Au Fondement des sociétés humaines*, Maurice Godelier advocates the renewal and reconstruction of anthropology as a science with even more rigour than before. Gilbert Herdt is among those contributors who identify explicitly the renewed scope of anthropology, in his case an increased understanding of sexuality as a multifaceted and multidimensional array of practices and structures. Concepts of 'sexual culture' with less discernible lines between the 'biological' and the 'cultural', sexual diversity, sexuality and human rights, the disruptive impact of migrations upon the sexual and social order, and an increased attention to transgender and complex subjectivities and emergent socialities, are all key to an understanding of the regulation of sexual behaviour which, as we have seen for the Baruya, is central in the reproduction and transmission of the inalienable. Complex subjectivities and emergent socialities are now, as Jonathan Friedman shows in his chapter, linked to the generalized cultural pluralism of different identities, albeit ethnic, religious or territorial. Culture undergoes a transformation from a structure of existence to a mere role set: the individual can practise culture, like sex, by choice (Friedman, this volume).

At least two aspects of social structure surround if not underpin the articulation of the inalienable with the sacred and the secret: gender and political structure. In these processes, at least among the several Papua New Guinean societies discussed in this volume, sexuality plays a central role in the embodiment of gender and domination or hierarchy. Herdt's chapter offers an overview of the important facets that need to be addressed in the realm of sexology in order to further understand the importance of sexual behaviour and representation in the reproduction of the social order. Gender and rank are organically linked but in a historically complex and non-exclusive way, as Margaret Jolly demonstrates in her chapter on Vanuatu. Christianization and Westernization have also had important consequences on the shift or dismantling of the centre, of the inalienable, as we have seen with Wiessner and Barker. In Vanuatu, the situation is rather complex since, according to some researchers, missions have introduced a new model of gender and rank while for others Christianization has built upon pre-existing forms of domination. Margaret Jolly discusses these issues: 'the historical transformations of rank in northern Vanuatu, the changing gendered configurations of rank and power and the central importance of Christianities in such transformations'.

Developing her earlier arguments which saw 'graded societies' not as unchanging institutions or as eternal manifestations of male *kastom* (heritage, tradition) but as diverse and dynamic processes of rank and power, responsive to, and constitutive of, indigenous histories, she critically discusses three recent contributions, all relevant to the question of rank and gender in North Vanuatu: John Taylor (2008), Lissant Bolton (2003) and Annelin Eriksen (2008). In Jolly's opinion, Eriksen's analysis is very rich but slightly problematic. According to the latter, graded society and church appear as alternative social models: graded societies are supposedly male dominated, hierarchical, and produce big men, while the church produces a 'feminine' community. Margaret Jolly takes another point of view and suggests that there is no, or a different type of, conjuncture of structures in this case, and that women were and are far more implicated in processes of rank-taking and *kastom*. Far from producing only feminine forms of 'communities', the Church has embodied contexts in which individualist, hierarchical and masculine forms have prevailed as well.

Other ethnographies, including Jolly's own, differ from Eriksen's hypothesis with respect to the gender-rank relationship in Vanuatu. Taylor (2008), for example, shows that male and female rank-taking are distinct processes, but remain critically and inalienably linked. Bolton (2003) demonstrates that *kastom* does not embody a social semantic that is only linked to masculine culture. She suggests that where *kastom* is used in a national discourse, women tend to be excluded from it. In everyday practice, however, men and women's *kastom* are far more blurred and are in some cases undistinguishable. There were

segregations between men and women, and the Church did attempt
to undo some of these separations, as was the case with the Enga as
described by Wiessner (this volume). In fact, however, it introduced
novel forms of segregations through a distinction of the female-
domestic and male-public domains. Margaret Jolly starts her analysis
with a report of a visit to the Musée du Quai Branly in Paris, where a
display on men's houses and figures of ancestral powers reveals the
unproblematized and simultaneous relationship between masculinity,
tradition and power: material elements substantiating masculinity
and domination, two elements that, as we have seen earlier, seem to be
at first sight those that underpin the reproduction and transmission
of the inalienable. Let us remember Wiessner's chapter, where women
had few inalienable rights, only support from the maternal kin and
the possibility to reject a proposed marriage partner, and Godelier's
work on Baruya initiations, where boys had to become men through
the acquisition of the secret and sacred character of the inalienable.
Margaret Jolly's chapter shows that, at least in Vanuatu, these are not
such tightly enclosed worlds: while genders are distinguished, both
women and men had different but related procedures for taking rank.

As Margaret Jolly recalls, Godelier (1978a, 1978b, 1984) refined
some of the fundamental notions of Marxist theory, asking if the '*idéel*'
was part of infrastructure, and thus prefiguring much later Melanesian
ethnography where objects are understood as materializations of
relations. What appear to be masculine objects do not represent
men as such, but are the material aspects of relationships, including
those between genders, that crystallize in modes of exchange or
non-exchange (see Strathern 1988). Goods and services materialize
in exchange systems, while inalienable objects and words appear in
non-exchange systems. In *The Making of Great Men* (1986), Maurice
Godelier had already prefigured this essential distinction, but he then
concentrated on what is exchanged (rather than kept) and focused his
research on the relationship between indigenous forms of leaderships
and varying modes of exchanges.

Mark Mosko's chapter reconsiders this important question. If the
inalienable, the sacred and secret constitutes the purpose of social
reproduction and is tied to politico-religious leaderships (or rank as in
Jolly's chapter), then it is necessary to analyse how these leaderships
are influenced by relationships produced by the exchanges of
alienable objects. In other words, leadership is to some extent the link
between the inalienable and the alienable. It concerns the question
of the 'personifications of power', to reuse the subtitle of the volume
published by Maurice Godelier and Marilyn Strathern in 1991.
Margaret Jolly (this volume) recalls the distinction between systems
of 'great men' and 'big men' as being based on two distinct systems

of exchange and of power and control. In 'great men' systems, where leaders are warriors, shamans, initiation leaders etc., these did not rely on the strategic accumulation of wealth, but on inherited ancestral powers within a ritual economy focused on male initiations. In 'big men' systems, on the other hand, leaders relied on the strategic accumulation of wealth and competition in ceremonial exchanges. In 'great men' systems, people can be exchanged only for people, such as in marriage; however, in 'big men' systems, things can stand for people, such as in transactions of bridewealth. In 'great men' systems, men depended on the appropriation of women's procreative power, whereas in 'big men' systems, they depended on the appropriation of women's labour force.

There is thus an apparent important distinction between great men and chiefly systems on the one hand, and big men systems on the other hand, which resides in the hereditary nature of access to power in the former, and control of labour and exchange in the latter. Mark Mosko critically examines this distinction and rearticulates the pattern of chiefly leadership in terms of categories of reciprocal exchanges. Hereditary succession in great men and in chiefly systems is not 'some kind of automatic one-way "inheritance" or transfer of status', he suggests, 'but rather a complex process wherein presumed successors strategically detach elements of their persons deemed to be effective in eliciting desired ritual elements of their predecessors'. Drawing on Marylin Strathern's work on the dividual and the partible person, he highlights how relationships are transportable. What Mark Mosko endeavours to demonstrate is that great men and big men systems are in fact 'variant expressions of one singular mode of sociality, that is gift exchange among partible persons'. Indeed, an analysis of ethnographic accounts of successions seems to show that the so-called inheritance based systems exhibit numerous exceptions, including strategies for disqualifying a person from becoming a chief. Mosko suggests that 'empirical instances of chiefly succession are the consequence of sustained series of complex interpersonal transactions mainly between chiefs and persons intent on becoming their heirs but also between the rivals for succession and other relevant persons'. Significantly, in their exchange systems North Mekeo leaders detach ritual knowledge and reattach it to the men they select to pass it on to. Succession, or in fact the transfer of succession, seems to operate in a blurred zone between the domain of exchange of goods and that of the exchange of the sacred and inalienable. Following Joel Robbins, what is transmitted here is again in the realm of ideology of language, of the secret.

We have seen how the chapters of this volume articulate a shift from a materialist to a more symbolic approach to social reproduction, in which the politico-religious is an integral part of infrastructure. We have seen that social reproduction is intimately tied to the inalienable, to objects and to knowledge that cannot be given but can only be transmitted. In the analysis of the inalienable, important questions recur, dealing with sacredness and secrecy, gender and the dynamics of rank-taking and systems of power. This shift is also one that Maurice Godelier has been undertaking in his own career. Very early on, in a methodologically significant chapter of his *Horizon, trajets marxistes en anthropologie* (1973), he already advanced the idea that kinship relationships and social organization may function as elements of infrastructure and of social reproduction. Analysing Yengoyan's (e.g. 1968) material on Australia's Pitjantjatjara's section systems, he suggested that classifications of kin operate in the distribution of access and control to means of subsistence (production). However, the more he analysed how aspects of the '*idéel*' structure and restructure a mode of production, the more he moved towards the distillation of the politico-religious domain as central. It is not sufficient that institutions of domination and control exist, it is also necessary for people to be able to accept these institutions; and to do so, they need to believe in a politico-religious complex that reproduces a holistic vision of society.

Centring his analysis on the inalienable as the nucleus of this holistic vision was an important step in Godelier's work. However, one further step had still to be taken in light of this shift: a discussion of why some societies seem to be organized around relationships of kinship rather than the politico-religious complex. In *Metamorphoses de la parenté* (2004) he addressed one of the strongest fortresses of our discipline: the idea of kin-based societies. The principal objectives of this work can be summarized in a few sentences. First, and most importantly, Godelier endeavours to demonstrate that kinship and the family are not the foundation of society and that there has never been such a thing as a kin-based society. He had previously (1973, vol.1: 38) expressed the idea that the family is not the basic unity of society, because a family cannot exist and reproduce itself through generations independently of other families. Formerly, however, Godelier thought this was due to the universality of the incest prohibition and the necessity of economic cooperation. In his later work Godelier rather observes that ties based on kinship are insufficient to create 'corporatedness'. It is, rather, adherence to a common and shared cultural web – which he calls the 'imaginary' content and which belongs to the politico-religious domain – that creates the social being as a member of a group. 'Imaginary' is understood as the world of conscious views, rules and norms imposed by a group with respect to its socio-political and religious order. In order to exercise some autonomy and durability, this imaginary anchors kin groups – however their members are recruited – in a territory. In other words, it is not kinship ties that produce a society, but rather politico-religious relationships that have this capacity when they produce and legitimate the sovereignty of a group of human beings over a territory and its material and socially constructed resources.

His other conclusions flow from the central aspect of the analysis of kinship mentioned above. In particular, they concern the observation that nowhere are humans considered sufficient to reproduce a human being, and that everywhere there are spiritual or religious agents that participate in the procreation process. A man and a woman fabricate a foetus, not a child. Importantly, it follows from this that the incest prohibition is not the passage from nature to culture and is not universal, but is rather a politico-religious strategy, a means for social reproduction. Following his analysis of the place of human reproduction and kinship in society, Godelier, like Gilbert Herdt (this volume), notes the emergent, abundant literature on reproductive technologies and their impact on the social order, especially that part of it which might be called sexual culture and sociality. What is at stake in the production of sexual culture is the regulation of sexual behaviour, both within individuals and outside in the cultural environment.

Métamorphoses de la parenté has provoked many responses and much scientific discussion; among the most prominent specialists on these questions are Jack Goody (2005) and Robert Barnes (2006), who have provided long and detailed reviews. While Jack Goody addresses yet another question in this volume to which we will return soon, Robert Barnes tackles these questions again and elaborates on some important aspects which were neglected in his earlier review. What is at stake for him is the definition of descent and of classification in particular, and the definition of anthropological concepts and their applicability in general terms. Descent is a particularly central notion since, according to Radcliffe-Brown (1952: 48), some form of unilineal institution is almost, if not entirely, necessary in any ordered social system. We touch here on the problem of the existence of corporate groups as based on kinship (Radcliffe-Brown) or as based on a politico-religious system for social reproduction (Godelier). Godelier showed in *Métamorphoses de la parenté* that Radcliffe-Brown's model did not represent the ethnographic reality. The question of what descent systems are, however, remains intact: 'there is after all no "true" definition of descent', Barnes writes in this volume, since ethnography reports the most diverse forms of successions, invoking many possible definitions by numerous researchers, 'but most seem not to have accepted that the variety is in fact the message'. Godelier's claim that religion or politico-religious systems are among the strongest forces even in the domain of change of kinship terminologies is backed up by Barnes' chapter, even though the 'history of evolutionary speculation in anthropology has never produced anything like certainty in our understanding of how and why such patterns change'.

Indeed, change, and the combination of structural and materialist approaches which are predominant throughout the chapters of this book and in Maurice Godelier's work, are the two major domains addressed in the last two chapters of our volume: Jonathan Friedman's work on cosmopolitanization and indigenization in the contemporary world system; and Jack Goody's short paper on the Asiatic mode of production. These chapters are to some extent distinct from the rest, since, as is the case with Gilbert Herdt's paper, the ambition is to look at the 'big picture'; and being able to detect the big picture while analysing local and particular phenomena has been the aim of Maurice Godelier's work as well. This is particularly explicit in *Au fondement des sociétés humaines: ce que nous apprend l'anthropologie*, which is being translated into English as we write. In this analysis, Godelier works against an anthropology that, in recent decades, has been thinking of itself as being emptied of its substance through the development of an overly relativistic attitude. He proclaims that anthropology is able to describe and understand aspects of social structure, be they local or general, and understand them in an expanding and recirculating way. Moving on from his former work on exchange systems and the metamorphosis of kinship, he points here to the universal weight of politico-religious symbolism as fundamental to social organization and order, whether in Tonga or the Western world.

The 'Asiatic mode of production' was, as Jack Goody recalls, a fundamental concept in the development of Marxist anthropology. It defied the uniform historical dialectics that were considered to lead the world to capitalism and thereafter to socialism. It had been declared unacceptable at the Leningrad conference in 1931 since it implied the impossibility of Eastern nations achieving socialism. Godelier reopened the question in 1970 by editing a volume that included Marx's study of pre-capitalist socio-economic formations, and by rehabilitating the notion of the 'Asiatic mode of production'. According to Marx, this mode of production succeeded the hunter-gatherer state of humanity by establishing sedentary and agricultural civilizations around waterways with centralized power structures. The major discussion that arose in Marxist anthropology concerned the question of whether this Asiatic mode was, or is, distinct from those social structures that in the West led to capitalist society. But the differences or absence of differences between the Oriental, the Asiatic and even the Western economic and political structures are not self-evident. As Jonathan Friedman recalls in his chapter, even the notion of 'class' has been heavily criticized and deemed by some (e.g. Harris 1992) to have been a failure in understanding social structure.

Combining Marxist and structuralist approaches, Jonathan Friedman reassesses these criticisms in order to work towards an understanding of class formation in what has come to be known as the era of globalization. In an attempt to find an alternative to the fragmentation produced by postmodernist analyses, he argues that it is impossible to dissociate questions of the structure of state societies and their reproduction from those of class or cultural identity. The global, he explains, is an emergent property produced by the articulation of numerous local processes that are not limited to the current modern era, but are embedded in a cyclical development of hegemonic expansion and contraction: he adopts a global systemic perspective. Analysing the fabrication of the cosmopolitanism of elites in different epochs, he convincingly concludes that this process takes place in periods of strong globalization such as we have today. These elites encompass the diversity that lies below, among the masses, without being part of it. The heterogeneous has become a goal in itself: 'a generalized cultural pluralism of different identities, ethnic, religious, territorial, gender and of political projects' (this volume).

Our introduction began with a quotation from Maurice Godelier about the scope of anthropology: 'From initiation rituals in Papua New Guinea to the Twin Towers'. One common theme in all the chapters in the present volume is that this scope is about understanding transformations of systems and structures, a theme that has remained central throughout Maurice Godelier's work.

Note

1. 'Economic anthropology is the comparative theoretical analysis of different actual and potential economic systems. In order to elaborate this theory, it takes its substance from concrete information produced by historians and anthropologists on the functioning and evolution of the societies they study. Alongside the field of "political economy" that, it seems, is devoted to the study of modern industrial societies, be they market or controlled, economic anthropology claims in a way to be the "extension" of political economy to those societies that have been neglected by economists... Hence, through its project, economic anthropology takes on the elaboration of a general theory of human beings' diverse social forms of economic activity, for one day comparative analysis should necessarily produce general anthropological knowledge'. (Our translation).

Bibliography

Alland, A. 1983. 'Review of "La Production des Grands Hommes"', *L'Homme* 23(3): 141–42.

Barnes, R.H. 2006. 'Maurice Godelier and the metamorphosis of kinship, a review essay', *Comparative Studies in Society and History* 48(2): 326–58.

Bolton, L. 2003. *Unfolding the Moon: Enacting Women's Kastom in Vanuatu.* Honolulu: University of Hawai'i Press.

Descola, Ph., J. Hamel and P. Lemonnier (eds). 1999. *La production du social: Autour de Maurice Godelier.* Paris: Fayard.

Dumont, L. 1967. *Homo hierarchicus. Essai sur le système des castes.* Paris: Gallimard.

Eriksen, A. 2008. *Gender, Christianity and Change in Vanuatu: An Analysis of Social Movements in North Ambrym.* Aldershot, Hampshire and Burlington VT: Ashgate.

Garelli, P. 1969. *Le Proche-Orient asiatique des origins aux invasions des peuples de la mer.* Paris: P.U.F.

Gernet, J. 1972. *Le monde chinois.* Paris: A. Colin.

Godelier, M. 1965. 'Objet et méthodes de l'anthropologie économique', *L'Homme* 5(2): 32–91.

———— 1966. *Rationalité et irrationalité en économie.* Paris: Maspéro.

———— 1977. *Horizon, trajets marxistes en anthropologie.* Paris: Petite collection Maspero (2 tomes, Nouvelle edition) [1973].

———— 1978a. 'Infrastructures, societies and history', *Current Anthropology* 19: 763–71.

———— 1978b. 'La part idéelle du réel. Essai sur l'idéologie', *L'Homme* 18(3–4): 155–88.

———— 1982a. 'Social hierarchies among the Baruya of New Guinea', in A. Strathern (ed.), *Inequality in New Guinea.* New York: Cambridge University Press, p.3–34.

———— 1982b. *La production des Grands Hommes. Pouvoir et domination masculine chez les Baruya de Nouvelle-Guinée.* Paris: Fayard.

———— 1984. *L'idéel et le matériel.* Paris: Fayard.

———— 1986. *The Making of Great Men: Male Domination and Power among the New Guinea Baruya.* New York: Cambridge University Press.

———— 1996. *L'Enigme du don.* Paris: Fayard.

———— 2005. *Métamorphoses de la Parenté.* Paris: Fayard.

———— 2007. *Au fondement des sociétés humaines: Ce que nous apprend l'anthropologie.* Paris: Albin Michel, Bibliothèque Idées.

———— 2008a [1997]. 'Aspects and Stages of the Westernisation of a Tribal Society', in S. Tcherkézoff and F. Douaire-Marsaudon (eds), *The Changing South Pacific: Identities and Transformations.* Canberra: ANU E-Press, p.27–42.

———— 2008b. 'Des rites d'initiation de Nouvelle-Guinée aux attentats des Twin Towers. L'anthropologie à la recherche des fondements des sociétés concrètes', in *Pensées pour le Nouveau Siècle.* Paris: Fayard, p.131–56.

———— and J. Hassoun (eds). 1996. *Meurtre du Père, Sacrifice de la sexualité. Approches anthropologiques et psychanalytiques.* Paris: Arcanes, 'Les Cahiers d'Arcanes'.

———— and M. Panoff (eds). 1998a. *La production du Corps: Approches anthropologiques et historiques.* Amsterdam: Edition des Archives Contemporaines, Overseas Publishing Association.

———— and M. Panoff (eds). 1998b. *Le corps humain, Supplicié, Possédé, Cannibalisé.* Amsterdam: Edition des Archives Contemporaines, Overseas Publishing Association.

———— and M. Strathern (eds). 1991. *Big Men, Great Men. Personifications of power in Melanesia.* Cambridge, Paris: Cambridge University Press, Editions de la Maison des sciences de l'Homme.

Goody, J. 2005. 'The labyrinth of kinship (a review of Métamorphoses de la parenté by M. Godelier)', *New Left Review* 36: 127–39.

Harris, D. 1992. *From Class Struggle to the Politics of Pleasure: the Effects of Gramscianism on Cultural Studies.* London, New York: Routledge.

Herdt, G. 1999. 'Rituels de sexuation et pouvoirs du corps en Nouvelle-Guinée: Essai comparatif en hommage à Maurice Godelier', in Ph. Descola, J. Hamel and P. Lemonnier (eds), *La production du social: Autour de Maurice Godelier.* Paris: Fayard, p.345–68.

Lévi-Strauss, C. 1947. *Les structures élémentaires de la parenté.* Paris: Mouton.

———— 1950. 'Introduction à l'œuvre de Marcel Mauss', in M. Mauss, *Sociologie et anthropologie.* Paris: PUF.

Mauss, M. 1923–24. 'Essai sur le don: forme et raison de l'échange dans les sociétés archaïques', *L'Année sociologique* 1923–24: 30–186.

Meggitt, M.J. 1989. 'Women in Contemporary Central Enga Society, Papua New Guinea', in M. Jolly and M. Macintyre (eds), *Family and Gender in the Pacific. Domestic Contradictions and the Colonial Impact.* Cambridge: Cambridge University Press, p.135–55.

Mosko, M. 1992. 'Motherless Sons: Divine Kings and Partible Persons in Melanesia and Polynesia', *Man* 27(4): 697–717.

Radcliffe-Brown, A.R. 1952. *Structure and Function in Primitive Society: Essays and Addresses.* London: Cowen and West.

Sahlins, M. 1985. *Islands of History.* Chicago: University of Chicago Press.

Strathern, M. 1988. *The Gender of the Gift: Problems With Women and Problems With Society in Melanesia.* Berkeley and London: University of California Press.

Taylor, J.P. 2008. *The Other Side: Ways of Being and Place in Vanuatu.* Honolulu: University of Hawai'i Press.

Vernant, J-P. 1962. *Les origines de la pensée grecque.* Paris: P.U.F.

Weiner, A.B. 1992. *Inalienable possessions: the paradox of keeping while giving.* Berkeley: University of California Press.

Yengoyan, A.A. 1968. 'Demographic and Ecological Influences on Aboriginal Australian Marriage Sections', in R.B. Lee and I. De Vore (eds), *Man the Hunter.* Chicago: Aldine, p.185–90.

Chapter 1

SOME THINGS YOU SAY, SOME THINGS YOU DISSIMULATE, AND SOME THINGS YOU KEEP TO YOURSELF: LINGUISTIC, MATERIAL, AND MARITAL EXCHANGE IN THE CONSTRUCTION OF MELANESIAN SOCIETIES

Joel Robbins

As is the case for so many others of my generation, Maurice Godelier's theoretical work and his Baruya ethnography have both been important parts of my thinking since the beginning of my education in anthropology. In the context of engaging his work here, it thus seems fitting to return to an ethnographic problem that has been with me nearly as long. The problem I am referring to is that of secrecy, the topic on which I originally planned to focus my research before turning to the study of Christianity, my direction changed by the primary concerns of the Urapmin people of Papua New Guinea, with whom I carried out fieldwork in the early 1990s. The kind of secrecy that initially interested me is what we might call 'culturally enjoined secrecy', or 'secrecy as a value'. In cultures organized around men's initiation and fertility cults – cultures like the ones that traditionally shaped Urapmin and Baruya life – initiates into various stages of the cults are taught knowledge that they are commanded to keep secret from women or younger men. Initiators explain to them that keeping such secrets is a crucial religious practice, one that helps to ensure that the world will keep functioning as it should, with gardens prospering, game abundant, and boys growing strong to become warriors. As construed in these cults, secrecy is not an aberrant form of communication or a negatively valued practice of dissimulation. It is instead a key feature of the most important of social practices, the ones that make the world function as it should. Little wonder then that amongst the Urapmin the word for secret, *awem*, is also the word for sacred (see also Jorgensen 1981). The human ability to keep secrets is an important part of what makes society possible.

By the time I began to think about secrecy, ethnographers of societies of the Mountain Ok region, of which the Urapmin are a part, had observed that the constant emphasis on secrecy in initiations, and the practice of protecting secrets by misleading initiates at various stages about knowledge they were not yet ready to receive, produced what Barth (1975) called an 'epistemology of secrecy' (see also Jorgensen 1981, 1990). This is a gloomy epistemology in which all knowledge is held to be liable to revision, and in which it is assumed that the more well known a piece of knowledge is, the less likely it is to be true. The latter consideration means that from an individual's point of view, the very fact that he/she knows something means it is probably not the last the word on the subject it treats. My original plan was to study how this epistemology influenced everyday life in Urapmin. How, outside of formal ritual contexts, could people live as radical sceptics; how could they get along in the world without any confidence in their knowledge of it? I think this remains an interesting question, but it turned out not to be the main focus of my research. The conversion of all adult Urapmin to charismatic Christianity in the late 1970s radically altered the course of their lives, and in doing so it changed in some ways their evaluation of secrecy. Christianity, as the Urapmin say, reveals all that is hidden (*bantap*), and brings everything into the 'open' (*kem diim*). For Christians, secrecy becomes profane. Under these conditions, with secrecy no longer central to Urapmin social life, it did not make sense to put it at the centre of my research. But key elements of the secrecy complex did linger on in Urapmin ideas about communication, what contemporary scholars would call their language ideology, and this is something I did attend to carefully in the field. In this essay I want to suggest that bringing the analysis of language ideology into conjunction with Godelier's theoretical programme in *The Enigma of the Gift* can allow us to approach the problem of secrecy in a new way, one that helps us to better understand how a phenomenon so negatively or at best ambivalently viewed in the West can sometimes play a crucial role in the construction of social life.

In developing this analysis, I want to start with Lévi-Strauss' (1963: 296) conception of society as made up of three dimensions of communication or exchange: one of women, one of goods, and one of messages or words. Through their studies of kinship and marriage, anthropologists have done extensive work on the exchange of people (or 'women' as it is usually phrased), and in the study of social structure and economy more broadly they have looked in detail at the exchange of goods. By comparison, the study of the exchange of words has never got off the ground. Certainly it is difficult to point to works in the structuralist tradition that develop the study of speech in terms of exchange. In the absence of such study, I will argue, the problem of how secrecy as a value helps to construct social life cannot be solved. And I will claim that some of Godelier's arguments in *The Enigma of the Gift*, when combined with work on language ideology, are precisely what we need to formulate a method of studying speech as the exchange of words.

In trying to bring Godelier's arguments about exchange in *The Enigma of the Gift* to bear on the completion of Lévi-Strauss' model of society as a tripartite system of exchange, I immediately come up against the problem that in that book Godelier (1999: 7) strongly criticizes Lévi-Strauss' move to make 'the entire social domain a combination of forms of exchange'. One of Godelier's criticisms of Lévi-Strauss' model is that it roots exchange in the universal faculties of the human mind, which for Godelier is part of Lévi-Strauss' general mistake of privileging the symbolic over the real and the imaginary. Another criticism, which Godelier develops in dialogue with Weiner's (1992) work, is that Lévi-Strauss' view of society as exchange does not take into account the finding that some things are defined precisely by the fact that they are not to be given, but are rather to be kept as inalienable possessions that anchor the identity and social standing of those who keep them but otherwise do relate to others through exchange. The keeping of things turns out to be as important to the construction of social life as is the exchange of them. These two criticisms of Lévi-Strauss' approach are threads that run throughout Godelier's book and make it difficult on the face of things to recruit his work for a project that would preserve the image of society as constituted by three domains of exchange.

Since Godelier's difficulties with Lévi-Strauss rest on two arguments, they require two responses. To the argument about Lévi-Strauss' reference to unconscious universals as the basis for this model of society, and the attendant privileging of the symbolic over the imaginary and real, I would argue that it is possible to keep the model but ignore Lévi-Strauss' arguments about the origins of the phenomena it treats and the way in which those supposed origins lead us to privilege the symbolic. Lévi-Strauss (1963: 296–309) himself does something similar in the section of his article 'Social Structure' that he devotes to this model, which is much less taken up with unconscious origins than is the *Introduction to the Work of Marcel Mauss* (Lévi-Strauss 1987), the text on which Godelier focuses. Indeed, I will be arguing that it is precisely by bringing to light the role of the imaginary in giving exchanges their meaning – a task Godelier has already carried out with great success in his own work in relation to the exchange of objects and women – that we can encompass speech within the model.

In response to the second criticism – that Lévi-Strauss' model of society as exchange utterly fails to grasp the significance of what is not and cannot be given – it is again possible to accept the charge as levelled without abandoning the model. After all, Mauss himself, in his earlier work on sacrifice, acknowledged a kind of exchange in which someone 'gives up something of himself but does not give himself' (Hubert and Mauss 1964: 100), indicating that it is possible to think about keeping under the rubric of exchange. If we accept the criticism but keep the model, it would then become necessary to discuss not only to what is exchanged on every level of society, and how it is exchanged (i.e. in what kinds of circuits and to what kinds of ends), but also what people keep on every level, what they assert cannot be given. We must attend, as Strenski (2002: 167) puts it in his very helpful study of Hubert and Mauss, to the way people give *of* the self but do not give *up* the self at all levels of society. Since secrets are precisely words or meanings that the self should not give, it should at this point be possible for readers to see where I am headed. But before reaching that conclusion, and establishing it ethnographically, I need to develop a model of speech as exchange. This is the task of the next section.

Exchanging Words

The study of speech and of people as speakers never made it onto the structuralist research agenda. This is an odd omission for a paradigm in which communication, exchange, and symbolic meaning are such key operators. But it is also an omission that can be relatively easily explained when we recall that one of Saussure's famous founding structuralist distinctions was between *langue*, language as a system, and *parole*, realizations of that system in the action of individuals. As something which is systematic, *langue* is, according to Saussure, a suitable object of study for a science of structure. *Parole*, by contrast, he defined as not amenable to study in such terms and so it was set aside. As Saussure's arguments were taken up in the formation of structural anthropological thought, this distinction between system and speech was largely preserved. To be sure, analysts could examine spoken 'texts' such as myths or verbal formulae for the evidence of underlying structures they instantiated, and could even study how some relatively fixed texts (e.g. spells) were given to others in various forms of exchange, but the chatter of everyday conversation, and the mechanics by which such chatter is passed, remained all but invisible to those working within the structuralist paradigm. We could perhaps consider this neglect of speech to be an allowable omission – all social theories leave some aspects of human life in the dark – except for the fact that it crippled the project of construing society as constituted out of the exchange of women, goods, and speech, thus leaving structuralism's primary social (as opposed to cognitive) vision radically incomplete.

The last two decades have seen the rapid rise of a new focus of research in linguistic anthropology that promises to help us to address the structuralist neglect of speech and to complete this part of the structuralist project that has been so long left unfinished. This new focus of research is 'language ideology' (Silverstein 1979; Woolard and Schieffelin 1994; Schieffelin, Woolard and Kroskrity 1998). A language ideology is a society's set of ideas about what language is and how communication works. Language ideological ideas are also connected to many other cultural domains, touching on ideas of person, relationship, and power among others. But they remain distinct from these other ideas by virtue of always taking up most prominently issues of language and communication. When we study a society's language ideology, we discover that the ideas that make it up evidence, like all socially shared ideas, some structure (not one that is closed or of necessity non-contradictory, but structure nonetheless). Those who study language ideologies have shown that these structures can be profitably examined as part of the more general study of a culture. On the basis of their work, we can say that even if *parole* itself may not be amenable to study using structuralist methods, language ideologies that provide actors with models for how *parole* operates are quite amenable to such study.

Having made this point, the next step of my argument is to suggest that the study of language ideologies can do for the study of speech as exchange what the study of prescriptive marriage rules did for the study of the exchange of women, or the study of rules of reciprocal exchange did for the study of the movement of goods. That is to say, I want to suggest that the study of language ideologies can finally bring speech as a domain of communication into the structuralist model of society.

In supporting this assertion, I am aided by the fact that language ideologies tend everywhere to take up issues that are relevant not simply to communication, but also to communication understood as exchange. Language ideologies always have things to say about what can be given in speech, what it means to receive speech, what needs to be given back in return when speech is received, who can give what kind of speech to whom, the turn-taking orders that should govern the commerce of speech between different kinds of people, etc. Indeed, it is hard to imagine that a language ideology in any society could fail to draw from and in turn provide feedback upon other ideas about exchange in the society in which it is found. Bambi Schieffelin, one of the pioneers of language ideological research, has made this point explicitly in the course of her study of the language socialization of children among the Kaluli of Papua New Guinea. As she puts it:

> Talk is not only instrumental, but is also a metaphor for what happens in exchange: Meaning is offered and taken, asked for and given. Children through ... exchanges of mediated or assisted talk are learning about reciprocity as well. They are learning about the form and functions of giving and taking, that reciprocity and social relationships are bound to one another (Schieffelin 2007: 126)

Here, finally, is a way of approaching speech as one among several orders of exchange, and of doing so without courting the difficulties of studying *parole* as Saussure conceived them.

Put in Godelier's terms, we might suggest that through the study of language ideology, we can analyse the exchange of words as it is constituted in a given society's imaginary. When we do so, we discover that there is great variation in how such exchange is construed, and that in some societies keeping is as much at issue as, or even more at issue than, giving when it comes to the imaginary constitution of communication. This is particularly apparent when we consider the growing body of literature that looks comparatively at Western and Melanesian language ideologies.

Keeping and Giving in Western and Melanesian Language Ideologies

Modern Western language ideology places heavy emphasis on speech as a form of giving, and in this respect Lévi-Strauss' own singular emphasis on what is given over what is kept may well show its influence. In this language ideology, what speakers give in speech are their intentions and the meanings these intentions create. In Reddy's (1993: 167–70, originally published 1979) famous account of the conduit metaphor that dominates Western models of communication, a brilliant analysis of language ideology carried out before the concept itself had been well established, one correlate of the metaphor in question is the idea that words are like boxes into which speakers put their meanings in order to send them to receivers, who open the boxes and take them out. We could not be closer to the terrain of the gift! The emphasis on the giving of intention and meaning is also evident in the purified Western folk models that constitute the analytic philosophy of language, for Austin (1975), Grice (1989), and Searle (1969) all anchor meaning in speakers' intentions. And finally, the model of speech as the gift of intention also reaches the explicit consciousness of speakers, where it appears as the modern value of sincerity (see Robbins 2001; Keane 2002 and 2007 – these works also trace the history of the language ideology I am discussing here in some detail). In order to realize this value, speakers struggle to make their intentions match what comes out of their mouths. Listeners, for their part, usually (that is to say, in unmarked situations), interpret what is said in light of this expectation, and failures to meet it are generally grounds for condemnation. Peters (1999) reminds us that as Westerners have imagined angels, these beings have no trouble realizing this value – for they are translucent and thus immediately transparent to one another. It is more difficult for human beings to give all that they mean to in speech, but in Western language ideology they are at least duty bound to try: in Western speech, the gift of intention must be given in order for communication to carry meaning.

There have long been hints in the ethnography of the Pacific that language ideologies in the region do not share the Western language ideological understanding that speakers' gifts of their intentions in speech are the basis of the meanings of their utterances. This has been particularly true in the literature from Melanesia, where many scholars have noted that in the societies in which they work people assert that they can never know what is in the 'mind' (i.e. 'heart', 'liver' etc. understood as the seat of thought) of other people, and that therefore one cannot interpret what they say on the basis of assumptions about the intentions they harbour there (see, for example, Eves 1998; LiPuma 2000: 166; Munn 1986: 68; O'Hanlon 1989; Schieffelin 1986, 1990; A. Strathern 1981; M. Strathern 1979). These often passing ethnographic observations have also been gathered into several more sustained arguments holding that in many Pacific language ideologies listeners are defined as more important than speakers in the process of 'giving' meaning to what is said (Duranti 1993a, 1993b; Robbins 2001; Silverstein 1998). Finally, in the last few years, the ways in which these indigenous language ideologies have clashed with Western ones based on sincerity have been a major part of the focus of two edited collections (Makihara and Schieffelin 2007; Rumsey and Robbins 2008).

This work on the Pacific language ideological claim that one cannot know what others are thinking and that such knowledge thus cannot be the foundation of meaning puts the long Melanesianist tradition of studying what I referred to above as culturally enjoined secrecy in a new light. The emphasis on secrecy as a positive practice also represents a challenge to Western language ideological assumptions. Secrecy in Melanesia is not about retaining one's thoughts or intentions, as in many Melanesian language ideologies these are never communicated regardless of whether or not one tries to protect them, so much as it is about making sure certain pieces of knowledge are never conveyed to others. With secrecy as a valued practice, we come to the idea of active withholding as a positive act – of the importance of keeping some things out of exchange. In the kinds of Melanesian language ideologies I am discussing, as far as intentions or meaning are concerned words are empty boxes that recipients have to fill. When it comes to secret knowledge, by contrast, the boxes are never sent at all. In Western language ideology, such withholding is the height of bad form, but in many Melanesian societies it is sacred practice.

Read together, all of the work on Pacific language ideologies I have been referring to has shown that communication as it is construed in Pacific imaginaries is not the same kind of exchange Western imaginaries take it to be. Indeed, the two cases appear to be inversions of one another, with Westerners ideally committed to giving up themselves completely in communicative exchange, and people in many Melanesian societies concerned to treat their intentions and thoughts ideally as in essence inalienable objects never to be sent over to their interlocutors, and acting in concerted ways to keep to themselves some information of interest to others. And the plot thickens if we bring in the realm of objects as another domain of exchange, for another inversion occurs at this level. Westerners, so determined to give their intentions away, are keen to keep as many material goods as they can for themselves, while Melanesians, so determined to keep their thoughts to themselves, give away most of the goods that ever come into their hands.[1] If society is made up of such exchanges, then Melanesian and Western societies must be considered as being quite different from one another. This is not, of course, a new discovery – but it is framed in somewhat novel terms. In order to begin the process of determining what value there might be in construing the difference in these terms, in the next section I will look in more detail at the entanglements of different levels of exchange in a single Melanesian case. In doing so, I return to the theme of keeping things out of exchange that is so important to Godelier's rethinking of the role of the gift in social life.

Secrecy and Exchange among the Urapmin of Papua New Guinea

The Urapmin are a group of 390 people living in the Sandaun Province of Papua New Guinea. As noted in the introduction to this essay, they are one of the Mountain Ok or Min group of societies well known in anthropology for their elaboration of ideas about the cosmological importance of secrecy. Godelier (1999: 179–85) discusses some important aspects of Min religion and mythology in *The Enigma of the Gift*, and analyses them for what they reveal about the origins of religion. I take up some of his concerns in that discussion in the conclusion of this paper. In this section, however, I want to examine how Urapmin people's understanding of the importance of secrecy and the impossibility of knowing other people's intentions can be interpreted in relation to their broader understandings of exchange at all levels of society.

As is the case in other Melanesian societies, Urapmin life appears at first glance to be almost wholly interpretable in terms of gift exchange. No one makes it through a day without giving some food to others and eating some that others have given to him/her. Kinds of relationships are defined by the kinds of exchanges that constitute them – be it of foodstuffs in generalized reciprocity, or of foodstuffs in balanced reciprocity, or of durable goods such as bows and string bags in delayed reciprocity, etc. Marriages are invariably understood either as sister exchange (which is an ideal but is also rare) or as a delayed exchange of women between social categories. All major rituals except male initiations, about which more below, feature exchanges as their primary content. This is true of marriages, funerals, and frequent and important rituals of dispute resolution (see Robbins 1999 for details on these kinds of exchange). In keeping with the importance of exchange in their lives, people in Urapmin regularly stress in both everyday and religious contexts the importance of generosity, and they praise one another by referring to themselves as people who extend their hands (*sigil*) with gifts to everyone they meet. As much as it makes sense to define any society as one built around gift exchange, the Urapmin surely qualify for this designation.

Yet as robust as the picture of Urapmin as a gift society appears when presented in traditional terms in the above paragraph (i.e. in terms of the exchange of women and goods), it becomes far more complicated when we bring the exchange of words into the analysis.

When it comes to the exchange of words, the Urapmin stress what is not given almost exclusively. If their hands are open, their hearts (*aget*, the seat of all thought, feeling, and intention) are decidedly not. This becomes clear when we review Urapmin language ideology, which tracks very closely the generalized description of Melanesian language ideologies I offered in the last section.

People in Urapmin routinely claim that one cannot know what another person thinks or feels in his/her heart. This is true even when people's speech might appear to reveal these things. 'Too much can happen between the heart and the mouth,' they say, to assume that what someone says represents what they feel or think in their hearts. Not only can one not know with any confidence what others think, but it is the height of impropriety to express guesses about such matters. There is a kind of psychic privacy to which everyone has a right, and violations of this are so unthinkable that when I, early on in my fieldwork, would occasionally ask people what they thought others were thinking or why they behaved in certain ways, they would not infrequently recoil in disgust at the mere thought of the mental operations that answering my question would entail. Given their views on the impossibility of knowing what others think, Urapmin people do not construe conversation as an exchange of intentions or meanings between people. It is instead a circuit in which people keep almost everything to themselves.[2]

In examining the men's initiation and fertility rituals that were formerly at the centre of Urapmin religion, we turn from considering a general background assumption that in conversation people give one another words but not the meanings or intentions they hold in their hearts, to the analysis of an explicit and highly elaborated theme of the importance of actively withholding things in verbal exchange.[3] The Urapmin men's cult had four major and a number of minor stages (*ban*) into which boys were inducted sequentially from their youth through as late as their young adulthood. If major Urapmin rituals are, as noted above, generally about the exchange of people and goods, initiations were a marked exception to the rule. Of course, one could find many different kinds of gifts and exchanges going on between initiators and between them and those who helped them carry out the rituals – gifts of services and goods that were necessary to carry out the rituals. But the main content of the rituals themselves was not about the exchange of people or things, but rather about the 'gift' of words and physical violence by the initiators to the novices. Setting aside the violence of the initiations – a topic that would take me far from my concerns here – I will focus on the words given. At each initiation stage, initiators presented novices with what they claimed was important mythical and cosmological information and at the same time insisted that this information was secret (*awem*) and must be kept from women and younger men. As the initiation stages progressed, however, the novices quickly came to realize that it was not only women and younger boys from whom secrets were kept. At each new stage, the initiates were told that the information that was given to them at the last stage was 'wrong' (*famul*) and was now being corrected, only to learn at the next stage that the corrected information was wrong as well. By the end of the initiation sequence, what initiates learned most fully was that they could not have confidence in what they knew, and that keeping secrets, rather than learning and knowing the truth about the world, was the key religious practice.

In the language ideology that shapes everyday Urapmin conversation, it is held to be a fact of life that people cannot convey their thoughts or intentions to others in speech. It is not that people actively withhold these things, it is simply in the nature of language not to convey them. This means that as a kind of exchange, conversation is one in which what is kept is more prominent than what is given. But this language ideology does not express a judgment on this fact; it simply represents it as the way things are. In the context of the men's cult, matters were quite different. Withholding, in this case the withholding of specific pieces of knowledge, was treated as an accomplishment. It was valued. It is as if the men's cults celebrated and promoted what the everyday language ideology only asserted as a truth about the world: that in the circuit of speech it is keeping that is really important.

Once we notice this particularity of the men's cult, it becomes possible to recognize that at the level of goods too it promoted a kind of keeping to oneself that everyday ideologies of generosity in Urapmin never charter. This is true in the way that Godelier and Weiner's analyses have led us to expect, for the distinctiveness and power of the Urapmin cult system as a whole, in the context of a regional ritual system of which it is a part, is based on their possession of the pelvic bones of Afek, the figure widely understood as the most important ancestress of all of the Min people (see Godelier 1999: 182).[4] These bones are, like the Baruya *kwaimatnie*, objects that are never given to anyone, and the Urapmin possession of them, together with the sacred, secret knowledge they also possess, anchors the cosmological identity of their community. But the cult emphasis on keeping goods is also true in a more mundane sense that speaks volumes about how exchange in the cult runs on principles counter to those that govern the exchange of women and goods outside of it. In support of this claim, I turn to Jorgensen's account of men's cult ritual among the Urapmin's Telefolmin neighbours. Jorgensen (1981: 77, 277) notes that marsupials are the game animals most frequently killed by Telefol hunters, and that a range of food taboos preventing men from consuming most marsupials makes these creatures the premiere food items given by men to women. Yet during one of the initiation rituals, cult leaders indulge in a meal of precisely those marsupials thought to be most taboo to them and to be the most appropriate gift for them to offer women. Ritual leaders consider this rite the 'essential act' of the entire initiation ritual (Jorgensen 1981: 466). Here we have, as a core secret act of the men's cult, a practice in which one keeps for oneself precisely the object one is most expected to give, and one does so as part of a sacred act that helps boys to grow into men, gardens to prosper, and game to be abundant. With goods as with words, the men's cult celebrates practices of keeping for oneself.

We can even suggest, though the argument is more tentative, that at the level of the exchange of women the men's cult also supports something like keeping to oneself, or at least the idea that marriage exchange might not be necessary. This is so because a central idea of the cult is that it is men that make men – women are not necessary to this process. The cult does not completely elide the fact of women's role in childbirth, but it does what it can to diminish it, and to suggest the viability of a world in which men interact only with one another, without the mediation of women. On this level too, then, the cult appears to assert the lack of importance of gift giving and exchange.

At this point, I hope to have established that if we understand Urapmin social life to be constituted out of three levels of exchange, we can see that as Godelier would predict practices of keeping things out of exchange appear to be more prominent than an analysis in terms only of reciprocity would lead us to expect. At the level of speech, keeping for oneself is everywhere the norm, and was actively promoted in the context of men's cults. At the level of goods and marriage, giving is most valued in everyday contexts, but in ritual contexts the keeping of objects and words, and a disregard for the importance of marriage exchange, is seen as proper.[5] Into this mixed situation, in which keeping and giving appear to jostle with one another for pride of place in the Urapmin imaginary of social relations, we now have to add the level of marriage exchange as it is understood outside of the men's cult. As we will see, such exchange makes a move to settle matters in favour of the value of giving rather than keeping more decisively than do the institutions we have hitherto considered.

I have already noted that the Urapmin idealize sister exchange marriages, and reward those who carry them out by relieving both sides of the obligation to pay bridewealth (*unang kun*, lit. 'woman's bones') in the form of shell money and other valuables. The vast majority of marriages, however, take their place in cycles of delayed restricted exchange, whereby a daughter of each marriage is expected to marry back into one or other of the social categories to which her mother belongs. In these cases, the side of the groom must pay bridewealth before a marriage is officially recognized. In return for the valuables given by the side of the groom to the side of the bride, the side of the groom receives pigs and other foodstuffs. Marriages are thus on the face of it as much focused on giving and receiving as the men's cult is on keeping to oneself. They are cycles of delayed reciprocity on the level of women in which are embedded more immediate exchanges on the level of goods that serve to keep the image of the gift very much in the forefront of people's concerns even before the daughters who will replace their mothers are born.

The strength of the emphasis on giving at the level of marriage is particularly marked in relation to two customs that surround it. The first is the custom by which families of a bride are expected at the outset to protest in rage over the possibility of losing their daughter to the man she will marry. It is on the basis of this rage that they demand bridewealth – it is to 'buy their anger' (*aget atul sanin*). Initially, they express their rage by asking for ridiculously large amounts of bridewealth – so large that no groom's family could afford to pay them. With time, their anger will cool down to the point that they will make reasonable demands and bridewealth will be paid, but it will often take them many months or more than a year to reach this point. And even when they do finally accept bridewealth, they will still insist that it is their due because of the anger they feel.

The belligerent drama that surrounds every marriage serves to air publicly the urge that families feel to treat their daughters as persons to be kept. Their anger at not being able to do so is given full expression, and they threaten time and again to arrange things such that they will not have to give up their daughters. But finally, an acceptable bridewealth is almost always negotiated and daughters are given in marriage. The pattern of every marriage thus unfolds as if the Urapmin both need to acknowledge the drive to keep women out of exchange, and also the need in the end to consent to giving them away. Following this pattern, people flirt with the possibility of keeping only to finally assert that giving must encompass it. The second marriage custom I will examine makes this point even more strikingly.

In Urapmin, it is women who decide whom they will marry and who initiate the marriage process. When a woman has decided on a prospective groom, she utters the name of the river from which his village gets water as she falls down on one of the muddy paths that criss-cross Urapmin territory. Upon hearing her, those who were with her arrange for a senior man of her family (often a mother's brother, though there is no rule requiring this) to come to ask her to 'call the name' (*win bakamin*) of her intended groom. Upon hearing the name, the senior man, along with others of her family, begin negotiations with the groom's family.

With respect to this part of the marriage process in Urapmin, I would like to point out that it is the one situation that I know of in which a person's speech is taken to convey their true intentions.[6] Once a woman has called the name of the man she wants to marry, people take her at her word that this is her intended groom and they act accordingly. The extent to which the process of a woman calling a man's name is ritualized, and the discomfort that men show over the task of hearing the name (few men are willing to take this on), indicate how unusual this kind of speaking and listening are in Urapmin experience. More than that, they treat the intention that is spoken by the woman as the kind of sacred, secret thing – the kind of normatively inalienable possession – that the Urapmin in all other cases hold intentions to be (see Robbins 2008 for a slightly fuller version of this argument). But the whole complex of practices associated with women calling the name of men they want to marry, even as it acknowledges the fact that intentions are usually kept to oneself, finally suggests that where marriage is concerned, even this most inalienable of possessions must be given away. Just as the import of marriage means that families will in the end have to give their daughters away, so too does it mean that at least once in their lives women will have to give their thoughts away in conversation. In marriage then, words, things, and women must all be given. Here is a total social fact that lets keeping for oneself take no hostages. If we take the incest taboo as the true origin of society, this is perhaps no surprise, but in the context of the analysis of Urapmin society I have developed in this section, it is perhaps more to the point to notice how marriage and the men's cult stand – or stood – as two opposed poles of Urapmin culture, allowing both centripetal and centrifugal forces of keeping and giving to play powerfully across the landscape of Urapmin life.

Conclusion: On Speaking, Keeping, and Alienation

One cannot simply state, as Durkheim did, that society is the source of the sacred. It also has to be shown that the *sacred conceals something from* the collective and individual consciousness, *something contained* in social relations, something essential to society, and in so doing the sacred distorts the social, makes it *opaque* to itself. It is even necessary to go further and to show that there is something in society which is part of the social being of its members and which needs *opacity* in order to produce and reproduce itself ... It is not *society* which conceals something of itself from men; it is real human beings who conceal something of their social relations *from each other* (Godelier 1999: 173 emphasis in original).

As Godelier moves toward the conclusion of *The Enigma of the Gift*, he introduces the theme of alienation, which quickly becomes as prominent as the theme of keeping to oneself that dominates the earlier part of the book. The kind of alienation on which he focuses is that which, he argues, produces the sacred. In this kind of alienation, people forget the role of humans in creating society, and instead attribute the power to do so to gods, who in creating the world give human beings gifts that leave people forever indebted to them. Godelier sees such alienation as both necessary, as it legitimizes the sexual, political, and economic exclusions and inequalities around which societies are formed (1999: 177), and as a ruse that the social sciences, if they are to realize their critical function, must help human beings see through (1999: 198–99). The crucial link between the earlier part of the book and this latter one is that the most important inalienable objects in a society tend to be ones that were divinely given to the human beings who now sequester them from exchange. This is certainly true of Afek's pelvic bones among the Urapmin, and Godelier turns to the mythology concerning Afek from other Min groups to help illustrate his point about the alienated nature of the sacred.

My essay has largely been taken up with two tasks unconnected to Godelier's discussion of alienation: (1) considering how the advent of work on language ideology has allowed us to revive the model of society as constituted out of three levels of exchange; and (2) asking how we can enhance this model by drawing on Godelier's work on the crucial role played by the act of keeping in the construction of society. In conclusion, I want to turn briefly to this second analytic focus of *The Enigma of the Gift* and ask how we might consider its key terms – alienation, opacity, and inequality – in relation to my focus on the ways in which speech can be understood as exchange.

Opacity is the obvious key term to start with here, for Melanesian language ideologies of the kind I have been discussing focus on the fact that people's minds are opaque to one another. In Melanesian societies in which such a language ideology is prevalent, people recognize each other as important sources of hiddeness and unpredictability in the world. In light of this, we might say that Melanesians come closer than those from other parts of the world to recognizing the human sources of opacity in society, even though they still give gods a good deal of play as well. Yet there is another reading of the Melanesian view of the opacity of minds that raises the question of alienation, a second key term, in a fresh way specific to the level of exchange of speech. This is relevant when we consider that just as anthropological science does not normatively allow us to treat gods as real, so too does it discourage us from accepting the idea that people can actually live together without constantly attempting, and with some success, to know what each other are thinking and what they are intending to say with their words. The notion that communication is the reading of people's intentions from what they say and do is so deeply embedded in anthropological, linguistic, and philosophical ways of thinking, that many scholars, when confronted with the data of Melanesian language ideologies, assume they must be misrepresentations of how Melanesian people actually behave when speaking and listening to the speech of others (Robbins and Rumsey 2008; Robbins 2008). If Melanesians really approached speech as they say they do, scholars often suggest, there would be no way for them to coordinate action and society would be impossible. In these debates, I have generally taken the side of trying to at least consider the possibility that Melanesian representations of their linguistic practice might be accurate, and I have suggested, among other things, that one reason why exchange at the level of goods is so elaborated in Melanesia is that it is doing a lot of the work of social coordination handled at the level of the exchange of speech elsewhere (Robbins 2008, 2007 and 2001). But my engagement with Godelier's arguments here has led me to want to consider, if only experimentally, where we might go if we do assert that Melanesian language ideologies are in fact fundamentally alienated, presenting the exchange of words as if it is not the speaker who by virtue of his/her intentions should control the meaning of speech.If we accept the analysis of Melanesian language ideologies as alienated representations of how linguistic practice operates in reality, the question that arises is that of how these misrepresentations are motivated: why would people mystify themselves about such a ubiquitous social practice? The misrepresentations that constitute the sacred, according to Godelier, exist to authorize various forms of inequality and domination, the third of his key concerns toward the end of *The Enigma of the Gift*. Might Melanesian language ideologies be in support of similar goals? It would be appealing to develop an argument along these lines, as it would help to round out an image of the fundamental role of inequality in social life that has very much dominated anthropology during the last several decades. But in fact the evidence points elsewhere. Unlike representations of the sacred, Melanesian language ideologies do not tend to bolster the position of one group in society over another, or to charter particular relations of inequality and dominance. They purport, instead, to deal with the human condition in absolutely general terms, without singling out any one group (say, for example, men) within it for special positive or negative attention. More pointedly, as Stasch (2008) has recently argued in an important article, these ideologies of opacity directly support political ideals of egalitarianism and autonomy. As he puts it, 'Melanesian sensitivity about not presuming to know others' minds is intertwined with sensitivity about not presuming to impinge on each other's self-determination' (Stasch 2008: 443). Without knowing what others are thinking, one cannot dismiss them in advance by claiming to know what they will do, nor can one claim to be acting on the authority of another. Each person equally possesses his/her own mind and as such is the origin of his/her own actions.

The ideal of personal autonomy and the emphasis on egalitarianism that Melanesian language ideologies foster fit well with claims that these are key aspects of Melanesian societies (even if they are not the sole realities). Such claims were once a staple of Melanesian ethnography, and the idea that Melanesians would go out of their way to 'misrepresent' how the exchange of speech works in their community in order to help realize values of autonomy and equality goes some way toward supporting them (Robbins 1994). Godelier is the leading figure of several generations of Melanesianists who turned away from the egalitarian argument, stressing the inequalities between men and women, and older and younger men, and showing how these produced various alienated representations at the level of specific Melanesian imaginaries. He carries out this task brilliantly in *The Making of Great Men* (1986) and then again in *The Enigma of the Gift*. The short concluding argument I have developed here suggests that an emphasis on keeping and giving at the level of speech might not only help us revive a model of society as a series of levels of exchange, but could also encourage us to carry forward the debate about inequality, equality, and the constitutive role of the imaginary in new ways.

Notes

1. I am hesitant to say much about the level of exchange of women here, not least because I do not think marriage is conceptualized in these terms in the West. But it is worth at least noting that families give their children freely in marriage in most Western folk models, in that they do not expect a person to come to them in return for the person given in marriage, while most Melanesians are concerned to keep cycles of marriage exchange fairly short. It is perhaps not surprising then that some Westerners formalize marriage with the exchange of sincere speech acts ('I do'), for them another form of 'pure' gift, while Melanesians most often do so with the binding exchange of goods.

2. I have elsewhere discussed in detail the way in which the Urapmin understand meaning to be made in conversation wholly by how the listener responds to what is said, rather than by what the speaker might have meant by saying it. Since my focus here is on what Urapmin language ideology can tell us about speech

as exchange, rather than Urapmin language ideology in all of its details, I do not review this argument here (Robbins 2001).

3. A note is in order here concerning the nature of my evidence on Urapmin men's cults. By the time of my fieldwork, initiation rituals had not been practiced for roughly fourteen years. Older men could discuss them with me at length, though they showed little interest in enumerating the fine details of each ritual as practiced. The importance of secrecy in the cults was still a topic of wide notice, however, and this for two reasons. First, people liked to point out a contrast which I noted in passing above, in which Christianity's emphasis on openness is in direct and welcome opposition to the importance of secrecy in their traditional religion. As a way of explaining what they liked about the present, many people found this a worthy topic of conversation. Second, to all intents and purposes the secret knowledge of the men's cult is still held only by the oldest men in the community – the last cohort to be fully initiated. While they too sing the praises of Christian openness, they do not in fact give this information away and their possession of it in part grounds the power several of them exercise as big men (*kamok*) (see Robbins 2004). Yet, even as there was a good deal of discussion of secrecy during my fieldwork for these two reasons, my analysis is not as rich as it would be had I been able to observe and participate in the rituals that were built around such secrecy. In order to partly remedy that gap, my discussion of Urapmin men's cults is also informed in a general way by my readings of work on men's cults as they were practiced in other Min groups (e.g. Barth 1975, Gardner 1981, Jorgensen 1981). As will be clear in the text, I also at one point draw on Jorgensen's (1981) exemplary work on the men's initiation rituals of the Telefolmin, the closest neighbours and allies of the Urapmin, to consider some data of a kind I do not have for the Urapmin themselves.

4. I take this opportunity to note that in Urapmin Afek's bones are kept in a secret cave (*wim tem*), rather than in a cult house, as Godelier suggests and as is the normal place to keep ancestral bones in other Min groups (thus rendering this cave another feature of their religious life that makes the Urapmin distinctive among their neighbours).

5. I should also note that a good deal of secret eating for oneself without sharing also goes on in daily life in all of the Min cultures, though it is not valued as such, as it is in the men's cult, and is generally publicly condemned (Jorgensen 1984: 119–20; Bercovitch 1994).

6. I say this while setting aside a number of novel Christian practices by which Urapmin have recently attempted to find ways of speaking that, in line with modern Western language ideology, allow them to express their intentions. I have discussed these practices at length elsewhere, most recently in an article that also provides a fuller account of the practice of women speaking the name of the men they want to marry (Robbins 2008).

Bibliography

Austin, J.L. 1975. *How to do Things With Words*. Cambridge: Harvard University Press.

Barth, F. 1975. *Ritual and Knowledge among the Baktaman of New Guinea*. New Haven: Yale University Press.

Bercovitch, E. 1994. 'The Agent in the Gift: Hidden Exchange in Inner New Guinea', *Cultural Anthropology* 9(4): 498–536.

Duranti, A. 1993a. 'Intentions, Self, and Responsibility: an Essay in Samoan Ethnopragmatics', in J.H. Hill and J.T. Irvine (eds), *Responsibility and Evidence in Oral Discourse*. Cambridge: Cambridge University Press, pp. 24–47.

———— 1993b. 'Truth and Intentionality: An Ethnographic Critique', *Cultural Anthropology* 8(2): 214–45.

Eves, R. 1998. *The Magical Body: Power, Fame and Meaning in a Melanesian Society*. Amsterdam: Harwood Academic.

Gardner, D. 1981. 'Cult Ritual and Social Organization among the Mianmin', PhD dissertation. Canberra: Australian National University.

Godelier, M. 1986. *The Making of Great Men: Male Domination and Power among the New Guinea Baruya*. New York: Cambridge University Press.

———— 1999. *The Enigma of the Gift*. Translation by N. Scott. Chicago: University of Chicago Press.

Grice, P. 1989. *Studies in the Way of Words*. Cambridge: Harvard University Press.

Hubert, H. and M. Mauss. 1964. *Sacrifice: Its Nature and Function*. Translation by W.D. Halls. Chicago: University of Chicago Press.

Jorgensen, D. 1981. 'Taro and Arrows: Order, Entropy, and Religion among the Telefolmin', PhD dissertation. Vancouver: University of British Columbia.

———— 1984. 'The Clear and the Hidden: Person, Self, and Suicide among the Telefomin of Papua New Guinea', *Omega* 14: 113–26.

———— 1990. 'Secrecy's Turns', *Canberra Anthropology* 13(1): 40–47.

Keane, W. 2002. 'Sincerity, 'Modernity,' and the Protestants', *Cultural Anthropology* 17(1): 65–92.

———— 2007. *Christian Moderns: Freedom and Fetish in the Mission Encounter*. Berkeley: University of California Press.

Lévi-Strauss, C. 1963. *Structural Anthropology*. Translation by C. Jacobson and B.G. Schoepf. New York: Basic Books.

———— 1987. *Introduction to the Work of Marcel Mauss*.Translation by F. Baker. London: Routledge and Kegan Paul.

LiPuma, E. 2000. *Encompassing Others: the Magic of Modernity in Melanesia*. Ann Arbor: University of Michigan Press.

Makihara, M. and B.B. Schieffelin (eds). 2007. *Consequences of Contact: Language Ideologies and Sociocultural Transformations in Pacific Societies*. Oxford: Oxford University Press.

Munn, N.M. 1986. *The Fame of Gawa: A Symbolic Study of Value Transformation in a Massim (Papua New Guinea) Society*. New York: Cambridge University Press.

O'Hanlon, M. 1989. *Reading the Skin: Adornment, Display and Society among the Wahgi*. London: British Museum Publications.

Peters, J.D. 1999. *Speaking into the Air: A History of the Idea of Communication*. Chicago: University of Chicago Press.

Reddy, W.J. 1993. 'The Conduit Metaphor: A Case of Frame Conflict in our Language about Language', in A. Ortony (ed.), *Metaphor and Thought*, Second Edition. New York: Cambridge University Press, pp. 164–201.

Robbins, J. 1994. 'Equality as a Value: Ideology in Dumont, Melanesia and the West', *Social Analysis* 36: 21–70.

——— 1999.'"This is Our Money": Modernism, Regionalism, and Dual Currencies in Urapmin', in J. Robbins and D. Akin (eds), *Money and Modernity: State and Local Currencies in Contemporary Melanesia.* Pittsburgh: University of Pittsburgh Press, pp. 82–102.

——— 2001. 'God is Nothing But Talk: Modernity, Language and Prayer in a Papua New Guinea Society', *American Anthropologist* 103(4): 901–12.

——— 2004. *Becoming Sinners: Christianity and Moral Torment in a Papua New Guinea Society.* Berkeley: University of California Press.

——— 2007. 'You Can't Talk Behind the Holy Spirit's Back: Christianity and Changing Language Ideologies in a Papua New Guinea Society', in M. Makihara and B.B. Schieffelin (eds), *Consequences of Contact: Language Ideologies and Sociocultural Transformations in Pacific Societies.* New York: Oxford University Press, pp. 125–39.

——— 2008. 'On Not Knowing Other Minds: Confession, Intention, and Linguistic Exchange in a Papua New Guinea Community.' *Anthropological Quarterly* 81(2): 421–9.

Robbins, J. and A. Rumsey. 2008. 'Introduction: Cultural and Linguistic Anthropology and the Opacity of Other Minds', *Anthropological Quarterly* 81(2): 407–20.

Rumsey, A. and J. Robbins. 2008. 'Anthropology and the Opacity of Other Minds', Special Journal Section, *Anthropological Quarterly* 81(2): 407–94.

Schieffelin, B., K.A. Woolard and P.V. Kroskrity (eds). 1998. *Language Ideologies: Practice and Theory.* New York: Oxford University Press.

Schieffelin, B.B. 1986. 'Teasing and Shaming in Kaluli Children's Interactions', in B.B. Schieffelin and E. Ochs (eds), *Language Socialization across Cultures.* New York: Cambridge University Press, pp. 165–81.

——— 1990. *The Give and Take of Everyday Life: Language Socialization of Kaluli Children.* New York: Cambridge University Press.

——— 2007. 'Found in Translating: Reflexive Language across Time and Texts', in M. Makihara and B.B. Schieffelin (eds), *Consequences of Contact: Language Ideologies and Sociocultural Transformations in Pacific Societies.* New York: Oxford University Press, pp. 140–65.

Searle, J. R. 1969. *Speech Acts: An Essay in the Philosophy of Language.* Cambridge: Cambridge University Press.

Silverstein, M. 1979. 'Language Structure and Linguistic Ideology', in P.R. Clyne, W.F. Hanks and C.L. Hofbauer (eds), *The Elements: A Parasession on Linguistic Units and Levels.* Chicago: Chicago Linguistic Society, pp. 193–47.

——— 1998. 'The Uses and Utility of Ideology: A Commentary', in B.B. Schieffelin, K.A. Woolard, and P.V. Kroskrity (eds), *Language Ideologies: Practice and Theory.* New York: Oxford University Press, pp. 123–45.

Stasch, R. 2008. 'Knowing Minds is a Matter of Authority: Political Dimensions of Opacity Statements in Korowai Moral Psychology', *Anthropological Quarterly* 81(2): 443–53.

Strathern, A. 1981. '"Noman": Representations of Identity in Mount Hagen', in L. Holy and M. Stuchlik (eds), *The Structure of Folk Models*. London: Academic Press, pp. 281–303.

Strathern, M. 1979. 'The Self in Self-Decoration', *Oceania* 49(4): 241–57.

Strenski, I. 2002. *Contesting Sacrifice: Religion, Nationalism, and Social Thought in France*. Chicago: University of Chicago Press.

Weiner, A.B. 1992. *Inalienable Possessions: The Paradox of Keeping-While-Giving*. Berkeley: University of California Press.

Woolard, K.A. 1998. 'Introduction: Language Ideology as a Field of Inquiry', in B.B. Schieffelin, K.A. Woolard and P.V. Kroskrity (eds), *Language ideologies: Practice and Theory*. New York: Oxford University Press, pp. 3–47.

Woolard, K.A. and B.B. Schieffelin. 1994. 'Language Ideology.' *Annual Review of Anthropology* 23: 55–82.

Chapter 2

THE ENIGMA OF CHRISTIAN CONVERSION: EXCHANGE AND THE EMERGENCE OF NEW GREAT MEN AMONG THE MAISIN OF PAPUA NEW GUINEA

John Barker

In his account of changes in Baruya society following European contact in 1951, Maurice Godelier writes intriguingly of 'a small group of young Baruya men who represent a new kind of great man' (Godelier 1986: 205).[1] These six or seven individuals were among the first generation to attend village schools run by the Lutheran Mission in the 1960s. Adopting the missionaries' contempt for indigenous rituals, mythology and shamanism, they excelled at their studies and in due course received mission sponsorship to attend secondary and tertiary schools elsewhere in Papua New Guinea, moving on to mainly secular professional careers as the country moved towards Independence. Once away from the villages, most had a change of heart concerning their ancestral culture. Eventually all but a pastor returned to their villages to undergo at least the main initial rituals. Indeed, most became avid supporters of both male and female initiations, viewing them as their cultural 'roots, their identity' (ibid.: 206). By the late 1970s, they had become 'folk heroes' to locals, exemplary in their command of English, their careers in the outside world, and their willingness to share their money to help kin and affines. In their success and through their example, they had come to replace 'great warriors' (*aoulatta*) at the top of the Baruya hierarchy of types of men (ibid.: 220).

Godelier draws a contrast with another type then emerging on the scene: local entrepreneurs setting up canteens and other small businesses. These individuals displayed attributes of the famed big men reported from elsewhere in New Guinea in their appeals to lineage and tribal members for supporting funds to set up shop, thus helping 'others while helping themselves' (ibid.: 216). However, Baruya provided poor ground for the emergence of true big men in part because the cash upon which the entrepreneurs depended came from outside the region, but mainly because the local social structure did not easily permit the conversion of money into traditional forms of wealth or the staging of large-scale secular exchanges upon which aspiring leaders could cement their reputations. In sum, while greatly impacted by the forces of modernity, Baruya as of the late 1970s remained a great man society.

Given the attention that anthropologists have devoted to traditional big men, it should not come as a surprise that they have tended to focus much more on his modern counterpart than on contemporary great men. Beyond the enduring fascination with figures like the Highlands leader Ongka (Strathern 1979), at least from the time of Marshall Sahlins' (1963) classic essay on Oceanic leadership, many observers have perceived an inherent commonality between big men and capitalist entrepreneurs (Finney 1973). Godelier's many writings on the subject of leadership, exchange and power suggest an evolutionary path from relatively egalitarian great man societies, through competitive big man systems, eventually to the stark inequalities and alienations of modern capitalism (Godelier 1986 and 1999). Several of the contributors to *Big Men & Great Man* (Godelier and Strathern 1991) agree, arguing that the introduction of capitalism both encouraged and expanded the scope for big men in Melanesia at the expense of great men systems (e.g. Schwimmer 1991).

All the same, most anthropologists working in contemporary rural Melanesia would readily recognize the types of modern great men sketched by Godelier. This is strikingly so for the Maisin of Oro Province who during the three decades I have worked with them have chosen their leaders from a pool of men (and to a much more limited extent, women) who had enjoyed relatively advanced education and professional careers elsewhere in the country before returning to their villages. All speak good English, have extended networks of relatives working elsewhere in the country, and are pillars of the Church and proud guardians of Maisin customs and traditions. Many have from time to time tried their hands at small businesses with limited success.

Their influence in the villages rests solidly upon their reputations as consensus-builders – a skill that in contemporary Maisin communities requires an ability to negotiate the three tiers of current identity: as villagers, citizens and Christians (Barker 2007).

In what follows, I will trace the cultural and historical roots of the contemporary great man system of leadership amongst the Maisin. As with the Baruya, much of the explanation rests with the indigenous exchange system. Drawing upon the brilliant insights of *The Enigma of the Gift*, I focus not only upon typical exchange patterns but specifically upon inalienable objects and their links to the sacred and the imaginary. I expand upon Godelier's analysis by arguing that the emergence of new great men among the Maisin, and likely elsewhere, was intimately associated with Christian conversion. Conversion for the Maisin has entailed change – often radical change – but change nevertheless requiring the conscious embrace of both tradition and modernity. The enigma of the gift thus leads us to consider the enigma of Christian conversion.

Kawo-Evovi: Keeping for Giving and Things that Must be Kept

Between 2000 and 2500 Maisin speakers live in four village clusters along the southern shore of Collingwood Bay near the border between Oro and Milne Bay Provinces. Since 1981, I have carried out most of my work in the largest of these. With a population of at least 800 people, Uiaku is made up of four villages straddling two sides of a broad, shallow river and stretching over 1.5 kilometres of coastline. The villages are all multinucleated, made up of contiguous hamlets named after the patrilineal clans that inhabit them. Through the colonial period up to the present, Collingwood Bay has remained an economic backwater in Papua New Guinea, accessible only by small coastal vessels and increasingly irregular airplane service to grass airstrips north of Maisin territory. Apart from decorated pounded barkcloth (tapa cloth), for which the Maisin are famous, villagers have been unsuccessful at developing products for sale in the cash economy. Since the late 1950s, hundreds of Maisin have migrated out of the area to advance their education and to attain jobs, mostly in urban centres. Their remittances of cash and commodities supplement the local economy, which by and large remains subsistence-based, dependent upon gardening, fishing, hunting and gathering from the extensive swamps and forests lying inland from the villages.

During the late 1990s, the Maisin garnered a degree of fame amongst international environmental activists when they refused to allow the commercial logging of their rainforest (Barker 2004 and 2008). The many visitors during that time were charmed by what they perceived as a 'tribe' that had steadfastly maintained its traditions. This was certainly understandable. To the extent one can ignore the clouds of biting sandflies and mosquitoes, the villages and villagers have an irresistible exotic charm. All but a handful of houses are made of bush materials and the grounds of the hamlets are carefully swept each day and beautifully adorned with shrubs, flowers and palm trees. Most women in their forties and older bear elaborate facial tattoos[2] and the Maisin speak proudly of the enduring importance of their traditions. Appearances, however, are deceiving. Few aspects of Maisin life have not been affected profoundly by more than a century of interactions with Europeans and the world beyond Collingwood Bay. A school has operated in Uiaku more or less continually since 1902 and Anglican Christianity has been thoroughly absorbed into the local culture. Almost all adults have spent time studying, visiting and working in urban areas and many villagers of all ages are fluent in Pidgin and English. While people are proud of their traditions and language, villagers also often express a profound sense of loss: an awareness that many customs have been forgotten and that what remains, not least the Maisin language itself, has become deeply corrupted by outside influences.

Like all but the most remote rural communities in Papua New Guinea, the Maisin live in a social world defined by both gift and commodity exchanges. Over the years, villagers have become increasingly dependent upon money to purchase an ever-broadening array of goods and to pay for services such as school fees and medical expenses. Discussions about cash – how to find it and properly use it – dominate village politics and many conversations after the day's work is done. All the same, gift exchange remains a key part of Maisin society. Virtually all major tasks, from clearing gardens to building houses, rely upon the frequent and open exchange of food, labour, betel nut and other items. A person's life course is still marked by major formal exchanges centred upon birth, adolescence, marriage and death. Maisin moral discourse revolves around central values of reciprocity, sharing, and balance. When the Maisin speak of 'tradition', they are often referring precisely to exchanges and the values that underlie them, drawing an implied (and often quite direct) contrast to a stereotype of European stinginess and individualism (cf. Bashkow 2006; Smith 1994).

When speaking about traditions in their own language, the Maisin speak of '*kikiki*'. In most cases, *kikiki* translates as 'story' and refers to the large corpus of popular folk tales (*amai kikiki*, 'ordinary stories') which can be told by and to anyone, and much more restricted *kikiki moturan,* 'true stories' – generally clan histories and stories legitimating prerogatives owned by clans or individuals, such as shamanistic powers or a certain tapa cloth design. The Maisin, however, also use *kikiki* in reference to non-discursive objects understood as reflecting or drawing upon ancestry, such as traditional songs and dances, dance costumes, tapa cloth, carved lime spatulas, and so forth. In contemporary Maisin usage, *kikiki* can be translated as something that embodies ancestral 'heritage' (Barker 2001). More importantly for this discussion, the category marks items as outside the range of ordinary exchange. They are inalienable possessions (Weiner 1992), 'those which concentrate the greatest imaginary power and, as a consequence, the greatest symbolic value' (Godelier 1999: 33). Specifically, they serve to 'affirm deep-seated *identities and their continuity* over time' (ibid., original emphasis). They thus exemplify the general principle defined by Godelier as 'keeping-for-giving' in that they serve to define the parameters of exchange and the social order that lies behind.

The most restricted of all *kikiki* are clan-owned designs painted onto barkcloth skirts and loincloths and, in the past, carved on wood. Such designs are believed to have been worn by the ancestors at the dawn of time, when the clans emerged in turn from an underground location far to the east of Collingwood Bay. The tapa emblems form part of a larger collection of decorations, objects, totems, histories, and ritual prerogatives that distinguish the clans, collectively known as *kawo-evovi.* Clan possessions may never be sold. While women may use either their fathers' or their husbands' *kawo-evovi,* rights of possession pass strictly down the male line. The only exception to the rule occurs during some initiation ceremonies, when maternal uncles may choose to allow a first-born child to use his or her mother's emblems and even, on very rare occasions, pass them to their own children.

Despite the clear rules – or perhaps in part because of them – *kawo-evovi* are a matter of great dispute amongst the Maisin. In part this is because the lines between clans are not nearly as clear as people often assume them to be, not least because of high levels of village endogamy and adoption. In addition, the Maisin believe that memory of many if not most of the clan emblems has been lost – the result of a steady decline in the frequency and scale of ceremonies in which they are displayed. Hence, decline and faulty memories have added to the confusion. Taken as a category, however, *kawo-evovi* are the oldest of the old things used by the Maisin. Like all old things, they do not just identify but embody the ancestors. When a Maisin decorates himself for the dance, donning his *kawo-evovi,* he merges with the original ancestor at the moment he emerged from underground at the dawn of time. Such sacra do indeed 'affirm deep-seated *identities and their continuity* over time' (Godelier 1999: 33), not least in the way in which the Maisin conceptualize traditional leadership.

Kawo and Sabu: The Making of Great Men[3]

Oral traditions and current practices suggest that pre-contact Maisin leadership closely approximated a great man system: that is, a system based upon distinct spheres of difference rather than one based upon a common measure, as in big man systems (Jorgensen 1991: 270), or inherited ranks, as in chieftainships. Certainly elements of big men type competition or notions of inherited rank were and are present as in many lowland societies (Liep 1991), yet the tendency was to stress difference, between men and women in general and between types of leaders in particular.

The Maisin recognized a diversity of possible kinds of exemplary persons in various spheres: warriors, feast-makers, magicians, gardeners, hunters, healers, and so forth. Almost all of these were men, the main exceptions being tapa and tattoo designers, who were female, and possibly healers, who today at least may be of either gender. At the present time, the most influential leaders combine several talents: as prolific gardeners, orators, and alliance-builders, for instance. This was almost certainly true in the past as well, but not the past as imagined by Maisin historians. The common identification of clans with distinctive and inalienable *kawo-evovi* inherited solely through the male line, as discussed earlier, reinforces a politics based upon a logic of difference.

This principle is most clearly exemplified in the case of the two most prominent types of traditional leaders: those Maisin today refer to (in English) as 'peace chiefs' and 'war chiefs'. Peace chiefs, it is said, hosted feasts and exchanged gifts of food, tapa, shell valuables, and spouses with erstwhile enemies, transforming them into allies by bringing them into a state of balanced reciprocity. War chiefs, on the other hand, took prominence in the face of threats from enemies or the organization of attacks on neighbours. As in other lowland Melanesian societies which make this distinction, the war/peace designation more exactly refers to a hereditary class system (Chowning 1979: 70). The Maisin distinguish between two types of ranked clans – *Kawo* and *Sabu*. The so-called 'chiefs' were actually the prominent men of each type of clan.

According to oral traditions, the Maisin migrated into Collingwood from the west in two, possibly three clan confederacies, each composed of higher ranked *Kawo* and lower ranked *Sabu* clans. As with clans, the identities of *Kawo* and *Sabu* were fixed in terms of a set of inalienable rights and emblems. As befits their higher rank, *Kawo* clans were far better endowed than their associated *Sabu*. As a class, they held the sole right to host feasts, dancing and large-scale exchanges in their hamlets. They possessed the right to use large lime pots and ornate lime spatulas when chewing betel nut and were the first to speak during public gatherings. While the specifics varied from clan to clan, *Kawo* in general possessed rights to wear a richer and wider assortment of ornaments than their *Sabu* counterparts. In contrast, *Sabu* clans held far fewer *kawo-evovi*. Their chief distinguishing trait was an uncompromising fierceness during times of battle. In a favoured metaphor, the *Sabu* represented a spear to the *Kawo*'s drum.

Kawo and *Sabu* existed in an asymmetrical relationship. The Maisin sometimes refer to the *Sabu* as 'servants' in light of their duty to provide food and perform dances at the feasts managed by *Kawo*. But the relationship goes deeper than this. *Sabu* are described in oral traditions as passionate, hot-headed and violent. One of the chief duties of the *Kawo* is to 'care for' their *Sabu* by giving advice, calming their passions, and channelling their energies into productive activities during peacetime (while unleashing them against enemies in times of conflict). In short, the idealized relationship was one of asymmetrical exchange in which *Sabu* showed 'respect' (*muan*) to their *Kawo* in exchange for advice that allowed the society to survival and prosper.

This sketch, it must be emphasized, is based upon stories the Maisin tell each other about the old days. Like all such idealizations, they reveal as much if not more about contemporary assumptions as they do about past arrangements. Seen in this way, the *Kawo/Sabu* relationship stands for a pervasive principle in the Maisin social order centred upon seniority. Thus parents, elder brothers, and clan elders stand respectively towards their children, younger brothers, and members of junior lineages in a relationship parallel to that imagined for *Kawo* and *Sabu* clans. They provide sound advice, care and nurturance to their juniors in order to shape their raw energies, to make them socially human. In return, juniors should listen to their elders respectfully and generously supply them with food and labour. Conflicts in Maisin villages are regularly attributed to people failing to fulfil their obligations under this scenario: juniors do not listen or obey their elders and thus act as selfish 'big heads' or elders fails to give good advice to control those under their watch (Barker 1998).

The distinction between the two types of clans determined the type of leader a man might become, but it could not determine who would actually become a leader or exactly how he might exercise his influence. That clearly rested upon ability and circumstances. Further, the general superiority of the *Kawo* clearly did not translate into a general dominance of *Kawo* over *Sabu* but instead pertained primarily to ritual moments, particularly alliance-building feasts. Indeed, many of the outstanding Maisin leaders over the past quarter century or more have been *Sabu* who have successfully drawn on the support of members across the villages. Nobody suggests that this is inappropriate or new.

To understand this apparent contradiction, one must consider a second principle to the Maisin social order exemplified by *Kawo* leaders and typical of great men systems: a strong preference for restricted and balanced exchange. While there was a strong competitive element in the feasts managed by *Kawo* leaders, their explicit aim was to form alliances by establishing balanced exchanges over time. By the same token, the favoured form of marriage was sibling exchange or, failing that, the presentation of children to wife-givers for adoption as balanced compensation for the loss of their sisters. The string of back and forth exchanges triggered by marriage, climaxing in a major ceremony marking the passage into puberty of a first-born child, also aimed at the creation of balance and stability between exchange partners. Again, as was typical in great man societies, this emphasis on balanced and restricted exchange was accompanied by a powerful ethical rhetoric of equivalence between men. Like the Tangu 'managers' of Madang Province, brilliantly described by Kenelm Burridge (1969), Maisin leaders had to perform a delicate balancing act of exercising influence while appearing to be the equal of their peers. The political order was thus inherently fragile.

Kawo and *Sabu* men were the most prominent types of great men in Maisin society a century or so ago, but before leaving this topic, a third major type needs to be briefly discussed: the *wea tamati*, or 'poison man'. One group of *Kawo* clans is said to have appeared at the dawn of time possessing a particularly deadly form of sorcery. They do not appear to have had *Sabu* associates or have sponsored feasts of their own, but instead worked in association with other *Kawo* when called upon as enforcers of their authority. They were greatly feared even by their associates because ultimately they could not be controlled or brought into equivalence. Their singular power to kill in secret presented the antithesis of a social order based upon exchange and its greatest vulnerability. The arrival of Europeans in general and missionaries in particular opened an opportunity to purge sorcerers and, in exploiting that opening, the Maisin would discover new kinds of great men.

Missionaries as Great Men

My central claim in this essay is that the conditions created by colonialism in general, and Christianity in particular, were more conducive in the case of the Maisin to the emergence of a new type of great rather than big man. The appearance of new types of great men in colonial Maisin society should not be understood in any simple sense as an expression of cultural continuity or resistance. Instead, it emerged as the product of indigenous and missionary moral and spiritual discourses, as a 'conjuncture of structures' in Sahlins' (1985) terms. I have already sketched the indigenous political system. A much briefer account must now be given of the mission's assumptions about leadership as well as the circumstances of its presence in Maisin villages.

The Anglican mission came to the north coast of what was then British New Guinea (after 1906, Papua) at the invitation of the Administrator, William Macgregor, who encouraged the entrance of missionaries as an adjunct to the task of pacification (Wetherell 1977). The mission almost immediately collapsed following the death of its founder within weeks of establishing the first station and inadequate support in staff or money from the mother church in Australia. It remained the poorest of the major missions throughout the colonial period, struggling to provide the rudiments of Christian services and education over the large district that Macgregor had allotted to it. The mission was also unusual in terms of the tolerance its leaders expressed for many aspects of indigenous culture, such as dancing and initiations, at that time fiercely opposed by the Methodist and Congregationalist missions operating elsewhere in Papua. In part, tolerance was born of necessity: the Anglicans depended much more than most other missionaries upon the material support of local villagers for their survival. Yet it also reflected the attitudes of the Anglican bishops and senior clergy, most of whom were strongly inspired by Anglo-Catholic Tractarianism of the mid-nineteenth century. Fiercely critical of the social costs of industrialization in Europe, the Anglican leaders romanticized about recreating in Papua a version of medieval Christendom in which the priest would serve as the guiding 'father' of his village parish in a hierarchy leading up through the Bishop to God Himself. Conversion was not meant to be disruptive, but to gradually 'Christianize' existing village society.

There were, of course, elements of indigenous society that the missionaries opposed such as warfare, cannibalism, the practice of sorcery, and the more violent rituals. For the Maisin, however, the attitudes of the church fathers, in combination with the poverty of the mission, made the transition to Christianity a relatively gentle experience. For all but a few years, the Uiaku station was run by Solomon Island and Papuan teachers under the loose supervision of overworked district missionaries stationed some twelve kilometres to the north in a different language group. While introducing the rudiments of Christianity, the teachers rarely challenged indigenous spiritual assumptions, which they largely shared (Barker 2005b). Baptized villagers were not expected to separate themselves from their pagan neighbours and continued to participate more or less fully in local rituals and exchanges, including those frowned upon by the white missionaries. Over time, a kind of dualism evolved in the Maisin's religious practices, with Christian services mainly located within the bounds of the mission station at the centre of Uiaku and 'traditional' ceremonies continuing in the surrounding villages (Barker 1993).

We cannot know in any detail how the Maisin regarded the missionaries in the early days, but there is little doubt that they conceived of their relationship in terms of exchange. From a very early date, district missionaries complained that villagers, including Christians, expected to be paid with tobacco and other goods for services rendered to the mission such as the upkeep of buildings or provision of food for the teachers. Many villagers thus treated the mission more or less as an outside entity, expecting immediate compensation for services rendered. Yet there is evidence from a remarkably early stage that the Maisin (like the missionaries) wished for a relationship based upon something more than bartering. Within a few weeks of the erection of the Uiaku station, made entirely from bush materials using local labour, villagers approached a very surprised teacher with a large collection of bundles and others materials indicating that they wished them to be destroyed. The same request was made to the district missionary when he arrived a few days later. Exhilarated by what he saw as the miraculous working of the Holy Ghost, he organized a huge public bonfire into which he and the teachers tossed the signs of, as they saw it, pagan superstition. As it turned out, this was only the first in a series of attempts to purge the villages of sorcery that have continued to the present. By far the most significant of these occurred in 1919–1920, when in an act of internal rebellion, villagers enlisted missionaries in a campaign to destroy the power of those *Kawo* clans possessing 'poison' as their *kawo-evovi* prerogative. In short order, the *sacra* of the sorcery clans – their large lime pots – ended up in the fires (Barker 2003).

Elderly Maisin in the early 1980s vividly recalled these early purges. They did not attribute their success, limited as it turned out to be, to the missionaries or God's power. Instead, they spoke of a partnership based upon a hierarchical exchange between villagers and missionaries (cf. Schwimmer 1973: 77–81). Their formulation boiled down to this. The missionaries brought the '*giu*': Christian knowledge as conveyed in worship services, sermons and the Bible.[4] In return, converts listened respectfully to the missionaries and the teachers, sent their children to the village school, attended services and accepted baptism. The missionaries' gift of the *giu* and the villagers' response of respectful listening – a poise that implies obedience – brought the partners into a state of balance, creating a condition of social amity moving beyond mutual obligation. It was that state, rather than the power of the Christian god *per se*, that enabled the purification of the community through the public destruction of the sorcerer's chief tool and emblem.

The partnership between missionaries and villagers was obviously modelled on that imagined between *Kawo* and *Sabu* clans. This parallel structure was reinforced repeatedly in my conversations with the Maisin. A much-loved story often performed in skits relates the arrival of the founders of the Anglican mission, the Reverends Albert Maclaren and Copland King, by whaleboat at Uiaku.[5] They are confronted by wild warriors. Just as they are about to spear the strangers, a spirit of peace comes over the warriors who lead them up from the beach to sit in the shade of a village house, hosted by the *Kawo* man. The *Kawo* leader presents them with food and in return the missionaries talk of the love of God, speaking the *giu*. The story always ends with the statement, 'And that's when we stopped fighting and were at peace'. Similar tales are told across coastal Papua New Guinea, all conveying the familiar division between the time of 'pagan darkness' and 'Christian light' (e.g. Errington and Gewertz 1994; Young 1977). The specific importance of the Maisin version lies in its identification of missionaries as a new, more powerful type of *Kawo*. They are identified in terms of their most sacred, inalienable object: the *giu*. This object legitimates and authorizes their higher status and their ability to give advice and calm the warlike passions of pagan villagers, here placed in the subservient position of *Sabu* and younger brothers.

The identity of missionaries as a type of great man – a more powerful *Kawo* – is furthered suggested in Maisin claims about the outcome of the partnership, the establishment of peace through the creation of social amity. The Maisin term for this valued condition is *marawa-wawe* which translates literally as 'giving of one's guts' or vitality. The term denotes a condition of perfect balance, one which transcends obligation. Significantly, this is the desired outcome of all major exchanges in Maisin culture, ranging from the series set off by marriage and ending in death and those sponsored by *Kawo* clans to create alliances. The difference here is one of scope. Village-level exchanges might create social amity between the exchange partners but at the same time reinforce clan and kin boundaries. The exchange with the missionary *Kawo*, however, is imagined as transcending local divisions to create a powerful embracing condition of *marawa-wawe*, one so powerful as to cleanse the community of the evil of sorcery.

Or so I was told. It is important to stress that my analysis here focused upon stories the Maisin tell each other about the sorcery purges. What 'really happened' was certainly much more complex and ambiguous, open to a variety of readings. Further, whatever degree of social unity was achieved, the state of *marawa-wawe* proved transitory; the evil of social division and the sorcery that accompanies it soon returned, setting up the basis for future purges. All the same, the evidence strongly suggests that the Maisin in the early 1980s thought of the missionaries as a new, powerful *Kawo*. This was probably true from a very early date. The missionaries themselves encouraged the association, although they could hardly have been aware of doing so. The strong paternalistic ethos of the mission and its structure resonated with the hierarchical nature of the *Kawo/Sabu* distinction. The missionaries' unwillingness and/or inability to insert themselves into the daily affairs of the Maisin also concurred with the limited nature of *Kawo* authority. Like a *Kawo*, the missionaries became 'great' in the context of ritual and exchange. They were not 'chiefs'. The mission thus brought something new to the Maisin while affirming received notions of leadership and the form of exchange they are based upon.

The Making of New Great Men[6]

In his celebrated book on cargo cults, *Mambu*, Burridge (1960) describes how the Tangu sought the 'moral European', that is to say the white man who would accept a balanced exchange relationship and thus restore their sense of dignity, alongside access to European wealth and power. It is not unlikely that in the early twentieth century the Maisin harboured similar dreams about the Anglican missionaries. If so, they were soon frustrated. The district missionary made only brief visits to the villages, working mainly with his teachers. 'Respectful listening' in the school and church services did not result in the arrival of European wealth and equality. The Maisin might dream of missionaries as a new type of great man, but they could not make them act the part.

The conditions of pacification provided young Maisin men with varying degrees of access into the colonial system and eventually opportunities to develop their own new forms of leadership. Beginning around 1912, all able-bodied men worked for at least one eighteen-month stint as indentured labourers on European run plantations and mines elsewhere in the colony. Within the villages, a few individuals were selected by the Resident Magistrate and district missionary respectively for the middleman offices of village constable and pupil teacher. Although their formal authority and effectiveness were quite limited, most are recalled as being petty tyrants in their spheres of action. The most select group of all was made up of a handful of men who left the villages to advance their education and training, eventually working as police and clerks with the government and as teachers with the mission. Much like the first generation of Baruya to 'make it' in the colonial system, these men enjoyed great prestige amongst those who remained behind.

As with Baruya, a new type of great man rose from the ranks of those who left the villages for professional careers and returned. Most village men served as labourers for Australian troops during the brutal Kokoda campaign of 1942–1943 and afterwards. At the conclusion of the Second World War, they returned home determined to improve the economic conditions of the villages. Rumours quickly spread through what was then the Northern District of a cooperative enterprise begun by the missionary at the village of Gona located on the central coast, spawning many imitators. The Maisin cooperative movement got its start in late 1946 when a mission teacher and a member of the Papuan Infantry Battalion abandoned their positions to return to Uiaku. Both were members of *Kawo* clans. One of their first acts was to organize meetings in which rival clan confederacies destroyed fighting clubs and spears, symbolizing a new era of peace and prosperity – of *marawa-wawe*. The district missionary was invited down to bless seedlings and tools. To the accompaniment of prayers and hymns, villagers enthusiastically expanded coconut plantations and established new plantings of cocoa and other cash crops.

The first cooperative soon floundered and collapsed. It was followed by several others over the next three decades. None enjoyed much financial success. Most of the managers proved incapable of keeping track of money, lending credit to relatives or spending it on parties for workers. The government periodically inspected the plantations and provided some technical assistance, but generally viewed the cooperatives with suspicion, as nascent cargo cults. Perhaps the greatest obstacle was the lack of regular shipping through Collingwood, making it difficult and expensive to get crops to market. In response to these obstacles and their need to get on with basic subsistence needs, villagers' enthusiasm for the cooperatives waxed and waned. By the time of my arrival in Uiaku, the cooperative had shrunk in scope to a small trade store which remained empty and locked during most of my stay.

Despite this long history of failure, the cooperative remained a subject of intense concern during 1981–1983. I attended several long village meetings where speaker after speaker lamented the poor state of the cooperative, not so much for failing to generate income but for what it revealed about the moral condition of the community. The rhetoric of the speeches directly replicated those heard during village meetings dealing with sorcery fears and accusations. While practical difficulties of getting goods to and from markets were mentioned, together with the pressures that managers faced from relatives seeking credit, the main cause of the cooperative's failings was attributed to gossip. People were whispering about the managers, jealous of their access to goods and prominent positions. Just as jealousy was the main cause of sorcery attack, the cooperative had become 'sick' because of incessant backbiting and division.

The Maisin were not able to simply write off the cooperative as a failure because by this time it had also become a potent symbol of *marawa-wawe*, of the condition of social amity that brings peace and prosperity. It had assumed this status in no small part because of its close association with the church and, more broadly, the ideal of unity at the community level. Villagers firmly believed that this unity had been created for a time and then lost. They pointed to one event in particular. During the late 1950s, leaders had used money earned through copra sales to purchase materials and build a semi-permanent church in Uiaku – the first in Collingwood Bay, I was told. The consecration was a huge celebration, lasting several days and marked by feasts and dances as well as long church services. The Bishop arrived to find the church surrounded by a low fence made of crossed sticks, a traditional marker of a tabooed area. This *oraa*, however, had a far greater significance for it was composed of a variety of woods that were the totemic possessions of the individual clans in the community. In effect, the church grounds provided a materialization of the *giu* (Christian knowledge) of the mission transcending and uniting the *sacra* of the clans.

This moment of Durkheimian effervescence proved to be short-lived. Still, it vividly displayed the stage upon which the new great men operated. Like the *Kawo* of old, they were expected to 'care for' ordinary villagers by offering sound advice drawn from their knowledge of traditions, of the Christian *giu* and, increasingly, the world of commerce outside the village. Unlike their ancestors, however, they were expected to serve the whole community, not just clan mates and kin. To the extent that ordinary villagers responded with respectful cooperation and refrained from gossip, conditions of social amity could be created to the benefit of all.

The first generation of the new great men strongly identified with the church. By the early 1980s, however, the modern varieties of great men were diversifying. Having had early access to schooling, the Maisin were positioned to benefit when the Australian administration accelerated Papua New Guinea's preparations for Independence during the 1960s. Virtually all village boys and a majority of girls left the villages to attend newly opened high schools and training colleges across the country. Many entered professional careers in the burgeoning civil service, private business, schools, and health care. During the late 1970s, a few of these men began to return to Uiaku to care for ailing parents. Villagers greatly admired them for their success in the outside world and knowledge of English and (so it was hoped) commerce. They very quickly assumed positions of leadership.

Over the past two decades as the national economy has declined, it has become increasingly difficult for young villagers to find employment and many remain in the villages. At the same time, large numbers of professionals have returned either because they have reached retirement age or because they want to raise families away from the dangers of the cities. The forms of great men – and to a much lesser extent, great women – have accordingly diversified to a certain degree. The Maisin today identify three general categories of leaders: village, church and government. Roughly speaking, village leaders are those elders responsible for managing 'traditional' events such as bridewealth exchanges or memorial ceremonies; church leaders support the work of the village priest; and government leaders work to maintain social order and to promote economic development. Several roles and positions are recognized within each of these categories. Some men and women are renowned as great healers; certain devout individuals are chosen to lead the church Mother's Union or youth fellowship 'crusades'; and other villages may find opportunities to exercise skills in grant writing or money management picked up during their former careers.

Many if not most of the new positions take the form of officers in various committees and associations, a reflection of the penetration of national bureaucratic forms into village society. Despite outward appearances, however, this penetration is very limited. With the partial exception of the priest,[7] no local official is paid and none are even remotely full-time specialists. All villagers spend the bulk of their waking hours engaged in subsistence activities and the daily and periodic exchanges that sustain the social order. With the return of so many former professionals who bring acquisitions from their time in town and in several cases enjoy pensions, villagers have become more tolerant of inequalities. That tolerance, however, has severe limits. Anyone flouting their good fortune risks sorcery attack. As much to the point, no matter what advantages an individual enjoys in terms of education or wealth from a career in town, villagers will not follow any individual unless he lives out an ideal of equality—making gardens, engaging in exchanges, living in a bush-material house. Local offices do not confer authority. Rather, influence depends very much on the degree to which villagers see a person as possessing superior skills but still remaining one of them.

Despite the explosion of types of leadership, the actual number of generally influential men and women in Uiaku remains small. Some are *Kawo* but several *Sabu* members have enjoyed great influence over the past two decades, particularly village councillors. Members of this smaller group are acknowledged for their skills across all three categories of leadership. As elders, they manage important exchanges; they play a prominent role in the church; they respond to conflicts in the community and play key roles in negotiating new projects. They are skilled mediators, whose influence rests upon their ability to forge consensus. In the intense egalitarian ethos of Maisin society, they are the frequent targets of malicious gossip and sorcery accusations and are widely assumed to provide a prime target for sorcery attacks. Their successes are always contingent and limited by circumstances. Thus the flood of environment activists arriving to work with the Maisin to stop logging in the late 1990s created conditions that favoured the rise of leaders skilful at dealing with outsiders at the expense of others. While competition is by no means absent in the rise and decline of modern Maisin leaders, their scope to act in the manner of big men is quite limited. A *Kawo* elder with the support of working relatives can occasionally mount an impressive bridewealth or first-born initiation ceremony, adding to his fame. Yet, unless he also excels in the government and church spheres, that fame will be limited and fleeting. Leaders today are great to the extent that they unite in their person the three pillars of Maisin identity – as villagers, as Christians and as citizens. And they are influential to the extent that they work towards the elusive state of *marawa-wawe* – the perfect balance that transcends obligation and creates the conditions for peace and prosperity.

Conclusion: The Enigma of Christian Conversion

In his seminal writings on power, inequality, gender and the gift, Maurice Godelier's ultimate subject has been the human condition. His approach, however, is grounded in superb ethnography. This is apparent in *The Enigma of the Gift*, which switches between rich detail about the Baruya and other groups, trenchant critiques of the inequities of late capitalism, and profound philosophical reflections on the relationships between humans and the sacred. Chapter 9 of The Making of Great Men reveals Godelier in a less familiar guise, as a historian of sensitivity and insight. His nuanced description of the new forms of Baruya big men emerging in the colonial system suggests that the transition to more competitive types of leaders, such as big men and nascent capitalists, is by no means automatic. Colonial incorporation offers new avenues for differentiated 'greatness' for a small number of young men while the structural basis of the traditional great man system, founded in exchange, proves resilient and flexible enough to foster the acceptance of the new leaders in the greatly altered situation of the present.

In the case of the Maisin, the emergence of new types of great men has been intimately associated with Christian conversion. This has to do in part with the particularities of the Anglican mission – its poverty and the paternal tolerance of its leadership which limited direct interference in local village society. Yet, this was only part of the reason. Across lowland Papua New Guinea, including areas in which white missionaries aggressively challenged local leaders and customary practices, very similar forms of great man leadership arose during the colonial period, associated with Christianity and cooperatives. This is not so surprising when one considers that practically up to the time of Independence (and in some areas, well after), the missions provided one of the few avenues open to villagers for long-term, prestigious employment, as teachers and clergy (Oram 1971). While the missionaries taught an individualistic dogma of personal salvation, in practice village congregations appear to have often embraced a collectivistic ethic, greatly curtailing the authority of indigenous clergy. It has long been thought that colonial incorporation encouraged the efflorescence of major exchange systems, enhancing the power of their chiefly and big man sponsors. There is growing evidence that the same conditions may have done much to stimulate the variety and influence of great men and the forms of exchange which support this type of political organization (e.g. Eriksen 2008).

That there should be a deep structural resonance between the forms of Christianity brought to Melanesia and indigenous exchange systems should not be completely surprising. Godelier argues that the enigma of the gift rests upon things that cannot be given away which serve to regenerate the social order and establish identities. The most powerful and mysterious of these are *sacra*, the objects imagined as belonging to the gods and thus the foundation of all things. The world imagined via an exchange regime founded upon clan *kawo-evovi* emblems was vastly smaller than that of the Christian imaginary, founded upon (as Maisin saw it) the *giu* – sacred Christian knowledge. Yet the underlying principles were the same: a hierarchical exchange partnership defined by inalienable objects which promised a transcendence of obligation and a 'heaven' of prosperity and equality free from the baleful evil of sorcery and division. Christian conversion as the Maisin experienced it confirmed an exchange-based universe while greatly expanding its scope. Hence Maisin elders insisted in their discussions with me that the missionaries did not bring God to their ancestors but rather an expanded awareness of the truth of things. 'Our ancestors were ignorant men', they told me. 'It was only after the missionaries arrived that they knew God was always here.'

The enigma of the gift, as analysed by Godelier, thus sheds light on the enigma of Christian conversion. Anthropologists' perspectives on Melanesian Christianity have tended to veer between two extremes: the view that conversion entails a severe rupture from the traditional past, as opposed to a view that local people wear their new Christian identities lightly, as a veneer over a continuing indigenous cultural core (Barker 1992; Douglas 2001; Robbins 2007). Such debates, however, are by no means limited to Melanesianists or anthropologists. For all students of culture, Christianity presents a puzzle. It is one thing: an internally varied but still instantly recognizable world religion with distinctive doctrines and rituals. And it is many things: 'a massing of historically and culturally contingent elements' whose success rests on an unparalleled capacity to absorb cultural differences (Wood 1993: 307). Applied to Christian conversion, Godelier's masterful treatment of exchange, and of the social and political forms arising thereof, allows us to approach the enigma of Christianity conversion from a fresh perspective with powerful comparative implications. We come to see Christianity as affirmed and transformed in its encounters with local peoples, not just at the conscious level of doctrines and practices but most profoundly as mediated by those inalienable 'words and things' defining the human relationship with the sacred (cf. Keane 2007; Rutherford 2006). In turn, Christianity serves as a revolutionary force in a thoroughly traditional way, at once confirming, translating and transcending the indigenous imagination of the sacred and the social order it engenders.

Notes

1. In 1999 and 2000, Maurice Godelier hosted in Paris two of the first international conferences on what would soon be known as the 'anthropology of Christianity'. With humour, a profound grasp of anthropological theory and apt examples from his beloved Baruya, Godelier encouraged and prodded a diverse group of Oceanists

to move beyond narrow ethnographic concerns to consider the bigger picture of conversion as a revolutionary social moment within which Pacific Islanders inscribed their own meanings and concerns. For most of us, the workshops were a wonderful gift that did much to put Christianity 'on the map' as a legitimate object of anthropological research. It is a pleasure and an honour to repay a small part of an accruing debt to Maurice Godelier for his many seminal contributions to anthropology, philosophy, political economy and Melanesian studies.

2. For a detailed account of women's tattooing, see Barker and Tiejten (1990). The custom was already waning by the early 1980s and abandoned completely by the end of the decade.

3. The following section summarizes a much more detailed account provided in Barker (2005a).

4. Like most missions in polyglot Papua, the Anglicans adopted a simplified version of the Wedau language spoken around their main station at Dogura for use in schools and churches across their district (Clarke 1976). It perhaps reinforces the notion of a gift from the mission that Maisin used the Wedaun *'giu'* to specify 'Christian knowledge' rather than adapting the equivalent vernacular term, *'saramon'*.

5. Albert Maclaren was in fact part of the government party that made first contact with the Maisin in 1890. Copland King would not arrive until two years later, long after Maclaren's death.

6. For much more detailed accounts of the cooperative movement and contemporary Maisin leadership, see Barker (1993, 1996 and 2007).

7. Papua New Guinean priests, based in Uiaku, have served the villages of southern Collingwood Bay since 1962. In recent years a number have been Maisin. While authorized to speak the *giu* in sermons that are occasionally harshly critical of the moral failings of the local community, in practice priests enjoy little authority in village affairs. Poorly and infrequently paid through offerings from villagers, few remain long at their posts.

References

Barker, J. 1992. 'Christianity in Western Melanesian Ethnography', in J. Carrier (ed.), *History and Tradition in Melanesian Anthropology*. Berkeley: University of California Press, p.144–73.

———— 1993. 'We Are "Ekelesia": Conversion in Uiaku, Papua New Guinea', in R.W. Hefner (ed.), *Christian Conversion: Historical and Anthropological Perspectives on a Great Transformation*. Berkeley: University of California Press, p.199–230.

———— 1996. 'Village Inventions: Historical Variations Upon a Regional Theme in Uiaku, Papua New Guinea', *Oceania* 66: 211–19.

———— 1998. 'To Hear Is to Obey: Changing Notions of Law among the Maisin of Papua New Guinea', *Jurnal Undang-Undang. Journal of Malaysian and Comparative Law* 25: 61–88.

———— 2001. 'Dangerous Objects: Changing Indigenous Perceptions of Material Culture in a Papua New Guinea Society', *Pacific Science* 55: 359–75.

———— 2003. 'Christian Bodies: Dialectics of Sickness and Salvation among the Maisin of Papua New Guinea', *Journal of Religious History* 27: 272–92.

———— 2004. 'Between Heaven and Earth: Missionaries, Environmentalists and the Maisin', in V. Lockwood (ed.), *Pacific Island Societies in a Global World*. Englewood Cliffs: Prentice-Hall, p.439–59.

———— 2005a. 'Kawo and Sabu: Perceptions of Traditional Leadership among the Maisin of Papua New Guinea', in C. Gross, H.D. Lyons and D.A. Counts (eds), *A Polymath Anthropologist: Essays in Honour of Ann Chowning*. Research in Anthropology and Linguistics, Monograph 6. Auckland: University of Auckland, p.131–7.

———— 2005b. 'An Outpost in Papua: Anglican Missionaries and Melanesian Teachers among the Maisin, 1902–1934', in P. Brock (ed.), *Indigenous Peoples and Religious Change*. Leiden: Brill, p.79–106.

———— 2007. 'Taking Sides: The Post-Colonial Triangle in Uiaku', in J. Barker (ed.), *The Anthropology of Morality in Melanesia and Beyond*. Aldershot: Ashgate, p.75–91.

———— 2008. *Ancestral Lines: The Maisin of Papua New Guinea and the Fate of the Rainforest*. Toronto: University of Toronto Press.

———— and A.M. Tietjen. 1990. 'Female Facial Tattooing among the Maisin of Oro Province, Papua New Guinea: The Changing Significance of an Ancient Custom', *Oceania* 60: 217–34.

Bashkow, I. 2006. *The Meaning of Whitemen: Race and Modernity in the Orokaiva Cultural World*. Chicago: University of Chicago Press.

Burridge, K.O.L. 1960. Mambu: A Melanesian Millennium. New York: Harper and Row.

———— 1969. *Tangu Traditions*. Oxford: Oxford University Press.

Chowning, A. 1979. 'Leadership in Melanesia', *Journal of Pacific History* 14: 66–84.

Clarke, E. 1976. 'Missionary Lingue Franche: Wedau', in S.A. Wurm (ed.), *Austronesian Languages*. Pacific Linguistics, Series C, No. 39. Canberra: Australian National University, p.953–66.

Douglas, B. 2001. 'From Invisible Christians to Gothic Theater: The Romance of the Millennial in Melanesian Anthropology', *Current Anthropology* 42: 615–49.

Eriksen, A. 2008. *Gender, Christianity and Change in Vanuatu*. Aldershot: Ashgate.

Errington, F. and D. Gewertz. 1994. 'From Darkness to Light in the George Brown Jubilee: The Invention of Nontradition and the Inscription of a National History in East New Britain', *American Ethnologist* 21: 104–22.

Finney, B.R. 1973. *Big-Men and Business: Entrepreneurship and Economic Growth in the New Guinea Highlands*. Hawaii: University of Hawaii Press.

Godelier, M. 1986. *The Making of Great Men: Male Domination and Power among the New Guinea Baruya*. New York: Cambridge University Press.

———— 1999. *The Enigma of the Gift*. Chicago: University of Chicago Press.

———— and M. Strathern (eds). 1991. *Big Men and Great Men: Personifications of Power in Melanesia*. Cambridge: Cambridge University Press.

Jorgensen, D. 1991. 'Big Men, Great Men and Women: Alternative Logics of Gender Difference', in M. Godelier and M. Strathern (eds), *Big Men and Great Men: Personifications of Power in Melanesia*. Cambridge: Cambridge University Press, p.256–71.

Keane, W. 2007. *Christian Moderns: Freedom and Fetish in the Mission Encounter*. Berkeley: University of California Press.

Liep, J. 1991. 'Great Man, Big Man, Chief: A Triangulation of the Massim', in M. Godelier and M. Strathern (eds), *Big Men and Great Men: Personifications of Power in Melanesia*. Cambridge: Cambridge University Press, p.28–47.

Oram, N.D. 1971. 'The London Missionary Society Pastorate: The Emergence of an Educated Elite in Papua', *Journal of Pacific History* 6: 115–37.

Robbins, J. 2007. 'Continuity Thinking and the Problem of Christian Culture: Belief, Time and the Anthropology of Christianity', *Current Anthropology* 48: 5–38.

Rutherford, D. 2006. 'The Bible Meets the Idol: Writing and Conversion in Biak, Irian Jaya, Indonesia', in F. Cannell (ed.), *The Anthropology of Christianity*. Durham, NC: Duke University Press, p.240–72.

Sahlins, M. 1963. 'Poor Man, Rich Man, Big Man, Chief: Political Types in Melanesia and Polynesia', *Comparative Studies in Society and History* 5: 285–303.

——— 1985. *Islands of History*. Chicago: University of Chicago Press.

Schwimmer, E. 1973. *Exchange in the Social Structure of the Orokaiva*. New York: St. Martin's.

——— 1991. 'How Oro Province Societies Fit Godelier's Model', in M. Godelier and M. Strathern (eds), *Big Men and Great Men: Personifications of Power in Melanesia*. Cambridge: Cambridge University Press, p.142–55.

Smith, M.F. 1994. *Hard Times on Kairiru Island: Poverty, Development, and Morality in a Papua New Guinea Village*. Honolulu: University of Hawaii Press.

Strathern, A.J. 1979. *Ongka. A Self Account by a New Guinea Big Man*. London: Duckworth.

Weiner, A.B. 1992. *Inalienable Possessions: The Paradox of Keeping-While-Giving*. Berkeley: University of California Press.

Wetherell, D. 1977. *Reluctant Mission: The Anglican Church in Papua New Guinea, 1891–1942*. St. Lucia: University of Queensland Press.

Wood, P. 1993. 'Afterword: Boundaries and Horizons', in R.W. Hefner (ed.), *Conversion to Christianity*. Berkeley: University of California Press, p.305–21.

Young, M.W. 1977. 'Doctor Bromilow and the Bwaidoka Wars', *Journal of Pacific History* 12: 130–53.

Chapter 3

ALIENATING THE INALIENABLE: MARRIAGE AND MONEY IN A BIG MAN SOCIETY

Polly Wiessner

A prominent theme in the work of Maurice Godelier is that humans have to create structured societies in order to live, and that society must adapt to a changing world. His best known illustration is the elegant contrast between equivalent versus unequivalent exchange in big man and great man societies based on the different ways that men dominate and exchange women in marriage (Godelier 1982). This formulation, grounded in years of meticulous fieldwork among the Baruya of Papua New Guinea, spurred major projects in re-examining systems of production, kinship and exchange, and their relationships to power (Godelier and Strathern 1991, Lemonnier 1990). During the process Godelier came to question his own construct as well as that of Lévi-Strauss (1949) on the exchange of women as the foundation of society as being too reductive, leaving many facts unexplained, and mutilating reality (Godelier 1996:8). Inspired by the work of Annette Weiner (1992), he went on to propose that no society can survive over time if there are no fixed points, the inalienable. The focus of his work then shifted from things that are given to things that are kept, and the role of religion and politics, rather than alliance and descent, in structuring society (Godelier 1999, 2005).

When Godelier conducted his fieldwork, the highlands of Papua New Guinea remained relatively isolated from developments in the rest of the world. The sacred and inalienable provided fixed points to guide society, as one Enga elder put it, a society with inalienable fixed points is like a garden of sprouting beans with straight stakes to climb and bear fruit. A garden without fixed stakes grows into a unproductive tangled mess. Following contact with Europeans, much of the inalienable was dismantled within two decades, while exchange flourished but became ever more entangled with new ties and new wealth. The subsequent waves of change took education out of the hands of parents, integrated the sexes, and placed cash over many human relationships. 'Money is life' became a common adage. This raises the question of what happens when the centre does not hold? What is truly inalienable and remains to guide people through a period of transition? How do sacred and inalienable points that are purely culturally constructed fare? Are those that are grounded in biology and ecology more robust? What is the role of kinship in times of transition? Here I would like to explore these questions among the central Enga of Papua New Guinea, a big man society, focusing on Godelier's original dimension: marriage.

The Enga

The Enga are a highland horticultural population numbering about 300,000 today; they are well known due to the work of Brennan (1982), Feil (1984), Lacey (1979, 1982), Meggitt (1965, 1974, 1977), Wiessner (2002),Wiessner and Tumu (1998), and others. Their staple crop is the sweet potato, which is extensively cultivated to feed the large human and pig populations. The sweet potato was introduced to Enga some 300 years ago; it grew well at high altitudes, in poor soils, matured quickly and was resistant to blight With these properties the new crop released constraints on production and allowed for substantial surplus production in the form of pigs for the first time. Since then pig production has fuelled some of the largest ceremonial exchange systems know in a non-centralized society, following paths created by the exchange of women for wealth (Wiessner and Tumu 1998). Prior to first contact with Europeans, goods, valuables and cults circulated along exchange networks including bachelors' and ancestral cults that homogenized values and beliefs throughout the Enga (Wiessner and Tumu 1999). By the 1950s, the largest exchange network, the Enga Tee Ceremonial Exchange Cycle, encompassed some 40,000 participants and over 100,000 pigs. In a society that flourished from the circulation of goods, beliefs, practices and ideas, what were the fixed points that allowed the centre to hold for men and women and structured relations between the two?

The Inalienable in Enga Society

Men inherited three inalienable rights from birth: clan membership and the support of clan brothers; potential equality with other men; and mutual obligations with maternal kin. The social organization of the central Enga conformed to a segmentary lineage system with patrilineal clans, sub-clans and lineages cooperating in agricultural enterprises, defence, war reparations, and organizing ceremonial exchanges and rites for the ancestors (Meggitt 1965). Men enjoyed inalienable rights to membership in their clans of birth that provided them with loyal clan brothers, lifelong security, and the land from which subsistence was derived. Land was owned both by individual families and by the clan. Clan land was parcelled out to families who passed it on to descendants of their choice. It was inalienable in the sense that it could be passed on to any relatives in the clan but not to outsiders; any infringement on the land of one member was considered to be an attack on the entire clan. The heritage of the clan was vested in ancestral stones for which periodic rituals were held in order to promote fertility and security. Unlike among the Baruya, however, power was acquired by managing wealth, not by handling sacred objects or administering secretive spells and rites.

A second inalienable right concerned social and political interaction, namely the strict separation of the sexes and potential equality between men. Values of potential equality and separation from women were inculcated in bachelors' cults when boys were educated for manhood and were believed to be transformed by a spirit woman into strong, mature men with keen intellects. The spirit woman tended to the handsome and the ugly alike, provided that they remained faithful to her during their bachelor years. Once young men had attended bachelors' cults and were deemed marriageable, they were challenged to compete, excel, and become big men through the production and management of wealth for *tee* ceremonial exchange, and through the development of skills in organization, oration, networking and mediation. If they ceased to provide benefits to the clan, their demise was rapid.

The potential equality of all men had a profound effect on women's marriage choices. In a sense, all men with hard-working wives could become wealthy men of some influence. While the very top positions as Great Kamongo – organizers for the Tee Ceremonial Exchange Cycle – were passed down from father to capable son (Wiessner 2010), all men could become 'wealthy' through household production with the support of socially competent and hard-working wives. When recounting their life stories (Kyakas and

Wiessner 1992), many women expressed the desire to raise pigs, cultivate ties, and make their families successful.

The third inalienable right of men was a relationship of mutual obligation with maternal kin. In Enga society clan membership could not cover essential needs such as securing allies in warfare, external finance for ceremonial exchange, access to trade routes, and alternate residences in times of crises. Such needs were met by a myriad of ties created via women who married outside the clan. Of these, maternal kin were of supreme importance. Relations with maternal kin were maintained by mandatory life cycle payments made by the husband's clan to his wife's clan for the growth of their children, compensation for their injury, and funerary prestations upon their deaths These payments recognized that biologically based maternal kinship was inalienable and that the transfer of reproductive and productive powers of women had to be compensated for throughout life. In turn, maternal kin found ways to assist the husband's clan when they were in need.

Women inherited few inalienable rights at birth with the exception of support from maternal kin. Further rights would come with marriage when a woman became a full member of her husband's clan, although these rights would terminate with divorce. A woman was given the right to land to cultivate by her husband, to receive support and protection from her husband's clan, and to receive regular gifts for her kin in exchange for her productive and reproductive efforts. In contrast to men, who ventured widely to participate in warfare, ritual and exchange, women were considered to be the belt that held the household together.

Women married and left their natal clans around the age of puberty. Marriage proceedings only allowed for passive female choice. Marriage proposals were initiated by the young man's parents with consideration for their son's preferences. However, if the marriage forged a crucial tie for trade, *tee* exchange, or peace, sons usually accepted their parents' choices. Women had the right to accept or reject a potential spouse. Of the thirty-three women we interviewed who grew up before first contact with Europeans, about half were eager to marry and half were reluctant to leave their homes and start a life of hard work (Kyakas and Wiessner 1992).

If both parties agreed, the two families met half way between their respective clans for the first bridewealth payment of pigs raised by the groom and his family. If there were not enough pigs, the bride's family might leave, but if they were too many, it might be taken as a sign that the groom had hoarded his pigs and was not generous in filling community obligations. At this point the bride was asked for her consent. If she said no, her refusal was accepted. If she said yes, over the course of the following weeks courtship parties were held night after night. The bride and her friends sang songs requesting bridewealth and charmed the groom's relatives into giving her pigs and valuables. The more pigs and valuables that were promised, the greater her status. Meanwhile the groom's family worked hard to make her feel content in her new home.

During the weeks that followed the bride, accompanied by the groom's relatives, brought the pigs and other gifts to her home where the bride and her family decided how to distribute them among their kin. The bride's family gave a few pigs or gifts in exchange to indicate lifelong support between the two families. The exchange pigs contributed by the bride's clan and others donated by the groom's relatives were then slaughtered during a joyous feast. The groom's female relatives dressed the bride in her wedding net bag, grass skirts and ornaments, and rubbed her all over with pig grease so she could preside over the distribution. Half of the pork was distributed to thank those who had contributed to the bridewealth. The other half was carried by a party composed of the groom, bride and his kinsmen to the bride's family where it was distributed. The party returned home, genuinely happy to have succeeded in recruiting a new clan member who would contribute to the prosperity of the clan.

From the time of the wedding feast, the bride became a permanent member of her husband's clan; a woman was told that her bones would be buried on her husband's land. His clan would provide the maternal relatives for her children. Divorce could occur if the bridewealth was repaid; however, divorce rates were low (Wiessner and Kyakas 1992), approximately seven per cent (Meggitt 1965) once the marriage was consummated. Couples were not supposed to marry for their own satisfaction but rather to fill socio-economic obligations and forge alliances between sub-clans and clans. The burden was on the couple and their close kin to make marriages work. Moreover, children belonged to the husband's clan, making women reluctant to divorce.

Women did not hold exclusive rights to their husbands. Successful men (around ten to fifteen per cent of men) sought to marry two or more wives to increase the productive power of their households, build political ties, and gain status. Younger women rejected polgynous marriage and had an arsenal of spells to drive away second wives. However, more mature women often shared their husband's ambitions, chose second wives for them, and helped raise the pigs for the bridewealth. Separate households were kept for each wife.

Relations between the Sexes

Relations between men and women were structured by separation of the sexes that assigned public roles to men and private ones to women. At the tender age of six to eight, young boys went to live in the men's house with their fathers. The basis for separation was that contamination with menstrual blood and other female influences would inhibit their physical and mental maturation. Throughout their lives men and women would maintain separate living quarters in women's and men's houses. Women who followed prescriptions and rites for the proper disposal of menstrual waste could work to promote the success of their husbands.

Spatial separation of the sexes supported cohesive patrilineal clans by allowing clan 'brothers', putatively linked by blood ties, to regularly discuss internal and external politics in the absence of women who were often from enemy clans. Clan secrets in turn bonded men. The division of labour allocating private roles to women and public roles to men permitted women to retreat to their natal clans during warfare, to be immune to the violence that claimed the lives of up to twenty-five per cent of men (Meggitt 1977), and to maintain external ties in times of war. The maintenance of such ties was essential for establishing peace and for the continuation of ceremonial exchange when hostilities ceased.

The Inalienable Dismantled

Kanopatoakali, the great Tee Cycle organizer of the Kalia clan and descendant of a long line of influential *kamongo* (leaders), was on his clan's ceremonial grounds in 1934 when the first party of Europeans, the Leahy brothers, came into central Enga prospecting for gold. The news that the mythical sky people had descended to earth and were travelling through Enga had already spread far and wide and so their arrival was anticipated. When one of their huge dogs urinated on Kanopatoakali's legs and the grass where he was standing, he took this as a sign of good fortune. After the party of White Men had passed by, he gathered the wet grass, killed a pig, and held a ritual for the sky people to commemorate the event. Little did he know that contact with Europeans would do much to dissolve the pillars of Enga society (Wiessner 2009).

The Leahy brothers were followed by Taylor's patrols into Enga in 1938–1939 that established a supply route and patrol post at Wabag in central Enga. Contact was disrupted during the Second World War and resumed in the late 1940s when the Colonial Administration began to pacify areas of Enga and pave the way for missions. Between 1948 and 1960 most areas of Enga were introduced to Christianity. Representations of the first pillar of Enga society – clan unity and brotherhood – began to be dismantled when the clan's sacred ancestral stones and objects were destroyed or relegated to Cultural Shows. Because Enga were more strongly oriented to the secular than the sacred, and because the idea of heaven had great appeal, the Enga gave up the better part of their traditional religious beliefs readily. The principles of Christianity that conformed to traditional norms and values were easily accepted. Others, for example, 'Do unto others as you would have them do unto you' were never internalized in Enga society. Reciprocity, whether positive or negative, remained the norm: 'Do unto others as they do unto you.' Polygyny was retained as a right of men and was used to achieve political and economic goals. Initially the solidarity promoted by ancestral cults remained because people of a single clan attended one church. Women were allowed to participate in religious activities for the first time.

Bachelors' cults were banned by some missions or performed in more secular contexts, for example to gather people for election campaigns. The spirit woman who transformed young men departed, so that bachelors' cults, where they still existed, seemed superficial and perfunctory. Missions downplayed menstrual taboos, encouraged family houses, and integrated boys and girls in schools. With the Colonial Administration's ban on warfare, defence, solidarity and secrecy were no longer as important; most men's houses were not rebuilt when their elder inhabitants died. Boys and girls interacted regularly at home and in school. A second pillar of Enga society – separation of the sexes – thereby crumbled.

Next to be eroded was the potential equality of men. During the colonial period, the few who worked for the colonial administration or obtained a good education were well poised to succeed in business, politics and the public service. In a country where business opportunities were wide open, some succeeded in becoming extraordinarily rich and passed that privilege on to their children. After independence those in politics and public service became skilled in diverting the huge pot of public funds for their private uses. Prior to first contact, any family who raised pigs could become 'wealthy' and those with charisma and skills in oration and mediation could attain the status of big men. Today men no longer enjoy potential equality; significant social inequalities with respect to the access to wealth have emerged. Such social inequalities in monetary wealth have also had a significant impact on marriage choices. Because women's agricultural work contributes less to family economic success than in the past, women prefer to marry men with education and monetary income.

Finally, between 1960 and 2008 the clan began to break down as activities that had previously united male clan members dwindled. As many as three to four different churches were established within single clans, with each denomination promoting different practices. For example, some churches encouraged the payment of war reparations and others forbade them, disrupting corporate group political action. Exchange systems that had initially expanded with the new wealth grew too large to be manageable. The Tee Ceremonial Exchange Cycle collapsed under its own complexity after 1979, leaving war reparation exchanges as the only major exchange at the clan level. By 1980 only two pillars of traditional Enga society held strong, both based on kinship: clan brotherhood and the accompanying rights to land, and the obligations of maternal kinship.

Clan brotherhood was further weakened in the 1990s by the entrance of the gun into tribal warfare (Wiessner 2006, 2010). The age hierarchy in politics was reversed as young men who could wield high-powered weapons took control. Clansmen who were not skilled in fighting with guns retreated with their families to live as war refugees for months or years; warfare was no longer an enterprise that incorporated all clansmen. In some areas gangs of mercenaries, who cut across clan boundaries, were formed. These gangs sought to fight out their own vendettas by colonizing the wars of other clans in the region. When one gang took one side, the other would ally with the opponents. According to our records, 573 wars with guns were fought in Enga between 1991 and 2009 leading to significant loss of life and destruction of property. Since 2006, there has been a trend towards peace as clans brothers become increasingly unwilling to go to war or pay compensation for troublemakers, brothers or not, further eroding the clan (Wiessner 2010).

In short, in the late 1980s and early 1990s there was a turning point as individuality and the pursuit of money overrode both traditional and Christian norms and values. The traditional adage 'You need a person', meaning that everybody has something to give, was replaced with to 'Money is life'. Cooperation within the clan decreased; individuals building new houses or gardens had to reward their helpers with cash or store bought foods. A 'sexual revolution' took place as young men and women made their own choices for partnerships and some women took their sexuality into their own hands. It is the changes that occurred in marriage patterns to adapt to the alienation of the inalienable that will be the centre of the rest of my discussion.

Marriage Choices

What happens to alliance and descent when the inalienable is dismantled? To answer this question it is necessary to look at both male and female strategies in marriage because, even under conditions of strong male dominance, women have always practiced strategic choices from the private realm or in unseen ways (Bonnemère 2004; Kyakas and Wiessner 1992; Strathern 1972). Data on marriage choices is taken from a study conducted in 2005 of 476 marriages of women and men between the ages of approximately sixteen and thirty-nine in four clans within 3 to 7 kilometres of Wabag, the Provincial capital of Enga (with a population of about 5000). Parents were interviewed about the marriages of each of their offspring and the following points recorded for both daughters and sons: approximate age of the offspring, spouse's clan and residence, who arranged the marriage, whether bridewealth was paid, whether divorce occurred and why, and number of children born. Marriage, as recognized by the Enga today, is defined as living with a sexual partner for months or years whether or not bridewealth has been paid or children have been born. When possible this information was cross-checked with the children themselves or with close friends and relatives.

Formerly, the choice of marriage partners by young people was constrained by minimal encounters between unmarried youths of the opposite sex. Single women were heavily chaperoned and rarely saw prospective spouses outside of *sing-sings* and courtship parties where interaction was formalized and brief. Young men and women expressed their preferences to parents and had the right to accept or reject marriage, but parents held the reins. With regular contact in church and schools from the 1960s to the 1980s, young women and men gradually became familiar enough with each other to make their own choices without parental participation and to pursue their own desires. In the 20–29 age group (n=130), seventy per cent of women had chosen their own partners without parental involvement and sixty-three per cent in the 30–39 age group (n=105). For men, the results were similar: seventy-six per cent in the 20–29 age group (n=67) had chosen their own partners and sixty-four per cent in the 30–39 age group (n=140).

With the decline in arranged marriages came a sharp reduction in the payment of bridewealth. Forty per cent of first marriages of the past two decades have been sealed by bridewealth in contrast to approximately ninety-five per cent in the past (Kyakas and Wiessner 1992; Meggitt 1965). Traditional marriage with bridewealth was chosen largely by women who had the prospect of marrying influential and well-connected men who would remain in the clan, or women from families with money who married wealthy men living in towns and held lavish weddings.

Wardlow (2006), in her fascinating study, proposes that Huli women who exchange sex for money (*pasinja meri*) and forgo bridewealth are expressing the individualistic modality of personhood and refusing to participate in the 'deployment of alliance'. This does not appear to be the case for most Enga women, though it is for some. Rather, with the weakening of clans and sub-clans, both men and women no longer feel that they are working together for clan prosperity; alliance does not have the same value today as when the Tee Ceremonial Exchange Cycle was in full swing. As a result, clan members are no longer as willing to contribute to bridewealth unless they see a connection that will bring valuable political or monetary connections. Young people often choose to forgo the struggles of parental participation and raising bridewealth, and simply begin living together for fear of losing a desired spouse or one with a salary. Thereafter it is unlikely that bridewealth will be paid. Enga society has always hosted both individualistic tendencies as well as a commitment to sacrifice for the clan or sub-clan. When clan unity breaks down, the individualistic tendencies remain and appear more prominent.

Second, what was considered desirable in a partner in the past has been altered with the decline of the exchange economy, the potential equality of men, and the cash economy. In traditional Enga society the way to a better, more secure life for a woman was to marry a man, work hard, and help increase his status so that the family would get more gifts, more helpers to join the household workforce, more supporters, and more allies. If the husband married a second wife with the permission of the first, it usually increased the status of the family, *tee* connections, and chances for the first wife and her children. Of course, not all marriage prospects were equal but all married women could work hard and make a name for their families. Today, with marked inequalities in education and access to wealth at the starting point, choices are quite different. Women desire men with money who can give them a more comfortable life with a reduced workload, desired material goods, and provide their children with more opportunities. But if the husband becomes wealthy from her hard work, he may seek a second wife with whom she must share her husband's income. Since women are no longer as valued for production and connections, many men abandon their first wives, or neglect them. Women no longer benefit from their own hard work as they did in the past and so many prefer to sit in the market and sell betel nuts or cigarettes to buy basic foodstuffs for their families.

The following excerpt from an interview with an educated Enga woman gives some idea of the growing importance of money and different strategies of some men and women:

As we all can see, money everywhere in the world is becoming a big problem, not only in Enga but also in the world. I think it is happening everywhere in the world. In 1985 when I did my grade 10 studies, money was not so important to us. We ate food from our gardens and my father was a Water Affairs officer and earned 60–70 kina a fortnight. We had such big money in the house that we could pay for all the things we wanted – bags of rice, cooking oil, and clothing. We still had money left over to help kin and pay school fees. We had food in the gardens, sweet potato, greens, banana, sugar cane and every weekend there were pig killings...

But now all of us can see there is not enough money. This money is – I don't know – just escaping or going away from us. Because everybody wants money you can see women and young girls, even those in 4th or 5th grade, walking up and down the streets and markets. When their parents give them K5 or K10, they go to second hand stores and buy six pocket pants or jeans. They try to look their best, but not so that people will say, 'That girl is a pretty girl', but just to attract men's attention so that they can have sex with them in exchange for money. And this sex is not for K50; K50 is very expensive. These days girls are just having sex with anybody for money, for fifty toea or one kina. When they get this money they do not bring it home, buy anything good, or spend it to have food in the house, but just to buy betelnut, cigarettes and to gamble. They don't care if the man is ugly, old, sick or paralyzed; they will do anything to attract that man to have sex with if he has money. Mothers used to have control over their daughters, but now they cannot tell them what to do because everything is money now: 'Money is life'.

Before, people used to bring sweet potato, greens and other foods and put all the food together and cook it in a big earth oven and share it among many households. But now people are suffering because they need money. And when they have some extra food they bring it to the market and sell it for money rather than share it with other people. When I sell my food in the market, I buy some betelnut, cigarettes, and play cards. Then I buy a packet of rice, take it home and just give it to my husband and kids, that's all. I don't buy for my brother's family or share it with other people because I need the money. Sharing has completely decreased in the last ten years.

Young women are not really a problem for their parents because when they want money to survive, they can exchange sex with men for money. When they get two kina from sex they can go buy betelnut or smoke or go to a second hand shop and by a shirt or a skirt. And then they are okay. They don't bother their parents. But for boys, oh, it is VERY hard for these boys nowadays. If a boy does not go to school or cannot find a job to work for his living, the only thing he is thinking of is: 'Where will I get money? What will I do to survive on this earth?' Some think about that and the only thing they can do to stop these worries from welling up in them is to go for marijuana. When they smoke they think that they are very big business men, that they are pilots who fly planes in the air, or men who steer very big ships in the ocean. And all kinds of thoughts like that come to these boys when they smoke marijuana.

Table 3.1 lists the frequency of reasons given by women for choosing partners. More than forty per cent of women said that they had been courting, fell in love, wanted to have sex and decided to marry with or without parental consent. In only ten per cent of cases parents and relatives arranged marriages and their daughters complied. In some of these arranged marriages, the parents forced their daughters to leave high school in order to marry an older, rich man for a large bridewealth payment. Seven per cent of women chose their own spouses because they were offered a large bridewealth. Another 17 per cent of women married men with money receiving little or no bridewealth because the men were wealthy and the women 'wanted to eat money'. Choosing a partner in order to establish social connections for inter-clan exchange, a major factor in past choices, plays a negligible role today. Seventeen per cent of women in the 20–29 age group and ten per cent in the 30–39 age group did not marry but exchanged sex for money.

Table 3.1. Reasons given by women in central Enga for choosing partners.

	AGE CATEGORY					
	20–29		**30–39**		**Total**	
	n	%	n	%	n	%
Courtship/Love/ Sex	43	42%	51	44%	94	44%
Arranged by Parents/Relatives	10	10%	11	19%	21	10%
Large Bridewealth	9	9%	7	7%	16	7%
Man had Money/ 'To Eat Money'	15	14%	21	20%	36	17%
To be Married/ Pregnancy	3	3%	2	2%	5	2%
Social Connections	5	5%	3	3%	8	3%
Did Not Marry: Sex for Money	17	17%	19	10%	36	17%
TOTAL	**102**	**100%**	**114**	**100%**	**216**	**100%**

For men choices have also changed. The average man still seeks a woman who can support the family and create ties outside the clan, but with the decline in exchange, surplus production is less important for making a name. The reasons cited by men for marriage include the sexual attractiveness of a woman, love, extended courtship and the desire to start a family, but rarely social connections or hard work. Men with money, even those with temporary jobs in mines, seek several wives for their status and pleasure. They enter into desired relationships with little concern for their permanence or value to the clan. Some men without jobs or money complain that they have a hard time finding wives because women prefer to become the second or third wife of a wealthy man rather than the first wife of a man without money.

The category of women who did not marry but exchanged sex for money is an interesting one. Because our research was carried out in rural areas near the provincial capital, it did not include women who were engaged in more professional prostitution like the women in Wardlow's (2006) study. These women stayed at home in their clans, living on their parents' land, gardening and getting extra income from sex with men they knew in their own clans and surrounding ones. They contributed part of their income to the obligations of their natal groups, remaining active members of their maternal clans. On the one hand, their parents did not approve and occasionally beat them, but on the other, they were happy to have their daughters nearby to help them.

Women who did not marry but exchanged sex for money to supplement their incomes talk about their situations with bravado. The following excerpts come from an interview with three women from families of high social standing who had decided to depart from the traditional way of life:

> No, we don't want to marry. We want to be free to go around to markets, visit and do what we want. If we are married, we must sit in the house, look after pigs, gardens and do all those things while the one who gets the name for our hard work is the man. Many women don't want to work for men any longer. They don't want to stay in the house while the man is roaming around doing nothing. If they are married, they must do all the jobs in the house like raising pigs, planting gardens, caring for kids, and fixing fences. Today in Enga if a man has plenty of pigs, he becomes a wealthy man. He will win a big name from the hard work of his wife and then roam around sleeping with or trying to marry all sorts of woman. Today women can work, raise pigs, and when they grow fat, she can give them away and make a name for herself or she can sell them for money. But as for us, we don't want to stay home and look after pigs; we prefer to roam around and earn money from sex. The only time we feel a bit uneasy is when we accompany a woman who is marrying in the traditional way to receive bridewealth...
>
> Our work is 'condom work'. Our lovers are mostly men from the community. During the day we joke, talk, and help each other; at night we slip off and have sex. But if we see a man from another place who has money, then we will go to him and say 'ppppssstt' and try to attract him. No money, no sex. If we give sex without money, how could we ask for money the next time?

When the wives of our lovers come to complain we just give them one hard blow and they usually go away. When community leaders come to talk to use about causing trouble, we ask, 'Do you want to give us money? If so give it to us; if not, then this is none of your business'.

The life histories of such women who live without a spouse, exchanging sex for money, tell a different story, that this lifestyle was not the intentional choice of mature women. Most began exchanging sex for money, cigarettes, clothes, betel nuts and other goods just before puberty, a time when they were still girls experimenting with their power to attract men and have an independent income. Some became sterile due to sexually transmitted infections and others got a bad reputation and so had few prospects for marriage. Although each woman had a different story, most gave the impression that if they could relive their lives, they would have made other choices.

Outcomes of Current Marriage Choices

The outcomes of modern marriage choices are threefold. First, there is an increased divorce rate; second, inter-clan ties are weakening; and third, because of lack of commitment from fathers, many children remain with their mothers when couples split. Let us start with divorce. At the time of Mervyn Meggitt's fieldwork in central Enga in the 1960s (Meggitt 1965), approximately seven per cent of marriages ended in divorce. In our study, 26 out of 123 (twenty-one per cent) women from the 20–29 age group had been divorced and 30 out of 124 (twenty-four per cent) from the 30–39 age group, indicating a threefold increase in the divorce rate. Bridewealth does not seem to make a big difference in securing marriage. Eighteen per cent of women who had received bridewealth were divorced, in comparison to twenty-four per cent of women who had not received bridewealth. This may be because wealthier men were more likely to pay bridewealth, but subsequently abandon or neglect their first wives.

Analyses of court cases and their outcomes give further insights into changing attitudes about marriage and the breakdown in traditional marriage practices. Today most domestic problems are handled by Village Courts, a division of the Papua New Guinea justice system that applies 'customary law' to achieve substantial justice, that is, justice that satisfies communities (Goddard 2009). Cases are held in the open air with large crowds attending, giving evidence and commenting. Magistrates are selected local leaders with little if any formal training. Often cases are first heard in informal Wari Courts (worry courts) that are not part of the national justice system, presided over by one magistrate. If they are not settled there, they are taken to Village Courts, with five magistrates present.

The data in Tables 3.2 and 3.3 come from participant observational study of disputes brought to Village Courts in three villages within 7 km of the provincial capital Wabag in 2008. Variables recorded included age, sex and clan of the plaintiff and defendant, the issue at stake, the discussion that ensued, and the court decision.[2] In informal Wari Courts (Table 3.1), theft was the most common complaint (twenty-eight per cent of cases, n=178), followed by marital problems/bridewealth disputes (twenty-two per cent) and land issues (twelve per cent). Theft is easily dealt with through compensation, but more complex cases such as marital problems and intra-clan land disputes are often referred to full Village Courts. Marital/bridewealth problems were the most frequent causes of complaints in Village Courts (thirty-eight per cent of cases, n=97) followed by intra-clan land disputes (seventeen per cent), and money issues (thirteen per cent) (Table 3.3).[3] Twenty-three out of thirty-seven complaints (sixty-two per cent) in Village Court cases concerning marriage problems were filed by women and fourteen (thirty-eight per cent) by men. This indicates that women expect fair treatment in Village Courts and are no longer judicial minors to be represented by men as has traditionally been the case.

Table 3.2. Wari Courts Categories Combined (n=178).

	n	Percentage
Property Not Returned	3	2%
Alcohol/Drug Abuse (with violence)	10	6%
Land Issues	22	12%
Marital Problems*	33	19%
Betrothal Broken/Bridewealth Issues*	5	3%
Theft	49	28%
Murder/Attempted Murder/Rape and Murder	1	1%
Other Family Problems (including personal injury)	6	3%
Accidental Death (human)	0	0%
Pig Death	5	3%
Insult/Personal Injury (non-family)	10	6%
Money/Credit Issues	18	10%
Destruction of Property/Destruction of Property and Violence	16	9%

Wari Courts are informal village courts with no official powers, presided over by at least one magistrate or local leader.

Table 3.3. Village Courts Categories Combined (n=97).

	n	Percentage
Property Not Returned	1	1%
Alcohol/Drug Abuse (with violence)	0	0%
Land Issues	16	17%
Marital Problems	30	31%
Betrothal Broken/ Bridewealth	7	7%
Theft	5	5%
Murder/Attempted Murder/Rape and Murder/ Molestation	3	3%
Other Family Problems (including personal injury)	7	7%
Accidental Death (human)	0	0%
Pig Death	5	5%
Insult/Personal Injury (non-family)	4	4%
Money/Credit Issues	13	13%
Destruction of Property/Destruction of Property and Violence	2	2%
Court Disturbance	4	4%

Village Courts are part of the national justice system and have five or more magistrates presiding with the authority to hand down fines of up to K1000 (ca. US$ 300) or jail sentences of up to six months.

Court decisions suggest the following. Adultery always requires compensation of a pig and a few hundred kina and may or may not be accompanied by divorce. In divorce cases, if bridewealth has been paid, it does not have to be repaid if the woman has children who will be left in the man's clan; otherwise it does. If divorce occurs for couples who have not paid bridewealth, the man has to pay a small amount of compensation for access to the woman's love and labour for the time he was with her and then let her return to her natal clan with her children if she so desires. Thus, the rights of maternal kinship prevail when bridewealth has not been paid. Men still maintain the right to marry second wives and often claim that their lovers are second wives-to-be, thereby avoiding adultery charges. Because tradition dictated that a man had to get permission from his first wife to marry a second, he must compensate his first wife for having a lover whom he claims will become his second wife; the court will give the first wife rights for divorce if she wishes. Compensation is required for abandonment and for any injury suffered during marital disputes. The rising divorce rates will reduce supportive inter-clan ties in the future and pull a central thread out of the social fabric.

What does lack of payment of bridewealth mean for inter-group relations? Interviews with women who had stable marriages in which bridewealth was not paid indicate that after the birth of children, husbands usually contributed when payments had to be raised by the wife's immediate kin, for instance, in the case of warfare compensation or funeral feasts. Sometimes these contributions were considered to act as delayed bridewealth. However, relatives of the women who married without bridewealth were generally upset with the liaison and did not contribute to the needs of her husband's clan unless he had contributed substantially to theirs in times of need. Marriage still forms the basis of inter-clan relations today but as the older generation passes away and the younger one ceases to pay bridewealth, there will be far fewer ties to raise support in times of need or to make peace after warfare. The Enga will have to rely increasingly on maternal kin for such assistance.

What happens to children when ten to fifteen per cent of women exchange sex for money and when many marriages are short-lived? Unless bridewealth has been paid or a paternal relative has taken in the children, young children usually return with their mother to her natal clan where they remain. Following Enga tradition, sons still have rights to land in their father's clan when they grow up, but often do not claim this land because the relationship with their father was fleeting or because paternity is uncertain. Rather, they seek land from their maternal uncles. This will bring a shift over the next decade from a strongly patrilineal and patrilocal society to a more cognatic one.

Concluding Remarks

The Enga case demonstrates both the importance of the inalienable in structuring cooperation and exchange in a big man society, and how quickly it can be dismantled. After contact with the outside world, the pillars of Enga society broke down as people were influenced by new religious beliefs and took advantage of new economic and political opportunities. What remained was largely rooted in kinship. Clan brotherhood, based in part on biological ties, persists today even though it is currently being eroded by individual interest. In contrast, maternal ties and accompanying obligations remain inalienable and are a steadfast source of support. As Godelier points out in the end of *The Enigma of the Gift* (1999: 210), one cannot choose one's parents; they are a given. When everything else appears alienable and negotiable, maternal kinship provides the inalienable to tide people over and channel alliance and descent while new structures emerge.

Acknowledgements

My heartfelt thanks go to members of our Enga Take Anda research team in Enga who collected much of the data presented here with persistence and perceptiveness: Nitze Pupu, Larson Kyalae, Lelyame Yongapen, Jarwe Munini, Wilhelminen Anton, and Regina Tanda.

Notes

1. Data collected in collaboration with Lelyame Yongapen, Jarwe Munini, Wilhelminen Anton, and Regina Tanda.
2. Data collected in collaboration with Nitze Pupu, Larson Kyalae, and Lelyame Yongapen.
3. Our interviews with 100 women who grew up prior to around 1950 indicate that marital problems were less frequent in the past owing to much lower rates of adultery. Past disputes were largely due to conflicts over payment to wives' kin, complaints about either sex not doing his or her job, and second wives (Kyakas and Wiessner 1992). Village Court data from the Saka Valley in 1976–1979 indicate that twenty-two per cent of court cases involved marital problems (Gordon and Meggitt 1985: 265), significantly lower than in 2008.

Bibliography

Bonnemere, P. 2004. *Women as Unseen Characters: Male Ritual in Papua New Guinea*. Philadelphia: University of Pennsylvania Press.
Brennan, P. 1982. 'Communication', in B. Carrad, D. Lea and K. Talyaga (eds), *Enga: Foundations for Development*, Vol. Enga Yaaka Lasemana, 3. Armidale: University of New England, p.198–216.
Feil, D. 1984. *Ways of Exchange: The Enga Tee of Papua New Guinea*. University of Queensland Press: St Lucia.
Goddard, M. 2009. *Substantial Justice: An Anthropology of Village Courts in Papua New Guinea*. New York: Berghahn Books.
Godelier, M. 1982. *La Production des Grands Hommes*. Fayard: Paris.
——— 1996. *L'énigme du don*. Paris: Fayard.
——— 1999. *The Enigma of the Gift*. Chicago: University of Chicago Press.
——— 2005. *Métamorphoses de la Parenté*. Paris: Fayard.
——— and M. Strathern (ed.). 1991. *Big Men and Great Men: Personifications of Power in Melanesia*. Cambridge: Cambridge University Press.
Gordon, R. and M. Meggitt. 1985. *Law and Order in the New Guinea Highlands*. Hanover: University Press of New England.
Kyakas, A. and P. Wiessner. 1992. *From Inside the Women's House: Enga Women's Lives and Traditions*. Brisbane: Robert Brown.
Lacey, R. 1979. 'Holders of the Way: A Study of Precolonial Socio-economic History in Papua New Guinea', *Journal of the Polynesian Society* 88: 277–36.

———— 1982. 'History', in B. Carrad, D. Lea and K. Talyaga (eds), *Enga: Foundations for Development*, Vol. Enga Yaaka Lasemana, 3. Armidale: University New England, p.8–22.

Lemonnier, P. 1990. *Guerres et Festins: Paix, Echanges et Compétition dans les Highlands de Nouvelle-Guinée*. Paris: Maison des Sciences de I'Homme.

Lévi-Strauss, C. 1949. *Les Structures Elémentaires de la Parenté*. Paris: Presses Universitaires de France.

Meggitt, M. 1965. *The Lineage System of the Mae-Enga of New Guinea*. New York: Barnes and Noble.

———— 1974. '"Pigs are Our Hearts!" The Te Exchange Cycle among the Mae Enga of New Guinea', *Oceania* 44: 165–203.

———— 1977. *Blood Is Their Argument*. Palo Alto: Mayfield.

Strathern, A. 1972. *Women in Between. Female Roles in a Male World: Mount Hagen, New Guinea*. London: Seminar Press.

Wardlow, H. 2006. *Wayward Women: Sexuality, Agency and Gender in a New Guinea Society*. Berkeley: University of California Press.

Wiener, A. 1992. *Inalienable Possessions: The Paradox of Keeping-while-Giving*. Berkeley: University of California Press.

Wiessner, P. 2002. 'The Vines of Complexity: Egalitarian Structures and the Institutionalization of Inequality among the Enga', *Current Anthropology* 43(2): 233–69.

———— 2006. 'From Spears to M-16s: Testing the Imbalance of Power Hypothesis among the Enga', *Journal of Anthropological Research* 62: 165–91.

———— 2009. 'The Power of One: Big-Men Revisited', in J. Eerkens, J. Kantner and K. Vaughn (eds), *The Evolution of Leadership. Transition in Decision Making from Small-scale to Middle-range Societies*. Santa Fe: SAR Press.

———— 2010. 'Youths, Elders, and the Wages of War in Enga Province, Papua New Guinea', *State, Society and Governance in Melanesia*. Discussion Paper 2010/3.

———— and A. Tumu. 1998. *Historical Vines: Enga Networks of Exchange, Ritual, and Warfare in Papua New Guinea*. Washington, D.C.: Smithsonian Institution Press.

———— and A. Tumu. 1999. 'A Collage of Cults', *Canberra Anthropology* 22(1): 34–65.

Chapter 4

ANTHROPOLOGY AND THE FUTURE OF SEXUALITY STUDIES: AN ESSAY IN HONOUR OF MAURICE GODELIER

Gilbert Herdt

Introduction

No field has contributed more to the understanding of human sexuality than anthropology, at least in the Academy, and in the twentieth century, not only did anthropological theory fundamentally alter the representation and understanding of sexuality across cultures, but it also contributed to a new way of thinking about the place of sexuality in late modern society. In this essay I wish to pay tribute to the work of Maurice Godelier in contributing to this development, especially in his New Guinea ethnographies, and suggest a future direction.

The field of sexuality in the nineteenth century began with a strongly medical orientation, prefigured by notions of 'disease' and sexual symptomology, so that only slowly did anthropological and sociological studies gradually succeed over intellectual hegemony of sexology (Herdt 2004; Irvine 2000), though this hegemony remains intact in certain quarters even today. Moreover, the early history of ethnographic studies of sexuality and gender, through the classics of Malinowski (1929) and Mead (1935) surely resonated across the social and psychological sciences for a half century, right up to the 'golden age' of anthropology (Mead 1961). Nevertheless, with the exception of Melanesia and New Guinea studies in recent decades, and then queer theory (Lewin and Leap 1996), sexuality study was generally distant from the centre of the discipline (Weston

1993; Boeslstorff 2007). Moreover, sexology – the more clinical, medical, and diagnostic study of 'sexual science' – retains significant intellectual influence, especially HIV/STD research, and reproductive health education. The rise of studies on structural violence, following Farmer (1992, 2003), has recently changed the situation, and helped us to understand the pitfalls and dilemma of an anthropological study of sexuality that would be truly interdisciplinary.

The story of that effort, in one sense, can be traced to my role in the organization of an 1993 Wenner-Gren conference on 'Theorizing Sex' (Cascais, Portugal). It was a critical moment in the transition to present concerns that post-date Foucault (1980) and yet anticipated the rise of structural violence as a paradigm. In the early 1990s, the accelerating explosion of international AIDS/STDs and sexuality research, in the context of globalization through forces such as sexual tourism, the human rights movement, and migration, were displacing both the earlier sexology and later anthropology. A new set of meanings and practices is coming into place regarding the social regulation of sexuality by communities and nongovernmental sources of power at the end of the century, as evidenced by subsequent conferences and the ever-growing international body of sexuality scholarship and activism (Herdt 1997a, 1997b).

Stated in its simplest form, the conference aimed to bring together leading scholars working from within the two great paradigms of sexual study, inaptly called (biological) essentialism and (cultural) constructionism. Perhaps we had hoped for a new breakthrough in bridging these seemingly oppositional perspectives; a kind of naive expectation that an historical moment of epistemological reconciliation might come from such a meeting of minds. Alas, that was not to happen. Sydel Silverman, then the President of the Wenner-Gren Foundation, has written a lucid and honest account of the conference (2002: 153–62). While positive developments have resulted from the Cascais conference, including the emergence of new networks of scholars cross-cutting disciplines that spanned biology, sociology, history, psychology, and so on, it was not, in my opinion, a very successful conference, and the reasons had more to do with the fact that many of the participants had to experience the events of the conference through the veil of a nasty strain of flu! Rather, I now think that the conference was ahead of its time for a new consensus to be achieved. The participants, many of them leaders in their fields, found it difficult to bridge the perspectives of colleagues in other fields. Subsequent conferences I have organized have taught me the hazards of attempting too much in bridging paradigms (Brummelhuis and Herdt 1995). To understand the role of anthropology in these debates, I will briefly review the history of the field.

A Short History of Sexology and Contemporary Sexuality

We ought to begin with the legacy of sexology. The fundamental intellectual tenet of sexology as an historical field of study is that sexual desire, gender roles (or performances), sex temperament, and sexual behaviour are largely, if not entirely, intrinsically driven by 'biopsychodevelopmental' factors. While it is true that 'environment' (adaptation, culture, social structure, and history) have often figured as a background to sexological studies old and new, seldom are such factors treated as significant sources of sexuality 'outcomes'. Such leading medical figures as Klaus Ulrich, Magnus Hirschfield, Havelock Ellis, Freud, and later Malinowski and Alfred Kinsey, respectively, exemplified the trend, or in the twentieth-century cases, at least did not significantly interrupt it (Robinson 1976; and see Freud 1905, Gagnon and Simon 1973, Herdt 1990, Rubin 1984, Tuzin 1994, Vance 1991). Kinsey, for instance, working to some extent in opposition to Freudian developmentalism, could embrace the ideas of population variation as a natural spectrum of sexual behaviour, and 'gender' as shaped by institutions and social roles, but he could not do without the notion of 'sex drives' as an underlying engine that was biologically intrinsic to the individual (Kinsey et al. 1948; see Herdt 1990). Foucault's (1980) critique of the ahistorical character of sexology (i.e. Freud's repressive hypothesis) still remains pre-eminent and basically sound in demonstrating the social influences upon sexuality discourse (though I disagree with Foucault's treatment of agency and desire: Hostetler and Herdt 1998). Clearly, sexology was to give way to holistic studies, particularly the 'sociocultural approach' – concerning sexual meanings and social practices, and their representation – to be useful to the study of human diversity. It was anthropology that helped to pioneer this intellectual transformation, even if it did not settle in it.

The efforts of American cultural anthropologists following the First World War to explore the developing concept of 'gender' (what was then called 'sex role temperament') were to become extraordinarily influential in the Academy, as well as in popular culture. They achieved their peak in the 1970s, following the second-wave feminist movement (Stimpson 1996), and the emergence of feminist social science, most especially in anthropology (Rosado and Lamphere 1974) and sociology (Chodorow 1978). Anthropological work early in the century followed upon the influential Boasian critiques of 'race' and 'intelligence'. Writing on 'gender' and sexuality slowly expanded up to the Second World War, but then retreated. The intellectual attacks on biological inheritance expanded to include social 'gender' task assignments, infrahuman primate and primate sociosexual organization, evolutionary models of inter-cultural speciation and sex typical differences in the fossil record, in addition to the continuing critiques of 'racial difference' which gradually encompassed the 'meaning of sexual (human) nature' (Benedict 1934, 1938; Herdt 1994; Suggs and Miracle 1999; Vance 1991). During this historical period we saw the production of the greatest ethnographies of sexuality in non-Western societies, by Malinowski (1929), and Margaret Mead (1927, 1935), respectively. They were intellectually influential enough that no serious textbook (including those by sexologists) could afford to ignore them. The recent biography of Malinowski reveals just how fully the sexual entered into the father of ethnography's critical thinking and fieldwork (Young 2004).

Here, an historical disruption occurred as a result of the Second World War. Unfortunately, European sexology, as conceived in Freudian psychoanalysis and British, German and Dutch medical sexual studies, did not reflect this environmentalist 'cultural' or 'gender' construct (and of course, neither did British social anthropology pursue ethnographies of sexuality). But this was to change completely. As John Gagnon and Richard Parker (1995: 5) have written, 'As a result of the catastrophes that befell Europe from 1914–1945 (and Eastern Europe to 1989), the centre of sex research moved from Europe to the United States.' The publication of the famed Kinsey studies clinched the trend toward the 'Americanization' of sexuality studies by 1950. The Freudian influence began its long decline. In the meantime, Parker and Gagnon (1995: 6) argue that 'even psychoanalysis, with its roots in Europe, [...] was unable to resist the more optimistic and individualist cultural traditions of the United States.'

After the Second World War, the relocation of sexuality studies, Gagnon believes, resulted in four key shifts: the loss of privilege of any single discipline in studying sex; the transcendence of the social survey method over other techniques, especially the clinical interview; the normalization of populations studies, previously focused upon 'deviants' but later on diversity; and finally, inclusion of the media in the dissemination of the results of sexual studies, allowing 'fake research' to contend with science in the 'marketplace for sexual information' (Parker and Gagnon 1995: 7).

In the later part of this transformation, following the second sexual revolution, in the 1960s (D'Emilio and Freedman 1988), the sociology of deviance achieved temporary hegemony (Gagnon 1990; Weeks 1985), only to be displaced by the liberationist movements that challenged the binary 'deviant/normal', first with respect to women (Chodorow 1978), and later, gays and lesbians (Kulick and Wilson 1995). The process would continue through to the mid-1990s, when first feminist theory would challenge 'androcentrism' in socio-cultural studies, and later 'queer theory' would posit 'heteronormativity' as the key fallacy of all social science, including sexuality studies, which assume the heterosexual norm to be central to all social life (Hostetler and Herdt 1998; Leap 1999).

Viewed very broadly, these instrumental changes in the Academy gradually moved away from regarding sexuality as a purely biological entity, defined diagnostically by Western medicine as a disease, and by moral theorists who defined sexuality in terms of 'good' and 'evil' rhetorical modes. In general, these approaches were anchored in modernist and evolutionary ideas that were chauvinistic and disregarded non-Western societies, thus precluding recognition of the immense range of sexual and gender 'variations' in the human record (I think Mead's remarkable book, *Male and Female: A Study of the Sexes in a Changing World*, 1949, lays out this transformation, which reaches its peak in Mead 1961; and see the critique of DiLeonardo 1998).

It is necessary to add, however, that this body of holistic anthropological work, from approximately 1925 to 1970, was conducted under the mantle of scientific positivism, with its associated positive methodology of 'participant-observation' following Boas and Malinowski (Friedl 1994; Herdt and Stoller 1990), including my own work on the Sambia of New Guinea (Herdt 1981). Subsequent 'interpretative' and 'postmodern' writings, which strongly inflected the historical influence of colonialism, the identity or positionality of the ethnographer, and the 'textual' currents popular in the epistemology of postmodern anthropology have shifted these frames of study (Di Leonardi 1998; Manderson and Jolly 1997; Parker and Aggleton 1999; Stoler 1995).

The Historic Place of New Guinea Anthropology

Michel Foucault (1980: 26ff) has discussed how sexual and gender ideas might be thought to result from what he calls 'historical networks' in bourgeois societies, which has come to be known as his critique of Freud's 'repressive hypothesis'. Domination comes from cultural institutions and modes of discourse, not from universal unconscious forces of the mind, Foucault has argued. In this model, historical circumstances shape gender discourse and, in turn, 'subjectify' people's 'ethical substances', in the sense of the value positions taken with respect to domination and gender hierarchy. I have already written of my disagreement with Foucault's complete rejection of repression in the Freudian sense, because I believe that repression is a powerful developmental process among the Sambia, and is a vital part of the symbolic compromise formations that facilitate male and female sexuality (Herdt 1993). While broadly agreeing with the role of history in shaping gendered institutions, it seems to me that Foucault has largely ignored individual agency and folk psychologies that construct ontologies; and this diminishes the role of cultural meaning systems that create reality for men and women in their relationships (Herdt 1991a, 1991b). Thus, Foucaultian theory remains too abstract and removed from the social practices which implement individual 'development' or implants cultural 'gender' in the folk psychologies of places such as New Guinea.

This area of culture and personality study has a long history in Melanesian anthropology, dating from the turn of the century, but began to take its present shape with the reactions to Freud's *Totem and Taboo* (1913), and later the semi-analytic work of Margaret Mead (1935, 1949), who suggested that pre-Oedipal envy of and identification with mother and the powers of women formed an important element of male development in these cultures (reviewed in Allen 1967; Bettelheim 1962; Herdt 1981, 1982, 1987, 1990; Stoller and Herdt 1982). Those who followed Freud, including Reik, Roheim, J. Layard, J. Whiting, Hyatt, Dundes, Spain, Spiro, Herdt and Stoller, have covered many of the features of the arguments raised, but have generally not explored the specific dynamics of male/female relations that lead to love, hostility, and sex, nor have they questioned the homosocial and homoerotic elements which are also created in the developmental contexts of the Sambia and a variety of similar societies that implement boy-inseminating rituals (reviewed in Herdt 1984, 1991, 1993). The feminist psychoanalytic perspectives of Nancy Chodorow (1978) are especially helpful here, as are some elements of the critical reinterpretations of the New Guinea literature in the work of Marilyn Strathern (1988).

While the role of the men's house as a social institution has long been identified as pivotal in understanding the development of sex roles and the male psyche in particular, its role in the creative production of culture and social reality has been less understood. As Godelier (1982: 34) famously wrote of the issue, 'Male domination remains the primordial basis of social organization and cultural reality.' The Baruya suggested that the purpose of male initiation and ritual secrecy is to achieve domination over women and children, although the reason why secrecy is required in addition to the physical strength and social power of men remains unclear (cf. Langness 1999). 'Domination' can be achieved in many ways in many societies, one might say. In New Guinea, the process of domination begins with warfare and extends to the psychocultural treatment of the individual body, invariably including not only material processes of production but also rituals, and, even more particularly, rituals that genderize the body. In the case of the body of the male, for example, what begins as more androgynous and soft is transformed through ritual into a more masculine and hard body.

Among Anga-speaking societies, including the Sambia and the Baruya, the inscription of vital meanings in thought as much as in the body is a matter of developmental change across the culturally constructed life-course of the individual actor. Thus, the body at birth is more 'hermaphroditic' (Herdt 1994), in spite of possessing genitals of one or the other sex, which gradually becomes gendered only through ritual initiations. This is because what matters ultimately are not the biological but the cultural genitals in these societies. So powerful are these rituals in the social consciousness of the Sambia that the most secret male myth of the founding of the cosmos tells that in the original state of nature, humans were hermaphroditic, and required ritual treatment through repeated inseminations in order to achieve the cultural state of being females and males (Herdt 1981).

This powerful cultural logic is structured through a variety of ritual initiations that take place over many years from childhood to adulthood. We might think of these rites and their gendered ideas as fundaments of these cultures (Herdt and Stephen 1989). That creates a kind of sexuality that is remarkable in its link to the body and social relationships and curiously, it has a flavour of the postmodern to it (Giddens 1992).

Ethnography of a Wenner-Gren Conference

The 1993 conference, organized by myself and psychologist Paul Abramson, was entitled: 'Theorizing Sexuality: Evolution, Culture and Development'. An account of this conference is contained in the appendix to Abramson and Pinkerton's[1] edited book, *Sexual Nature, Sexual Culture* (1995), which also contains some of the conference papers. As Sydel Silverman noted in her opening statement, the conference was the first of its kind to be sponsored by the Wenner-Gren Foundation, both in terms of the focus on sexuality, as well as the range of disciplines (nine anthropologists, two psychologists, an evolution psychologist, four sociologists, two primatologists, a philosopher, a developmental geneticist, a historian, an operations researcher, and an endocrinologist).[2] All the participants had been invited in advance to address three critical questions: 1) What are the received assumptions within each field and how can we incorporate non-reproductive sex into our paradigms? 2) How can we move past the influence of constricting dichotomies of sex/gender and biology/culture and essentialism/constructionism?

3) How can we create a dialogue that asks new questions across disciplines?

In terms of these three broad questions, I think the aim of the conference was to interrogate and then bridge the more purely biological approaches to sexuality with those of the social and cultural sciences. The division of labour of the conference organizers reflected this utopian ideal: Abramson was primarily responsible for the 'biological' side, and Herdt for the 'cultural' side, with nominations for participants and negotiations regarding the mixture influenced by all sides, including the Foundation. This utopian ideal was a very bold – perhaps too ambitious – intellectual goal. In retrospect, it seems to me that a perusal of the participant list suggests that the stellar group of scholars invited typically represented people who were at the top of their field, and thus represented the epitome of these countervailing epistemologies. Bringing them together in such a context had probably never been attempted before; certainly not in an intimate, intellectual exchange, which the Wenner-Gren format created. At any rate, the conference, again in my own personal view, did not achieve this grand goal. I would like to provide a brief 'postmortem' on the reasons for this. My 'data' are drawn from interviews I have conducted (three in person) with conference participants over the past several months, as well as upon my own reflections of the events. As noted a little later, I now believe that these experience-near accounts are only part of the picture; while the larger picture of transformation was going on globally and was hardly reflected at all in the conversations occurring in the conference room.

In a nutshell, one aspect of the 'problem' that confronted the conference project is reflected in the table of contents of the Abramson and Pinkerton (1995) book, which lists four parts: 'Evolutionary origins', 'Crossroads: biology and behavior', 'Cultural dimensions', and 'Quantitative Models and Measurement'. This set of neat-and-tidy boxes is left over from the historical epistemology of sexology. Notice that the book begins with 'evolution', with non-human species, a tried and tested approach to sexuality forums. The primary linkage between the first two sections and the later ones is not located in social or cultural entities as such, but in sociobiology, as is reflected in later chapters. Otherwise, there is little overlap between the first two parts of the book and the third part (on culture). Moreover, all three parts are disconnected from the last part, on quantitative measurement. This disconnection of theory and method is itself highly troubling and again, hastens back to the sexological heritage that the conference could not shrug off. In short, the approaches are presented as 'competing' paradigms. Likewise, it seems to me now, there were not enough scholars 'linking' the two paradigms as represented in the

1993 conference room. There were few 'bridgers' or 'connectors', people who are able to wear more than one hat in their research; and none of the later were in the 'postmodern' presentational mode, where neither 'biology' nor 'culture' and are clear, and where very different ideas, jargon, and textual and rhetorical approaches are rampant (anarchistic, some would say). The one exception was a junior colleague at the conference (Cohen 1995), who had recently returned from the field, and had not yet distilled his findings.

The primary register of this contention and inability to bridge came out in the debates and definitional arguments about terms. Time and again one found the basic tenets of a paper, a model, or an explanation challenged on the grounds of scientific terms or jargon. This is described in the appendix to Abramson and Pinkerton (1995), written by two students of Abramson (Okami and Pendleton 1995: 389), as follows: 'Meanings and uses of terms such as "sex", "gender", "science", "biomedical", "homosexual", "adaptation", "intersex", "function", and "reproduction", became points of heated contention. Even the notion of "sexual pleasure" was questioned: was it a socially constructed category, or did it exist autonomously within human biology and experience?' The passage that follows suggests that Abramson defined sexual pleasure as 'functionally specific positive responses in the genitals'. Herdt could not seem to persuade his co-organizer to reconsider the issue that, whatever the individual or subjective experience of these sensations, their meanings and practices in communities and societies were of a different order. Indeed, after a time I despaired of how to bridge my own position, which suggests that these are separate levels of understanding. Now I realize that the two levels – individual difference theories versus cultural difference theories – are always present in these larger scholarly gatherings, though seldom made explicit (Herdt 2004).

The conference featured a big idea debate on nature versus nurture accounts – the so-called 'biological' presentations vs. the 'cultural constructionism'. For example, one commentator spoke thus of Carole Vance's remarkable paper at the conference: 'Vance offered a social constructionist view of the history of anthropological involvement in the study of sexuality' (p.389). I do not think that this sentence describes what she did, nor does it do her justice, since her entire presentation was aimed at refining the meanings of constructionism. I think that the resulting impasse was common to many such gatherings before. As Suggs and Miracle (1999: 39) have recently noted the same problem as it emerged from a totally different conference: 'Those from the hard-line, hardwired behaviour schools are not talking about the social uses of biology. They are talking about the motive forces of biology'. Thus, I hope that the reader has begun to understand the historical and epistemological barriers confronting not only the participants but also the organizers themselves.

Permit me to provide a wider description of the conference discussion through the comments of conference participants, whom I shall call 'informants' below; they represent three views of the conference: positive, negative, and in-between. I will start with the negative. One of the most significant and renowned of the socio-cultural participants, who have contributed enormously to the field, was quite negative. When asked what was the overall effect upon her work and subsequent intellectual development, she remarked without pause: 'I never want to be in a room with sociolobiologists again!' She went on to say that she felt the biologists were unable and unwilling to 'listen to' and 'feel genuine interest' in the theory and findings of their cultural colleagues. She did not contribute to the book mentioned above because she felt that the editor was unable to 'get it' and recognize that sexuality is not all 'hard wired'.

A story circulated towards the end of the conference that sums up the 'shock' of this scholar's experience at the conference. It was the fourth night of the conference, at cocktail time. She was approached by the one of the most senior 'biological' scholars and a noted (meaning a nominee for a Noble prize) geneticist. He remarked to her, 'You don't believe in genes, do you?' She replied: 'Excuse me?' 'You just don't believe in the existence of genes, do you?', he said again. She was so flabbergasted at his remark, that her response that she had taught in a medical school for years, that her writings always acknowledged the existence of material forces, including genes, was lost in the conversation. She came away feeling that if he could imagine that – after several days of intellectual discussion and exchange, including the reading of her own paper – there was something deeply wrong. Others have repeated the story in making the point about a 'listening' gap that seemed to prevail, especially later on in the meeting.

One of the senior biological participants, an eminent person in his field outside of anthropology, had a more positive reading of the conference. However, it is clear that his experience was primarily concerned with his own learning experience. He said that he was very curious about anthropology and had always wanted to participate in something of the kind. 'I had read the old text, like Margaret Mead's, but didn't have a real grasp of what was happening now.' In his view, the primary problem with the conference was that there was almost no 'overlap between anthropology and sexology' in 1993. He felt that this has changed somewhat in recent years. He definitely felt that the conference was important in his own intellectual (late career) development. He noted that because of the conference, he and a colleague were motivated to include 'qualitative methods and teaching' on these issues at the major centre which he co-heads. He thought of this as a change in his views. Finally, he remarked that there are more intellectual spaces now, and people can go to professional conferences without meeting each other or confronting each others' paradigms, as happened in Cascais. This is a very telling insight and also reveals the explosion in international conferences on sexuality that have emerged in recent years.

The third and final informant presented a more balanced, in-between view. She is a leading socio-cultural anthropologist who now heads one of the most important centres of its kind in the world, and she is directly involved in social, medical and sexuality research and education. She felt that the conference attempted a great deal, perhaps too much, in bridging the biological and cultural: 'Two camps quickly got set up and withdrew to their corners.' She alluded to the 'genes' story mentioned above as the manifestation of the failure to communicate or understand. For this scholar, however, the experience was highly influential, and perhaps even fundamental, in changing her career. She claimed that it opened a whole world of intellectual contacts that were important to her, and definitely changed her work in the direction of sexuality. For her, the conference 'defined a moment in time – always what came before and after.' She felt it was deeply problematic that there were two 'sides' that could not be bridged, and yet that 'it would have been impossible to bridge this if postmodernism had been present'. This was an insight that had not occurred to me before, and she responded to this comment by stating: 'Don't you think it was remarkable that not a single presentation was confessional – in the postmodern mode?' I had to agree, although Cohen's (1995) original paper was a step in that direction. She remarked that the direction of the past five years has led ever more deeply into the new 'confessional' mode on sexual anthropology, and this was highly problematic. Finally, she remarked that the vicissitudes of 'biology' and 'culture' have changed in recent years. Perhaps the AIDS work, so prominent in many fields, she said, 'has made cultural people more sensitive to the biological, and biological and medical people a bit more sensitive to cultural context'. Interesting enough, neither of the other two informants quoted above agreed with her on this score.

These narratives give a sense of the broader context of the conference experience, and the reader may consult the published papers for further reflection. Stated crassly, there was an unfortunate tendency for both 'camps' to think that the other was devoted to its approach as if it were a 'religion'. There is something very ironic in this thought, since most of the scholars in this conference, I would venture to say, were either atheists or humanist secularists, and probably bring less of 'religion' to understanding human sexuality than just about any gathering of scholars that one might imagine. In point of fact, it is difficult for me to say how much headway was actually made in 'theorizing sex', or in the more restrictive goal of including non-reproductive sexuality and notions of sexual pleasure into models of human sexuality. Clearly, many good things came from the conference, including much that I learned and have subsequently been able to draw upon in my own work. I do not think that the 1993 conference fully recognized the centrality of anthropology as a kind of 'mother discipline' in orienting the paradigmatic study of sexual theory, although this might have been one outcome. Whatever the case, the hiatus between the biological and cultural areas of sexual study has always been great, and was not bridged to any discernable extent by the conference. However, I think the concerns of the field have shifted beyond this 'competing paradigms' idea, and the remainder of my paper is devoted to exploring this idea.

The Past is Not the Future of Sexuality Study

I would now like to claim that the future of sexuality studies in the social and cultural sciences actually began a decade ago, before the Cascais conference. It was not born in the lab or the sex clinic, or even in the classroom, but in Europe, with the demise of the Cold War. Its icon – the Berlin Wall – was besieged and dismantled, literally stone by stone by Berliners, which was followed by the reunification of Germany, the collapse of the Soviet Union, and the eventual independence of Eastern Europe. The collapse of the Wall in 1989 set off a series of watershed events which began to finish off the central intellectual themes of modernity set in place late in the nineteeth century as reviewed above.[3] I do not think that any of us present at Cascais, with the possible exception of Igor Kon (1995), appreciated this changing understanding, simply because it was still emergent, and diffuse.

Since 1990, and each year seems to accelerate the process, a new historical trend – a kind of global democratization of sexuality – has fanned out from Western European and North American states, to the Third World. Within a short space of time, the meanings and social practices associated with 'private sex' and 'sexual liberation movements' had begun to change. This was true both within the Western European and North American states (Weeks and Holland 1996), as well as in non-Western countries, where 'sexual diversity' began to blossom in the former colonies (e.g., South Africa; see Gevisser and Cameron 1995). Today, what we might call this post-Cold War social change is exploding the boundaries of traditional sexual cultures, infused by the AIDS epidemic and the study of STDs, and the advance of structural violence as a new grand theory (Farmer 1992). Additionally, the import of new advances in reproductive technologies and contraceptives, information technologies that export sex,[4] the associated approval of sex research in many places that formerly tabooed this, as well as a new-found but by no means universal respect in the Academy, created what was once called the dirty science (Gagnon and Parker 1995). In the twenty-first century, a new and growing rhetoric claims international human rights for all sexual cultures/sexual minorities (Parker et al. 2002).

As the world opens its borders to trade and commercial exchange, sex research, knowledge transfers, and sexual migration, there is a possibility of homogeneity – a single, worldwide 'sexual culture' (Altman 2000). The question of difference theories of sexuality arise: are we all to become the same or homogeneous in our sexual meanings and practices? The record of anthropology makes it clear that such a formulation is far too simple and short-sighted (Herdt 1997). Not only has historical change in sexual cultures been noted since at least the time of the Roman Empire, but also sexual diversity and the emergence of new sexual cultures in Europe remains surprising robust and impressive today. Moreover, as democratization spreads to many corners that were previously suppressed, as well as in the United States, formerly oppressed people, including transgender, bisexuals, gays and lesbians, among others, have increased their visibility and upheld their claims for full social personhood and citizenship as the century closes. This historical trend, while emerging in 1993, was still nascent and did not fundamentally impact on the discussions at Cascais. In this 'postmodern' sexuality, it is not that the biological-versus-cultural debate is any less important to theory or relevant to methodology, it is just less pressing to the politics of science and popular culture (Appadurai 1993; Gagnon 1997; Herdt 2004).

This view led me to reflect upon several new and emerging themes of research, education and policy in sexuality studies, and others that are 'old' but are being critically altered in the historical transformation mentioned above. (This list is not meant to be exhaustive.)

First: the emerging concept of sexual culture, which comes out of the AIDS/HIV work (Parker et al. 1991), and which has become of increasing importance (Herdt 1999a; reviewed in Teunis and Herdt 2006). In this model, the line between 'biology' (phylogeny and ontogeny) and 'culture' (shared meanings and social practices) is less discernible, and less important, than the signal function of regulating sexual behaviour within human groups (biology/culture). This line of conceptual change was presaging in theory work by Connell and Dowsett (1993) and DiMauro (1995).

Second: the growing body of work on sexual diversity set within the larger context of population and human variation models, which seeks to understand the courses and outcomes of sexuality variation. A good deal of this comes out of gay and lesbian studies, both within anthropology, and in other disciplines (Jacobs et al. 1997; Lewin and Leap 1996; Weston 1993). The methodological difficulties facing this work, including the problem of 'natives studying natives', and being sexually involved with people in the research project, are formidable and the subject of much debate and critical thought (Herdt 1999a; Kulick and Wilson 1996; Markowitz and Ashkenazi 1998).

Third, a new rhetoric of sexuality as human rights, which is displacing a very powerful 'biological' preoccupation in sexology with the 'causes' of sexual orientation. Rather than asking, 'Why heterosexual?', or 'Why homosexual?', this approach asks, 'How are the rights and laws of heterosexuals and homosexuals different or the same? Who is not protected? Why or why not? What is regarded as privileged, e.g., procreative heterosexuality'.

Forth: the disruptive impact of migrations upon the sexual and social order, which poses the fundamental problem that when someone moves from one place to another, they may not know the 'rules of the sexual culture', and are therefore placed at greater risk, e.g., of infection to STDs, of sexual violence, etc. (Herdt 1997). The plight of refugees, and the terrible vulnerability of refugee women and children to sexual assault, have only just begun to be conceptualized in this way (Long and Long 1997).

Fifth: the emergence of increasingly greater attention to 'transgender' categories and individual people, formerly coded in the terms of sexual binaries and third sex/gender classifications (Herdt 1994). Today, however, these discussions are going beyond either the puerile 'nature vs. nurture' arguments of before, to increasingly identify very complex subjectivities, and emergent socialities (Besnier 1994; Lang 1996).

Sixth: the emerging literature on reproductive technologies, and the impact of these meanings and practices on social order, especially that part of it which might be called sexual culture and sociality. The important contribution by Rayna Rapp and Faye Ginsburg, in this conference, provides a significant discussion for this critical area of work (Martin 1987).

Last but not least is of course the work on sexually transmitted diseases, and the AIDS pandemic. The vast explosion of this work is difficult to comprehend, let alone, conceptualize (see Gagnon 1990; Herdt 1997; Levine et al. 1997; Lindenbaum 1992; Parker and Aggleton 1999; Teunis and Herdt 2006). The impact on theories and methodology, including the virtual irrelevance of sexology to understanding the pandemic, are notable. The great dangers posed to many non-Western populations by the spread of HIV/AIDS, particularly in Asia and Africa, are the subject of enormous concern in many quarters. A recent contribution by Manderson, Bennett and Sheldrake (in press) represents a comprehensive and extraordinary effort to think through what is known about the cross-cultural work on sexuality and AIDS.

Convergence

What many of these conceptual themes have in common is the difficulty of bridging the old schism between individual and cultural difference theories. In addition, these new theoretical and methodological issues have to confront an explosion of sexual diversity, what I call new and emergent sexual cultures, all over the world. How are these entities to be conceptualized in the time and space world? What cultural reality do they claim and how are these realities situated by culture makers and stakeholders in power relations?

By default, sexologists originally treated sexuality as part of nature, but not as natural, since they typically studied the abnormal; and they certainly did not conceptualize the sexual as the product of culture or cultural realities. Without the construct of sexual culture – locating the meanings and practices of persons and relationships at least partly in the social world – the default condition always dominated both the discourses and study of the sexual. Thus, while Kinsey's (1948) study of American sexuality was enormously influential in changing attitudes about sex, and indeed, in paving the way for the Baby boomers' gender and sexual studies a generation later, it left intact the idea of sex as a natural development, with no fits and starts, or disjunctions in society.

Since the Cascais conference I have struggled with this intellectual problem and my work in the past several years is a direct result of the epistemological *ennui* I had to confront as a result of this. Critical to this effort in my work are the constructs of sexual culture and sexual lifeways, the means of my theory building of confronting both the cultural difference and individual difference dimensions of the sexual (Herdt 2004, 2009). I define sexual lifeways as the culturally specific erotic ideas and emotions, sexual/gender categories and roles, theories of being and becoming a full social person (in the Maussian sense) that constitute life course development within a particular sexual culture (Herdt 1997: 20, 2003). Sexual cultures, in turn, are the specific discursive and material fields by which systems of power relationships are used to control sexual behaviour or conduct, and thus sexual lifeways are instituted, enculturated, enacted and reproduced.

Sexual cultures, as historical formations, are distinct from those that border them, or form the imports of colonization. Moreover, at a time of increasing migration and changes in the post-9/11 world system, the flux of sexual cultures through migration and transplantation remains an issue of sexual change. Sexual cultures are formulas for gender performances and the control of gender roles in sexual relations. Sexual lifeways thus overlap with but can be conceptually distinguished from gendered lifeways. While sexual lifeways have traditionally been gendered as male, female or according to some alternative or third-sex/gender category (Herdt 1994), what is at stake in the production of sexual culture is the regulation of sexual behaviour, both within individuals and beyond in the cultural surround.

Sexual lifeways provide a cultural template or script that, once internalized by the individual, moulds an amorphous array of thoughts, feelings, needs and desires into specific attractions, fantasies, behaviours, understandings of the self, roles, rights, duties, ontologies, deontologies and teleologies. This is not to suggest that specific sexual desires, such as for same-sex or cross-sex persons, are something the individual is simply socialized into as part of a larger package. Some of the components of sexual lifeways are more accurately described as 'learned' and are therefore more voluntary than others. The concept is not intended to be exhaustive of all processes of sexual development; there are potential slippages between sexual lifeways and other processes that produce sexual subjects, and these slippages can produce discordances and mismatches between the different components of any given sexual lifeway. For example, most individuals in the contemporary West continue to be socialized in the direction of erotic and emotional attachments to members of the opposite sex, with the expectation that they will marry heterosexually, raise a family and, eventually, become a grandparent. But despite the existence of one officially-sanctioned sexual lifeway, there are a myriad of possible developmental outcomes, including the adoption of a gay or lesbian identity and social role – a sexual lifeway that presents itself as a viable option in adolescence, at the earliest.

Clearly, if a biopsychological/developmental perspective familiar from the sexological tradition is to be relevant to contemporary socio-cultural theory and research, it must not simply recycle the universalistic, essentialist, and reductionist assumptions of nineteenth-century sexology. And if such a perspective is to make productive use of taxonomies, these taxonomies must be culturally and historically grounded (Herdt and Stoller 1990). Existing concepts

– such as 'sexual preference', 'sexual orientation' and even 'sexual identity' – are inadequate in describing the forms of social life and subjectivity that have been attached to particular sexual desires. In addition to being too individualistic and internal, obscuring the social and cultural levels from view (Herdt 1997a), these concepts reduce to one or, at most, two dimensions (i.e., sexual object choice, and the subjective identifications that follow from it) what is in fact a multi-dimensional, multi-faceted phenomenon (though, of course, all concepts homogenize diversity to some degree). Obviously it is inadequate to reduce all of the meanings to one entity such as 'identity', which does not effect developmental and cultural change as part of itself, but rather instantiates a permanence that is foreign to people's lives (Herdt 1990).

This is not just to say that identity is a social and ontogenetic process. I also mean that the phenomena typically glossed as 'sexual identity' include a narrative of origins (an ontology), a fantasy of an ultimate purpose and future fulfilment (a teleology), and a theory of and/or plan for moral action in the world (deontology). The problem with globalization, as well as queer theory formulations of this issue, is the tendency to dismiss the ontological and teleological components as 'biological' or 'essentialist' (see for example Patton 1993; Herdt and Boxer 1996; Herdt and McClintock 2000). However, I would contend that all three of these dimensions are important to the formation and sustenance of meaningful human life patterns – a claim long supported by the cross-cultural record (Schweder et al. 1989). The idea of sexual lifeways has the merit of avoiding the triumvirate of 'isms' listed above.

Summing Up: The Past is Not the Future

The history of sexuality studies over the past century and a half has seen a shifting of three orders of things: the definition of the phenomenon, and the knowledge related to it (epistemology); the changing of disciplines empowered by the state and popular culture to socially regulate the phenomena of sex; and the locus of power or control that is shifting from local sexual cultures and states to international and nongovernmental organizations. Today, as a consequence, sexuality theory is open to scrutiny from multiple disciplines beyond the Academy, with multiple audiences or publics in the waiting. Some of these include local people, the sexual groups and sexual cultures that ethnographies are reporting on. And they have formed their own committees and human rights promotions and lobbied for the increasing respect of each discipline for each other's way of seeing the world. Thus it is no longer accepted that medicine or biology are privileged ways of explaining sexuality, and reductionistic thinking is changing.

Sexology arose in response to the definitional understanding of sexuality as a phenomenon of disease, located in individual bodies, and diagnosed accordingly. It was located as much in the 'secular' domain of doctor's offices, clinics and hospitals, as in the Academy. Psychoanalysis, for example, never succeeded in being institutionalized in the Academy in the United States. The focus of this discourse was 'biology' and the 'body'. The sexual reform movements that intended to ameliorate the conditions of suffering and the laws related to sexuality disrupted this historical system.

However, the epistemology that focused on sex as 'internal secretions' and 'biology' did not fundamentally change, and the methodology that took individual sexual behaviour as the unit of analysis has continued through epidemiology and demography to this day. The invention of the construct of gender, with its associated attention to social context and later, historical period, was located in the Academy but took advantage of twentieth-century reform movements, including the early women's emancipation movement. Today the human rights/sexual rights movement is the epitome of this postmodern transformation (Parker et al. 2002). The focus of study then shifted away from sex to gender roles, and remained thus for a long time.

The disciplinary focus upon anthropology and sociology, and later history and to some extent social psychology, moved sexuality studies into the Academy, with the locus of its meanings in social things, not in individual bodies as such. Only in the last quarter of this century have we seen the controversial attempts of some feminist writers and sexuality scholars to theoretically link sexuality with gender. Whereas sexology and its legacy in the biological sciences understood 'sex' to be inside the individual person, the later socio-cultural approach generally understood 'sex' to be outside the person in social roles and institutions. Thus, I think we can appreciate the intellectual burden involved in the effort to bridge the biological and the cultural at Cascais.

But the new shift to sexuality studies now locates the meanings and practices of sex in something that is neither in the body nor in society. It is related to the spread of disease and the worries of contagion, both real and imagined, but is not being approached solely through medicine, epidemiology, or individual bodies. The creation of a network of NGOs – nongovernmental organizations throughout the world – may be the purest manifestation of this new attention to what we might call power. But the meanings associated with this attention to the social regulation of sex and sexual behaviour were built upon over a century of sexual reform and emancipation movements, including the feminist, subsequent homosexual, later gay and lesbian, and now transgender social movements. The legacy of rhetoric and liberationist ideas associated with individuals and groups, more like imagined communities that sometimes become face-to-face sociological communities of individuals residing in proximity together, lends a popular concern with human rights to this change (Parker et al. 2002). This transformation is now primarily located outside of the Academy and no discipline, including ours, has control over it. As globalization and the internationalization of sexual movements and knowledge accelerates, we can expect that the social regulation of sexuality will be contested in other domains, such as religion, where old debates will become enfolded into new discussions about the human and civil rights of sexual persons and diverse sexual cultures.

Anthropology is better suited than any other academic discipline to conceptualize these total systems of meanings, knowledge and practices, and to think through the implications of their changing contours around the globe, especially in the Third World. That is the challenge, which could not have been articulated at Cascais. That is the future that lies before us.

Notes

1. Pinkerton is a colleague of Abramson's and was not present at the 1993 conference.
2. A second historian, besides John Fout, had been invited to attend, but Jeffrey Weeks from England cancelled shortly before the conference began.
3. There are many possible historical markers of this change. The one which I like to use is the emergence of the historical identity categories 'homosexual' (c. 1869–1870, attributed to Ulrichs) and later 'heterosexual' (often attributed to Havelock Ellis between 1890 and 1892). By the time that 'heterosexual' came into popular coinage in the later 1890s, following the wide newspaper coverage of the Oscar Wilde sodomy trial scandals, modernist attitudes toward sexual identity, sexual liberation, individual sexual identity, and related themes were well formed (see Robinson 1976; Weeks 1985).
4. The emergence of incredible information technologies, such as the cell phone, personal computer, fax machine, and internet make the transport of sexual imagery across the globe probable. Virtual reality means sex can travel across the continents; it is explored in a chat room but may be consummated through sexual expression in the social world.

Bibliography

Abramson, P.R. and S.D. Pinkerton (eds). 1995. *Sexual Nature, Sexual Culture.* Chicago: University of Chicago Press.

Allen, M. R. (1967). *Male Cults and Secret Initiations in Melanesia.* Melbourne, Australia: Melbourne University Press.

Altmann, D. 2000. *Global Sex.* Chicago: University of Chicago Press.

Appadurai, A. 1993. 'Consumption, Duration and History', *Stanford Literary Review* 10 (1–2): 11–23.

Benedict, R. 1938. 'Continuities and Discontinuities in Cultural Conditioning', *Psychiatry* 1: 161–7.

Besnier, Niko. 1994. 'Polynesian Gender Liminality through Time and Space', in G. Herdt (ed.), *Third Sex, Third Gender.* New York: Zone Books, p.285–328.

Bettelheim, B. (1962) *Symbolic Wounds.* New York: Collier Books.

Boelstorff, T. (2008) *Coming of Age in Second Life.* Princeton, NJ: Princeton University Press.

Brummelhuis, H.T. and G. Herdt (eds). 1995. *Culture and Sexual Risk.* New York: Gordon and Breach, Inc.

Chodorow, N.J. 1978. *The Reproduction of Mothering.* Berkeley: University of California Press.

Cohen, L. 1995. 'The Pleasures of Castration', in P. Abramson and S. Pinkerton (eds), *Sexual Nature, Sexual Culture.* Chicago: University of Chicago Press, p.276–304.

Connell, R.W. and G.W. Dowsett (eds). 1993. *Rethinking Sex: Social Theory and Sexuality Research.* Philadelphia: Temple University Press.

D'Emilio, J.D. and E.B. Freedman. 1988. *Intimate Matters: A History of Sexuality in America.* New York: Harper and Row.

Di Leonardo, M. 1998. *Exotics at Home.* Chicago: University of Chicago Press.

DiMauro, D. 1995. *Sexuality Research in the United States.* New York: Social Science Research Council.

Farmer, P. 1992. *AIDS and Accusation: Haiti and the Geography of Blame.* Berkeley: University of California Press.

——— 2003. *Pathologies of Power: Health, Human Rights, and the New War on the Poor.* Berkeley: University of California Press.

Foucault, M. 1980. *The History of Sexuality.* Translation by R. Hurley. New York: Viking.

Freud, S. 1905 [1962]. *Three Essays on the Theory of Sexuality.* New York: Basic Books.

——— 1913. *Totem and Taboo.* Leipzig-Vienna: Hugo Heller.

Friedl, E. 1994. 'Sex the Invisible', *American Anthropologist* 96: 833–44.

Gagnon, J.H. 1990. 'The Explicit and Implicit Use of the Scripting Perspective in Sex Research', *Annual Review of Sex Research* 1: 1–44.

——— 1997. 'Others Have Sex with Others: Captain Cook and the Penetration of the Pacific', in G. Herdt (ed.), *Sexual Cultures and Migration in the Eras of AIDS.* Oxford: The Clarendon Press, p.23–40.

——— and R. Parker. 1995. *Introduction, Conceiving Sexuality.* New York: Routledge.

———— and W. Simon. 1973. *Sexual Conduct: The Social Sources of Human Sexuality*. London: Hutchinson.

Gevisser, M. and E. Cameron (eds). 1995. *Defiant Desire: Gay and Lesbian Lives in South Africa*. New York: Routledge.

Giddens, A.1992. *The Transformation of Intimacy: Sexuality, Love and Eroticism in Modern Societies*. Darby: Diane Publishing Co.

Godelier, M. 1982. 'Social Hierarchies among the Baruya of New Guinea', in A. Strathern (ed.), *Inequality in New Guinea*. New York: Cambridge University Press, p.3–34

Herdt, G. 1981. *Guardians of the Flutes: Idioms of Masculinity*. New York: McGraw-Hill.

———— 1982. 'Fetish and Fantasy in Sambia Initiation' in G. Herdt (ed.), *Rituals of Manhood*. Berkeley, CA: University of California Press, p.44–98.

———— 1984. 'Ritualized Homosexuality in the Male Cults of Melanesia, 1862–1982: An Introduction', in G.H. Herdt (ed.), *Ritualized Homosexuality in Melanesia*. Berkeley: University of California Press, p.1–81.

———— 1987.'The Accountability of Sambia Initiates', in L.L. Langness and T.E. Hays (eds), *Anthropology in the High Valleys: Essays in Honor of K. E. Read*. New York: Novato, Chandler and Sharp, p.82.

———— 1990. 'Developmental Continuity as a Dimension of Sexual Orientation across Cultures', in D. McWhirter, J. Reinisch and S. Sanders (eds), *Homosexuality and Heterosexuality: The Kinsey Scale and Current Research*. New York: Oxford University Press, p.208–38.

———— 1991a. 'Representations of Homosexuality in Traditional Societies: An Essay on Cultural Ontology and Historical Comparison', *Journal of the History of Sexuality* Part I(1): 481–504.

———— 1991b. 'Representations of Homosexuality in Traditional Societies: An Essay on Cultural Ontology and Historical Comparison', *Journal of the History of Sexuality* Part II(2): 603–32.

———— 1992. 'Ten Years after Ritualized Homosexuality in Melanesia: Introduction to the New Edition', in G. Herdt (ed.), *Ritualized Homosexuality in Melanesia*. Berkeley, CA: University of California Press, p.1–82.

———— 1993. 'Sexual Repression, Social Control, and Gender Hierarchy in Sambia Culture', in B. Miller (ed.), *Sex and Gender Hierarchies*. New York: Cambridge University Press, p.193–210.

———— 1994. 'Mistaken Sex: Culture, Biology and the Third Sex in New Guinea', in G. Herdt (ed.), *Third Sex, Third Gender: Beyond Sexual Dimorphism in Culture and History*. New York: Zone Books, p.419–46.

———— 1997a. 'Inter-Generational Relations and AIDS in the Formation of Gay Culture in the United States', in M. Levine, P. Nardi, and J. Gagnon (eds), *In Changing Times: Gay Men and Lesbians Encounter HIV/AIDS*. Chicago: University of Chicago Press, p.245–82.

———— 1997b. 'Sexual Cultures and Population Movement: Implications for HIV/STDs', in G. Herdt (ed.), *Sexual Cultures and Migration in the*

Era of AIDS: Anthropological and Demographic Perspectives. New York: Oxford University Press, p. 3–22.

———. 1999. *Sambia Sexual Culture: Essays from the Field*. Chicago: University of Chicago Press.

——— and A. Boxer. 1993. *Children of Horizons: How Gay and Lesbian Youth are Forging a New Way Out of the Closet*. Boston: Beacon Press.

——— and R.J. Stoller. 1990. *Intimate Communications: Erotics and the Study of Culture*. New York: Columbia University Press.

———. 2004. 'Sexual Development, Social Oppression, and Local Culture', *Sexuality Research and Social Policy*, 1: 1–24.

———. 2009. *Moral Panics/Sex Panics*. New York: NYU Press

——— and M. Stephen (eds). 1989. *The Religious Imagination in New Guinea*. New Brunswick, NJ: Rutgers University Press.

——— and M. McClintock. 2000. 'The Magical Age of 10', *Archives of Sexual Behavior*, 29(6): 587–606.

Hostetler, A. and G. Herdt. 1998. 'Culture, Sexual Lifeways, and Developmental Subjectivities: Rethinking Sexual Taxonomies', *Social Research* 65: 249–90.

Irvine, J. 2000. *Disorders of Desire*. Philadelphia: Temple University Press.

Jacobs, S.-E., W. Thomas and S. Lang (eds). 1997. *Two-Spirit People: Native American Gender Identity, Sexuality, and Spirituality*. Urbana: University of Illinois Press.

Kinsey, A. et al. 1948. *Sexual Behavior and the Human Male*. Philadelphia: W. B. Saunders.

Kon, I. 1995. *The Sexual Revolution in Russia*. New York: Free Press.

Kulick, D. and M. Wilson (eds). 1996. *Taboo: Sex, Identity, and Erotic Subjectivity in Anthropological Fieldwork*. London: Routledge.

Lang, S. 1996. 'Travelling Woman: Conducting a Fieldwork Project on Gender Variance and Homosexuality among North American Indians', in E. Lewin and W. Leap (eds), *Out in the Field*. Urbana: University of Illinois Press, p. 86–110.

Langness, L.L. 1999. *Men and "Woman" in New Guinea*. Novato: Chandler and Sharp Publishers Inc.

Leap, W. 1999. *Public Sex, Gay Space*. New York: Columbia University Press.

Levine, M., J. Gagnon and P. Nardi (eds). 1997. *AIDS and the Gay Community in the United States*. Chicago: University of Chicago Press.

Lewin, E. and W. Leap (eds). 1996. *Out in the Field*. Urbana: University of Illinois Press.

Lindenbaum, S. 1992. 'Knowledge and Action in the Shadow of AIDS', in G. Herdt and S. Lindenbaum (eds), *The Time of AIDS*. Newbury Park: Sage, p. 310–34.

Long, L. and D. Long. 1997. 'Refugee Women, Violence, and HIV', in G. Herdt (ed.), *Sexual Cultures and Migration in the Era of AIDS*. Oxford: Oxford University Press, p. 87–106.

Malinowski, B. 1929. *The Sexual Life of Savages in North-Western Melanesia*. New York: Harcourt, Brace and World, Inc.

Manderson, L. and M. Jolly (eds). 1997. *Sites of Desire, Economies of Pleasure: Sexualities in Asia and the Pacific*. Chicago: University of Chicago Press.

Markowitz, F. and M. Ashkenazi (eds). 1998. *Sex, Sexuality, and the Anthropologist*. Urbana: University of Illinois Press.

Martin, E. 1987. *The Woman in the Body*. Boston: Beacon Press.

Mead, Margaret. 1927. *Coming of Age in Samoa*. New York: Dutton.

———— 1935. *Sex and Temperament in Three Primitive Societies*. New York: Dutton.

———— 1949. *Male and Female*. New York: Dutton.

———— 1961. 'Cultural Determinants of Sexual Behavior', in W.C. Youn (ed.), *Sex and Internal Secretions*. Baltimore, MD: Williams and Wilkins, p.1433–79.

Okami, P. and L. Pendleton. 1995. 'Appendix: Theorizing Sexuality', in P. Abramson and S. Pinkerton (eds), *Sexual Nature, Sexual Culture*. Chicago: The University of Chicago Press, p.387–97.

Parker, R. and P. Aggleton (eds). 1999. *Culture, Society and Sexuality: A Reader*. London: UCL Press.

Parker, R., R. Barbosa and P. Aggleton. 2002. *Framing the Sexual Subject: The Politics of Gender, Sexuality and Power*. Berkeley: University of California Press.

Parker, R., M. Carballo and G. Herdt. 1991. 'Sexual Culture, HIV Transmission, and AIDS Research', *Journal of Sex Research* 28: 75–96.

Patton, C. 1990. *Inventing AIDS*. New York: Routledge.

Robinson, P. 1976. *The Modernization of Sex: Havelock Ellis, Alfred Kinsey, William Masters and Virginia Johnson*. Ithaca, NY: Cornell University.

Rosaldo, M. and L. Lamphere. 1974. *Woman, Culture and Society*. Stanford: Stanford University Press.

Rubin, G. 1984. 'Thinking Sex: Notes for a Radical Theory of the Politics of Sexuality', in C.S. Vance (ed.), *Pleasure and Danger: Exploring Female Sexuality*. New York: Routledge and Kegan Paul, p.267–319.

Silverman, S. 2002. *The Beast at the Table*. New York: Alta Mira Press.

Stigler, J., R. Shweder and G. Herdt (eds). 1989. *Cultural Psychology: The Chicago Symposia in Culture and Human Development*. New York: Cambridge University Press.

Stimpson, C.R. 1996. 'Women's Studies and Its Discontents', *Dissent* 43: 67–75.

Stoler, A. 1995. *Race and Education of Desire*. Chapel Hill: Duke University Press.

Strathern, M. 1988. *The Gender of the Gift*. Berkeley: University of California Press.

Suggs, D.N. and A.W. Miracle. 1999. 'Theory and the Anthropology of Sexuality: Toward a Holistic Anthropology in Practice', in D.N. Suggs and A.M. Miracle (eds), *Culture, Biology and Sexuality*. Athens, Georgia: University of Georgia Press, p.33–48.

Teunis, N. and G. Herdt. 2006. 'Introduction', in N. Teunis and G. Herdt, *Sexual Inequality and Social Justice*. Berkeley: University of California Press, p.1–30.

Tiefer, I. 1991. 'Social Constructionism and the Study of Human Sexuality', in E. Stein (ed.), *Forms of Desire: Sexual Orientation and the Social Constructionist Controversy*. New York: Garland Publishing, p.295–324.

Tuzin, D.F. 1994. 'The Forgotten Passion: Sexuality and Anthropology in the Ages of Victoria and Bronslaw', *Journal of the History of the Behavioural Sciences* 30: 114–37.

Vance, C.S. 1991. 'Anthropology Rediscovers Sexuality: A Theoretical Comment', *Social Science and Medicine* 33: 875–84.

Weeks, J. 1985. *Sexuality and its Discontents*. London: Routledge and Kegan Paul.

———— and J. Holland (eds). 1996. *Sexual Cultures. Communities, Values and Intimacy*. New York: St. Martin's Press.

Weston, K. 1993. 'Lesbian/Gay Studies in the House of Anthropology', *Annual Review of Anthropology* 22: 339–67.Young, M. (2004) *Malinowski: Odyssey of an Anthropologist, 1884–1920*. New Haven, CN: Yale University Press.

Chapter 5

MATERIAL AND IMMATERIAL RELATIONS: GENDER, RANK AND CHRISTIANITY IN VANUATU

Margaret Jolly

Illuminations in the Dark:
Musée du Quai Branly Paris, 15 June 2008

In the darkened recesses of the Musée du Quai Branly, in a section dedicated to men's houses and male figures of ancestral power, I encounter several slit gongs from Malakula, in a style reminiscent of photographs in John Layard's *Stone Men of Malekula* (1942).[1] These do not have the famous carved faces of those from North Ambrym, with their huge hooked noses and their bulbous, compelling eyes but are starker, simpler embodiments, more barely anthropomorphic. But the body of one gong is not so bare. This is a distinctive *tambour des deux visages* (drum with two faces) from North East Malakula: on one lip its wood is etched with an image of a fish and beneath, the words 'Americans' and 'Red Cross', and a very indistinct, almost indecipherable date: 19 September 1945.[2] On the other lip, aeroplanes are etched. Does the image of the fish creolize ancestral and Christian meanings? And how might this written evocation of 'Americans' and 'Red Cross' relate to the momentous experiences of the Second World War, to the huge presence of American troops on the island of Espiritu Santo, their relations with ni-Vanuatu and their potent influence in shaping anti-colonial and millenarian movements which both preceded and succeeded their presence in the archipelago (see Lindstrom and Gwero 1998; Tabani 2008).[3] In the Western

Figure 5.1. *Tambour des deux visages* (drum with two faces), permanent collection Musée du Quai Branly. Collected by Jean Guiart 1960s. Photograph courtesy of Martin Maden.

imagination, as in the curatorial vision of the Musée du Quai Branly, wooden slit gongs and the rituals in which they resound (canonically the rituals of grade-taking in Northern Vanuatu) are associated with an ancestral past of an exclusively male cult, rather than a *kastom* which embraces women, and with the historical irruption of the Second World War and the complex articulations which developed between indigenous men and the extraordinary efficacy of these strangers.

The Coombs Building, 26 August 2008

I am sitting in the dark in Seminar Room A in the Coombs Building at the ANU, captivated by a powerpoint presentation by Chris Ballard apropos his conjoint research project with Elena Govor on the famous Russian explorer Nikolai Miklouho-Maclay. They focus on his journeys in the New Hebrides (Vanuatu) in 1879. His diaries of this voyage are lost, many of his papers have been dispersed but his sketch book albums remain, aged but safe in the archives of the Russian Geographical Society in Saint Petersburg. A complete digital record of these sketches, his recently discovered journal from 1879 and exchanges with ni-Vanuatu *filwokas* at the Vanuatu Cultural Centre have enabled illuminating reconstructions of the experiences of that voyage. From his sketches in pencil and his scribbled surrounding marginalia in a mess of Russian, German, English, early Bislama and indigenous languages – word lists, comments from onlookers and personal reflections – some of the contours of those earlier cross-cultural conversations can be discerned. Two sketches of tattooed women especially intrigued me. One showed the tattooed buttocks and upper thighs of a woman of Tongoa Island, probably Leisavtina, leading wife of the paramount chief Tinabua Mata. These marks were seen as a sign of her very high status and were reserved for the wives of chiefs. Another sketch drawn in Vuorbalasa village in Vanua Lava showed a woman from behind. Her entire back was covered with geometric tattoos, imaging rows and rows of pigs' jaws and tusks, signifying that all these pigs were killed in grade-taking ceremonies to achieve her high rank.

Histories of Gender, Rank and Christianities in Vanuatu

These two vignettes graphically distil and exemplify my concerns in this chapter: the historical transformations of rank in northern Vanuatu, the changing gendered configurations of rank and power, and the central importance of Christianities in such transformations. This chapter follows on from my earlier writing on 'the graded society' of North Vanuatu (1981, 1984, 1989, 1994) and especially in a volume dedicated to exploring Maurice Godelier's famous distinction between 'big men' and 'great men', as different figures of power in Melanesia (Godelier and Strathern 1991). To recapitulate Godelier: in the first, great men – warriors, shamans, initiation leaders – did not rely on the strategic accumulation of wealth, but on inherited ancestral power within a ritual economy focused on male initiation; persons were exchangeable only for other persons, such that the direct exchange of women prevailed in marriage; in the second, big men relied on the strategic accumulation of wealth and competition in ceremonial exchanges and persons could be exchanged for things, such as pigs and shells, in transactions of bridewealth, for example. In the first, great men primarily depended on the appropriation of women's procreative labours; in the second, big men pre-eminently relied on the appropriation of women's productive labours (Godelier 1982, 1986, 1991).

In my chapter in that volume (Jolly 1991a), I compared three examples of the 'graded society' in north Vanuatu – in Vao, South Pentecost and East Ambae – suggesting they might be plotted on a continuum between great men and big men systems with Vao most akin to the first and East Ambae approximating the second. In propounding that analysis (1991a, 1994) I critiqued some earlier anthropologies which tended to reify 'the graded society' as a static institution rather than seeing rank-taking as a dynamic process. I argued for an historical approach to transformations of rank rather than one which posited teleologies in evolutionary time or psychoanalytic development (e.g. Allen 1981a, 1984; Layard 1942). Finally, I addressed the paradox of how women were crucial to such 'personifications of power',[4] albeit defined by different figures of men.

I intimated how models embedded in Western theories of psychoanalysis (e.g. Layard 1942) or historical materialism (e.g. Godelier 1977, 1982, 1984, 1986) were vulnerable to the deconstructive critiques of Marilyn Strathern's *The Gender of the Gift* (1988), which queried the relevance of exogenous Western distinctions between nature and culture, individual and society, subjects and objects, persons and things (and thus procreative and productive labour) for the world of 'Melanesia'. Strathern championed a new approach to gender not as the construction of culture built on the 'nature' of sexed bodies (cf. Butler 1990) but as a labile and fertile code which marks relations and materializations of relations as much as bodies and persons. Her approach will be addressed here through analyses of gender, rank, personhood and Christianity in some recent ethnography of Vanuatu. I also reconsider the crucial contributions of Godelier on relations between the 'material' and the 'immaterial' in Melanesia.[5] In a brief conclusion, I return to Maurice Godelier's work, not so much his vast corpus of texts in English and French produced over several decades, or his broader influence in French and global anthropology, but his more recent engagement in the world of museums and material culture (see Price 2007; Godelier 2009).

This chapter develops my earlier argument for seeing 'graded societies' not as unchanging institutions, as eternal manifestations of male *kastom*, but as diverse and dynamic processes of rank and power, responsive to, and constitutive of, indigenous and exogenous histories. As such, it benefits from the passage of time between then and now. Not only have we seen the maturation of theoretical discussions of questions of rank, power, gender and indigenous Christianities in the anthropologies of 'Melanesia' but we also have exciting new ethnographic insights deriving from the research of both foreign and indigenous researchers in Vanuatu (including the *filwokas* associated with the Vanuatu Cultural Centre, see Taylor and Thieberger 2011). I am especially indebted here to the writings of Lissant Bolton (2003), John Taylor (2008a) and Annelin Eriksen (2008) for insights apropos the changing configurations of rank, power, gender and Christianities in northern Vanuatu: in East Ambae, North Pentecost and North Ambrym respectively.

My re-analysis in this chapter has been sharpened by Annelin Eriksen's arguments. She contends that the graded society and the church are alternative social movements: 'whereas the graded society produced big men, the church produces communities ... The church is dominated by the collective/non-personified and female gendered social form, whereas the graded society is dominated by the personification/male gendered social form' (2008: 121). She thus links the graded society with individualism and hierarchy, and the church with collectivities and egalitarianism.

Eriksen's formulation owes something to Marilyn Strathern: she cites *The Gender of the Gift* (1988: 177), but the notion of 'personification' she deploys is rather different to Strathern's concept as articulated therein and she moves the argument into the terrain of history and indigenous Christianity (cf. Hess 2006, 2009; Mosko 2010a, 2010b).[6] But, as we shall see, Dumont is a more dominant, perhaps eclipsing influence, even as she reverses his associations of individualism and egalitarianism, and hierarchy and holism. And how far can Eriksen's opposition between the collective, egalitarian practice of the Christian church, gendered feminine, and the individualist, hierarchical practice of the graded society, gendered masculine, be sustained when we examine the complicated historical transformations of gender, rank and power in the context of Christian conversion in North Vanuatu? I suggest that women were and are far more implicated in the process of rank-taking and *kastom* than Eriksen's depiction admits and that Christian churches have also been contexts in which more individualist, hierarchical and 'masculine' forms have prevailed.[7]

John Taylor in North Pentecost: *The Other Side*

At the outset I need to eschew the idea that the 'history' I relate here privileges that Western genre of narrative and the telling of stories in which historical dynamism is primarily attributed to foreign agents and exogenous influences (see Hau'ofa 2000). As John Taylor has so eloquently shown in his book, *The Other Side* (2008a), there is a profoundly indigenous mode of historical consciousness in Vanuatu (see also Taylor 2004, 2010a, 2010b). In his analysis of 'ways of being and place in North Pentecost' he discerns recurrent patterns which 'permeate Sia Raga historical and social consciousness, kinship and spatial practices, and items of material culture' (2008a: 5). These patterns are not the static structures of earlier anthropologies, they are 'emergent and regenerative processes connecting ideas of place and time through biological idioms of movement and growth' (2008a: 5). They are especially apparent in the image of the 'land-tree', communicated to him as a blackboard diagram by Jif Ruben Todali soon after his arrival, which blends cosmography and social topography (2006, 2008a: 74). Such patterns are apparent both in the stories of the movement of indigenous persons (*atatun vanua*) across land and ocean and the movements of foreigners (*tuturani*); they model both the indigenous relations of men and women and the relations of ni-Vanuatu with foreigners. One side is perforce connected, entangled, even 'stuck together' (*wasi*) to 'the other side' in dialectical relations of attraction and repulsion, sameness and difference.

In his analysis of rank and gender in North Pentecost, based on fieldwork from 1999 to 2006, Taylor sees male and female rank-taking as distinct but crucially linked. 'Not only do they incorporate what are essentially the same ritual and economic processes to similar ends, but also both men and women who attain the highest levels in their respective systems are in some cases, if rarely, able to participate in the other' (2008: 48). In its present form, although the men's system is most often called *bolololi* and the women's *lihilihi*, they both 'involve the acquisition of pig names (*ihan boe*) through the ritual sacrifice of pigs, and the right to wear particular emblems through the strategic exchange of pigs and textiles. Such emblems include elaborate textile skirts and belts, feather headdresses, hair combs, pig tusk bracelets, ankle straps, necklaces and tattoos' (2008a: 48).

Thus, the marking of individual status in this social hierarchy, and its relation to the embodiment of spiritual power and expert knowledge, is shared by both men and women. Still, it seems, Sia Raga men thereby attained more rights than women – to have certain architectural structures built on the ceremonial ground (*sara*), to dance to particular slit gong rhythms and to drink kava. Moreover, at the apex of *bolololi* were elaborate ritual performances in which men sacrificed pigs with varying degrees of tusk curvature and achieved upward mobility through a series of named grades (Taylor 2008a: 48; cf. Jolly 1991a, 1994). This was 'the basis for social hierarchy and authority, but also served to regulate flows of knowledge, skills and spiritual power' (Taylor 2008a: 49).

Taylor insists, following Layard (1942), that the graded society constitutes not just a form of secular power but a sacred mystery, that the sacrifice of pigs and the system of sacred fires in the *gamali* ('men's house') was a form of social rebirth for the celebrant who was thus increasingly and exponentially endowed with the spiritual power of the ancestors. It was core to ancestral religion in this part of Vanuatu. The graded society, even at its most hierarchical male apex, in those 'ladder grades' which marked the potent, dangerous differences of men of rank, thus also constituted a powerful collective practice pervaded by the shared values of sacrifice central to the ancestral religion and of the intimate connection between the living and the dead. In his view, women were and are an integral part of this – in both the past and the present.

What then happened when Sia Raga became Christians? From the 1860s, Sia Raga converted to Anglicanism (through the Melanesian Mission) and today about eighty-four per cent still adhere to that denomination, with smaller numbers of adherents to Roman Catholicism (10.5 per cent), Seventh Day Adventism (1.4 per cent), Neil Thomas Ministries (1.4 per cent) and Ba'hai (c. 1.6 per cent; 2008a: 12). From the late nineteenth century the project of conversion engaged the Anglican hierarchy, such as Bishop Cecil Wilson and Bishop George Selwyn and more humble foreign missionaries, but was pre-eminently the result of an indigenous mission, with many labourers returning from Queensland and Fiji and promoting conversion. Despite the rhetorical opposition towards the labour trade by most Protestant missions, there was also complicity: the experience of plantation labour often catalysed conversion to Christianity, mission stations relied on plantation production and missionaries routinely enticed prospective converts by distributing cloth, knives, axes, hoop iron and tobacco. As Taylor stresses, Sia Raga like all ni-Vanuatu, perceived material and immaterial, spiritual power as integrally connected, indeed indistinguishable, and this is evinced in many histories of conversion: Louis Tariwali, the first Sia Raga convert, was sent to the Melanesian Mission station on Norfolk Island by his uncle to get a steel axe (tellingly called a *bisope*, 'bishop', see Taylor 2010a) while oral historians of Lamalanga recount how Bishop Selwyn came ashore with metal fish-hooks secreted in his top hat (Taylor 2008a: 57).

How did the adoption of Christianity impact on indigenous rank-taking? While the first generation of Anglican missionaries was relatively tolerant of indigenous practices, Bishop John Patteson and others later adopted a far tougher attitude to the practices of pig killing and kava drinking, realizing that the graded society – although a source of peace and social integration – was integrally connected to the 'old religion' and generated debilitating debt (Taylor 2008a: 75). In the early 1930s pig killing, kava drinking and polygyny were banned by an Anglican synod, and locally kava plants were uprooted and kava-grinding stones shattered. This precipitated tense divisions between those designated 'clean' (*melmelo*) and the 'drinking' (*mwinminu*) who continued to imbibe kava, kill pigs and practise polygyny. The latter, though baptised, were denied a Christian burial. Despite the eloquent efforts of local Christian catechists, such as Louis Lolo, to reconceive these divisions through the indigenous cosmography of two entangled sides, in this period, conflict and dissension rather than visions of necessary complementarity, prevailed (2008a: 76–78).

Yet, ultimately, Christianity was embraced as part of *aleñan vanua* ('the ways of the place'; see below). As Allen (1969) has argued for Ambae, the hierarchical divisions of the Christian church – for Anglicans, catechist, pastor and priest – were seen as mirroring the graded society, and the valued qualities of the *ratahigi* (high-ranking men, often later also *jifs*)[8] – eloquence, generosity, humility, decisiveness, and the capacity to make peace and access esoteric knowledge – were very similar to that of the priest. 'This résumé of the archetypical *ratahigi* is to all intents and purposes identical to that of the Sia Raga Anglican priest today' (Taylor 2008a: 62). Clearly then hierarchy and a more individualist, masculine embodiment of power have characterized Christian churches as much as the graded society. Women have been effectively absent from the top levels of both these hierarchies. But the gendering of both the indigenous hierarchy and of the Christian churches is a rather more complicated affair than the demographic absence of women at the apex of both *kastom* or *jos* (church).

Taylor explores these questions primarily through the historical reconfiguration of the twin places of dwelling in North Pentecost, *imwa* and *gamali*, often translated as 'household dwellings' and 'men's houses' (see Jolly 1989, 1991a, 1994 on *im* and *mal* in South Pentecost). In the past, *imwa* in North Pentecost typically accommodated nuclear families or one wife and her children in polygynous households; whether men regularly ate and slept with their wives in *imwa* is uncertain. The patterns of eating and sleeping in North Pentecost *imwa* and *gamali* were likely closer to those of South Pentecost (Taylor 2008a: 156) than the pre-Christian situation described by Rodman for East Ambae where women ate and slept in the *valei* while men always ate and slept in the *na gamal* (1985a). In North Pentecost, in the past, probably only older men of high rank (pursuing an idealized abstinence, cf. Jolly 2001) and younger, unmarried men routinely slept in the *gamali*. The sequence of twelve sacred fires/ovens (*matan gabi*) in the *gamali* marked the sequence of grades and men cooked and ate only from the fire of their respective rank; according to Codrington, any man who intruded into a division of the *gamali* 'above his own would be clubbed or shot' (cited in Taylor 2008a: 158). These fires were considered *gogona* (parallel to the Sa *kon*), a sanctity created by living humans as distinct from *sabuga*, a sacred power emanating from the ancestors.[9] Significantly, older men and women insisted that high-ranking women could enter the *gamali* in the past, and indeed could eat from the *matan gabi* which corresponded to their grade.[10] Taylor alludes to the probable earlier existence of separate houses for women who were menstruating or birthing, described by Speiser (1991 [1923]) and Layard (1942) but strangely not documented by missionaries. Their very existence suggests to him that men did routinely share the *imwa*. Women in such states were *sabuga* (not *gogona*), an inherent power emanating from the ancestors, and not so much polluting as dangerously sacred and potent (see Jolly 2002a, 2002b, after Hanson 1982).

Following my arguments apropos *im* and *mal* in South Pentecost (1989), Taylor insists that we should not conceive the first as domestic, feminine spaces and the second as public, masculine spaces. Men live/d in *imwa* as much as women and *gamali*, although they may in the past have been pre-eminently 'men's houses', forbidden to women, are now rather places where large collective projects are pursued – by both men and women, separately and together. They are sites for cooking large communal feasts on the giant earth oven in the front section, while the back section of the *gamali*, used by men for storing kava equipment and for nightly drinking sessions, is not much frequented by women. But the vast interior of *gamali* dwellings is routinely used by men and women together in making thatch for houses, by women separately while plaiting pandanus baskets and textiles, and even for meetings of the local branch of the Vanuatu National Council of Women. Taylor thus concludes: 'the term "men's house" may no longer be so apposite to these structures' (2008a: 142).

Like the landscape in general, both house forms are for Sia Raga not just inert places of human presence, but animated historical agents, activated by the movements of people in space and time. Contra Margaret Rodman's view (1985a, 1985b) for Ambae that domestic dwellings have been sites of historical dynamism and innovation while 'men's houses' have remained spaces of entrenched convention, Taylor reveals dramatic movement in both, in construction materials and in their gendered patterns of use.[11] Changes in settlement and dwelling patterns resulted less from the urgings of early missionaries than the edicts of the colonial government and local leaders like Dr Phillip Ilo, who returned from education as a doctor in Fiji in the 1950s, and encouraged 'development' through the greater concentration of village settlements and a head tax to support the development of roads, air strips and piped water.

Christian conversion, as elsewhere, was marked by the suspension of segregated patterns of dwelling, eating, sleeping and movement. Thus, although men and women still take rank, this is not manifest in the same quotidian patterns as before. Sia Raga (like traditionalist Sa speakers in the 1970s and 1980s; see Jolly 1989) still avoid conjugal beds, since this is thought to jeopardize a man's strength and spiritual power, especially if he has drunk kava that night. Men often sleep in a partitioned space within the *imwa*, separate from women and children. But men and women now cook and eat together in the *imwa*, although there is a tendency towards gendered specialization in communal feasts, as men prepare the ovens and manipulate the hot volcanic stones, butcher the meat and prepare it for cooking while women usually prepare the vegetables and coconut cream. Each hamlet has its own *gamali*, typically in the centre of the settlement, flanked by a *sara* or ceremonial ground. The *gamali* is linked with a particular *ratahigi* and embodies his authority to settle disputes and levy punishments. In this sense then, it has sustained some elements of a decidedly masculine power even though clearly no longer a 'men's house'. As distinct from Christian churches which are perhaps more akin to 'public' spaces, open to all, *gamali* are strongly identified with the hamlets in which they are located (Taylor 2008a: 151; cf. Bolton 2003: 82–85).

Whereas each hamlet typically has only one *gamali*, there may be several *sara*, proximate ceremonial grounds typically linked with a set of brothers and their sons. The *sara* is 'a microcosmic field of exchange' (Taylor 2008a: 148), the locus for many transactions, daily

conversations, games and dances and the quintessential locale for
major ceremonies like marriage and 'the lavishly complex ceremonies
called *bolololi* in which men exchange and kill pigs in the process of
acquiring status' (Taylor 2008a: 148). In giving or receiving pigs,
men perform the canonical dance style, imitating a soaring hawk,
zigzagging across the *sara* in configurations suggestive of surveillance
and mastery (cf. Jolly 1991a, 1994; Layard 1942). But, as Taylor
insists, women are a forceful presence at *bolololi*, asserting, contesting
and transforming their status, through the vigorous exchange of
literally hundreds of *bwana* and *bari* (plaited pandanus textiles dyed
red and used for exchange). Women interrupt male performances
with 'spectacular displays of female wealth, knowledge, and prestige'
(Taylor 2008a: 148). Moreover, this is not just a manifestation
of their egalitarian collectivity since women also proudly display
the leaf emblems of their own specific rank in the dances of *havwa*
(Taylor 2008a: 148). So women are part of what Eriksen labels
'personifications' of power. Moreover, the processes of avoidance,
sequestration and cleansing in *bolololi* closely parallel those of
childbirth, and thus both men and women are able to 'effect similar
processes of ancestral regeneration through different means' (Taylor
2008a: 168).

Like other ethnographers of Vanuatu (e.g. Rodman 1985a, 1985b;
Jolly 1989) Taylor discerns much about the transformations of
gender, rank and power associated with Christian conversion from
the materializations of relations in dwellings and the architectonics
of houses. But he critiques Margaret Rodman's analysis for East
Ambae (1985a, 1985b) which associated the contrast of household
dwellings and men's houses (*valei/na gamal*) with a series of binaries:
female and male, private and public, mats and pigs, and especially
with the contention that, responding to missionary influence, the
household dwellings came to represent individualism and innovation
and the men's houses communalism and conservatism (cf. Eriksen
2008). Taylor insists that the dramatic transformations in North
Pentecost pertain to both places of dwelling and have been most
influenced by local leaders like Louis Tariwali and Dr Phillip Ilo. Thus,
he insists on blurring the boundaries of *imwa* and *gamali*, and on
seeing these houses, like the gendered persons of Marilyn Strathern,
not as marking an essential, radical binary but rather emergent and
dialectical processes engaging sameness and difference. In his view,
Sia Raga houses, like persons, are permeable and partible (Taylor
2008a: 142). 'Thus, the relationship between *imwa* and *gamali* – and
by extension, men and women – is better viewed in terms of fluid
relationality and linked encompassment rather than rigid dichotomy
and opposition' (Taylor 2008a: 170). Both dwellings are talkative,

animated historical agents, mnemonic spaces which incorporate the 'space-time principles of trajectory and branching' that Jif Ruben Todali imaged in the 'land-tree'.

There is a constant association between human anatomy and the house: a house has a face, mouth and ears, teeth and shoulders, a forbidden anus and rows of rafters representing men and women, the 'two sides of the house'. Houses are seen to breathe and speak, ingest and defecate; they are not just symbols of persons but embodied, sentient agents, 'personifications' in the sense deployed by Strathern (Taylor 2008a: 181). A similar patterning and agency pertains to *bwana* pandanus textiles. The woven body of the textile is its torso, the tassels its fingers, and the central seam dividing and connecting the two sides its backbone. These two sides are variously interpreted as representing the two moieties of Bule and Tabe, or male and female. Ultimately, Taylor's analysis draws not just on the insights of the 'new ethnography' of Melanesia (see Foster 1995) but also on profoundly indigenous models, like that of the 'land-tree', which entangle bodies and houses, persons and things, concrete materializations and abstract structures in cosmographies of fertility and regeneration. In the worldview of Sia Raga, as much in the Christian present as the ancestral past, the feminine and the masculine, the material and the immaterial, the corporeal and the spiritual are irrevocably entangled, and often indistinguishable.

Lissant Bolton between East Ambae and Port Vila: *Unfolding the Moon*

I now turn to the ethnography of Lissant Bolton who, in her considerations of gender, rank, and Christianity, has focused attention not so much on houses but on valued pandanus textiles, like the *bwana* of North Pentecost. In her book (2003) and several related papers (1996, 1999, 2001a, 2001b), Bolton offers a compelling account of the way in which the women of Vanuatu, and most particularly those of East Ambae, through their revaluation of the knowledge and practice of making pandanus textiles, asserted this as a valued part of *kastom*, locally and nationally throughout the archipelago. Her analysis is based on long-term and continuing fieldwork, focused not just in the remote hamlets of East Ambae, but also in the national capital of Port Vila, particularly in the Vanuatu Cultural Centre where she collaborated with Jean Tarisesei in the development of the Women's Culture Project.[12] Whereas anthropologists typically celebrate and even fetishize our processes of participant observation, Bolton rather depicts her work as 'participant engagement', since she has been working not just to document but to collaborate in a revival and revaluation of women's knowledge and creative practice, especially apropos pandanus textiles and *kastom*. She has not been a detached, disembodied observer of these processes, but an engaged, even evangelical proponent of the notion propounded by the Vanuatu Cultural Centre from 1991, through the Women's Culture Project, that 'women have *kastom* too' (Bolton 2003: xiv–xv, xxxiii–xxviii). She has been an exemplary *animateur* of ni-Vanuatu women in general and her primary collaborator Jean Tarisesei in particular.

What of the intriguing title of her book? This is not, Bolton observes, an English translation of some metaphor in the language of East Ambae (unlike Taylor 2008a). Indeed, women in East Ambae often greeted her proposed title with bemusement, observing that one cannot speak of 'unfolding the moon' but only of its rising. The phrase is her creation. Firstly, it suggests the way in which East Ambae women, at an exchange event, remove and unfold a pile of textiles from their baskets: at the base, lies the most valuable *maraha* of different kinds, which they then alternate with less valuable *qana* of different kinds until, finally, on top of each pile is placed either a *qana vivi* or the clothing textile *sakole*, which are both decorated with designs of the moon, stencilled in blood red on the plaited white pandanus. Secondly, the phrase describes the 'movement in which women unfolded an aspect of their knowledge and practice and laid it out in the national arena, asserting and defining it for the first time as *kastom*' (Bolton 2003: xxxiv). I will return to that crucial term in a moment but let me first portray the text, as Bolton does for her reader, as paralleling the construction of a textile.

Women make textiles by plaiting strips of prepared pandanus outwards from one side, creating a panel and then joining new pandanus to the starting edge and plaiting outward from the other direction to create a second side. The longitudinal central seam is not only diacritical but highly valued. Similarly, Lissant plaits an argument which first develops a side which engages with the broader questions about notions of *kastom* in Vanuatu, then moves to a more dedicated ethnography of the making, exchange, efficacy and agency of textiles on Ambae. These chapters are conjoined by a central seam – a discussion of both the notion and the value of *ples* – a word in Bislama which, though derived from its homophone in English 'place', has a rather distinct and louder resonance in the place of Vanuatu.

From the dense fabric of Bolton's text I tease out the dominant threads relevant to my focus on transformations of gender, rank and power in the context of Christian conversion. First, let me consider her approach to the concept of *kastom*.[13] Cutting through the tightly coiled, even tangled, debates of the 1980s and 1990s, she suggests that the crucial context for the emergence of the concept of *kastom* was the process of missionization. Following Strathern (1990), she doubts that the mere advent of Europeans was sufficient to 'invoke a new-self-consciousness of difference' (Bolton 2003: 8) since a self-conscious recognition of difference was intrinsic to the extensive indigenous networks of trade and cultural exchange in the archipelago. I agree (see Huffman 1996 and Jolly 1994). It is important to acknowledge how the concept of *kastom* is used both to highlight local differences within the archipelago and to stress the similarity of ni-Vanuatu practice vis-à-vis outsiders (and see Jolly 1992a). The assumption of a profound difference and of the trauma of 'first contact' is perhaps rather a symptom of European hubris (see Jolly and Tcherkézoff 2009); indigenous perceptions of a large gulf between locals and strangers probably derived not from difference per se but from European presumptions to power, in the combined effects of the sandalwood and labour trades, land alienation, colonial government and missionary activity.[14] But 'missionization' was a part of that colonial process and, surely, the most crucial part. The pervasive opposition between *kastom* and *skul* (signifying Christianity and not just education), which marked the early stages of Christian conversion and persisted until the 1970s–1980s, suggests that the relation with Christianity was pivotal. Patterson depicts the opposition between *kastom* and *skul* in North Ambrym in the pre-independence period as 'bitter and at times murderous' (2001: 42). Such agonistic opposition was later transformed into the lived complementarity of 'two sides' in many local Christian contexts (see Taylor on North Pentecost above) and in the discourse of Christian nationalist politicians and church leaders in the period leading up to independence in 1980 and after (Bolton 2003: 15; cf. Jolly 1982, 1994).

Bolton argues that although *kastom* seems proximate to the English and canonically anthropological concept of 'culture', conventionally used to refer to a whole way of life, it rather refers only to certain practices, to 'customs' in the nomenclature of early missionaries and anthropologists.[15] There is no doubt that particular practices were and are privileged in the contrast between *kastom* and *skul* (or *jos*, church): ancestral versus Christian rituals, divergent styles of clothing, housing and cooking, and the Christian claim of improving women's status.[16] For the overwhelming majority of ni-Vanuatu who are Christians (as indeed for those few who still identify themselves as *kastom* adherents), *kastom* is thus a matter of selective perpetuation from past to present to future, of distinguishing good from bad *kastom*, between those practices thought worthy of continuity or revival and those which should be left to expire.

Bolton asserts that *kastom* has no 'direct cognates in the indigenous languages' (2003: 10). Yet, this is at odds with idioms in several languages akin to *aleñan na vanua*, 'ways of the place' in Raga, as described by Taylor, where images of divergent 'ways' or 'roads' are deployed (cf. Jolly 1982, 1994: 21, on Sa and especially quoting Bumangari Kaon). So it seems that it is not just the small enclaves of traditionalists, in South Pentecost, North Ambrym, Malakula and Tanna who in certain contexts mobilized such strongly contrastive notions of the 'ways of the place' and of foreign ways, even if Christianity is now seen by most ni-Vanuatu Christians as an intrinsic part of those 'ways of the place' (unlike *bisnis, lo* and *politik*, all still usually seen as *blong waetman*, see Forsyth 2009). Intriguingly Taylor observes that while *kastom* and *jos* are often today opposed in Bislama, in the indigenous language of Raga, Christianity is rather embraced as part of *aleñan na vanua*. Perhaps this indigenous propensity to recognize 'two sides' or 'two roads' was early in dialogue with a Christianity which tried to enforce a binary division, between the 'clean' (the baptised) and the 'dirty' drinking heathens, between the 'time of darkness' and the 'time of light'. But, extrapolating from the example of Sia Raga, discussed above, rather than accepting that 'one side' perforce eclipsed the other, ni-Vanuatu often articulated a desire to sustain both, in complementary and dialectical relations, rather than accept the hierarchical encompassment of Christianity over *kastom* for instance (see Taylor's Epilogue in 2008a, 2010a).

In such indigenous plotting of relations, ni-Vanuatu typically privilege place rather than time (see Curtis 1999, 2002, and for discussion of spatio-temporal connections in ni-Vanuatu philosophies, see Rodman 1992; Jolly 1999). This is clear in the Bislama concept and value of *kastom* and its intimate connection to the concept and value of *man ples* (see Bolton 2003: 67–77; Patterson 2006a). Arguably there was in earlier writing on *kastom*, including my own (1982, 1992a, 1992b), an undue association with time, the past and tradition. Those of us who lived and worked with anti-Christian traditionalists (like Keesing with the interior Kwaio of Malaita, and myself with the traditionalist Sa speakers of South Pentecost) probably unduly absorbed not just the pervasive oppositional rhetoric within such communities about *kastom* versus *skul* in that period, but also the strong moral value associated with the ancestors, such that our ethnographies were unduly suffused with an anthropological nostalgia for the past and a lament for the demise of *kastom*, too narrowly conceived as pre-colonial practice (see Keesing 1992; Jolly 1989, 1994; but cf. Keesing and Jolly 1992). Still, in some of his later, more general formulations, Keesing emphasized that *kastom* represented 'discourses about the past situated in the present and oriented towards the future' (1993: 587–97).

In the pervasive practices of revival and renewal, among Christians as much as traditionalists, discourses of *kastom* are as much, perhaps more, about the present and the future than the past. In the Vanuatu context, this was highlighted by Tim Curtis in his doctoral thesis (2002). In collaborative research on Tomman and South West Malakula, with the talented *filwoka* Longdal Nobel Maasingyau, Curtis discerned that *kastom* was primarily a rhetoric of alternative development, a future-oriented project. Similarly, the *yia of kastom ekonomi*, celebrated in Vanuatu in 2007 and extended into the future, offers an alternative model of 'development', grounded in non-commoditized economies and promoting objects of value in *kastom*, like pigs and pandanus textiles, rather than money.

Bolton acknowledges that 'it *is* the past that provides ... legitimation' (2003: 40, emphasis in the original; cf. Rousseau 2004 on legitimation). But, a future-oriented *kastom* is core to Bolton's approach and the project of reviving the practice and value of making pandanus textiles, and of women's value in *kastom*. *Kastom*, especially as it developed as a political discourse associated with independence, even in the *filwoka* programs of the VKS, had become a male monopoly. Grace Mera Molisa, personal secretary to the first Prime Minister Father Walter Lini from 1980 to 1991, lamented that the value women had in *kastom* and Christian churches in rural villages and the significant role women had played in the independence movement was not reflected in the independent state (see Molisa 1987). The discourse of *kastom* in her view thus threatened to become 'a Frankenstein's corpse, used to intimidate women' (Jolly 1991c, 2005). Molisa forcefully confronted that spectre.

Like Molisa, Bolton eschews any generalized portrait of male domination in Vanuatu, as suggested in most writings by foreign observers and especially missionaries. She rather adopts Strathern's view of persons as 'the plural and composite sites of the relations who produced them' (1988: 13, cited in Bolton 2003: 54). The changing contexts of symmetry and asymmetry between the subject positions of men and women, usually defined by kinship, for her negate the suggestion that 'all men have power over all women' (Bolton 2003: 55; cf. Jolly 1992c). But does contextual diversity in gendered power negate the possibility of ultimate male domination and does the latter necessarily imply the power of 'all men' over 'all women'? Bolton avoids implicating male domination in pre-colonial practices by highlighting how the hierarchical valorization of male public domains and female domestic domains is a foreign, missionary importation (Bolton 2003:

56; cf. Jolly 1989; Jolly and Macintyre 1989). She contends that it was Christian churches rather than indigenous hierarchies which offered such a model of pervasive patriarchy: 'they also almost universally enshrined their own assumptions about male superiority in the structures they introduced' (2003: 56). The same was true for the colonial state, staffed primarily by expatriate men and appointing indigenous men as assessors and *jifs*. 'For all the rhetoric criticizing the status of women in indigenous practice, it was expatriates who established a formal inequality between all men and all women' (Bolton 2003: 56). I rather suggest that gendered inequalities predated such introduced institutions, even if they did not conform to the 'formality' of the Western opposition of public and domestic (Jolly 1989, 1991b). Unarguably men have dominated the formal hierarchies of the church and the introduced state and, despite valiant efforts by the late Grace Mera Molisa, Hilda Lini, and many others since, that pattern clearly persists to the present in Vanuatu.

Insofar as *kastom* had become a national political discourse, deployed by the state, women tended to be excluded from it. Using her position in the Vanuatu National Council of Women (which she co-founded) and her role on the Vanuatu Cultural Council governing the Vanuatu Cultural Centre (VKS) in the 1980s and 1990s, Molisa was determined that the *filwoka* programme of the VKS should not further exclude women from *kastom*. Molisa was a prime mover behind the introduction of women *filwokas* at the VKS and, despite initial, rather muted opposition from one male *filwoka*, the others all embraced this change (Bolton 2003: 64). In *kastom* as articulated and practised locally, as distinct from *kastom* as articulated and practised nationally, *filwokas* acknowledged that women played a crucial, if neglected, part. Thus, through a combination of indigenous pressures and the support of foreign aid agencies, the Women's Culture Project was born. After a rather faltering start with initial staff resigning, Jean Tarisesei was appointed co-ordinator and Bolton the training officer on that project. Their first programme as part of that was the documentation and revival of women's textile production on Ambae, Tarisesei's island of residence, and based in Lovonda, the Anglican village to which Tarisesei had moved at marriage.

At the outset, Bolton eschews the usual English and Bislama translation of these textiles as 'mats'; because the English term denotes a coarse textile, often a floor covering, and thus suggests 'an extremely low status in the system of relative value established by museums' (Bolton 2003: xxxi). She describes the extraordinary diversity of these textiles, in their forms, in their uses, and in their names (1996, 2001a, 2001b, 2003: 104ff). Origin stories, like that of Tahigogona's nine sisters, explain the commonality and the diffusion of different types of textiles across Ambae (Bolton 1996, 2003: 110) while contemporary commentators like Roslyn Garae see plaiting as 'the reason that women came into the world' (Bolton 2003: 109). All textiles are plaited from pandanus, most are long and narrow with a central seam; some are white, while some are dyed blood red (or purple, especially when using commercial dyes), with either a single block of colour and/or stencilled geometric patterns; some have openwork designs at either end; some have designs plaited into the pandanus or overweave designs; some have long, fine fringes while others have short, stubby fringes; still others have a plain selvage edge.

Textiles of similar form and use may be given different names in different districts; fifty different names for textiles were recorded on Ambae. Moreover, all these differences interact such that one Ambae woman may plait up to twenty-five different named types, each with specific uses. 'There are pandanus textiles used in exchanges, to wrap the dead, to present to honored guests, to wear to mark achieved status in the *huqe*, textiles on which to sit or to use as blankets, textiles for specific points in rituals, textiles that are the focus of rituals' (Bolton 2003: 111). These uses establish some of the main categories: *maraha*, textiles of higher value used in exchange and to wrap the dead; *qana*, textiles of lesser value, used in exchange when new and later to sit on and sleep under (through which they become the non-exchangeable *buresi*); textiles used as clothing in the past, such as the women's *sakole*; and *singo*, textiles used to confer and symbolize rank. Within each of these categories there are finer distinctions but, as Bolton points out, the system of classification is not neatly hierarchical but dynamic and contextual. *Qana* may be everyday blankets but a certain kind, *qana hunhune*, is used to cover and protect the head of a bride (cf. Taylor on *bwana hunhuniana* 2008a: 130–33). Another kind of *qana* may be used to cover the body of a dead person before they are wrapped in a precious *maraha*. Like Taylor, Bolton draws inspiration from Strathern (1988) and Gell (1998) in seeing these textiles not as objects but as the materialization of relations, as animated agents, like persons; their importance is 'not what they mean, but what they do' (2003: 129).

Clearly their efficacy both derives from and enhances women's agency. Bolton stresses how on Ambae it is only women who plait and dye pandanus textiles (unlike Central Pentecost, where men take part in the stencilling and dyeing process, see Walter 1996). In the past, men were forbidden to touch a textile until it was finished on pain of going bald; today some men may offer some casual assistance to their wives, but only in preparing pandanus, never in plaiting.[17] Still, men wear and use these textiles and, on occasion, as in the *huqe*, exchange them. The production of textiles from locally growing pandanus plants secures a woman's attachment to her *ples* on Ambae (as does bearing children to the land) and both reaffirms and transforms her relations with others.

All married women need to make textiles to contribute to those exchanges which mark significant life events. Women typically sit down to plait together and this quotidian production through common techniques creates female sociability, sometimes co-operative work (Bolton 2003: 124) and 'an equality of plaiting' (2003: 117). Yet, textile production also creates hierarchies between women. Whereas plaiting 'binds women together in relationships of assistance, obligation and shared labor' (2003: 130), dyeing textiles evokes very different associations. It is pervaded by anxieties and restrictions, not just because dyeing is a technique with inherent technical risks but because dyeing imbues dangerous powers in such textiles and creates distinctions between women. Dyeing in itself is dangerous and a woman should avoid sex and not be menstruating when she is dyeing, for example, the *maraha* textiles, bathed in blocks of blood red.

Although women never explicitly associated this red with the blood of their menstruation, sexuality and childbirth, perhaps out of Christian modesty, Bolton argues for the link, paradoxically evidenced by how 'dyeing is linked to both menstruation and sexual relationships by the very effort with which they are kept separate' (Bolton 2003: 136). Women should abstain from sex while preparing to dye textiles while menstruating women should avoid being close to any dyeing process lest they sicken. A common story tells of a woman so preoccupied with plaiting that she neglected her children who both died (Bolton 2003: 136; cf. Taylor on *bololili* and birthing above). Only some women have the knowledge to make the restricted stencil type *gigilugi* and to plait the most powerful textiles in the *singo* category (2003: 117), which deploy diamond and zigzag designs, in which the red dye enhances the raised pattern of an overweave. These are used both to mark the ranks of the male *huqe* and the status women assume in *huhuru* (see below). Women without such inherited knowledge need to commission a *singo* specialist to create such textiles, which must always be attached to *maraha*, to make them complete.

When women present and exchange textiles there is collective female satisfaction, as up to a hundred women pour onto a *sara* and 'let the baskets fall from their heads with a satisfying thud, expressive of the labour they have invested in their contribution to the exchanges' (Bolton 2003: 126). Today, women invidiously contrast their hard work of textile production and exchange with men's preoccupation with kava consumption; one woman alleged that 'men drink kava at exchanges since they have nothing to do, since women are the principal actors' (2003: 122). Bolton comments, 'Of course, in the past, when men were absorbed by the *huqe* [graded society] and devoted much of their energy to the production and acquisition of pigs, their presentation of pigs would have balanced women's presentation of textiles' (2003: 122).

Despite this contemporary rather combative stress on the distinctive solidarity of women as producers of valued textiles (versus kava-consuming men), pandanus textiles also manifestly mark differences and distinctions between women. In the past, women also gained status and honour through acquiring tattoos, which signified both their father's wealth and the status of their prospective husbands (Bolton 2003: 143). A woman might be tattooed from neck to ankle, but the designs on her inner thigh should be known only to her husband. Tattooing was abandoned in the 1940s at the instigation of Christian missionaries (Anglicans in East Ambae and Church of Christ in the West) and so the exchange of textiles is now the primary means whereby women acquire status, seniority and respect (Bolton 2003: 143).

Since high-ranking women and men both acquire the right to eat restricted food associated with that grade, Evelyn Malanga, a textile specialist, described *huhuru* as 'the women's *huqe*' (Bolton 2003: 150; cf. Rodman 1981: 97). Bolton says little about the male *huqe* on Ambae (but see Allen 1972, 1981a, 1981b, 1984, 2000; W. Rodman 1973), suggesting only that the production, sacrifice and exchange of pigs is far less common than in the past. By contrast, the exchange and presentation of pandanus textiles seems to have increased; one woman observed how whereas only one or two *maraha* were presented at weddings in the past, at a recent wedding forty were presented (Bolton 2003: 121). Textiles are significant in several Ambae ceremonies, but their most crucial and valued use is in *huhuru*, which literally translates as 'to make red'. For this ceremony a married woman produces textiles and commissions *singo* to be presented to her husband and his family in return for the textiles they gave at her marriage. Women thus acquire the right to eat restricted food and become a 'person of greater substance, worthy of respect' (Bolton 2003: 148).

Bolton deploys the phrase 'status-alteration ceremonies' (cf. Patterson 1981 on 'status acquisition') to refer to *huhuru* and a range of other ceremonies which transform status, including rituals of taking rank, for both men and women. In her view there has been an undue focus on male hierarchies, neglecting 'the widespread existence of equivalent systems by which women achieve status' (2003: xxxii). This is no doubt true, although in some places men and women's systems are intimately articulated.[18] In East Ambae the day before a woman marries, her father arranges for her to acquire a junior grade in the *huqe* by killing a pig; the day after she marries she offers textiles to her husband, prefiguring her later prestations in *huhuru* (Bolton 2003: 146; cf. Rodman 1981: 85). This echoes the separate sequences of grades conferred on women by their fathers and brothers as opposed to their husbands and his agnates in South Pentecost (Jolly 1991a: 66). The senior men interviewed by Bolton saw *huhuru* as far more closely linked to the *huqe* than women, even suggesting that only women married to men of high rank could attain high status themselves. Women rather stressed the autonomy of *huhuru*.

Bolton suggests, despite parallels between the ranking of pigs and textiles, of men and women, and reciprocal references between them, that *huqe* and *huhuru* are distinct. Moreover, she asserts that unlike the *huqe*, with its ten sequential titles, *huhuru* are not necessarily taken in a fixed sequence and the particular designs chosen are a matter of ambition and availability rather than a set sequence. (She admits a regional difference: in Longana the grades are not seen as sequential while in Lombaha women described five sequential ranks; Bolton 2003: 149). But, this argument eerily echoes critiques of earlier anthropologies of the 'graded society' as reifying the sequence and occluding flexibility, dynamism and innovation (Allen 1981b, Jolly 1991a). Men frequently 'skip' grades on South Pentecost in response to the exigencies of the sorts of pigs available and their particular ambitions (see Jolly 1991a: 61; 1994: 178 and 225–26). Still, there is more of an ideal of a male hierarchy of titles, materialized in the sequence of sacred fires, of ladders built onto domestic dwellings and *nakamal*, and of names suggestive of higher and higher elevation.

Both in the context of the practices of *kastom* in East Ambae and *kastom* articulated in the context of the *filwoka*'s workshops in the Vanuatu Cultural Centre (VKS), the distinction of men and women seems to have been increasingly emphasized. Bolton acknowledges that in everyday practices, men's and women's *kastom* is far more blurred, overlapping and complementary. She highlights how the very phrase 'women have *kastom* too' presumes both the prior distinction of men and women and women's exclusion from *kastom* (Bolton 2003: 170ff). Doubtless there was a profound segregation of men and women in indigenous ni-Vanuatu societies, but Christian churches, in trying to undo what they perceived as the male domination underlying that segregation, introduced novel forms of segregation predicated on the distinction of public and domestic domains. The very aim of improving women's status in the church, and of forming women's clubs and committees, created a unitary category of 'women', whereas before the diversity of gendered, kin-based relations prevailed (see Jolly 2003a).[19] In similar fashion Bolton acknowledges that in the VKS's project of extending the concept and the value of *kastom* to women and their valued creations of pandanus textiles, a similar dynamic has occurred. Even as they tried to defy the idea of an immutable gender hierarchy in *kastom*, they perforce distinguished between 'all men' and 'all women'.

Annelin Eriksen: *Gender, Christianity and Change in Vanuatu*

Like Bolton, Eriksen's ethnography derives both from experiences in a remote village location and the national capital Port Vila (from the mid-1990s to the present). But whereas Bolton focuses on the national, annual congregation of *filwokas* from all over the archipelago at the Vanuatu Cultural Centre, Eriksen focuses rather on the experience of women between the village of Ranon in North Ambrym and the town of Port Vila. Both are concerned with historical transformations in the configuration of gender, rank and power, and especially in that complex and sometimes fraught relation between *kastom* and Christianity. But rather than witnessing and promoting the extension of *kastom* to women, Eriksen suggests that *kastom* has been gendered masculine and Christianity feminine. The pronouncement by a feisty man, in espousing *kastom* ways at a meeting in Ranon, prefigures her argument: 'We are not women. We can make no use of the Bible here' (2008: 2).

This is a contemporary configuration of the broader gendering of social life which Eriksen discerns in North Ambrym, between two alternative logics, contrasting yet complementary, gendered male and female. In a reanalysis of concepts of kinship and marriage in relation to *ples*, she suggests that in the voluminous literature on the famous six-class system of North Ambrym since Rivers (who posited an ideal structure of three agnatic groups, *buluim*, cross-cut by two matrimoieties), there has been an undue emphasis on the 'men of the place'. In her view, the 'system' has been defined by the male-focused *buluim* and *batatun*, and not enough emphasis has been given to the alternative matrilateral roads for tracing relations and the movement typically associated with women in marriage (but see Patterson 1976, 2001, 2002). Her stress on the crucial question of perspective in actualizing one of several potential 'roads' in kinship relations is welcome, as is her attempt to see such relations from a woman's or, perhaps better, a feminine perspective. But this has been attempted before. Contra Patterson (1976) who has stressed the indigenous idiom of passage in the notion of *buluim/bulufatao* (the 'doorway' to the house or literally 'the hole in front of the house'), Eriksen paradoxically stresses the closed, inherently male character of the 'house' (significantly *im*, not *mal*). She also portrays the central concept of *batatun* as male-centric: Eriksen translates this as 'brother'. In the cognate context of the Sa language of South Pentecost, I prefer to translate *batatun* as sibling set; the word for brother *selan* is the generic for a same-sex sibling, i.e. for both brothers or sisters. But, in practice, *batatun* is most often deployed to refer to alternate generations or 'layers of men' (Jolly 1994: 103, following Patterson 1976: 90, but see Layard 1942: 123 who after Deacon translates as 'matrilineal moiety'). All of these are 'brothers': in the ascending generation of fathers' fathers, 'elder brothers' and in the descending generation of son's sons, 'younger brothers'. Women do not have a comparable distinction of seniority for their sisters.

The recognition of the eternal or 'ontological' debt created by maternity in the systems of North Ambrym and South Pentecost, which Eriksen discerns in the ceremonies of male initiation (*malyel*) and the corresponding female ceremony (*yengfah*), has long been recognized in the literature (most notably by the Marist priest Elie Tattevin in his insightful analysis of *lo sal*, 1926–1927, 1928; but see also Jolly 1991a: 63–66 and 73; 1994: 83 and 109–13; Patterson 2001).[20] But that debt, though owed to the mother, is primarily mediated through her brother; hence the dangerous power of the mother's brother over the life of both men and women and his central place in all life-cycle ceremonies.[21]

Eriksen observes how the undue stress on structure and descent in earlier anthropology occluded both these gendered 'relational codes' and the centrality of place (see also Taylor 2005). This is not true of Patterson (1976) who earlier challenged descent models with a stress on indigenous idioms of alternation, alliance and residence. Like Patterson (1976, 2001, 2002) and myself (1994, 1999), Eriksen highlights the centrality of the concept of *ples*. In 'ideal typical' terms, she sees men as iconic of place; linked to places of *buluim* origin, to a *harl* (*nasara* or ceremonial ground), men hold the power to transmit and control land, while women are associated with 'roads' (*hal*) through their movement in marriage and in the broader movement of persons, ideas and institutions. But later she stresses that place is not just about 'roots' but about 'routes', such that place is portable (2008: 33), 'place is brought along not left behind' (2008: 35). Itineraries of movement from an origin place are crucial in the life histories of persons and collectivities. Both men and women tell stories of detailed sequences of movements across the landscape, ordered itineraries echoing both Fox's conception of topogeny (1997, see Patterson 2006a) and more proximately the concept of the 'land-tree' for North Pentecost, as discussed by Taylor (2006, 2008a and above).

But although men and women move, Eriksen suggests that, in the logic of North Ambrymese kinship, movement is gendered feminine (cf. Jolly 1999, 2003b). Daughters and sisters embody *metehal* – the 'end' of the road (in the sense of its rationale rather than its terminus). Whereas in the nineteenth-century movements of the 'people trade' to Fiji and New Caledonia, in which women from North Ambrym constituted a small minority, in contemporary migration to town they constitute over a third. In stark contrast with the *kastom* communities of South Pentecost in the 1970s and 1980s (Jolly 1994: 10–11), women have been migrating from the Christian villages of North Ambrym in large numbers to Port Vila for decades and choosing to stay in town: for short-term or long-term wage labour, to provide child care for female relatives, and to marry men from other islands.

Once in town North Ambrymese women often become a 'road', like Annelin's interlocutor Rose, linking village and town, providing a base for relatives to stay in town, sending children, goods and cash back home and selling goods from the island in town (2008: 59ff). They may seek to secure continuing rights to land on the island by sending remittances back to be used in the ceremonial economy. Eriksen suggests that a novel ceremonial economy has developed in urban weddings: *sakkam presen*, a ceremony which superficially resembles a dowry payment since these are gifts given solely to the bride by her brother. Weddings and other life-cycle rituals on North Ambrym – *malyel* for male circumcision and *yengfah* for first menstruation (but see Patterson 2001) – still involve large prestations of tubers, pigs and pandanus textiles alongside money and cloth. However, *sakkem presen* requires chests stuffed with consumer goods – cloth, soap, mattresses, household utensils, furniture (perhaps to the value of c.100,000 vatu) – with lesser contributions of *kastom* food and valuables, such as a wedding laplap and perforce a red pandanus textile placed over the head of the bride, adorned in several 'Mother Hubbard' dresses and decorated with white powder and deodorant. Consumer goods are much treasured but are not thought to 'grow' as do indigenous valuables. In the ceremonial economy on North Ambrym, the crucial relation between brother and sister is mediated (as in gifts to the mother's brother for the debt to the mother). But in *sakkem presen*, the brother-sister relation is made central and unmediated. Eriksesen sees this as a visible response to the significance of women's wage labour in town and the large remittances they send back to North Ambrym (far more than young men).[22] *Sakkem presen* is in Eriksen's view a new kind of ceremonial economy, 'a conjucture of capitalist structures on the one hand and Ambrym principles of kinship and marriage on the other' (2008: 81, but cf. Taylor 2008a: 126–34 re Sia Raga weddings). There are emerging class divisions between North Ambrymese in town, between those of the urban middle class and those living humbly in squatter settlements, differences which are both evinced in and reinscribed by such ceremonies. And yet, in Eriksen's view, the gift ultimately encompasses the commodity; as money undergoes a kind of 'ceremonial laundering'.

The importance of women on the move is clear not just in this recent migration to town but in the longer history of movement associated with Christian churches. Eriksen counterposes what she calls the 'loud' and the 'silent' stories of mission history and Christian conversion. The 'loud' stories, which she finds privileged in ethnography to date (by Keesing 1992; White 1991; Jolly 1982), tell of men of importance who either resisted or appropriated the mission message. One such was Magekon, who tried to acquire rights to the Seventh Day Adventist church from Lonwe in West Ambrym; he offered pigs in a way akin to gaining a *mage* title. But, the German missionary who came later to Magekon's village of Linbul, proved too strong; he prohibited pork and required daily church attendance and so Magekon moved to Fanla, and back to *kastom* (Eriksen 2008: 84–86). Eriksen is right; such 'loud' stories do tend to privilege both foreign male missionaries and high-ranking indigenous men and their mutual relations. Charles Murray, the first Presbyterian missionary from 1887, reported parlous progress in conversion (and a horrific sequence of deaths – his wife, children and brother), until he established a relation with the high-ranking Malnaim of Ranon. Murray linked the church with the male graded society and Malnaim converted, using the church as a novel emblem of his own power. Murray called the church the *im kon*, the name of the house to which the highest *mage* men retreated, when they had become so high as to be dangerous to others.[23] But Murray wanted women present in this new *im kon*; Malnaim refused, banned the mission, and ordered food supplies to Murray be stopped. Only fearless male converts from Queensland, like James Kaun and Peter Ramel who built the church at Melkonkon before Murray even arrived, are seen to have risked the material and spiritual revenge of the *mage* men (Eriksen 2008: 87–90). So, perhaps the privileging of male missionaries, high-ranking men, and early male converts reflects their greater power and consequence in such historical contests.

But, Eriksen argues, silenced by this 'loud' story is the other story of the Presbyterian mission, whereby the church at Ranon became a refuge for women, runaways and the sick, an 'alternative movement of the powerless' (2008: 90). At least by the 1920s, women were being baptised in large numbers and the church had become an arena for 'women, peace-making and alliance' (2008: 90). Eriksen suggests that women were central in spreading the word; from the time that a woman called Rebecca returned from Queensland, women aided the diffusion of the church, as they moved for marriage and their husbands converted, and as the itineraries of migration from older villages in the interior to the coastal Christian settlements gathered pace.

Despite the loud resistance of *kastom* adherents and *mage* men like Tainmal and Tofor of Fanla into the late twentieth century (cf. Patterson 2003), Eriksen charts the historical eclipse of the *mage* by the Christian church. And, despite the prominence of men in leadership positions in the Presbyterian Church (only one of six elders are women), Eriksen sees the church not just as the major arena for women's agency but as a place which is indubitably 'feminine'. Both men and women religiously attend Sunday service, but it is women who support the church through their fundraising activities and women's groups meetings every Tuesday (which are part of the island-wide and powerful national organization of the Presbyterian Women's Mission Union, PWMU). She suggests that in the 'open' aesthetics of these church relations, food and company are pooled and shared and households merge into a 'social whole'.

Eriksen acknowledges that Christian churches are not overarching social wholes but rather smaller communities of Presbyterians, Catholics, and now adherents of the Neil Thomas Ministries (NTM) which are sealed off from each other by church endogamy. Her focus is firmly on the majority Presbyterians. But regardless she still asserts they are 'open' collectivities, in contrast to the 'closed' collectivities of *kastom*; generalized exchange in the church is egalitarian sharing, whereas the generalized exchange of past grade-taking ceremonies was eclipsed by the personification of the one man who took rank.

She illustrates this with a description of the transformation of the New Yam ceremony from an exclusivist male first-fruits ceremony to a church ceremony in which women dominate and men have been reduced to 'spectators' (2008: 120). Unlike the tree fern figures on the *nasara* representing the *mage* men of the past, there is no room for such objectifications of one person's achievement in the church: 'The church does not emphasize singular men the way older ceremonial institutions did' (2008: 113). 'The priest or the elder can never achieve a position of a big man as men in the traditional graded society did' (Eriksen 2008: 120); their position is merely 'rhetorical', with speech-making powers but with no control over amassed food, valuables or people like the *mage* men of old.[24]

Eriksen is not claiming that the domain of *kastom* is exclusively male nor the church exclusively female, since women are involved in *kastom* just as men are involved in the church. This is not an argument about demographic presence but about the gendering and value of domains. Yet her portrait dramatically differs from Taylor's depiction of North Pentecost and Bolton's of East Ambae. The aporetic position of the Presbyterian elder in North Ambrym seems very distant from those Anglican pastors of North Pentecost whom Taylor depicts as closely akin to *ratahigi* in their power. And Bolton's description of women on East Ambae and in the national sphere of Vanuatu, as keenly involved in celebrating and reviving their place in *kastom*, seems far removed from the gendered historical trajectories that Eriksen describes for North Ambrym. Are these differences of *ples* or perspective?

It is important to stress the limits of Eriksen's model. Although she makes a strong distinction between the domain of the church and the *mage*, she also suggests that in other moments in the ceremonial economy of Ambrym – in the life-cycle rituals of birth, puberty, marriage and death – there is a 'shift between emphasizing the community, or the social whole, on the one hand, and the achievements of a particular person who eclipses the collective contribution – what we might call personifications (M. Strathern 1988: 177)' (Eriksen 2008: 2001, citation in the original). So in these contexts she sees alternation and oscillation between these gendered relational codes.

But then, in the final chapters, she deploys this binary in an expansive analysis of other social movements in North Ambrym and nationally, such that different national organizations and movements are linked with these alternative gendered logics (Eriksen 2008: 121–58). For her, Nagriamel primarily exemplifies a closed, hierarchical male form, like the *mage* (with a fixation on the 'personifications' of power of Jimmy Stephens and Olsen Kai, which occludes the involvement of many women in this movement). In contrast, in her view, the New Hebrides National Party (later the Vanuaku Pati), grounded in the Christian churches and led by Presbyterian and Anglican pastors like Father Walter Lini, was a more 'communal, democratic and "flat" movement' (2008: 170). One wonders then how she assesses the extraordinary power that *kastom* assumed in the later political platform of the Vanuaku Pati and the independent state, the recognition of the Malvatumauri, the National Council of Chiefs in the constitution adopted at independence and the continuing, perhaps increasing, tendency of male politicians and *jifs* of many persuasions to legitimate their power in the state by taking ranks in the *nimangki* (see Lindstrom 1997).

Finally, she suggests the reasons for the relative lack of success of the Vanuatu National Council of Women (VNKW), the Vila-based organization, compared to the Presbyterian Church in mobilizing village women (in North Ambrym at least): 'The feminist movement is more comparable to the exclusive movements of men, like the graded society ... it was the structural similarity of the feminist movement to the *kastom* movement which made it foreign. The feminist movements seemed to create personifications in the same way as the exclusive male movements had done' (2008: 172). But this is at odds with Patterson's depiction of how the Presbyterian Women's Missionary Union was vitally engaged in the local women's rights movement alongside the local chapter of the VNKW who promoted women's practical participation in development and not just the 'empty posturing' of political parties apropos gender equity (Patterson 2001: 46–47). Although Eriksen applauds the work of VNKW in calling for equal rights for women, in promoting an 'egalitarian state' project and as a movement of 'great significance for many urban women' (2008: 171), I read this as a thinly-veiled critique of the 'personifications of power' exercised by its founders and prominent leaders, like the late Grace Mera Molisa and Hilda Lini, a critique which may echo those of some women in North Ambrym. Yet, it seems that any suggestions of female leadership, unlike the male leadership comfortably assumed by men like Father Walter Lini, condemn such women to be seekers after 'individual glory' (see Jolly 2003a, and Taylor 2008b on how some Santo men are reasserting their exclusive *raet* to power, against those women espousing gender equality). Eriksen admits that her application of the gendered alternative logics of North Ambrym to the zones of broader social movements and national politics in Vanuatu is perforce 'oversimplified' (2008: 170). So it is. What puzzles me is why she stretches her analysis in this way, so that there appear to be few limits to her 'comparative perspective'. But how persuasive is her model of gendered historical transformation even for North Ambrym?

Eriksen's book is perceptive in many ways, apropos the gendered patterns of kinship and place, Christian conversion, the transformation of rituals, and the movements of women, especially in recent migration to town. But ultimately her abstract arguments about gendered alternative logics and historical shifts in 'encompassment' from masculine to feminine forms overwhelm her material and restrict the creative purchase of her insights. I offer three major criticisms.

First, despite her historical and comparative intentions she tends to extrapolate backwards from the present configuration of the relation of *kastom* and Christian churches to the past, and to unduly extrapolate from the North Ambrym example to the whole of North Vanuatu. She sees herself as offering an historical argument as to how the 'the traditionally encompassed social form [female] has become primary, and how the male form is losing ground' (2008: 3). But in making this argument she unduly equates *kastom* with the male *mage* (cf. Bolton 2003), and does not offer a persuasive account of what that encompassing 'male form' was in the past.

The *mage* in its present form is perhaps as marginal to the ceremonial life of North Ambrym as it was once central. But although Eriksen paints an abstract image of the encompassing value of this masculine hierarchy in the past, she simultaneously diminishes its past material, everyday significance in two ways: firstly, by emphasizing the late historical importation of the *mage* from Malakula (see Patterson 1981, 2002) and secondly, by unduly privileging the 'out-worldly' nature of the spiritual power that men attained at its greatest heights.

Since Layard (1942) we have known that there was a vibrant regional exchange in the titles, chants and dances, the ceremonial insignia of rank, and indeed the all important pigs and pandanus textiles in North Vanuatu. But although foreign origins were often celebrated in each different locale, such ceremonies did not remain totally esoteric but became intimately imbricated with particular local patterns of gendered kinship and place, production and exchange. For North Ambrym, Patterson (1976) talks of the *mage* rites as being grafted onto the 'indigenous kinship rituals' in which 'titles are taken, boars sacrificed and a tree-fern monument erected' (Patterson 1981: 230). The *mage* became the apex of rites of status acquisition, but the indigenous rites in which women had a more influential presence persisted, and in Patterson's view the rites were mutually reinforcing. This entailed a complex articulation of indigenous and exogenous forms and a creolized imbrication of symbols and structures, although kinship structured the performance of indigenous rites but not the *mage* (see Patterson 1981, 2001).

Despite the variety of forms generically called *nimangki* in contemporary Bislama, high rank has everywhere entailed material as well as spiritual efficacy and evinced collective potency as well as that of individuated men. For Vao in the early twentieth century, Layard described how men did not take grades as singular men but as alternate generations of agnates representing the 'two sides of a stone'. Their sacred potency increased with the slaughter of pigs, as did that of women who had titles conferred upon them both in the male *maki* and their own separate ceremonies, conjointly assuring regeneration from the ancestors. For South Pentecost in the 1970s to 1980s, I observed (1991a, 1994) that groups of brothers typically took titles together while women related as sisters or wives did so in the same ceremony as their brothers or husbands, and that grade-taking ceremonies were necessarily combined with the kinship rituals of *lo sal*. High-ranking men could enforce taboos on major resources, be more efficacious in their magical practices to grow crops, nurture pigs and ensorcel people, exercise authority in local disputes and, in the past, make peace rather than war. With reference to East Ambae in the 1960s and 1970s, Allen (1981b) talked of *ratahigi* in more singular terms, as both efficacious entrepreneurs and autocratic leaders, able to organize punitive raids, settle civil disputes, and punish ritual offences (with gangs of young men acting as both a source of labour and police force).

By contrast, Eriksen only summarily acknowledges the material sources and signs of the power of *mage* men (the food, the pigs, the pandanus textiles) and their secular authority alongside their dangerous spiritual potency. Curiously, in view of her earlier contrast between the broader secular authority of *mage* men and that of the merely 'rhetorical' power of pastors and priests, she ultimately stresses their 'extraordinary' 'out-worldly' power, in approaching the volcano, the land of the ancestral spirits (2008: 145–46). She thus concludes that 'the graded society existed to some extent outside of the wider community' (2008: 145).

It is important not to overplay the significance of the 'graded society' in North Vanuatu, but it is equally important not to underplay its significance, especially in the past, and its deep grounding in what were simultaneously material and immaterial relations. Across North Vanuatu, the capacity to take titles (by men and by women) depended on being able to amass food, crucial valuables (pigs and panadanus textiles), and people for a ceremony. The legitimacy of the power attained by both men and women in such ceremonies was palpable in quotidian patterns, most obviously in patterns of restricted eating, but also in the materiality of house forms, pigs, textiles and the materiality of people's bodies, their punctuation with tattoos and their more evanescent adornment with pigs' tusks, bracelets, feathers and valued textiles. Across the region, high-ranking men did assume powers beyond the *nimangki*, powers which could be punitive, deviant and destructive (see Allen 1981b) as well as peaceful, legitimate and positive. Although the power of the very highest men was seen as so 'extraordinary', so 'out-worldly', that they lived and ate separately, and posed a mortal danger to their living kin, we have to ask what this 'out-worldliness' means. Given the precepts and values of the ancestral religion, it was surely the intimate presence of the dead among the living, of ancestral efficacy, for good and evil, witnessed in this world. Perhaps the 'out-world' was, in Sia Raga idiom, simply 'the other side of the leaf'.

Eriksen's notion of 'out-worldly' derives from Dumont on Indian religion and his related concepts of renunciation and purification. But this introduces distinctions between 'this' world and 'that' world, between the living and the ancestors, between material and immaterial efficacy which are inappropriate to the ancestral religions of Vanuatu. I am not denying the widespread perception of such high-ranking men as extraordinary and as dangerous, but rather querying how that extraordinary power was and is perceived in relation to the living in both past and present. At several points Eriksen alludes to the rather tragic figure of Tofor, a *kastom jif* of Fanla, North Ambrym, 'both a superhuman and an outcaste at the same time' (2008: 146). Patterson (2002) offers a far more detailed and sympathetic account of Tofor's life, acknowledging that this charismatic *kastom* leader and successful entrepreneur of the 1970s also committed 'murder by both occult and overt means' (2003: 130). His eldest son, whom he sent to school, migrated to Switzerland and in the national revival of *kastom* which accompanied independence Tofor lost his seemingly unassailable status as custodian of *kastom* to the Presybterian Willy Bongmatur who subsequently became head of the Malvatumauri. It would be deceptive to draw links between the disempowered figure of the elderly Tofor, constituted by his very marginality in a profoundly Christian island, and the figures of the *mage* men of the pre-Christian past. And yet Eriksen concludes: 'as the *mal* of the *mage* in the past had no strong influence in matters beyond the *mage*, the *kastom* chief today has no say in matters beyond *kastom*' (Eriksen 2008: 158). Forsyth's comprehensive national survey of the powers of *kastom jifs* cogently demonstrates otherwise (2009).

Secondly, in depicting not just the *mage* but indeed *kastom* movements in Vanuatu as 'masculine' in character, Eriksen has failed to acknowledge those women who are vitally involved in practising and promoting *kastom* and perpetually crossing over (or not even seeing!) the boundaries between church and *kastom*. Most ni-Vanuatu women are engaged in a series of mundane daily and ritual practices which are core to *kastom*, even if they have not been as celebrated as the remarkable revaluation of pandanus plaiting and dyeing on East Ambae. In that process, as Bolton insists, the materiality of the textile made visible crucially important relations between women and between women and men, and their relative value. By re-emphasizing *huhuru* in their lives, the women of East Ambae hardly became re-encompassed by the masculine value of *kastom* but rather insisted on the value of their hard work, the efficacy of the valuables they made and their power and status in *kastom*. They thus challenged the undue monopoly which men had assumed with respect to *kastom*. That process also created distinctions between women, on the basis of expert knowledge. In the plaiting of pandanus textiles Bolton discerns women's egalitarian collectivity but in the dangerous business of dyeing she detects strong distinctions between women; and the ceremony of *huhuru* manifests not just 'status alteration' but elevation, as certain named women attain seniority over others. Women may be cautioned not to go 'too high', and not to display the excesses of men aspiring to individual glory; however, the 'feminine' here embraces hierarchical distinctions of deference and *rispek* between women and not just egalitarian collectivity.

And is the 'feminine' space of the Christian churches so uniformly a space of egalitarian collectivity, as Eriksen suggests for the Presbyterian church at Ranon? It may be that women are demographically dominant in the churches and that their extraordinary collective efficacy eclipses that of men, either as lay members of congregations or as leaders – elders, pastors and priests. But this also underestimates the power of the masculine hierarchies of those churches as observed by Bolton and Taylor both nationally and locally. Moreover, from the early post-independence period, some men, like the Sia Raga Anglican Father Walter Lini, moved from a high position in the church to the state, where he 'personified' power in the position of the first Prime Minister of the independent state. As well as these persisting embodiments of power witnessed in the predominantly male hierarchies of the Christian churches, are distinctions between women absent from Christian churches? Female patterns of leadership are surely evident in Christian churches and local Christian women's groups, even if they are muted by an overall stress on women's solidarity and equality. Why should these 'personifications of power', like those of the leaders of VNKW, be dismissed as 'un-feminine' or even 'masculine' forms?

Finally, I turn to how Eriksen's model of gender in social change in Vanuatu ultimately owes a debt less to Marilyn Strathern and more to Dumont. Although Eriksen acknowledges Strathern's central stress on relation as a way of avoiding the Western antinomy between individual and society, in the plotting of her gendered 'alternative logics' or 'relational codes' Eriksen ultimately opposes individual and collective in a way that is far closer to Dumont. Yet in an unsettling reversal of the values Dumont deployed in his comparison of India and the West, individualism is here associated with hierarchy and collectivism with egalitarianism; the first is gendered masculine and the second feminine. In other ways Eriksen is more faithful to Dumont, for example in her insistence on the premise that in any social whole there must be one dominant value, which encompasses other submerged values at lower levels. Thus, we arrive at her historical formula for North Ambrym that whereas the masculine, personified, hierarchical form was the encompassing value in the past, today the encompassing value is feminine, communal and egalitarian (2008: 159ff). Since I have already elaborated my problems with this Dumontian approach to Oceania in some detail (Jolly 1994b, which Eriksen cites at its most rhetorical!), I will not repeat them again here. I simply lament that whereas Strathern's model, like Jif Riben Todali's 'land-tree', sustains a sense of 'fluid relationality', contextual dynamism, and movement forward in the energetic relation of masculine and feminine, the excessive abstraction in Eriksen's approach leads her to rather static and even ahistorical binaries, which ultimately betray her best intentions.

Some Final Thoughts on Historical Materialism and Material Culture

In conclusion, I return to Maurice Godelier, not to his reflections on big men and great men alluded to above, but to some of his earlier thoughts on the relation of the material and the immaterial, or as he expressed it in the language of French Marxist anthropology at the time, the '*matériel*' and the '*idéel*' (1984). And I do that partly by revisiting the Musée du Quai Branly where I started out.

In much of Godelier's corpus we find him astutely and eloquently grappling with the concepts of a European Marxism with its model of 'levels', of infrastructure and superstructure, of forces of production, social relations of production and ideologies, in the light of the vast historical and anthropological evidence of ancient Greece and Rome, Africa, the Americas, Australia, Japan and China, and of course, the site of his extensive and intensive fieldwork, the Baruya of the Papua New Guinea Highlands. The universal aspirations of that vision are for me deliciously French. But in that protracted labour, Godelier also challenged and refined some fundamental Marxist notions in asking, for example, whether 'ideas' might be seen as part of infrastructure, and not just as ideologies. Thus, he posits that the '*idéel*' is not just part of an ideological superstructure but that material things and relations are embedded with, indeed are indissociable from, the immaterial, from abstract thoughts and ideas (Godelier 1984: 168–220). This proposition, though expressed and elaborated in the language of historical materialism, and at certain points converted to algebra (1984: 202), might be seen to prefigure some more contemporary approaches to 'things' as the materializations of relations.[25] Throughout this chapter we have witnessed the ways in which abstract structures of thought, gendered models of relations between persons, and sacred ideals of ancestral regeneration are materialized in the houses, the pandanus textiles, the slit gongs and, indeed, the pigs of Vanuatu, both as living personifications and in their seemingly 'dead' ivory tusks.

And so let us return to those slit gongs which sit in the Musée du Quai Branly as part of the universal patrimony which France is protecting. The very materiality of these objects, transplanted from the *nasaras* of North Vanuatu to Quai Branly, embodies abstract thoughts and personifies relations. They are, as I intimated at the start, exhibited primarily as a manifestation of a profoundly male *kastom*, an ancestral cult from which women have been excluded and extruded and which lives on rather removed from our shared history, remote from the 'Americans' of the Second World War or 'Red Cross'. The overall layout of the Musée du Quai Branly has of course been extensively criticized for its undue emphasis on exotic primitives, removed from their complex colonial and historical relations with Europe but available for metropolitan aesthetic enjoyment. In her witty and controversial book *Paris Primitive* (2007), Sally Price has elaborated some of her earlier claims about 'primitive art in civilized places' through the example of this museum. She documents the important role that both Maurice Godelier and Lorenzo Brutti played in arguing that the materiality of these objects could not be so easily divorced from immateriality – the meanings, the ideas, the relations, the values, the agency with which they were endowed by their creators, users and original spectators (see Godelier 2009). The long, protracted and ultimately futile battle between ethnographic and aesthetic approaches in French museums is considered elsewhere (see Clifford 2007; Jolly 2011). But without denying the current museological orthodoxy that moving objects can and should change their immaterial values and their efficacy in social life through curatorial recontextualization (see Jolly 2012), I here wish to honour the role that Maurice Godelier and Lorenzo Brutti played in keeping faith with the peoples of Oceania in insisting on the inseparable connection of material and immaterial relations and revealing the animated agency of objects like that *Tambour des deux visages*.

Figure 5.2. Details of *Tambour des deux visages*, showing date, permanent collection Musée du Quai Branly. Collected by Jean Guiart 1960s. Photograph courtesy of Martin Maden.

Acknowledgements

I thank John Taylor, Lissant Bolton and Annelin Eriksen, the authors of the trio of books I chose to discuss in this chapter for their comments and generous responses. I also thank Chris Ballard, Miranda Forsyth, Katherine Lepani, Rachel Morgain and Anna–Karina Hermkens for their helpful comments. I thank Mary Patterson for her critical responses to the section dealing with Eriksen's book, received very belatedly just as this chapter was going to press. I thank colleagues both at CREDO in Marseille and St Andrews in Scotland for stimulating discussions of this chapter in earlier drafts, and the editors of this volume and the anonymous referees for their helpful suggestions. A special thanks goes to Martin Maden for his stunning photography of the *Tambour des deux visages* at my request and permission to publish these here.

Notes

1. The preferred spelling of Malekula has changed to Malakula. Aoba became Ambae at independence.
2. I deciphered this date only on a return visit on 20 March 2009.
3. The slit gong was collected by Jean Guiart in the 1960s.
4. The sense of 'personification' used in this edited volume is rather different to that advanced by Strathern in *The Gender of the Gift*.
5. Mark Mosko (this volume) similarly poses the question of the relation between Strathern's text and Godelier's earlier analysis. On the divergent meanings of gender as applied to individuals by psychologists and gender as applied to relations see Théry, in the collection edited by Pascale Bonnemère and herself (Théry and Bonnemère 2008).
6. Eriksen suggests that we label an emphasis on 'the achievement of a particular person who eclipses the collective contributions' a 'personification' (2008: 121). This diverges from Strathern's conception which rather sees personification in relation to objectification in the divergent logics of commodity and gift economies: 'in a commodity economy things and persons take the form of things ... in a gift economy, objects act as persons in relation to each other' (1988: 176). She contrasts the way in which objects create mediated relations in exchange, with the unmediated form of exchange in the work of production, where one person has a direct influence on the minds or bodies of another, e.g. through conjugal labour or a mother's capacity to grow a child. This contrast between mediated and unmediated exchanges is later discussed by Eriksen (2008: 160–61) in terms closer to Strathern's original. But Strathern does not stress the contrast between a particular person and a collectivity, as does Eriksen, which rather reinscribes the dichotomy between individual and society which Strathern challenged: 'the female social form (the communal and unmediated) has gained in prominence, and the male social form (the personified and mediated) has become marginalized' (Eriksen 2008: 162). Her stress on communal versus personified owes more to Dumont's privileged binary of holism and individualism, and his theory of the necessary hierarchizing of values in relation to a whole (see Eriksen 2008: 162ff).

7. Many other ethnographers of Papua New Guinea have been pondering similar transformations from 'dividuals' to 'individuals' in the process of Christian conversion and whether and how such transformations are gendered (e.g. Mosko 2010a, 2010b; Robbins 2004; Tuzin 1997). Robbins's model of Christian conversion as radical rupture has been much debated (see Mosko 2010a, 2010b; McDougall 2009, Taylor 2010a). In future work I hope to reconsider these debates.

8. See Lindstrom (1997) on the complex relation between indigenous and introduced colonial concepts of chiefs, his important reflections with Geoffrey White on 'chiefs today' (1997) and Forsyth's more recent study on *kastom* and state justice in Vanuatu (2009, see Jolly 2011b for a review).

9. Compare Jolly (1996) on the distinction of *kon* and *loas* in Sa, the language of South Pentecost and my speculations about Tattevin's translation choice for the Catholic church, as *im kon* to differentiate it from the exclusively male *mal*.

10. Taylor (2008a) suggests that at certain points in the past high-ranking women gained admission to the *gamali* and more recently notes continuity in this practice. In 2009 he observed the ritual of *hororoana gamali* in which two elderly women gained entry to the *gamali* and 'more importantly the sacred fire of a man who had just killed pigs at a *bolololi*' (email to author 12 February 2009).

11. The shape and materials of *imwa* have dramatically changed, with higher sides of woven split bamboo and windows now replacing the bamboo poles and the long thatch roofs of the past which brushed the ground. Dr Ilo also promoted pit toilets and separate kitchens (*imwa gabi*) in which everyday cooking is now done, to alleviate the dangers of accidents with fire and respiratory problems from daily exposure to smoke in the *imwa*. Pandanus textiles, however, unlike people, need the smoke of cooking fires to be well-preserved and sustain their suppleness, and so are typically suspended in great baskets above the fires of such kitchens. Unlike *imwa* used for sleeping, which have a closing door, kitchens are wide open to visitors, who can be invited to eat or simply partake of leftovers available in the kitchen.

12. From 1994 to 2009 they organized annual workshops of women *filwokas* akin to those of men from the late 1970s led by Kirk Huffman (the curator of the museum from 1976) and later by Darrell Tryon from 1981 to 2010 (see Bolton 2003: xvi–xviii, 1999). Jean Tariseisi left the Vanuatu Cultural Centre in 2009.

13. This word, current in Bislama and the pidgins of Papua New Guinea and the Solomon Islands, has been the subject of vast anthropological and linguistic debate. See Rousseau (2004) for a recent appraisal for Vanuatu. The essay by White (1993) is rare in attempting a sophisticated socio-linguistic study. Bolton quotes Tryon's assessment that the word probably entered Bislama in the 1920s, was not very current till the 1960s, and was not recorded in a dictionary until 1977, although its use and meaning rapidly expanded in the decades before and after independence in 1980 (Bolton 2003: 11, 14ff). I heard it used constantly in Bislama in South Pentecost and in Luganville and Port Vila throughout the 1970s and 1980s.

14. Bolton has perhaps failed to acknowledge that in most of the writing which imputes a 'trauma' consequent to colonialism, it is not the knowledge of difference but rather differences of power which are highlighted. So, in an early formulation Keesing suggested 'Perhaps it is only in the circumstances of colonial invasion, where peoples have had to come to terms with their own powerlessness and peripherality, that allow such an externalization of power as a symbol' (1982: 23). Bob Foster (1995) rather thought, on the basis of his experience of Tanga in Papua New Guinea, that rather than 'the noisy confrontation with colonizers', that quieter internal conversations had linked matrilineages with *kastom* and

households with *bisnis*. See Jolly (1992a, 1992b) where I stressed the universal human capacity for self-conscious recognition of difference, and disputed the characterizations of 'inauthentic', 'spurious' or 'invented' traditions contra Keesing (1989) and Philibert (1986). Neither separately nor in writing with Nicholas Thomas (Jolly and Thomas 1992) did I accept self-consciousness as a basis for distinctions between *kastom* and culture (as Bolton suggests 2003: 23) but rather argued it was supercilious, even racist, to suggest that some people passively perpetuated an 'unconscious cultural inheritance'. Culture is always created and always changing. In this debate I rejected the 'invention' approach of Hobsbawm and Ranger, but accepted it in the sense used by Wagner in *The Invention of Culture* (1981).

15.   Although I concur with Bolton that *kastom* 'developed as an indigenous concept', I am less persuaded that this was 'quite distinct from anthropological notions of culture or tradition'. This seems at odds with her overall stress on the relationality of the term, and with the influence of concepts of 'culture' on those ni-Vanuatu who were educated in English and French, the influence of the Vanuatu Cultural Centre through the *filwoka* program and the radio broadcasts nationally, she describes so well (2003: 27–32), as well as linguists and anthropologists, including herself, both at the national and local level.

16.   Bolton suggests that 'cooking techniques were not made the explicit focus of morally evaluative comparison' (2003: 51). Yet the contrast between the earlier separation of cooking and eating on the basis of gender and rank (on sacred fires/ ovens) and the Christian pattern of eating together was stressed both by *kastom* adherents and Christians in South Pentecost (Jolly 1989,1994) and by Anglicans in North Pentecost (Taylor 2008).

17.   However, Bolton notes that this protocol was broken when at the conclusion of the project on Ambae 'a number of men cut stencils and helped their wives dye the textiles they hoped to sell to me', at inflated prices (2003: 117). In this 'stampede', men deployed unrestricted stencil designs and developed novel designs based on sand-drawing.

18.   See Taylor (2008a) on Sia Raga, Layard (1942) on Vao and Jolly (1991a: 66; 1994) on South Pentecost but compare Deacon's depiction of women's separate, secret system in Seniang, Malakula (Deacon 1934: 478).

19.   Apart from her statements about Christian churches in general at the start, Bolton tells us little about the relation of women and men in the churches on Ambae.

20.   Eriksen's interpretation of *yengfah* as a ceremony of menarche is dramatically at odds with Patterson's recent depiction of this ritual. Patterson suggests that this ritual (*yengfa* in her transcription) was neither 'mandatory nor performed necessarily at puberty' (2001: 42) but rather entailed the sacrifice of a tusked boar which the girl had raised herself (in other contexts a practice forbidden to women) and thereby the acquisition of the Yengfa title. Patterson interprets this rite as enhancing the girl's fertility, her agency and her capacity for embodied self-reflection (performed with a bowl of water or a mirror), such that she is 'both a producer of life' and a 'vector of the blood that sustains life' (2001: 44). Until its cessation in the early twentieth century – 'it was banned to Christians by the missionaries' (Patterson 2001: 45) – it was a distinctive expression of women's status independent of fathers and husbands. Its revival in the post-independence era was, Patterson suggests, connected to the 'urban national rhetoric of gender equality' and the manifestation of a 'local "women's rights" movement' (2001: 48) which engaged both the Presbyterian Women's Missionary Union and the local chapter of the Vanuatu National Council of Women (VNKW). The ritual was revived in both national festivals and local contexts and the local branch of the VNKW was called the Yengfa Women's Council (2001: 49).

21. On the basis of her fieldwork prior to and after independence, Patterson suggests that the role of the mother's brother, who was earlier but one of many matrilateral kin seen as 'harbourers', has become more central in recent rites (personal communication by email 17 November 2010). Eriksen did fieldwork on North Ambrym with her husband Knut Rio whose monograph *The Power of Perspective* develops many cognate and related arguments. Patterson is critical of Rio's interpretations of kinship, agency and history apropos a sand drawing (2006: 217). I have chosen to consider only Eriksen's book in detail here since it is focused on my central questions apropos gender, Christianity and social change. Two other recent studies based on doctoral fieldwork in the Banks Islands (Hess 2009; Kolsus 2007) deserve consideration alongside the trio discussed here since they focus on Christianity but were perforce omitted due to space and time.

22. Patterson disputes the fact that only brothers are involved and observes that prestations of trade goods appeared far earlier in Christian weddings in rural contexts as part of provisioning the bride with her domestic equipment (personal communication by email, 17 November 2010).

23. Patterson suggests that both high-ranked men and their wives could aspire to an *im kon* or sacred house and the associated restrictions on commensality (2002: 203). See my analysis of Tattevin's translation choices in his use of this term for the Catholic church on South Pentecost (Jolly 1996). I am not aware of *im kon* as a designation for a special house for a high-ranking man or woman in Sa and rather stressed how by associating the church with the dwelling shared by men and women (*im*), Tattevin was distinguishing it from the *mal*. Tattevin may, however, have been aware of Murray's earlier translation.

24. Eriksen does not really engage with the debate about differences between big men and great men, catalysed by Godelier (1982).

25. On the evidence of more recent publications, Godelier has distanced himself from his earlier Marxism (2007, 2008).

References

Allen, M.R. 1969. *Report on Aoba.* Port Vila: British Residency.

―――― 1972. 'Rank and Leadership on Nduindui, Northern New Hebrides', *Mankind* 8: 270–82.

―――― 1981a. 'Rethinking Old Problems: Matriliny, Secret Societies and Political Evolution', in M.R. Allen (ed.), *Vanuatu: Politics, Economics and Ritual in Island Melanesia.* Sydney: Academic Press Australia, p.9–34.

―――― 1981b. 'Innovation, Inversion and Revolution as Political Tactics in West Aoba', in M.R. Allen (ed.), *Vanuatu: Politics, Economics and Ritual in Island Melanesia,* Sydney: Academic Press Australia, p.105–34.

―――― 1984. 'Elders, Chiefs and Big Men: Authority, Legitimation and Political Evolution in Melanesia', *American Ethnologist* 11(1): 20–41.

―――― 2000. *Ritual, Gender and Power: Explorations in the Ethnography of Vanuatu, Nepal and Ireland.* Sydney Studies in Society and Culture. New Delhi: Manohar Publishers.

Bolton, L. 1996. 'Tahigogona's Sisters: Women, Mats and Landscape on Ambae', in J. Bonnemaison, C. Kaufmann, K. Huffman and D. Tryon (eds), *Arts of Vanuatu*. Bathurst, NSW: Crawford House, p.112–19.

———— 1999. 'Women, Place and Practice in Vanuatu: A View from Ambae', in L. Bolton (ed.), *Fieldwork, Fieldworkers: Developments in Vanuatu Research. Oceania,* Special Issue 70: 43–55.

———— 2001a. 'What Makes *Singo* Different: North Vanuatu Textiles and the Theory of Captivation', in C. Pinney and N. Thomas (eds), *Beyond Aesthetics: Art and the Technologies of Enchantment*. Oxford: Berg, p.97–115.

———— 2001b. 'Classifying the Material: Food, Textiles and Status in North Vanuatu', *Journal of Material Culture* 6(3): 251–68.

———— 2003. *Unfolding the Moon: Enacting Women's Kastom in Vanuatu*. Honolulu: University of Hawai'i Press.

Butler, J. 1990. *Gender Trouble: Feminism and the Subversion of Identity*: New York: Routledge.

Clifford, J. 2007. 'Quai Branly in Process', *October* 120 (Spring): 3–23. Republished in edited form in *Le débat: Le moment du Quai Branly* 147: 29–39.

Curtis, T. 1999. 'Tom's *Tambu* House: Spacing, Status and Sacredness in South Malekula, Vanuatu', in L. Bolton (ed.), *Fieldwork, Fieldworkers: Developments in Vanuatu Research. Oceania* Special Issue 70: 56–71.

———— 2002. 'Talking about Place: Identities, Histories and Powers among the Na'hai Speakers of Malakula (Vanuatu)', PhD thesis. Canberra: Australian National University.

Deacon, A B. 1934. *Malekula: A Vanishing People in the New Hebrides*. Edited by Camilla H. Wedgewood with a Preface by A.C. Haddon. London: George Routledge and Sons.

Eriksen, A. 2008. *Gender, Christianity and Change in Vanuatu: An Analysis of Social Movements in North Ambrym*. Aldershot, Hampshire and Burlington, VT: Ashgate.

Forsyth, M. 2009. *A Bird that Flies with Two Wings: Kastom and State Justice Systems in Vanuatu*. Canberra: ANU E-Press. (http://epress.anu.edu. au/kastom_citation.html).

Foster, R. 1995. *Social Reproduction and History in Melanesia*. Cambridge: Cambridge University Press.

Fox, J.J. 1997. 'Genealogy and Topogeny: Toward an Ethnography of Rotinese Ritual Place Names', in J.J. Fox (ed.), *The Poetic Power of Place: Comparative Perspectives on Austronesian Ideas of Locality*. Canberra: Australian National University, p.91–102.

Gell, A. 1998. *Art and Agency: An Anthropological Theory*. Oxford: Clarendon Press.

Godelier, M. 1977. *Perspectives in Marxist Anthropology*. Cambridge: Cambridge University Press.

———— 1982. *La Production des Grands Hommes*. Paris: Fayard.

———— 1984. *L'Idéel et le Matériel: Pensées, économies, sociétés*. Paris: Fayard.

———— 1986 [1982]. *The Making of Great Men: Male Domination and Power among the New Guinea Baruya.* Cambridge and Paris: Cambridge University Press and Maison des Sciences de l'Homme.

———— 1991. 'An Unfinished Attempt at Reconstructing the Social Processes which May Have Prompted the Transformation of Great-Men Societies into Big-Men Societies', in M. Godelier and M. Strathern (eds), *Big Men and Great Men: Personifications of Power in Melanesia.* Cambridge: Cambridge University Press, p.275–304.

———— 2007. 'Death of a Few Celebrated Truths and Others Still Worth Restating', *Journal de la Société des Océanistes* 125(2): 181–92.

———— 2008. 'Community, Society, Culture: Three Keys to Understanding Today's Conflicted Identities', Huxley Memorial Lecture, London, 7 November.

———— 2009. 'Excursus: Combining the Pleasures of Art and Knowledge for the Museumgoing Public', in *In and Out of the West: Reconstructing Anthropology.* Charlottesville: University of Virginia Press, p.177–91.

———— and M. Strathern (eds). 1991. *Big Men and Great Men: Personifications of Power in Melanesia.* Cambridge: Cambridge University Press.

Hanson, A. 1982. 'Female Pollution in Polynesia', *The Journal of the Polynesian Society* 91: 335–81.

Hau'ofa, E. 2000. 'Epilogue – Pasts To Remember', in R. Borofsky (ed.), *Remembrance of Pacific Pasts: An Invitation to Remake History.* Honolulu: University of Hawai'i Press, p.453–71.

Hess, S. 2006. 'Strathern's "Dividual" and the Christian "Individual": A Perspective from Vanua Lava, Vanuatu', *Oceania* 76(3): 285–96.

———— 2009. *Person and Place. Ideas, Ideals and Practice of Sociality on Vanua Lava, Vanuatu.* Oxford: Berghahn.

Huffman, K. 1996. 'Trading, Cultural Exchange and Copyright: Important Aspects of Vanuatu Arts', in J. Bonnemaison, K. Huffman, C. Kaufmann, and D. Tryon (eds), *Arts of Vanuatu,* Bathurst: Crawford House Publishing, p.182–94.

Jolly, M. 1981. 'People and their Products in South Pentecost', in M.R. Allen (ed.), *Vanuatu: Politics, Economics and Ritual in Island Melanesia.* Academic Press: Sydney and New York, p.269–93.

———— 1982. 'Birds and Banyans of South Pentecost: *Kastom* in Anti-Colonial Struggle', in R.M. Keesing and R. Tonkinson (eds), *Reinventing Traditional Culture: The Politics of* Kastom *in Island Melanesia. Mankind* (Special Issue) 13(4): 338–56.

———— 1984. 'The Anatomy of Pig Love: Substance, Spirit and Gender in South Pentecost, Vanuatu', *Canberra Anthropology* 7(1–2): 78–108.

———— 1989. 'Sacred Spaces: Churches, Men's Houses and Households in South Pentecost, Vanuatu', in M. Jolly and M. Macintyre (eds), *Family and Gender in the Pacific: Domestic Contradictions and the Colonial Impact.* Cambridge: Cambridge University Press, p.213–35.

———— 1991a. 'Soaring Hawks and Grounded Persons: The Politics of Rank and Gender in North Vanuatu', in M. Godelier and M. Strathern (eds), *Big Men and Great Men: Personifications of Power in Melanesia*. Cambridge: Cambridge University Press, p.48–80.

———— 1991b. '"To Save the Girls for Brighter and Better Lives": Presbyterian Missions and Women in the South of Vanuatu: 1848–1870', *The Journal of Pacific History* 26(1): 27–48.

———— 1991c. 'The Politics of Difference: Feminism, Colonialism and Decolonisation in Vanuatu', in G. Bottomley, M. de Lepervanche and J. Martin (eds), *Intersexions: Gender/Class/Culture/Ethnicity*. Sydney: Allen and Unwin, p.52–74.

———— 1992a. 'Specters of Inauthenticity', *The Contemporary Pacific* 4(1): 49–72.

———— 1992b. 'Custom and the Way of the Land: Past and Present in Vanuatu and Fiji', in M. Jolly and N. Thomas (eds), *The Politics of Tradition in the Pacific. Oceania* (Special Issue) 62(4): 330–54. (Republished in R. Borofsky (ed.), *Remembrance of Pacific Pasts: An Invitation to Remake History*. Honolulu: University of Hawai'i Press, 2000).

———— 1992c. 'Partible Persons and Multiple Authors' (contribution to Book Review Forum on Marilyn Strathern's *The Gender of the Gift*), *Pacific Studies* 15(1): 137–49.

———— 1994a. *Women of the Place: Kastom, Colonialism and Gender in Vanuatu*. Reading: Harwood Academic Publishers.

———— 1994b. 'Hierarchy and Encompassment: Rank, Gender and Place in Vanuatu and Fiji', in M. Mosko and M. Jolly (eds), *Transformations of Hierarchy: Structure, History and Horizon in the Austronesian World. History and Anthropology* (Special Issue) 7(1–4): 133–67.

———— 1996. 'Devils, Holy Spirits, and the Swollen God: Translation, Conversion and Colonial Power in the Marist Mission, Vanuatu, 1887–1934', in P. van der Veer (ed.), *Conversion to Modernities: The Globalization of Christianity*, Routledge, New York and London, p. 231–62.

———— 1999. 'Another Time, Another Place', *Oceania* 69(4): 282–99.

———— 2001. 'Damming the Rivers of Milk? Fertility, Sexuality, and Modernity in Melanesia and Amazonia', in T. Gregor and D. Tuzin (eds), *Gender in Amazonia and Melanesia: An Exploration of the Comparative Method*. Berkeley: University of California Press, p.175–206.

———— 2002a. 'Introduction: Birthing beyond the Confines of Tradition and Modernity?', in V. Lukere and M. Jolly (eds), *Birthing in the Pacific: Beyond Tradition and Modernity?*, Honolulu: University of Hawai'i Press, p.1–30.

———— 2002b. 'From Darkness to Light? Epidemiologies and Ethnographies of Motherhood in Vanuatu', in V. Lukere and M. Jolly (eds), *Birthing in the Pacific: Beyond Tradition and Modernity?*, Honolulu: University of Hawai'i Press, p.148–77.

———— 2003a. 'Epilogue', in B. Douglas (ed.), *Women's Groups and Everyday Modernity in Melanesia. Oceania* (Special Issue) 74(1&2): 134–47.

——— 2003b. 'Spouses and Siblings in Sa Stories', *The Australian Journal of Anthropology* 14(2): 188–208.

——— 2005a. 'Beyond the Horizon? Nationalisms, Feminisms, and Globalization in the Pacific', in M. Kaplan (ed.), *Outside Gods: History Making in the Pacific. Ethnohistory* (Special Issue) 52(1): 137–66.

——— 2011. 'Flying with Two Wings: Justice and Gender in Vanuatu'. *The Asia Pacific Journal of Anthroplogy* 12(2): 195–201.

——— 2012. 'Becoming a "New" Museum: Contesting Oceanic Visions at Musée du Quai Branly', *The Contemporary Pacific* 23(1): 108–39.

——— and R.M. Keesing. 1992. 'Epilogue', in J. Carrier (ed.), *History and Tradition in Melanesian Anthropology*. Berkeley: University of California Press, p.224–47.

——— and M. Macintyre. 1989. 'Introduction', in M. Jolly and M. Macintyre (eds), *Family and Gender in the Pacific: Domestic Contradictions and the Colonial Impact*. Cambridge: Cambridge University Press, p.1–18.

——— and S. Tcherkézoff. 2009. 'Oceanic Encounters: A Prelude', in M. Jolly, S. Tcherkézoff and D. Tryon (eds), *Oceanic Encounters: Exchange, Desire, Violence*. ANU E-Press. (http://epress.anu.edu.au/oceanic_encounters_citation.html).

——— and N. Thomas. 1992. 'Introduction', in M. Jolly and N. Thomas (eds), *The Politics of Tradition in the Pacific. Oceania* (Special Issue) 62(4): 241–48.

Keesing, R.M. 1982. 'Introduction'. *Mankind*. Special Issue. *Reinventing Traditional Culture: The Politics of* Kastom *in Island Melanesia* 13: 297–301.

——— 1989. 'Creating the Past: Custom and Identity in the Contemporary Pacific', *The Contemporary Pacific* 1: 19–42.

——— 1992. *Custom and Confrontation: The Kwaio Struggle for Cultural Autonomy*. Chicago: University of Chicago Press.

——— 1993. '*Kastom* Re-Examined', *Anthropological Forum* 6(4): 587–97.

Kolsus, T. 2007. 'We Are the Anglicans: An Ethnography of Empowering Conversions in a Melanesian Island Society', Dr. polit thesis dissertation, Oslo: University of Oslo.

Layard, J. 1942. *Stone Men of Malekula*. London: Chatto and Windus.

Lindstrom, L. 1997. 'Chiefs in Vanuatu Today', in L. Lindstrom and G. White (eds), *Chiefs Today: Traditional Pacific Leadership and the Postcolonial State*. Stanford: Stanford University Press, p.211–28.

——— and J. Gwero (eds). 1998. *Big Wok: Storian blong Wol Wo Tu long Vanuatu*. Christchurch and Suva: Macmillan Brown Centre for Pacific Studies and Institute of Pacific Studies, University of the South Pacific.

McDougall, Debra 2009. 'Christianity, Relationality, and the Material Limits of Individualism: Reflections on Robbins' *Becoming Sinners*'. *The Asia Pacific Journal of Anthropology* 10(1): 1–19.

Molisa, Grace Mera 1987. *Colonised People*. Port Vila: Black Stone Publications.

Mosko, M. 2010a. 'Partible Penitents: Dividual Personhood and Christian Practice in Melanesia and the West', *Journal of the Royal Anthropological Institute* 15(2): 215–40.

——— 2010b. 'Partible Penitents: A Response to Comments', *Journal of the Royal Anthropological Institute* 16(2): 253–9.

Patterson, M. 1976. 'Kinship, Marriage and Ritual in North Ambrym'. PhD thesis, Sydney: University of Sydney.

——— 1981. 'Slings and Arrows: Rituals of Status Acquisition in North Ambrym', in M.R. Allen (ed.), *Vanuatu: Politics, Economics and Ritual in Island Melanesia*. Sydney: Academic Press Australia, p.189–236.

——— 2001. '"Breaking the Stones": Ritual, Gender and Modernity in North Ambrym, Vanuatu', *Anthropological Forum* 11(1): 39–54.

——— 2002. 'Moving Histories: An Analysis of Place and Mobility in North Ambrym, Vanuatu', *The Australian Journal of Anthropology* 13(2): 200–18.

——— 2003. 'Leading Lights in the "Mother of Darkness": Perspectives on Leadership and Value in North Ambrym, Vanuatu', *Oceania* 73(2): 126–42.

——— 2006a. '"Finishing the Land": Identity and Land Use in Pre and Postcolonial North Ambrym', in T. Reuter (ed.), *Sharing the Earth, Dividing the Land: Land and Territory in the Austronesian world*. Canberra ANU E Press, p.323–43. (http://epress.anu.edu.au/sharing_citation.html).

——— 2006b. 'Agency, Kinship, and History in North Ambrym', *Journal of the Royal Anthropological Institute* (N.S.) 12: 211–17.

Philibert, Jean-Marc. 1986. 'The Politics of Tradition: Towards a Generic Culture in Vanuatu', *Mankind* 16(1): 1–12.

Price, S. 2007. *Paris Primitive: Jacques Chirac's Museum on the Quai Branly*. Chicago: University of Chicago Press.

Robbins, J. 2004. *Becoming Sinners: Christianity and Moral Torment in a Papua New Guinea Society*. Berkeley: University of California Press.

Rodman, M. 1981. 'A Boundary and a Bridge: Women's Pig-Killing as a Border-Crossing Between Spheres of Exchange in East Aoba', in M.R. Allen (ed.), *Vanuatu: Politics, Economics and Ritual in Island Melanesia*. Sydney: Academic Press Australia, p.85–104.

——— 1985a. 'Contemporary Custom: Redefining Domestic Space in Longana, Vanuatu', *Ethnology* 24: 269–79.

——— 1985b. 'Moving Houses: Residential Mobility and the Mobility of Residences in Longana, Vanuatu', *American Anthropologist* 87: 56–72.

——— 1992. 'Empowering Place: Multilocality and Multivocality', *American Anthropologist* 94(3): 639–56.

Rodman, W. 1973. 'Men of Influence, Men of Rank: Leadership and the Graded Society on Aoba, New Hebrides', PhD thesis, Chicago: University of Chicago.

Rousseau, B. 2004. 'The Achievement of Simultaneity: *kastom* in Contemporary Vanuatu', PhD thesis, Cambridge: Cambridge University.

Speiser, F. 1991 [1923]. *Ethnology of Vanuatu: An Early Twentieth Century Study*. Honolulu: University of Hawai'i Press.

Strathern, M. 1988. *The Gender of the Gift: Problems with Women and Problems with Society in Melanesia*. Studies in Melanesian Anthropology, No. 6. Berkeley and Los Angeles: University of California Press.

———— 1990. 'Artefacts of History: Events and the Interpretations of Images', in J. Siikala (ed.), *Culture and History in the Pacific*. Transactions of the Finnish Anthropological Society 27. Helsinki: Finnish Anthropological Society.

Tabani, M. 2008. *Une pirogue pour le paradis: le culte de John Frum à Tanna (Vanuatu)*. Paris: Maison des Sciences de l'Homme.

Tattevin, E. 1926–1927. 'Sur les bords de la mer sauvage', *Revue d'Histoire des Missions* 3: 370–413, 4: 82–97, 407–29, 557–79.

———— 1928. 'L'organisation sociale du sud de l'île Pentecôte (N.H.)', *Anthropos* 23: 448–63.

Taylor, J.P. 2004. 'The Story of Jimmy: The Practice of History in North Pentecost, Vanuatu', *Oceania* 73(4): 243–59.

———— 2005. 'Paths of Relationship, Spirals of Exchange: Imag(in)ing North Pentecost Kinship', *The Australian Journal of Anthropology* (Special Issue) 16(1): 76–94.

———— 2006. 'The Ways of the Land-Tree: Mapping the North Pentecost Social Landscape', in T. Reuter and J.J. Fox (eds.), *Sharing the Earth, Dividing the Land: Territorial Categories and Institutions in the Austronesian World*. Canberra: ANU E Press, p.299–322. (http://epress.anu.edu.au/sharing_citation.html).

———— 2008a. *The Other Side: Ways of Being and Place in Vanuatu*. Honolulu: University of Hawai'i Press.

———— 2008b. 'The Social Life of Rights: Gender Antagonism, Modernity and *raet* in Vanuatu', *The Australian Journal of Anthropology* (Special Issue, *Changing Pacific Masculinities*) 19(2): 165–78.

———— 2010a. 'The Troubled Histories of a Stranger God: Religious Crossing, Sacred Power and Anglican Colonialism in Vanuatu', *Comparative Studies in Society and History* 5(2): 418–46.

———— 2010b. 'Janus and the Siren's Call: Kava and the Articulation of Gender and Modernity in Vanuatu', *Journal of the Royal Anthropological Institute* 16(2): 279–96.

———— and N. Thieberger (eds). 2011. *Working Together: Vanuatu Research Histories, Collaborations, Projects and Reflections*. Canberra: ANU E-Press.

Théry, I. 2008. 'Pour une anthropologie comparative de la distinction de sexe', in I. Théry and P. Bonnemère (eds), *Ce Que Le Genre Fait Aux Personnes*. Paris: Éditions de L'École des Hautes Études en Sciences Sociales, p.15–43.

Tuzin, D. 1997. *The Cassowary's Revenge: The Life and Death of Masculinity in a New Guinea Society*. Chicago and London: University of Chicago Press.

Wagner, R. 1981. *The Invention of Culture*. Second edition. Chicago: Chicago University Press.

Walter, A. 1996. 'The Feminine Art of Mat-Weaving on Pentecost', in J. Bonnemaison, C. Kaufmann, K. Huffman and D. Tryon (eds), *Arts of Vanuatu.* Bathurst, NSW: Crawford House, p.100–9.

White, G. 1991. *Identity through History: Living Stories in a Solomon Island Society.* Cambridge: Cambridge University Press.

———— 1993. 'Three Discourses on Custom', in L. Lindstrom and G. White (eds), *Anthropological Forum* Special Issue 6(4): 475–94.

Chapter 6

THE MAKING OF CHIEFS: 'HEREDITARY SUCCESSION', PERSONAL AGENCY AND EXCHANGE IN NORTH MEKEO CHIEFDOMS

Mark S. Mosko

Maurice Godelier's *The Making of Great Men* (1986) has achieved deserved renown in Pacific ethnology for having identified the 'great man' as a type of Pacific leader as different from the classic pair of 'big man' and 'chief'.[1] Our ethnographic analyses and comparisons across Oceania will consequently never be the same. But Godelier's great man is theoretically innovative in refocusing anthropological understandings of indigenous leadership to varying modes of exchange – in particular, the differing implications of exchanging women for other women or for goods – to the presence or absence of collective initiations, and in raising anew issues of hereditary succession in social contexts other than where they have previously been encountered, that is, outside of supposedly chiefly polities.

Godelier's writings on great man societies and the parallel accounts of most subsequent commentators (e.g., Godelier and Strathern 1991), however, have tended to focus on the two former of these connections with the result that the big man–great man contrast, and thereby Melanesia as a region, has received the most attention. The implications of Godelier's great man for chiefly societies across all regions of the Pacific – most significantly as regards the shared feature of hereditary succession to positions of power and influence

– has received comparatively little notice or critique. In this chapter, I seek to add some clarity to the notion of 'hereditary succession' which great man and chiefly systems evidently share, concentrating ethnographically on the Austronesian-speaking North Mekeo (Amoamo) chiefdoms of the upper reaches of the Biaru River in the Central Province of Papua New Guinea. But rather than examine North Mekeo patterns of chiefly leadership in terms of initiations or exchange between affinally tied groups, which I have discussed elsewhere (Mosko 1985, 1991, 1992), I do so here in terms of certain categories of reciprocal transaction involving chiefly officials and the 'inheritors' of their positions.

This shift of focus from initiation and affinal reciprocities to those involving chiefly succession and inheritance involves more than a substitution of relational contexts, however. It entails the adoption of a perspective on personhood, sociality and reproduction which differs in fundamental ways from Godelier's. I refer here to what has become known as the 'New Melanesian Ethnography' (Josephides 1991) which has emerged from elaborations of the Maussian theory of gift exchange in key works by Marilyn Strathern (1988), Roy Wagner (1986, 1991) and others. In this view, persons are composite beings, 'partible' or 'dividual' beings rather than 'individuals' as encountered canonically in legalistic contexts of Western society. Agency is implicated inasmuch as persons strategically detach the part of themselves which is gauged likely to elicit the desired or anticipated detachment or counter-prestation. Counter-intuitively to most Westerners, agents are here effective in their relations when they decompose or de-conceive themselves – when they reduce their own persons subtractively rather than augmenting or expanding them.[2] Interest and calculation are thus implicit in this mode of sociality through the capacity of actors to anticipate which detachments and attachments are likely to elicit the desired responses in exchanges with other related persons. In this regard, the New Melanesian model of personal partibility and agency encompasses elements of strategizing and calculation which parallel the 'achievement' aspect of chiefly performance which has characterized most standard accounts of Pacific leadership until now (see below). But also, it is assumed from this viewpoint that the 'things' given and received in elicitory gift exchanges, whether in Melanesia or elsewhere, are not categorically differentiated from the persons transacting them.

The Making of Great Men appeared in its original French version in 1982, several years prior to Strathern's paradigm-setting *The Gender of the Gift* (1988). Thus Godelier did not have available for his analysis such notions as personal partiblity, detachment, elicitation and so on, which form the core of the New Ethnography. Nonetheless, these radically different conceptualizations of personhood and sociality have profound implications for each of the three key distinguishing features in Godelier's model of Pacific variability. His contrast of great man and big man societies is premised on a categorical distinction between systems, on the one hand, where women as persons are given for other women and, on the other, where objects or things – items of bridewealth that are neither persons nor parts of persons – are exchanged for women. From the vantage of the New Melanesian Ethnography which I adopt here, articles of brideprice or bridewealth that marriage transactors exchange in big man societies are characteristically construed as inalienable but detachable parts of the transactors as persons, much the same as are women exchanged for women in great man societies.[3] Similarly, male initiates are not merely incomplete persons in the process of being made or grown to completeness by their initiators but are already complete, partible agents who, in the process of reciprocal elicitory detachments and attachments with their mentors, reproduce them (Godelier 1986: 31–76; cf. Strathern 1988: 98–132). Accordingly, in neither great man nor chiefly societies does hereditary succession consist in some kind of 'automatic', ' one-way' 'inheritance' or transfer of status, but rather in a complex process wherein presumed successors strategically detach elements of their persons deemed to be effective in eliciting desired ritual elements of their predecessors, just as the latter did in relation to their predecessors, and so on. Reconfiguring Godelier's typological model of Pacific variation in terms compatible with the New Melanesian Ethnography thereby converts the disparate key variables he has identified for differentiating big man, great man and chiefly systems into variant expressions of a singular mode of sociality, that is, of elicitory gift exchange among partible persons. Focusing on the processes by which North Mekeo chiefs are made and succeed one another, therefore, I shall consider the material and immaterial items exchanged between chiefly officials and their prospective heirs as elicitory transactions of the parts of their respective persons.

It is worth noting incidentally that the kind of personal detachability I describe for North Mekeo chiefly succession and inheritance is strongly implicit in Godelier's accounts of the transmissions between Baruya great men and their successors. The supernatural powers embodied in 'great warriors' (*aoulatta*) and their powerful weapons, for example, are regarded as gifts originally obtained by ancestors from benevolent spirits and transmitted to descendants (1986: 106). Shamans' (*koulaka*) spiritual powers are seen to lie in their own persons, including knowledge of the invisible supernatural realm, which they have acquired as parts of their persons through soul- or spirit-exchange with spirits (1986: 113, 118). Cassowary hunters (*kayareumala*) are understood to be possessed by spirits detached from cassowaries (1986: 128). Salt-makers (*tsaimaye*) transact their salt-making magic with 'anyone who expresses an interest in the subject' (1986: 133), meaning, I suggest, anyone who elicits the magic from its possessor through personal gifts – a process closely paralleling North Mekeo chiefly succession which I discuss at length below. Most dramatically of all, the *kwaimatnie* sacred bundles containing 'superhuman powers that govern the universe' which are controlled by *kwaimatnie* initiation leaders have been 'inherited' from ancestors, and those powers of the spirits are transferred directly by the leaders from the bundles into the initiates' bodies (1986: 90–91, 112).

'Hereditary Succession' in Comparative Oceanic Perspective

Most of Godelier's (1986, 1991) deliberations over the variability of Pacific polities have focused on the comparison of big man and great man societies to the relative neglect of chiefdoms, even though it is chiefs who share with great men the feature of 'hereditary succession'. Before turning to the North Mekeo case, it is necessary to examine briefly from the perspective of the New Melanesian Ethnography additional anthropological understandings of chiefly succession which have tended to centre on the distinction between criteria of ascription versus achievement.

From the time of first European encounters to the present, the societies of the Austronesian-speaking peoples of the Pacific have been perceived by most European observers as 'chiefdoms', meaning in general terms that a society's constituent kinship, political, legal, economic and religious relations are organized ideally in accordance with formalized differences of rank, and in particular that functions of politico-ritual leadership and authority over relatively large groupings are exercised by persons occupying discrete hereditary offices (Scaglion 1998). For societies such as these in pre- and early post-contact circumstances, succession to chiefly positions has been typically perceived in terms of rules of inheritance formulated in accordance with principles of ascription combining either patrilineal or matrilineal descent (usually depending upon the principle by which members of groups are recruited), primogeniture and, for the preponderance of examples, gender, inasmuch as it is men generally who are eligible to occupy chiefly offices but not women. Thus stereotypically in patrilineal systems the eldest son of the previous chief should inherit the position of chief, while in matrilineal systems it should be the chief's eldest sister's eldest son.

For several decades now, most anthropological accounts of indigenous leadership and authority in the Pacific, including Godelier's (1986: 162–66), trace their inspirations to Sahlins's classic essay, 'Poor man, rich man, big man, chief' (1963). For Sahlins, chiefdoms encountered mainly in Polynesia and Micronesia consist in relatively large societal scales of organization, with hereditary rank and ascribed status calculated in terms of genealogical seniority. The big man type supposedly characteristic of most Melanesian societies appears in smaller scale settings with leadership qualifications based on achievement. Although Sahlins' formulation has been subjected to considerable critique and refinement (e.g. Meggitt 1967; Douglas 1979; A. Strathern 1982; Allen 1984; Jolly 1987; Thomas 1989), it continues to inform ongoing description, comparison and debate including the most recent syntheses (Marcus 1989; Feinberg and Watson-Gegeo 1996; Lindstrom and White 1997; Scaglion 1998; Kawai 1998; Peterson 1999; Guo 2004). Of particular significance is the manner in which the ascription and achievement criteria used to differentiate chiefs from big men have been carried forward respectively in subsequent analyses and critiques. Whereas the addition of Godelier's great man as a new political type has produced substantial reformulations of the Melanesian big man, the Polynesian chief and the criterion of ascription it shares with the Melanesian great man remain relatively unscathed (see Godelier and Strathern 1991; Sahlins 1963; Goldman 1970; Douglas 1979; Marcus 1989; Bakel 1986; Feinberg and Gegeo-Watson 1996; Lindstrom and White 1997; Scaglion 1998; Linnekin 1990; Mosko 1994; Hirsch 1995; and below).

Nonetheless, as often as ethnographic accounts of chiefly Oceanic polities have been represented in terms of ascription and idealized hereditary succession, many investigators have been careful to record empirical 'deviations' of particular sorts. It has frequently been noted, for example, that persons other than designated heirs as stipulated by rules of genealogical seniority actually succeed to chiefly positions. Firth (1964), for example, observed that among Tikopians, chiefs were elected, and some forty-five per cent or more of Tikopian chiefs were not the eldest sons of their predecessors. On nearby Anuta, dying chiefs named their successors (Feinberg and Gegeo-Watson 1996: 77, 79–80). Hooper (1996: 250–51, 253), Walter (1974) and Toren (personal communication; 1989: 153; 1999) report that chiefly positions in Fiji are frequently transmitted by processes of selection to a range of potential claimants, often in deviation from strict patrilineality. In Samoa, *ali'i*, *tulefale* and *matai* are more or less elected to their titled positions by their *kainga*, so any member of the cognatically constituted descent group may succeed to chieftainship (Marcus 1989: 194; Shore 1989; Tcherkézoff 2000: 152–53). On Tokealu, *aliki* chiefs were selected from the membership of the aristocratic patrilineage and were not necessarily the eldest sons of previous chiefs (Hooper and Huntsman 1996: 157). Among the Tabalu of northern Kiriwina in the Trobriand Islands, the *guyau* chief is succeed by the male member of his matrilineage who successfully organizes his mortuary feasts and reconstitutes his predecessor's network of marriage and yam exchange relations (Malinowski 1932: 114; Powell 1960: 127–29, 131; Weiner 1976: 201; 1988: 105–8). Similarly among Rotumans, ranked chiefly titles were distributed among cognatic descent groups (*ho'aga*), and all adult males of a given group were eligible for succession to its title on criteria of seniority, personal character and 'other pragmatics' (Howard 1966: 64–65). Maori chieftainships were ideally inherited patrilineally and through primogeniture, but an incompetent chief could fall from power and, proven effective, low-ranking persons could aspire to positions of political, even chiefly power (Bowden 1979: 50, 52). In the complex ranking system of contemporary Tonga, successors to titles are not necessarily recruited by patrilineal descent or primogeniture (Kaeppler 1971), and Biersack (1982: 196) reports that the latter principle, where it is invoked, applies to sibling or collateral relationships, not consanguineal ones. Among Mekeo peoples of Papua New Guinea as reported by Seligmann (1910: 344–51), Hau'ofa (1981: 2–3, 207–14), Bergendorff (1996: 26) and myself (Mosko 1985: 193; but see below), eldest sons as ideal successors can be passed over in favour of younger or even adopted sons, and pretenders to patriclan and patrilineage chiefly office must receive the endorsement of opposite moiety chiefs (*pisaua, ufuapie, kofuapie*) at formal installation feasts if they are to legitimate their successions. Peterson (1999: 393–94) goes so far as to claim for Micronesia that genealogies of chiefly entitlement are ex post facto ideological justifications for the facts of political domination established on other grounds.

These examples, I suggest, are altogether typical of those Oceanic polities which anthropologists have accepted as 'chiefdoms'. The explicit rules of ascription that have been used to designate such systems as chiefly seem just as consistently to acknowledge a fairly standard lists of 'exceptions'. Ideal successors are commonly passed over, for example if they are incompetent or maybe just too young (or too old) to perform their duties. Or to be legitimate, even ideally entitled heirs to chieftainship must be endorsed by the elders of the descent group, by the wider community or by specially designated affinal or other allied groups. Despite idealized inheritance rules, claimants to high office are frequently expected to have elicited the public support of their predecessors before the transmissions of office are accomplished. Women may become chiefs in special circumstances, as when there are no genealogically qualified male successors available. In some cases, what really appears to matter is the scale of physical force that rivals can muster in support of their candidacies. In others, the contours of chiefly organization have demonstrably changed under the influence of colonialism and national independence, giving rise to many novel criteria of chiefly office which appear to be antithetical to ascription generally (e.g. success in business, attainment of Christian or secular educational distinction).

Not only do these 'deviations' from criteria of chiefly ascription appear to be standardized, many of them closely resemble the achievement criteria supposedly distinctive to big men and, thereby, challenge the dominant anthropological typologies. Sahlins (1963), for example, tried to take account of systems which appeared to combine criteria of both ascription and achievement by designating them as 'intermediate'. Douglas (1979) then critiqued Sahlins's comparative schema for failing to differentiate ideal expectations from actualities, but she nonetheless retained the achievement/ascription opposition as the key axis along which Oceanic leadership systems varied, arguing that empirical systems consisted of differential combinations of the two principles. Goldman's (1970) comparative study of Polynesian chiefdoms in terms of 'status rivalry' similarly consisted in varying combinations of achievement and ascription criteria. Basically the same perspective is contained in Marcus' (1989) treatment of variations in Polynesian chieftainship as admixtures of kingly (ascription)and populist (achievement) sides. Other influential comparative treatments of Oceanic leadership have similarly continued to orient their typologies toward variations of achievement and ascription (e.g. Firth 1964; Peterson 1999; Kirch 1984: 63–64, 68; Marcus 1989; Scaglion 1998).

For me, the issue is the following: if such empirical anomalies or exceptions constituting 'achievement' are or appear to be consistently standardized across many locales, how accurate is the presupposition that Pacific chieftainship is 'ascriptive' and 'hereditary' or, for that matter, 'chiefly' in the first place? Quite justifiably, many pragmatically minded analysts have argued that Oceanic chiefly systems, like other highly elaborated formal codes, must incorporate sufficient flexibility to enable them to respond effectively to the exigencies of historical processes and in so doing enable their own reproduction. Rigid adherence to ascriptive criteria of succession would, of course, inhibit this (Goody 1966: 1–39; Douglas 1979; Goldman 1970: 7–17; Shore 1989: 138). A few ethnologists have appreciated, however, that the seeming deviations from idealized ascription in contexts closely tied to leadership and succession are themselves structured into the dynamics of those systems' reproduction. Certain contradictions inherent to Hawaiian-type kin terminologies and descent calculations produce divergent claims to genealogical seniority and rank, and, hence, to chiefly office (see, for example, Panoff 1965; Sahlins 1958, 1985; Goldman 1970; Walter 1974; Mosko 1994; Shore 1989; Peterson 1999; Toren 1999). Similarly, although *mana* is usually understood in systems where it is encountered to be transmitted in accordance with genealogical seniority, it is also widely acknowledged that *mana* is only to be known by its perceptible manifestations and proofs, which frequently deviate from strict genealogical lines of descent and transmission (e.g. Hocart 1927; Firth 1940; Sahlins 1981: 31; Keesing 1984; Shore 1989; Hooper 1996: 257–62). These and other indications suggest that there is something systemic regarding the seeming 'deviations' from idealized rules of succession that makes them non-deviational. The self-evidentiary basis of hereditary chieftainship in the Pacific is more complex than varying admixtures of ascription and achievement or the tempering of idealized rules by pragmatic necessities.

In this chapter, therefore, I examine the grounds on which one case of supposedly 'hereditary chieftainship' is or has come to be regarded as both 'hereditary' and 'chiefly'. I use this opportunity of acknowledging and modifying Godelier's insights into the connections between modes of leadership, gift exchange and initiation in order to augment earlier arguments that hereditary chieftainship, as it is customarily understood in standard anthropological accounts of the Pacific, does not exist as such (see Mosko 1991, 1992, 1994, 1995; cf. Walter 1978). Rather, I argue, what have frequently been taken as the definitive diagnostics of chiefly leadership and the complementary principle of achievement both consist in long-sustained patterns of interpersonal transaction characteristic of Melanesian and, I suspect, pan-Pacific sociality more broadly. In formal terms, I suggest that empirical instances of chiefly succession are the consequence of sustained series of complex interpersonal transactions mainly between chiefs and persons intent on becoming their heirs but also between the rivals for succession and other relevant persons, most especially those people who will eventually become their subjects. Very simply, under close scrutiny chiefly ascription consists in long series of performative, elicitory personal detachments and attachments resulting in the transmission of the chiefly parts/relations of the predecessor's person to that of his successor. Hereditary chieftainship in the Pacific, therefore, does not consist in a combination of opposed principles of ascription and achievement, for satisfaction of the criteria of hereditary succession itself requires satisfactory performance of a long-sustained and wide-ranging series of interpersonal transactions and exchanges.

North Mekeo 'Hereditary' Chieftainship and Official Sorcery

I now illustrate these propositions by reference to the North Mekeo peoples of Papua New Guinea, who from the earliest ethnographic accounts have been described as possessing hereditary chiefs and sorcerers.

The North Mekeo constitute one of four dialectically distinguished groupings of Mekeo-speaking peoples at the western edge of the Central Province of Papua New Guinea. The earliest account of their system of chieftainship is contained in Seligmann's *The Melanesians of British New Guinea* (1910), based on his observations in 1896 and 1904 shortly after Catholic (Mission of the Sacred Heart) missionization and the imposition of colonial control in 1890. The system of functionaries he described as 'chiefs', 'sorcerers' and 'departmental experts' was the most distinctive feature of Mekeo culture and that of their coastal neighbours, the Roro. Subsequent anthropological and historical accounts of Mekeo peoples conducted over the ensuing century are notable for the extent to which they emphasize the continuing importance of chiefly practices in village life generally, and, until fairly recent times, the persistence of chiefly patterns of authority in customary domains of activity (see Guis 1936; Hau'ofa 1971, 1981; Monsell-Davis 1981; Stephen 1974, 1995; Bergendorff 1996; Mosko 2005).[4]

At the time European colonial control was initiated, villagers were organized into four politically autonomous tribal groups with members of each tribe occupying a contiguous territory. The two 'Central' Mekeo tribes, the Biofa and the Ve'e, were concentrated along the floodplain of the Angabanga River. The two 'Bush' (later 'North') Mekeo tribes, the Amoamo and the Kuipa, lived along the tributaries of the adjacent Biaru River. The mainly endogamous Amoamo tribe consisted of exogamous patrilineal moieties, each of which was composed of two named clans. Members of a clan were divided into named patriclans that were dispersed among one or more villages. Most villages were thus composed of the male members of two clans – one from each moiety – minus their married sisters plus their wives and children. Relations between members of the same tribe were expected to be peaceful, at least on the surface, since violence was prohibited and sorcery attacks were conducted in secret. By contrast, relations between members of different tribes were for the most part warlike.

According to the most authoritative ethnographic accounts (Seligmann 1910: 342–48; Hau'ofa 1971, 1981; Mosko 1985, 1991, 1994, 2005), politico-ritual functions were divided among four types of titled hereditary officials which were ideally duplicated in each local branch of a patrilineal clan. These were the 'peace chief' (*lopia*), 'war chief' (*iso*), 'peace sorcerer' (*ungaunga*), and 'war sorcerer' (*faika*) (Figure 6.1). Peace chiefs were responsible for organizing the two dominant contexts of intra-tribal exchange in which their respective clans participated: exogamous intermarriage and reciprocal mortuary feasting. Peace sorcerers were ritual specialists who supported their clan peace chiefs by punishing, through sickness and death, those villagers who disobeyed the chiefs. Peace sorcerers were also expected to protect the members of their respective clans from the illicit depredations of sorcerers from other clans. A similar division of labour obtained between the war chief and war sorcerer, the former organizing the warriors of his clan branch in actual battle, the latter performing the ritual necessary for the war chief and his party to be effective when attacking enemies and to protect them from injury.

To be recognized as a legitimate chief or sorcerer of his clan, a successor was expected to be formally installed during large public

INTERNAL RELATIONS	EXTERNAL RELATIONS	
lopia peace chief	*iso* war chief	**CHIEFLY AUTHORITY**
ungaunga peace sorcerer	*faika* war sorcerer	**SORCERY AUTHORITY**

Figure 6.1. Structure of North Mekeo politico-ritual authority (after Mosko 1991: 103). © Cambridge University Press.

ceremonies attended by their counterparts in the domains of peace and war throughout the remainder of the tribe. Thus all peace chiefs and peace sorcerers attended one another's installation ceremonies, as war sorcerers and war chiefs did amongst themselves. In all accounts from Seligmann onward, it has been confirmed that the peace chief has been regarded as the most genealogically senior of the four chiefly titles, serving as the 'chief' of the entire clan, including the lineages otherwise headed by the three other officials. Therefore, when I discuss North Mekeo chiefly inheritance and succession, I am not referring just to the reproduction of peace chiefs but to all four categories of politico-ritual authority.

Among all Mekeo, the four categories of chiefs and sorcerers are known as 'Akaisa Men' (au akaisa or au a'aisa, depending on dialect), referring to the culture hero and deity, Akaisa. It was Akaisa who in mythical times bequeathed to the Mekeo all of their cultural and social institutions, including their system of chiefly and sorcery authority. It is thus from Akaisa that all installed chiefs and sorcerers are supposed to trace their ritual pedigrees, back through all of the intermediary office-holders to Akaisa himself (Mosko 1985: chap.8, 1992). Very importantly for the discussion below on the topic of chiefly inheritance, the power or agency of an installed chief or sorcerer is thereby understood to be, or to embody, the spiritual capacities of all of his predecessors, including Akaisa's own formidable personal powers.

Succession to chiefly and sorcery positions among all Mekeo peoples has been characterized in terms of 'heredity' or genealogical seniority, specifically patrilineality and primogeniture (Seligmann 1910: 344, 346); Hau'ofa 1971: 164–68, 1981: 207; Mosko 1985: 114; Stephen 1974: 13; Bergendorff 1996: 26). For war chiefs, war sorcerers and peace sorcerers, only males are eligible to exercise au akaisa powers, for as men they alone are equipped to ritually 'close' or 'tighten' their bodies sufficiently to prevent the dangerous 'dirty' ingredients of their ritual charms intended for their victims from entering their own bodies and causing harm. Since the ritual capacities of the peace chiefs do not rely on the manipulation of these categories of dirty substances in the same manner as the other officials, women are not categorically excluded from becoming peace chiefs, and in historical times a few fully installed women chiefs in both Central and North Mekeo tribes have been reported. Villagers stress, however, that women have been installed as peace chiefs only when there were no other surviving male members of their clans to succeed to these positions, and that ordinarily women are ineligible to become even peace chiefs because their own children, even their sons, are by definition members of a clan and moiety different from their mothers, and au akaisa positions must not and cannot pass between clans. Even so, female claimants to chiefly positions are expected to engage in the same sorts of personal transactions as male contenders, as outlined below. It is significant too that in cases where a female peace chief has been the last living member of her clan branch, upon her death other branches of the same clan are expected to continue making important mortuary prestations in her name, even though that branch of the wider clan is extinct. In such cases, the surviving chief who acts on behalf of a vacant chieftainship is understood to embody the latter chief's ritual capacities and entitlements.

Thus according to extant ethnographic accounts, it is by men who ideally are linked patrilineally along lines of primogeniture and genealogical seniority that chiefly and sorcery positions are inherited. From my knowledge of the genealogical ancestry of several North Mekeo clans, I would estimate that, as often as not, *au akaisa* inheritance fails to conform to these ideal expectations. I shall argue, however, that these deviations cannot simply be dismissed as expected or predictable discrepancies between ideal rules of ascription and historical realities of performance. For, despite appearances, the very nature of chiefly agency and the manner of its transmission, regardless of patrilineality and primogeniture, suggest that there are alternative processes at play.

Fundamental to these processes are the basic mechanisms of interpersonal agency, chiefly and otherwise, as villagers understand them in indigenous terms. All customary human activity (*etsifa*: 'skill', 'knowledge' or 'cleverness') is regarded as 'hot' or 'effective' (*etsiabu*). So, for example, the skills of gardening are hot for producing vegetable foods, and love magic, wielded by men, is hot for changing the minds of women to love or like them. The effectiveness of these skills is always context specific, so gardening skills are 'cold' (*ekekia*) when it comes to seducing women, and love magic is insufficient to grow crops (Figure 6.2).

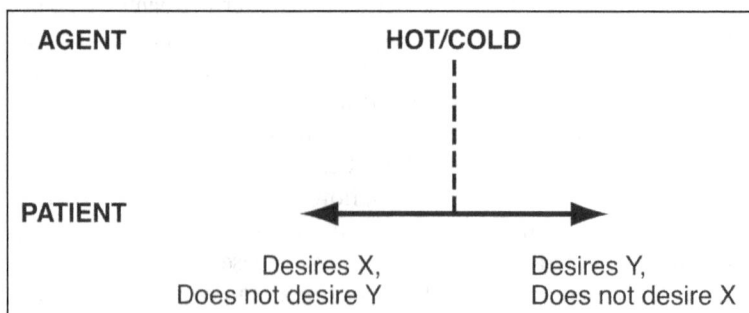

Figure 6.2. Hot/cold agency upon desires of patient (after Mosko 1985: 41–51). © Cambridge University Press.

All of the skills which human beings are able to use in their relations with one another involve direct transfers of a particular bodily substance or quality – *ngaka* 'vital energy' – from one person as agent upon another, the recipient or patient (Gell 1998: 21–23). The entities which are regarded as possessing human *ngaka* include all human body parts, but also the products of bodily exertion as personal detachments. Thus the *ngaka* necessary for human life that is contained in garden food is partly derived from *ngaka* elements of the gardener's own person which are transferred to the food he/ she grows, eventually to become assimilated to the persons who eat that food. This is an example of 'clean' or 'good' (*velo*) *ngaka* which is supportive of life and upon which all life depends. Most kinds of human agency which villagers adjudge to be morally 'bad' (*abala*) – what Western outsiders have characterized as harmful 'magic' and 'sorcery' – involve interpersonal transfers of dirty *ngaka*, that is, the detached bloody remains of dead human persons or human-like beings. These dirty parts of persons are regarded as hot in human interactions inasmuch as, along with or as part of the bad *ngaka* they contain, they incorporate the 'spirit' or 'soul' (*tsiange, lalau*) of the person from whom they were originally extracted. Thus it is with reference to the specific kind of reaction they desire in their fellows – whether for good or for evil – that people detach from their own persons the appropriate parts for transfer and attachment to others. Therefore the agencies which animate the interpersonal relations between North Mekeo villagers conform to the model of personhood and sociality that Strathern and others have formulated in terms of partibility and elicitation.

The distinctive kinds of agency which installed chiefs and sorcerers affect in their official relations with fellow villagers are connected to particular ritual transactions focused upon the prestations exchanged among Akaisa Men at *umupua* mortuary feasts and *kumau* feasts of installation. In the former ceremonies, the people of all the intermarrying clans of a tribe effectively unmix or 'de-conceive' (*engama*) themselves, through their peace chiefs, of the cognatic or matrilaterally-derived bloods (*ifa*) which they had heretofore shared with one another by common kin relationship with the deceased. People refer to these prestations as *pange*, or the 'lost blood/flesh of the deceased' traced to the deceased's two grandmothers' clans. For every deceased person, the bloods of the deceased's two grandfathers – father's father and mother's father – are not given away, at least on that occasion (Mosko 1985: chaps. 6–7; Figure 6.3).

However, for every such mortuary de-conception and distribution performed by the peace chief of the sponsoring clan, there is an additional prestation known as *iunge fanga* consisting of blood, slices of fatty back-skin and pieces of certain internal organs taken from a sacrificed village pig. But peace chiefs are not the only persons entitled to exchange *iunge fanga*. It is a mark of all four categories of installed Akaisa Men that they and only they can either give or receive *iunge fanga*. At formal feasts of installation (*kumau*) for peace chiefs

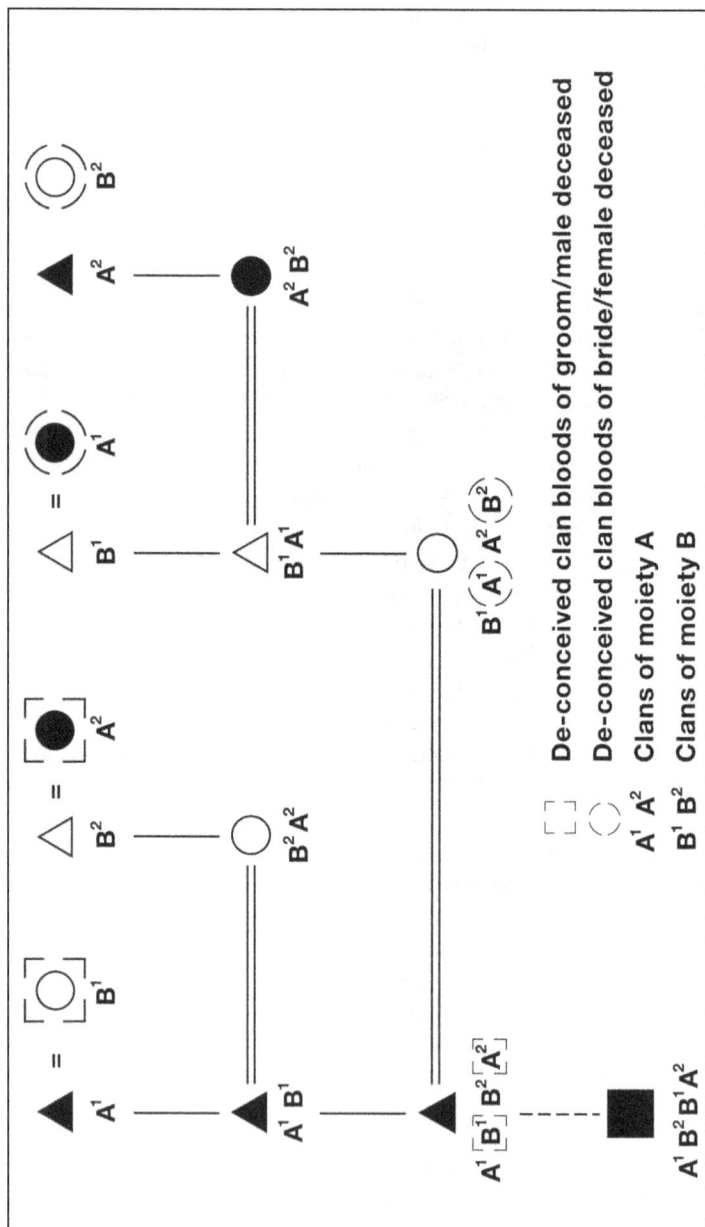

Figure 6.3. Mortuary feast de-conception (after Mosko 1992: 705). © Royal Anthropological Institute of Great Britain and Ireland.

and peace sorcerers, initiates must give portions of *iunge fanga* to the peace chiefs and peace sorcerers of other clans of the tribe. Similarly, at installation feasts for war chiefs and war sorcerers, designated heirs distribute *iunge fanga* to their chiefly and sorcery counterparts. Indeed, the performance of these *iunge fanga* transactions are the definitive ritual acts which qualify selected successors to inherit *au akaisa* capacities from their *au akaisa* predecessors. But just as it is only Akaisa Men who can give and receive *iunge fanga*, they must never eat it themselves or they would instantly become *ulalu* 'commoners' and abdicate their offices. Akaisa Men thus distribute the *iunge fanga* they receive from one another among the people of their respective clans and their families. Thus all commoner or non-chiefly villagers (*ulalu*) are obliged to eat the *iunge fanga* that they are given by their clan officials.

Now *iunge fanga* is classified as the detached *pange* or 'lost bloods' of deceased persons, but not the persons ordinarily celebrated at mortuary feasts. Rather, *iunge fanga* incorporates certain lost bloods identified with the officiating Akaisa Man himself: specifically, the bloods of his mother (or mother's father's clan) which he had embodied in his own conception and the procreative blood of his son and heir obtained from that son's mother (i.e. the officiating chief's wife) and, thereby, his wife's clan. In short, by giving away *iunge fanga*, an officiating *au akaisa* de-conceives himself of all his maternally-derived bloods and associated *ngaka*. These include his own mother's blood (equivalent to a third grandparent, his maternal grandfather) and his wife's blood as incorporated in the body of his future heir. By performing these rites of *iunge fanga* de-conception, Akaisa Men become extraordinary persons sharing strictly pure agnatically derived blood traced through their line of predecessors all the way back to Akaisa, who mythically performed the first *kumau* feast with the flesh of his mother and son at the inaugural installation of the tribe's Akaisa Men. In comparison with the de-conception of grandmothers' bloods which ordinary villagers (*ulalu*) undergo upon their deaths, Akaisa Men de-conceive themselves of one of their two grandfather's clan bloods in their own life-times, retaining in their persons only the pure agnatic blood of their forth grandparent, their father's father (see Mosko 1985: chap. 8, 1992).

These detachments of *iunge fanga* are particularly significant inasmuch as they prescribe the grounds of chiefly and sorcery agency and inheritance. As implied above, an installed chief or sorcerer must ensure that his chosen heir from infancy onward is never given *iunge fanga* to eat, even inadvertently, or he will be forever disqualified from becoming an Akaisa Man. Thus if a chief or sorcerer wishes to permanently disqualify a particular son or other member of his clan from succeeding him, he merely gives that person some *iunge fanga* to eat, and that person must obey. The stated reason that installed Akaisa Men cannot eat *iunge fanga* is that, by eating it, they become vulnerable to the hot agency of other Akaisa Men; in effect, they become commoners embodying matrilaterally acquired bloods which inhibit their capacity to perform the hot skills distinctive to Akaisa Men's pure masculine agency. It is by eating the detached *iunge fanga* parts of chiefs' and sorcerers' persons and assimilating them into their own persons, in other words, that commoner villagers are made vulnerable to the specific powers of their tribal Akaisa Men. And since Akaisa Men de-conceive themselves from the detached parts of the persons embodied in *iunge fanga* blood and flesh, they become relatively immune to the powers of other Akaisa Men, thereby acquiring a measure of immortality like their ritual ancestor Akaisa himself (see Mosko 1985: chaps. 7–8; 1992).[5]

With these contextual considerations in mind, I can turn directly to the subject of North Mekeo chiefly 'hereditary succession' by noting first the frequently repeated claim that Akaisa Men should pass their offices to their chosen heirs before they themselves die. As villagers explain, it is not impossible but still very difficult for an intended successor to inherit his predecessor's *au akaisa* position, even his own father's, if he has to obtain it from anyone other than the immediately preceding occupant. The implication here is that no one can succeed to *au akaisa* status automatically but must be formally installed in the appropriate type of *kumau* installation ceremony, consisting, as I have indicated, of interpersonal detachments and elicitory transactions. If an Akaisa Man dies before his office is formally handed over to his successor, it becomes particularly difficult to recruit another chief or sorcerer of the same dispersed clan to perform the installation transaction, as noted above in the case of extinct clans. Because of fear of dying prematurely, many chiefs and sorcerers relinquish their positions when they are still relatively young and active and when their successors are still adolescents or even boys.

Knowledgeable villagers stress even more forcefully, however, that living incumbents typically pass on their offices to successors as the consequence of numerous prior elicitory transactions between them. There are several aspects to this. Whenever people have recounted to me the procedures of formal chiefly or sorcery installation, they almost always point out that the successor must present his antecedent with 'something big or important' (*kangu apounga*), typically a large slain village pig. This gift of a pig is quite separate from the *iunge fanga* pork which successors distribute publicly to other chiefs and sorcerers attending their installations, as described above. Rather, the *au akaisa* initiate is understood to be giving this pig to his predecessor in order to elicit from him the material token or tokens of his office. In the case of a retiring peace chief, for example, the successor is understood to pay his pig to his predecessor so that the latter will relinquish to him his 'knife' (*atsiwa*), the key symbol of his chieftainship, which has been transmitted along the chain of his predecessors to him through the same sort of transactions. The other categories of Akaisa Men have their own ancestral heirlooms of office which are similarly transmitted to their successors through elicitory gifts of pigs or other wealth. If a newly installed chief or sorcerer wishes to acquire additional ancestral relics of office from his predecessor – pig-tusk ornaments, string bags, lime-gourds, weapons, ritual charms, and so on – then he must organize additional *kumau* feasts at which he must make additional elictory gifts.

There are several important points that require emphasis here. These tokens of *au akaisa* status are regarded as parts of the installed chief's or sorcerer's own person, as well as embodying the hot and powerful bodily residues of his predecessors and, hence, their detached spirits or souls. In some instances, I have been told, these surviving articles of *au akaisa* status were the original paraphernalia of office handed out by Akaisa himself to the first chiefs and sorcerers of particular clans. By possessing these heirlooms, it is believed that Akaisa Men can call upon their ritual ancestors as spirit allies to assist them in their projects. The point is that chiefs and sorcerers are expected to transfer these material tokens of *au akaisa* agency to their successors, even their eldest sons, but again only when the latter have given them the appropriate elicitory payments.

The requirement for initiation transactions of this nature bears directly upon villagers' claims about the difficulty of succeeding to vacant *au akaisa* positions. Only chiefs and sorcerers of the appropriate category in other branches of the same clan can ritually install someone in this manner, and the formal payments they typically demand are supposedly much greater than when living Akaisa Men install their own successors. That, at least, is one reason why old officials should pass on their positions before they die. Another is that Akaisa Men in possession of numerous spirit-laden relics of their offices, as described above, can expect to receive as many separate gifts from their successors over the course of a series of feasts taking place over years or even decades. The main reason for Akaisa Men to transmit their positions to their successors in their own lifetimes, therefore, is that the most important aspects of their positions and their persons that they have to transmit consist in the secret knowledge they have obtained from their ancestors. For all Akaisa Men (and similarly for all commoner magicians), this knowledge consists of the verbal spells (*menga*) which Akaisa Men use to direct the spirits of the dead and Akaisa himself to do their bidding, and the ingredients (*fuka*: 'medicines') contained in ritual charms (*toli, polu*). A key feature of all North Mekeo spells is that they include the names of the persons who previously possessed the knowledge of the spell and who are called upon to affect the desired results. The spells of chiefs and sorcerers are, in other words, detached parts of the persons who previously possessed and used them, including the deity Akaisa. The species of plants, animal parts and minerals which qualify as Akaisa Men's ritual medicines are similarly regarded as containing traces of the detached bodily remains of ancestral or other spirits. By acquiring these bits of secret ritual knowledge, Akaisa Men are thought to embody parts of those powerful ancestors and spirits and thereby to possess the capacity to manipulate them into doing their bidding in the performance of their offices.

Thus the clan chiefs and sorcerers who may be entitled to install young men in vacant chieftainships in other branches of their clans will rarely be in a position to possess or transmit the magical spells, genealogies, knowledge of medicines, and so on that the deceased chief or sorcerer received from his predecessors. It is this knowledge, obtained originally from Akaisa, which is the source of Akaisa Men's ritual powers over life and death. Those officials who possess this knowledge, acquired in unbroken chains of reciprocity from their ancestors, are regarded as hot and effective; those who have lost or forgotten this knowledge are regarded as cold and ineffective. Therefore, 'hereditary succession' among North Mekeo consists essentially in elicitory reciprocity involving the successive detachment of ritual knowledge from Akaisa Men and its attachment to the men successfully eliciting it. And despite the explicit rule that chiefs and sorcerers should install their eldest sons to succeed them, the critical issue is whether the prospective heir has made the appropriate gifts to the incumbent in order to elicit the critical hot knowledge and paraphernalia from him.

From all the reports I have received, it seems that Akaisa Men keep their ritual knowledge in utmost secrecy until such times as they transmit it to their successors. They then give it out bit by bit, and usually only to the one person they select to succeed them. As with the bequests of official insignia and heirlooms that chiefs and sorcerers give to their predecessors, Akaisa Men do not give away their knowledge 'for nothing'. They transmit their ancestral knowledge as gifts of *ngafengafe* kindness or generosity to intended successors only when the latter have duly paid for them with numerous prior elicitory personal gifts of *ngafengafe* kindness of their own – areca nut, betel, tobacco, fish, meat, and nowadays cash and commodities. *Ngafengafe* gifts of kindness comprise not only things but any kinds of devotion of labour, such as the regular performance of mundane household chores, frequent hunting and fishing, and obedience to the old man's instructions. Typically *ngafengafe* reciprocities between an Akaisa Man and his successor stretch out over many years, from the novice's boyhood to well after he has formally succeeded as chief or sorcerer, as long as his predecessor is alive and willing to divulge additional secret knowledge. In normal situations, a given chief or sorcerer will have several sons or other junior clan members competing (*kepipalau*) for their favours, and they will play them off against one another to elicit from each of them generous *ngafengafe* gifts. Whenever people have rationalized to me why a given chief or sorcerer has passed over an eldest son in favour of a junior or adoptive son, or even some other member of the clan – and even when their eldest son is selected – it is usually because the chosen heir was more generous and attentive to the old man's desires.

These *ngafengafe* reciprocities are understood to be effective in accordance with the same logic by which magic and sorcery skills operate. By making personal *ngafengafe* gifts to their elders, young men seek to 'change their minds' (*minotsi kelove*) and make them sufficiently happy that they will hand over knowledge that they would otherwise keep to themselves (see Mosko 1999, 2007). And when it comes to a given chief's or sorcerer's choice of heir, villagers are quick to point out that a junior son – even a classificatory or adoptive son from another lineage of the clan, as long as he has effectively elicited the favour of the chiefly father – will be favoured over an inattentive elder brother.[6]

As noted above and elsewhere (Mosko 1985: chaps. 5–8), North Mekeo regard the products of people's labours as parts or extensions of their persons. Thus the foods grown in gardens that a man cultivates are understood to embody detached parts of him as a person. Accordingly, eating food grown from one's own labours is considered bad or morally reprehensible. The food one produces should instead be given to others in accordance with any number of categories of kin relationship. And since food exchanges among North Mekeo are in the main reciprocal, villagers of different clans and moieties effectively become constituted of one another's persons in addition to the connections and identities of kinship and clanship established through procreative transactions. Therefore, the *ngafengafe* gifts of food, betel, meat, fish, money and so on which intending heirs give to their predecessors are viewed as detachments of their persons and attachments to the persons of their fathers. Similarly, the elicited items of official secret chiefly or sorcery knowledge which intending heirs acquire also qualify as personal detachments from their immediate predecessors and, through them, previous generations of Akaisa

Men. There is nothing automatic about 'hereditary' inheritance or succession in North Mekeo chieftainship, nor is this a process simply regulated by abstract rules of genealogical seniority merely tempered by historical contingencies. Rather, the *ngafengafe* reciprocities between *au akaisa* and their intending heirs that underpin chiefly succession consist in the identical logic of personal partibility and elicitation which I have described elsewhere for other categories of North Mekeo relationships and exchange (Mosko 1985, 1992, 2002, 2007, forthcoming).

It is for this reason that empirical cases of succession to Akaisa Man positions frequently fail to conform to the strictures of patrilineality and primogeniture which have been stressed in Mekeo ethnography generally. In an earlier publication (Mosko 1985: 117–23), I noted a number of cases whereby vacancies in specific *au akaisa* offices were filled from outside the Nganga clan of Akabe village, as an uninstalled but knowledgeable adept married to a female clan member founded a lineage of specialists which enabled the clan to achieve its ideal four-fold balance of politico-ritual functions. Presumably in cases such as this, installed office-holders of the appropriate *au akaisa* categories in other branches of the clans involved had to be compensated for their services in reviving the extinct offices (see above). More commonly, though, living chiefs and sorcerers transmit their official positions to younger members of the clan or lineage other than eldest sons. The detailed examination of these practices in particular cases, to which I now turn, reveals most definitively the mechanism of personal partibility, detachment and attachment by which chiefly agency is transmitted.

Akaifu Clan Peace Chiefs and War Sorcerers: A Case Study of North Mekeo Chiefly Inheritance

I have chosen for this demonstration an extended case study of the peace chief and war sorcerer lineages of Akaifu clan of Nganga village.[7] This narrative is a composite of stories and oral traditions stretching over most of the past century which I have pieced together from a wide range of informants, often with competing interests, on the basis of nearly four years of ethnographic study beginning in 1974. The characters belonging to the earliest two generations are people I never met but of whom I have learned from oral accounts, historical sources and Sacred Heart Mission genealogies. I have known personally Akaifu clan members of the three subsequent generations. While all elements of this narrative are part of the village's public domain, some episodes are strongly contested by various parties involved, so I have endeavoured to include in this account the main alternative versions.

The peace chief lineage of Akaifu clan is composed of two patrilines founded by apical ancestors, Mini and Iko, who lived roughly at the time of the arrival of European government and missionary officials in the late nineteenth century (Figure 6.4). Mini was the installed peace chief of the clan, and his branch was 'senior' (*fakania*) to the 'junior' (*eke*) patriline headed by Iko.[8] Being the most genealogically senior member of his patriline, Iko was the junior peace chief (*uibina*: literally 'string giver') of the clan and designated as the senior peace chief's 'younger brother' (*atsina*). It is the *uibina*'s responsibility to assist the peace chief in the performance of the ritual preparations and distributions of mortuary feast foods at feasts, specifically to tie up the pieces of *iunge fanga* ritually butchered by his peace chief.

The other relevant Akaifu clan patriline is that of the 'war sorcery' (*faika*) lineage. Apepe was the apical ancestor of the junior branch of this lineage, and he possessed the ritual knowledge of war magic which, in the pre-colonial era, was essential for protecting the clan as a whole in its perpetual hostilities against enemy tribes. Apepe, however, was never officially installed as the clan's war sorcerer (see below).

Before the installed peace chief, Mini, died, he was succeeded by his only son, Fokama. At the same installation ceremony, the string-giver, Iko, passed his position to his son, Atsiua. At the time, the Akaifu clan, and particularly the peace chief lineage, was relatively small in numbers, so soon after assuming the peace chieftainship, Fokama was concerned to pass his chiefly knife to a younger man before he died for the reason noted above – that it is extremely difficult to install a chief if the predecessor dies before he can do it himself. At the time, Fokama's only son, Bepeapu, was just a 'little boy' and too young either to acquire the knowledge necessary for official performance of his duties or to engage in the complex series of *ngafengafe* transactions that would be necessary to elicit them from his father. Thus at a mortuary feast, in front of all the other chiefs and sorcerers of the tribe, Fokama passed his knife and other chiefly paraphernalia to his own younger brother, Lopo, with the understanding that when Bepeapu was old enough he would pass along the office to him. When he became old enough, Bepeapu gave Lopo the expected *ngafengafe* gifts of kindness and was eventually installed to succeed him. By this time, however, Lopo's wife had given birth to his only son, Aueke, who was younger than Bepeapu by some eight years and genealogically junior to him.

When Bepeapu was installed as chief, Ito, the only son of Atsiua, the string-giver, received his new responsibilities as *uibina*. According to reports of contemporary clan members, Ito was very generous

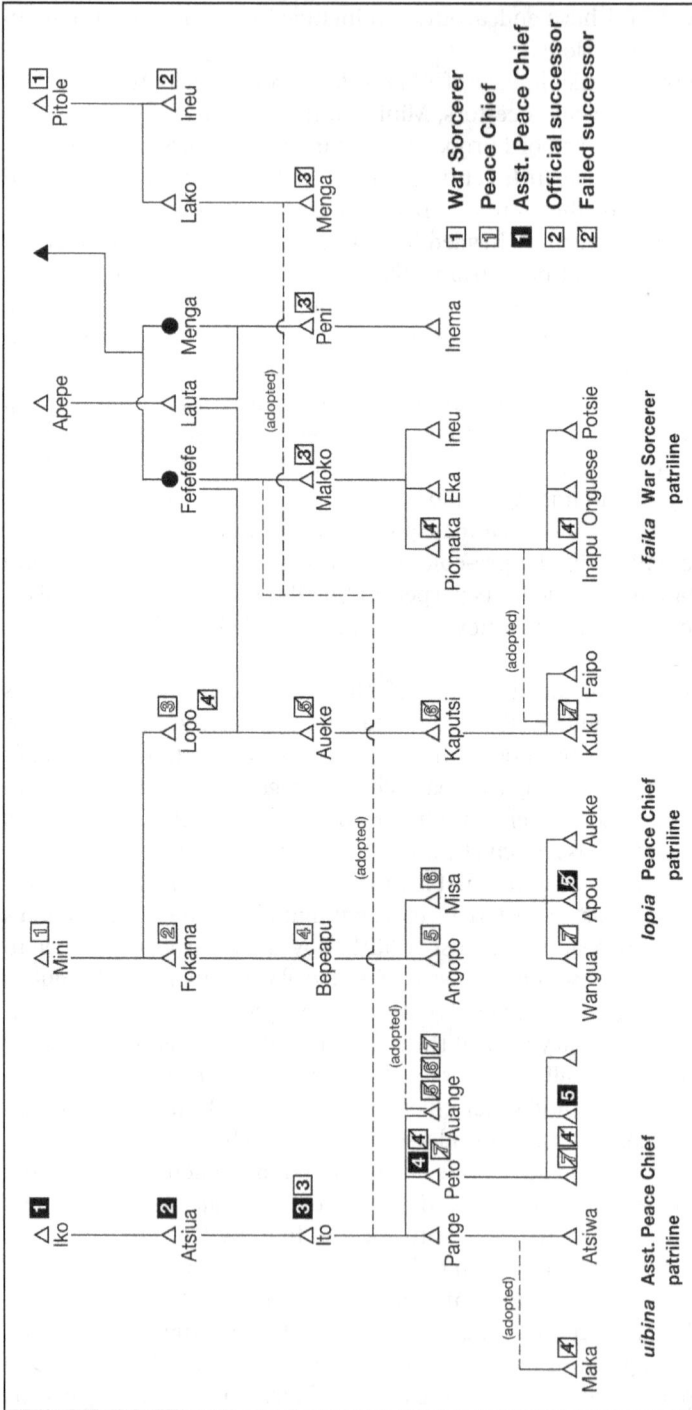

Figure 6.4. Succession of Akaisa Men (Peace Chief and War Sorcerer), Akaifu clan.

(*ngafengafe*) in his youth, both in providing numerous gifts of meat, fish, betel nut, tobacco, and so on to his own father, Atsiwa, but also to Apepe, the clans uninstalled war sorcerer and his only son, Laufa, and other elders. The war sorcery lineage, as noted above, had been headed by Apepe, the apical ancestor of the lineage's junior branch. Apparently, Apepe had acquired the knowledge and paraphernalia of war sorcery during the pre- and early colonial eras of fighting but he never became the clan's official war sorcerer; this office had been passed instead to a man, Aisanga, of the senior war sorcery branch (not represented in Figure 6.4). After being installed as war sorcerer in his youth, Aisanga married a Kuefa (Goilala) mountain woman and left the Mekeo area permanently to live at her village in the distant mountains. Thus the war sorcery lineage that remained in the clan and village was the junior war sorcery branch. The unofficial war sorcerer, Apepe, passed his war sorcery knowledge to his son, Laufa, who like his father was not installed into that position himself.

When Laufa reached middle age, his several sons by his two wives, Fefefefe and Menga (who were themselves sisters), were regarded as too young to acquire the very dangerous and powerful skills of war sorcery. But the young man Ito, who was already the clan's string-giver in the peace chief lineage, because he had always been generous to Laufa, was gradually given the clan's war sorcery knowledge and the paraphernalia. Laufa's own sons, Maloko and Peni, being supposedly too young at the time, have frequently complained that when Laufa handed the war sorcery over to Ito, it was with the understanding that when Maloko and Peni were old enough, Ito would pass the knowledge and paraphernalia back to them, that is, to the senior members of the remaining war sorcery lineage of the clan. By the time that Laufa died, Ito was a young married man, and he and his wife adopted Maloko and Peni as their sons while also producing many other children of their own.

Nevertheless, Ito never gave his war sorcery over to Maloko and Peni for two apparent reasons. On one hand, before he died, Ito told me that in the view of the Christian God (*Deo*), war sorcery, like peace sorcery, was evil, and he wanted that knowledge to die with him.[9] Other villagers have repeated this explanation to me even fifteen years after Ito had died. On the other hand, Ito reported to me – and I have heard it from many other villagers – that Maloko and Peni never engaged in the sorts of elicitory *ngafengafe* transactions with Ito that he had undertaken in his youth vis-à-vis their father, so Iko was never obliged to give Maloko and Peni their father's war magic 'for nothing'.

At this point, I was myself implicated in this narrative, for during my initial fieldwork of 1974–1976, I was adopted by Ito and his wife as their son and a member of the peace chief and string-giver patrilines of Akaifu clan. Ito accordingly became one of my key informants, and he spent many hours with me, teaching me North Mekeo customs in the context of my frequent gifts of tobacco, tinned meats, rice, and so on. Several villagers have thus indicated to me over the years that as I had spent so much time with Ito in private as well as public conversation in such circumstances, Ito must have given to me his secret war sorcery knowledge – which is not true, and I never asked for it.

By that time, Ito's own eldest son, Pange, had spent most of his youth in missionary schools, so by the mid-1970s he had moved to the Highlands, married there, and attenuated his relations with everyone in the village including his parents. Ito's wife and my adoptive mother, Muniapu, complained to me on occasion that Pange never sent them any money from his job, and to this day he has not returned to visit the village. My point is that none of the young men of the chiefly or war sorcery lineages of the clan ever went through the process of elicitory *ngafengafe* gift-giving necessary to persuade Ito to give them his knowledge. Thus Akaifu clan's war sorcery went extinct with Ito's death in 1985.

Returning to the senior peace chief line, Bepeapu formally succeeded his father's brother, Lopo, as peace chief and received from him his knife and other peace chief paraphernalia in a series of mortuary feasts when he was still a relatively young man. Soon after marrying, Bepeapu was taken away by the Catholic priests at Veifa'a to be educated and trained as the first primary school teacher for the young children of the village – in those days a policy of the Church officials regarding the eldest sons of many Mekeo peace chiefs. At that time in North Mekeo, primary school education lasted only two years and included instruction in reading and writing in the indigenous language as developed orthographically by the missionaries. Bepeapu's own eldest son, Angopo, was several years younger than his father's younger brother's son, Aueke, whose own father, Lopo, had been chief before Bepeapu. When I knew him in the mid-1970s, Aueke had frequently expressed concern publicly and to me privately that the peace chieftainship of the clan should have gone back to him rather than to Bepeapu's son. However, Aueke was never formally trained in European culture or language, unlike Bepeapu, and he never engaged in the appropriate forms of *ngafengafe* generosity with either his own father, Lopo, or with Bepeapu in order to elicit the peace chieftainship from them. Although Aueke was regarded as a man of extraordinarily talents by other villagers, he never acquired the ritual knowledge of clan peace chief, which he thus claimed should be given to his only son, Kaputsi.

The peace chief, Bepeapu, had two sons, Angopo and Misa. As the elder of the two, Angopo was designated early on as Bepeapu's heir.

However, in the course of his high school education he contracted leprosy and was forced to live outside the Mekeo region in a sanatorium near Port Moresby. Initially, Bepeapu and his family moved to Port Moresby where they could take care of Angopo, only visiting the village occasionally and hosting relatives when they arrived in town on visits. Because Angopo was unable to travel to the village for many years, Bepeapu could not install Angopo at the appropriate *kumau* feast, and there was considerable concern in the clan over the transference of the chieftainship to him, given his condition. His younger brother, Misa, having being raised in town, was deemed unlikely ever to return to live in the village and thus was initially regarded as unsuitable to succeed Bepeapu.

Therefore, without a clearly designated heir, the junior peace chief, Ito, gave to Bepeapu his third eldest son, Auange, for adoption, with the expectation that he would be mentored by Bepeapu and, when old enough, would return to the village to become the clan's next senior peace chief. Nowadays Auange maintains that throughout his late childhood and youth, he was frequently told by Bepeapu and others that he was to become Bepeapu's chiefly successor. There is a disagreement between him and others of the clan, however, over the extent to which he engaged in the sorts of *ngafengage* transactions which would have elicited from Bepeapu the knowledge and skills he would need to serve as peace chief. And in any event, Bepeapu ended up installing both of his sons to the peace chieftainship, one after the other.

As I understand it, while living at the sanatorium in Moresby, Angopo received a high school qualification and certification for primary education. When his disease was regarded as being sufficiently under control with antibiotics, Angopo was allowed to take a primary teaching job in one of the Port Moresby suburbs. At this stage, he took on primary responsibility for providing for the subsistence of his natal family, including his aging father, Bepeapu, and his mother. This support consisted in precisely the sort of gifts of *ngafengafe* kindness which proved effective in eliciting his father's knowledge of peace chieftainship and his support in succeeding him. Thus at the clan's next mortuary feast in the late 1960s, Bepeapu turned his chiefly knife over to his eldest son, Angopo. Since Angopo was able to procure only a single pig to give his father, Bepeapu only passed on his knife and no other paraphernalia or heirlooms of his office – his *bako* chest ornament, his lime-pot and lime-stick, string bag, etc. Also, it is rumoured that since by this time Angopo was well into his thirties, of uncertain health and not expected to marry, Bepeapu had decided not to turn the entirety of his office over to his eldest son.

Since both Bepeapu and Angopo were living in Port Moresby for most of the 1950s and 1960s, Akaifu clan's senior peace chiefs, father and son, were unable perform their chiefly duties in the village on a daily basis. In the early 1970s, however, a new elementary school station was established by the mission at Akufa, a location central to all North Mekeo villages. Angopo therefore applied for a transfer to Akufa and in 1975 he was successful, moving there and bringing with him his father, Bepeapu the old chief, who he continued to look after with regular *ngafengafe* support and generosity. Being close to the village for the next three or so years, Angopo was able to serve his clan as peace chief on ceremonial occasions, and with his salary at Akufa he was a regular host to most of the villagers whenever they travelled between village and town. When his teaching responsibilities at Akufa interfered with his village feasting duties, his assistant, the junior string chief, Ito, stood in for him as peace chief.

Without regular access to his medications, however, Angopo's leprosy became infectious in late 1976, and over the next two years he gradually declined and died. By then, his adopted brother, Auange, had married and returned to the village with his Central Mekeo wife. After Angopo's death, his younger brother, Misa, returned to the village from town with a wife, a non-Mekeo woman from the Gulf. For the next four years or so, old Bepeapu continued to serve as Akaifu peace chief, inasmuch as he still retained the ritual paraphernalia that Angopo had never elicited from him. At the large mortuary feast staged by the clan in around 1986 for all of its recently deceased, including Angopo, Bepeapu handed the chiefly knife and heirlooms to his second son, Misa, rather than the adopted son, Auange, who earlier had been expected to become peace chief even before the knife went to Angopo. Over the years, Auange has complained to me and others about his bitter sense of betrayal. Others, however, argue that despite his high school education he lacks the personal qualities which they would prefer to see in their next chief – qualities which Misa was considered to demonstrate in the manner in which he regularly expressed sentiments of *ngafengafe* kindness both to his parents and to other members of the clan and village from the moment of his return. It is presumed that in the short interval between Misa's arrival in the village and his father, Bepeapu's, death, he was given the secret knowledge needed to lead the clan as peace chief. So in the late 1980s after Ito and Bepeapu died, Misa performed their mortuary feast as peace chief, installing Ito's second son, Peto, as assistant string-giving chief, passing over Ito's third-born son and his own adoptive brother, Auange.

Over the subsequent years that Misa served as peace chief, he proved in most people's estimation to be a most effective leader of his clan and the village as a whole. In around 1990, Mission authorities persuaded him to undergo formal training to become the village's catechist – a position vacated with the death of the previous long-serving catechist from the opposite clan of the village. For two years Misa and his family relocated to the Catholic mission station at Kubuna at the edge of Mekeo territory where he received his training.

Soon after he left the village, however, Aueke, whose father had long ago been installed as peace chief before Bepeapu, died. Because Aueke's mother, Fefefefe, married the clan war sorcerer, Laufa, when his father, Lopo, died, Aueke was adopted by Laufa and developed close fraternal ties with Laufa's sons, Maloko and Peni. Maloko's and Peni's respective mothers were sisters, and one of them, Fefefefe, was also the mother of Aueke. Thus Maloko was Aueke's half-brother through a mother in common, and, along with Peni, step-brother through adoption by Laufa. Over the course of the clan's subsequent political history, until his death, Aueke tended to support the aspirations of his adoptive war sorcery kin over the interests of his own genealogical relatives in the peace chief lineage, and his son, Kaputsi, has followed suit. In particular, before his death in 1990, Aueke supported the claims of Maloko and Peni against Ito for the return of the clan's war sorcery to their lineage, and Maloko and Peni and other members of the war sorcery lineage have supported Kaputsi's aspirations to succeed Misa as peace chief on the basis of Aueke's earlier claims.

For five years or so in the mid-1990s, Misa served as peace chief and catechist, bringing a degree of unity to the clan and village that it had not known for many years (see Mosko 2001). In 1998, however, Misa grew seriously ill and died rather suddenly, leaving three sons amongst his seven children. While he was still alive, he had declared that his eldest son, Wangua, was unqualified to succeed him as peace chief – a view endorsed by other clan members – inasmuch as the boy was consistently disobedient toward his father and made no attempts to solicit his indulgences. On one occasion while I was in the village, Misa publicly beat his son when he was caught smoking marijuana. It was thus Misa's apparent intention to install his second son, Apou, to the chieftainship. But at the time, Apou was still enrolled in primary school down-river at Akufa station and was too young to endear himself to his father through regular acts of *ngafengage* kindness.

In around 1994, however, Aueke's son, Kaputsi, who had spent a number of years living in Samarai, returned to the village, married and started to raise a new family. His first marriage in the 1970s to a North Mekeo woman had produced two sons, Kuku and Faipo. He had left the village for Samarai when his first wife died, and his sons were 'given food' or adopted during his years of absence by Piomaka, eldest son of Maloko in the war sorcery lineage of the clan. Although neither Kuku nor Faipo had been given any official knowledge or ritual from an incumbent peace chief when they were young men, closely related members of the war sorcery lineage had been (and still are) supporting Kaputsi's aspirations for one of his sons to become installed as peace chief after Misa.

Within a year of Misa's death in 1998, however, Misa's widow, while still in mourning, was discovered to be pregnant from an affair with a resident Central Mekeo widower whose first wife – a woman in yet another branch of Akaifu clan – had died in 1997. Many of the women and men of the village were outraged, as she had been the wife of their beloved chief and catechist. After they beat her, the widow was driven from the village, whereupon she and her paramour eloped to live in his village, taking with her Misa's children, including Misa's two eldest sons. Therefore once again the supposedly ideal heir to the peace chieftainship of Akaifu clan was residing away from his own village. And with Misa's death occurring before he could install his successor, it is now very difficult for the clan to stage a *kumau* installation feast with a peace chief of another branch of Akaifu clan from Central Mekeo brought in to do the honours.

Under the circumstances, however, on my last visits in 2001, 2003, 2005, 2006 and 2009, the situation had become even more uncertain. In the peace chief lineage, not only are all of Misa's sons living away from the village, but Peto, old Ito's second son and the installed assistant string chief, now argues that he should become the next peace chief as he possesses the most knowledge of the position, which he obtained from his father, Ito. His younger brother, Auange, who was earlier adopted by the old chief, Bepeapu, however, occasionally contends that the peace chieftainship should have gone to him long ago. Others in the clan and village point out, however, that Peto's three young sons never acquired the ability of speech and so are completely unqualified to become peace chief, and that Auange is childless. The members of the war sorcery branch of the clan continue to support the claims of Kaputsi, that one of his sons should become the next peace chief. Confronted with this challenge, Auange and Peto have been arguing on my last two visits that the knife should perhaps be given to Misa's second eldest son, Angopo, rather than allowing it to pass to Kuku, Kaputsi's eldest son. In the context of these discussions between members of the peace chief and war sorcery branches of the clan, people were raising the old issue that both I and the current assistant string-giver, Peto, have not passed onto them the war sorcery previously held by Ito which is rightfully theirs, and of course Peto claims, as do I, that as far as he knows, Ito carried that knowledge to his grave.

Conclusion

As with prior analyses of chiefly systems elsewhere in the Pacific, this case study illustrates the importance of candidates' performative achievements as necessary conditions of succession to presumably ascribed chiefly positions. The narrative also illustrates the inherent contradictions of genealogical seniority informing, for example, Aueke's and Peto's claims to the clan's peace chieftainship. However, at numerous junctures, these materials demonstrate that even the expressed ideal of ascription in terms of genealogical seniority, patrilineality and primogeniture hinges on the complex, extended interpersonal exchanges which pretenders to high office affect in relation to both their predecessors and their constituents. To this extent, my analysis of North Mekeo chiefly inheritance follows Godelier's model of the Melansian great man, wherein patterns of leadership are tied to particular structures of exchange. However, the sorts of exchanges implicated in the transactions of North Mekeo Akaisa Men and their successors are premised on distinct notions of personal partibility and elicitation, so that the items transacted are viewed as parts of the persons involved. To this extent, therefore, the dynamics of North Mekeo chiefly succession and agency diverge from the model of exchange which Godelier has employed with the Baruya and are closer to the kinds of sociality which have been hypothesized to underlie the non-chiefly seemingly achievement based systems of the rest of Melanesia.

Rather than assume, as many have for chiefdoms elsewhere, that these complications arise among from a combination of ascription and achievement criteria of succession, or from some compromise between ideal rules and contingent necessities, I suggest that there are at play here fundamentally different notions of personhood and agency. Long-standing debates over Pacific leadership in terms of achievement and ascription have relied on exogenous notions of bounded persons and the corollary Euro-centric distinction between subjects and objects. In the case of North Mekeo chiefly succession, however, the various elements of Akaisa Man status, as well as the items of exchange that are given in reciprocation for them, can be seen more accurately as particulate and detachable elements of the persons and relations who transact them. Consequently, the seeming empirical 'deviations' from idealized rules of succession that commentators have consistently reported, as well as the admixtures of opposed ascriptive and achievement criteria, no longer appear as such; they are intrinsically systemic. Even in supposedly patrilineal systems like North Mekeo where primogeniture is expressly valued, first-born sons of chiefs must engage in the same sorts of *ngafengafe* elicitations as subsequent born or adoptive brothers. In this view, 'ascription' *is* 'achievement', and vice-versa.

The extended case study of Akaifu clan also illustrates that the process of chiefly succession involves a much wider field of interpersonal transaction than just the relation of predecessor and successor. Also included are relations of office holders and rivals to succession to other persons within the clan, living and dead, their formal feast exchange partners in other clans, the deity Akaisa, and at certain junctures even the inquisitive ethnographer.

If the North Mekeo case proves not to be unique, this analysis may constitute an important advance for Pacific ethnology in more than one respect, for it implies, on one hand, that systems which have been radically contrasted with one another in previous typologies may actually operate according a common mode of sociality and can thus be construed as more closely akin to one another than was previously imagined. On the other hand, this analysis points to the new expansion of the New Melanesian Ethnography itself; that is, in her own epitomizing accounts of Melanesian sociality, Strathern (1988, 1991) has restricted her horizon to supposedly non-chiefly relations and contexts, thereby leaving unexamined the implications that her model of personal partibility and elicitation might have for the leadership dynamics supposedly characteristic of the large remainder of Oceania.

This leads to one final consideration: if the conventional definitions of Pacific chieftainship have relied so heavily on the notion of ascription, what does it imply about the nature of chiefly leadership forms once that criterion is removed? Perhaps without ascription, we do not have 'chiefs' in the Pacific at least as we have long envisioned them.

Acknowledgements

This essay is based upon forty-six months of ethnographic fieldwork conducted among North Mekeo over the past thirty-seven years. Numerous funding agencies have generously supported this endeavour, including the National Institute for General Medical Sciences, the National Institutes of Health, the Wenner-Gren Foundation for Anthropological Research, the Hartwick College Board of Trustees, the National Institute for the Humanities, Auckland University Research Committee, the Marsden Fund of the Royal Society of New Zealand, the Australian Research Council, and the Research School of Pacific and Asian Studies at the Australian National University. Earlier versions of this essay were presented at a workshop, 'Making Rights in Indigenous Property "Self-evident" in Regimes of Inheritance', at Cambridge University in 2001, at the 2002 Vienna meetings of the European Society of Oceanists in Vienna, at the 2002 Canberra meetings of Australian Anthropological Society, and at a 2004 seminar at Academia Sinica in Taipei. I am grateful to the many colleagues who have offered their comments and criticisms. Many North Mekeo villagers, living and dead, including those named in this essay, have given of their knowledge and expertise merely from their *ngafengafe* kindness, creating debts which I can never repay. In this regard, Kaiva Muniapu, Pafifi Menga, Ameaua Wangu'u, Mariano Peniamo, Adolo Mangemange and Martin Ae deserve special acknowledgement. I, however, am solely responsible for all deficiencies contained herein.

Notes

1. Some of the authoritative anthropological statements on big man, chiefly and great man societies in the Pacific include Sahlins (1963), Goldman (1970), Douglas (1979), Allen (1984), Godelier (1986), Marcus (1989), Godelier and Strathern (1991), Feinberg and Watson-Gegeo (1996), White and Lindstrom (1997), and Scaglion (1998). Several of these will be discussed in the course of this chapter.

2. Space allows me to merely note that elsewhere I have explored this precise juxtaposition between subtractively vs. expansively effective chiefs in a critique of Sahlins's (1981, 1985, 1991) recent analyses of Polynesian chieftains as 'divine kings' in accordance with the structuralist principles of Dumontian hierarchy; see Mosko (1992, 1995).

3. It is not my intention to critique Godelier's formulation of the differences between great man and big man societies as alternate modes of affinal exchange and initiation, which I have addressed elsewhere from a somewhat different perspective from the one I adopt here; see Mosko (1991).

4. This is not to imply that Mekeo chiefly practices and functions have not changed over the past century. I have elsewhere (Mosko 1999, 2005, 2009) argued that the system of chiefly authority observed by the earliest European arrivals, including Seligmann, had already been greatly transformed over preceding decades as a consequence of depopulation arising from introduced epidemics and various policies of early colonial domination (cf. Stephen 1974; Bergendorff 1996). The specific contribution of chiefly agency and exchange dynamics to processes of Mekeo historical change and transformation, however, lies beyond the bounds of this chapter, but fine-grained analyses of the dynamics of North Mekeo personal agency in contexts of change are examined in recent works (Mosko 1999, 2002, 2007, forthcoming).

5. These transactions of *iunge fanga* compare with analogous rituals concerning the entitlements and agency of chiefly personages in Micronesia and Polynesia, as for example in kava ceremonies (e.g. Leach 1972; Toren 1989). The novel implication of this analysis, based on the model of Melanesian personal partibility and sociality, is that people not only receive the life-giving powers of the deities through their chiefs but they are also made vulnerable through the ingestion of chiefs' ritual detachments to the death-dealing powers of the gods.

6. North Mekeo sibling classification conforms closely with generational Hawaiian terminology, so that all men of a given generation within a clan are 'elder/younger brothers' (*anga/atsina*) to one another and classificatory 'fathers' (*ama*) to one another's offspring; see Mosko (1985: chap. 6).
7. The clan, village and personal identities that appear in the following narrative are pseudonyms.
8. According to Sacred Heart mission genealogies extending back another four generations, these two patrilines did not emerge from a single male source. This is a situation altogether typical of the composition of North Mekeo clans (*ikupu*). Most residential clan groups are composed of several patrilineage (*ikupu*) units, distinguished according to specialized ritual *au akaisa* functions as described above, but which do not link up genealogically by remembered connections to a single male ancestor.
9. Early in the present century, Mekeo peoples were converted to Catholicism; see Stephen (1974) and Mosko (2001, forthcoming).

Bibliography

Allen, M. 1984. 'Elders, Chiefs and Big Men: Authority, Legitimation and Political Evolution in Melanesia', *American Ethnologist* 11: 20–41.

Bakel, M. van. 1986. 'Samoa: Leadership between Ascribed and Achieved', in M. van Bakel, R. Hagensteijn and P. van de Velde (eds), *Private Politics: A Multi-disciplinary Approach to 'Big-man' Systems*. Leiden: Brill, p.96–104.

Bergendorff, S. 1996. *Faingu City: A Modern Clan in Papua New Guinea*. Lund: Lund University Press.

Biersack, A. 1982. 'Tongan Exchange Structures: Beyond Descent and Alliance', *Journal of the Polynesian Society* 91: 181–212.

Bowden, R. 1979. 'Tapu and Mana: Ritual Authority and Political Power in Traditional Maori Society', *Journal of Pacific History* 14: 50–61.

Douglas, B. 1979. 'Rank, Power, Authority: A Reassessment of Traditional Leadership in South Pacific Societies', *Journal of Pacific History* 14: 2–27.

Feinberg, R. and K. Watson-Gegeo (eds). 1996. *Leadership and Change in the Western Pacific*. New York: Athlone Press.

Firth, R. 1940. 'The Analysis of Mana: An Empirical Approach', *Journal of the Polynesian Society* 49: 483–510.

——— 1964. 'Succession to Chieftainship in Tikopia', in R. Firth, *Essays on Social Organization and Values*. New York: Athlone Press, p.145–70.

Gell, A. 1998. *Art and Agency: An Anthropological Theory*. Oxford: Clarendon Press.

Godelier, M. 1986. *The Making of Great Men: Male Domination and Power among the New Guinea Baruya*. Cambridge, Paris: Cambridge University Press, Maison des Sciences de l'Homme.

——— 1991. 'An Unfinished Attempt at Reconstructing the Social Processes which May Have Prompted the Transformation of Great-men Societies into Big-men Societies', in M. Godelier and M. Strathern (eds), *Big Men and Great men: Personifications of Power in* the Pacific. Cambridge, Paris: Cambridge University Press, Editions de la Maison de Sciences de l'Homme, p.275–304.

—— and M. Strathern (eds). 1991. *Big Men and Great Men: Personifications of Power in Melanesia*. Cambridge and Paris: Cambridge University Press, and Editions de la Maison des Sciences de l'Homme.

Goldman, I. 1970. *Ancient Polynesian Society*. Chicago: University of Chicago Press.

Goody, J. 1966. 'Introduction', in J. Goody (ed.), *Succession to High Office*. Cambridge Papers in Social Anthropology No. 4, 1–56. Cambridge: Cambridge University Press, p.275–304.

Guis, J. 1936. *La Vie des Papous*. Paris: Dillen.

Guo, P. 2004. 'Rethinking Ascribed/Achieved Status: Hierarchy and Egality in Oral Histories among Langalanga, Solomon Islands', presented at 18th conference of The International Association of Historians of Asia, Taipei.

Hau'ofa, E. 1971. 'Mekeo Chieftainship', *Journal of the Polynesian Society* 80: 152–69.

—— 1981. *Mekeo: Inequality and Ambivalence in a Village Society*. Canberra: Australian National University Press.

Hirsch, E. 1995. 'The "Holding Together" of Ritual: Ancestrality and Achievement in the Papua Highlands', in D. de Coppet and A. Iteanu (eds), *Cosmos and Society in Oceania*. London: Berg, p.213–34.

Hocart, A.M. 1927. *Kingship*. London: Oxford University Press.

Hooper, A. and J. Huntsman. 1996. *Tokelau: A Historical Ethnography*. Auckland: Auckland University Press.

Hooper, S. 1996. 'Who Are the Chiefs? Chieftainship in Lau, Eastern Fiji', in R. Feinberg and K. Watson-Gegeo (eds), *Leadership and Change in the Western Pacific: Essays Presented to Sir Raymond Firth on the Occasion of His Ninetieth Birthday*. London: Athlone, p.239–71.

Howard, A. 1966. 'The Rotuman District Chief: A Study in Changing Patterns of Authority', *Journal of Pacific History* 1: 63–78.

Jolly, M. 1987. 'The Chimera of Equality in Melanesia', *Mankind* 17: 168–83.

Josephides, L. 1991. 'Metaphors, Metathemes, and the Construction of Sociality: A Critique of the New Melanesian Ethnography', *Man* (n.s.) 26: 145–61.

Kaeppler, A. 1971. 'Rank in Tonga', *Ethnology* 10: 174–93.

Kawai, T. (ed.). 1998. *Chieftainships in Southern Oceania: Continuity and Change*. Hyogo, Japan: Japan-Oceania Society for Cultural Exchanges.

Keesing, R. 1984. 'Rethinking Mana', *Journal of Anthropological Research* 40: 137–56.

Kirch, P. 1984. *The Evolution of Polynesian Chiefdoms*, Cambridge: Cambridge University Press.

Leach, E. 1972. 'The Structure of Symbolism', in J. La Fontaine (ed.), *The Interpretation of Ritual: Essays in Honour of A. I. Richards*. London: Tavistock, p.239–84.

Lindstrom, M. and G. White (eds). 1997. *Chiefs Today: Traditional Pacific leadership and the Postcolonial State*. Stanford: Stanford University Press.

Linnekin, J. 1990. *Sacred Queens and Women of Consequence: Rank, Gender and Colonialism in the Hawaiian Islands*. Ann Arbor: University of Michigan Press.

Marcus, G. 1989. 'Chieftainship', in A. Howard and R. Borofsky (eds.), *Developments in Polynesian Ethnology*. Honolulu: University of Hawai'i Press, p.175–209.

Meggitt, M. 1967. 'The Pattern of Leadership among the Mae-Enga of New Guinea', *Anthropological Forum* 2(1): 20–35.

Malinowski, B. 1932. *The Sexual Life of Savages*. London: Routledge and Kegan Paul.

Monsell-Davis, M. 1981. 'Nabuapaka'. PhD dissertation, Sydney: Department of Anthropology, Macquarie University.

Mosko, M. 1985. *Quadripartite Structures: Categories, Relations and Homologies in Bush Mekeo Culture*. Cambridge: Cambridge University Press.

———— 1991 'Great Men and Total Systems: Hereditary Authority and Social Reproduction among the North Mekeo', in M. Godelier and M. Strathern (eds.), *Big Men and Great Men: Personifications of Power in Melanesia*. Cambridge and Paris: Cambridge University Press, and Editions de la Maison des Sciences de l'Homme, p.97–114.

———— 1992. 'Motherless Sons: "Divine Kings" and "Partible Persons" in Melanesia and Polynesia', *Man* (n.s.) 27: 697–717.

———— 1994. 'Junior Chiefs and Senior Sorcerers', in M. Jolly and M. Mosko (eds.), *Transformations of Hierarchy: Structure, History and Horizon in the Austronesian World. History and Anthropology* (special edition) 7: 195–222.

———— 1995. 'Rethinking Trobriand Chieftainship', *Journal of the Royal Anthropological Institute* (n.s.) 1: 763–85.

———— 1999. 'Magical Money: Commoditization and the Linkage of Maketsi ("Market") and Kangakanga ("Custom") in Contemporary North Mekeo', in D. Akin and J. Robbins (eds.), *Money and Modernity: State and Socal Currencies in Melanesia*. ASAO Monograph, Pittsburgh: University of Pittsburgh Press, p.41–61.

———— 2001. 'Syncretic Persons: Sociality, Agency and Personhood in Recent Charismatic Ritual Practices among North Mekeo (PNG)', in J. Gordon and F. Magowan (eds), *Beyond Syncretism. The Australian Journal of Anthropology* (special edition) 12: 259–76.

———— 2002. 'Totem and Transaction: The Objectification of "Tradition" among North Mekeo', *Oceania* 73: 89–109.

———— 2005. 'Peace, War, Sex and Sorcery: The Escalation of Chiefly Authority and Sorcery in Early North Mekeo Contact History', in M. Mosko and F. Damon (eds), *On the Order of Chaos: Social Anthropological Theory and the Science of Chaos*. New York: Berghahn Books, p.166–205.

———— 2007. 'Fashion as Fetish: The Agency of Modern Clothing and Traditional Body Decoration among North Mekeo of Papua New Guinea', *The Contemporary Pacific* 19: 39–83.

———— 2009. 'Black Powder, White Magic: European Armaments and Sorcery in Early Mekeo-Roro encounters', in M. Jolly, S. Tcherkézoff and D. Tryon (eds), *Oceanic encounters: Exchange, desire, violence.* Canberra, Australian National University E-Press, p.259–94.

——— Forthcoming. *Gifts that Change: Personal Partibility, Agency and Religion in a Changing Melanesian Society.* New York: Berghahn Books.

Panoff, M. 1965. 'La Terminologie de la Parente en Polynesie: Essai d'Analyse Formelle', *L'Homme* 3: 60–87.

Peterson, G. 1999. 'Sociopolitical Rank and Conical Clanship in the Caroline Islands', *Journal of the Polynesian Society* 108: 367–410.

Powell, H. 1960. 'Competitive Leadership in Trobriand Political Organisation', *Journal of the Royal Anthropological Institute* 90: 118–45.

Sahlins, M. 1958. *Social Stratification in Polynesia.* Seattle: University of Washington Press.

——— 1963. 'Poor Man, Rich Man, Big Man, Chief: Political Types in Melanesia and Polynesia', *Comparative Studies in Society and History* 5: 285–303.

——— 1981. *Historical Metaphors and Mythical Realities: Structure in the Early History of the Sandwich Islands Kingdom.* Ann Arbor: University of Michigan Press.

——— 1985. *Islands of History.* Chicago: University of Chicago Press.

——— 1991. 'Return of the Event Again: With Reflections on the Great Fijian War of 1843 to 1855 between the Kingdoms of Bau and Rewa', in A. Biersack (ed.), *Clio in Oceania: Toward a Historical Anthropology.* Washington, DC: Smithsonian Institution Press, p.37–100.

Scaglion, R. 1998. 'Chiefly Models in Papua New Guinea', *The Contemporary Pacific* 8(1): 1–33.

Seligmann, C. 1910. *The Melanesians of British New Guinea.* Cambridge: Cambridge University Press.

Shore, B. 1989. 'Mana and Tapu', in A. Howard and R. Borofsky (eds), *Developments in Polynesian Ethnology.* Honolulu: University of Hawai'i Press, p.137–73.

Stephen, M. 1974. 'Continuity and Change in Mekeo Society 1890–1971', PhD dissertation, Canberra: Research School of Pacific Studies, Australian National University.

——— 1995. *The Gifts of A'aisa.* Berkeley: University of California Press.

Strathern, A. 1982. 'Two Waves of African Models in the New Guinea Highlands', in A. Strathern (ed.), *Inequality in New Guinea Highlands Societies.* Cambridge: Cambridge University Press, p.35–49.

Strathern, M. 1988. *The Gender of the Gift: Problems with Women and Problems with Society in Melanesia.* Berkeley: University of California Press.

Tcherkézoff, S. 2000. 'The Samoan Category Matai ("chief"): A Singularity in Polynesia? Historical and Ethnological Comparative Queries', *Journal of the Polynesian Society* 109: 151–90.

Thomas, N. 1989. 'The Force of Ethnology: Origins and Significance of the Melanesia/Polynesia Division', *Current Anthropology* 30: 27–34.

Toren, C. 1989. 'Drinking Cash: The Purification of Money through Ceremonial Exchange in Fiji', in M. Bloch and J. Parry (eds), *Money and the Morality of Exchange*. Cambridge: Cambridge University Press, p.142–64.

———— 1999. '"All Things Go in Pairs, or the Shark Will Bite": The Antithetical Nature of Fijian Chieftainship', in C. Toren, *Mind, Materiality and History: Explorations of Fijian Ethnography*. London: Routledge, p.163–81.

Wagner, R. 1986. *Asiwinarong*. Princeton: Princeton University Press.

———— 1991. 'The Fractal Person', in M. Godelier and M. Strathern (eds), *Big Men and Great Men: Personifications of Power in Melanesia*. Cambridge and Paris Cambridge University Press, and Editions de la Maison des Sciences de l'Homme, p.159–73.

Walter, M. 1974. 'Succession in East Fiji: Institutional Disjunction as a Source of Political Dynamism in an Ascription-oriented Society', *Oceania* 44: 301–22.

———— 1978. 'An Examination of Hierarchical Notions in Fijian society: A Test Case for the Applicability of the Term "Chief"', *Oceania* 49: 1–19.

Weiner A. 1976. *Women of Value, Men of Renown*. Austin: University of Texas Press.

———— 1988. *The Trobrianders of Papua New Guinea*. New York: Holt, Rinehart and Winston.

White, G. and L. Lindstrom (eds). 1997. *Chiefs Today: Traditional Pacific Leadership and the Postcolonial State*. Palo Alto: Stanford University Press.

Chapter 7

WHAT IS LEFT OUT IN KINSHIP

Robert H. Barnes

Godelier's extensive survey of metamorphoses of kinship broaches many issues of recent topicality, yet also addresses many topics for which there is a long anthropological lineage (Godelier 2004). I have tried to present a reasonably representative summary of his views accessible to Anglophone readers (Barnes 2006). Inevitably there were some matters which had to be left aside simply because the space available dictated that some selection be made. I think one or two of these points deserve reverting to, and would like to discuss them briefly in the following. In particular I would like to consider some loose points in our understanding of descent and of classification, surely two central topics in the history of the subject.

Terms such as descent, descent group, marriage, alliance, corporations and so on with which we discuss kinship have been offered many definitions. Whatever the intrinsic merits of individual definitions are, the fact is that the various definitions are incompatible among themselves. More important is that any given definition defines its own field of relevance. Societies with descent groups are those societies which have groups which fit a specific definition of descent groups. The value of any given definition depends on its purpose and the degree to which it helps to achieve that purpose. What is more, given the great variety which exists in approaches by societies to each of the topics listed above, any definition also defines a large field of irrelevance. The question not often addressed which arises implicitly is what is to be done with societies that lack the feature in question? The obvious and easy answer is to use other methods than those suited for the given topic. For societies which lack marriage alliance, do not use the methods appropriate for studying marriage alliance. But what do we do with examples of societies which have, for example, descent groups by one definition, but lack them by another? And in general why should we feel sure that societies which lack, say, descent groups are uninteresting for that reason?

That puzzle has always struck me when I have thought of the following comment by Radcliffe-Brown (1952: 48): 'Unilineal institutions in some form, are almost, if not entirely, a necessity in any ordered social system.' This necessity derived from two sociological laws, which were, 'the need for a formulation of rights over persons and things sufficiently precise in their general recognition as to avoid as far as possible unresolved conflicts'; and 'the need for continuity of the social structure as a system of relations between persons, such relations being definable in terms of rights and duties'. Further, 'If any society establishes a system of corporations on the basis of kinship – clans, joint-families, incorporated lineages – it must necessarily adopt a system of unilineal reckoning of succession' (Radcliffe-Brown 1952: 46–47). These views represent Radcliffe-Brown's explicit positivism, in which he emulated Durkheim, and today are not accepted by many, perhaps most, anthropologists, although there will always be those who wish to argue for the relevance of scientific method to the social sciences.

Radcliffe-Brown conceded that these laws may be truisms. The problem is, however, that they are neither laws nor true. Radcliffe-Brown's definition of a corporation (1952: 45) is reasonably comprehensive: 'A corporation is here defined as a collection of persons who jointly exercise some right or rights.' Using figures taken from Roger Keesing, Godelier (2004: 115) estimated that forty-five per cent of societies had patrilineal groups, twelve per cent matrilineal groups, four per cent an arrangement of double unilineal descent, and thirty-nine per cent were cognatic in some way without unilineal groups. These figures in fact derive from the World Ethnographic Sample (Aberle 1961: 663). There are always difficulties about what units count as a society for comparative statistical purposes, but these results suggest that Radcliffe-Brown's generalization may not stand up. Of course the question remains as to whether any of the examples in the thirty-nine per cent of the sample in the cognatic category form a system of non-unilineal corporations on the basis of kinship. In a well known article Firth (1957) observed that in most Polynesian societies descent groups are not unilineal. In any case, if the figures are truly representative they, as well as Firth's examples, demonstrate that unilineal institutions are not necessary. Why therefore should non-unilineal groups be of no interest?

In reaction to a tradition deriving from Radcliffe-Brown and continued by Fortes, Kuper (1982: 92) asserted startlingly that 'there do not appear to be any societies in which vital political or economic activities are organized by a repetitive series of descent groups'. Of course this conclusion comes at the end of a detailed argument, but depending upon what it means, it does appear to be contradicted by a considerable body of ethnographic literature. I do not know how to reconcile it with knowledge of the workings of descent groups in three sites of intensive field research in eastern Indonesia, where named patrilineal descent groups come together, to varying extent, for political or economic purposes. That is to say that I do not see what are the operative words in Kuper's statement which by some shoving and pushing would permit apparent counter examples to be accommodated.

In the 1950s Fortes (1953: 25) told an American audience that 'the most important feature of unilineal descent groups in Africa brought into focus by recent field research is their corporate organization'. This is a rather odd statement in a summary of work which certainly includes that of Evans-Pritchard on the Nuer. In his book about them and in an article included in a collection which he co-edited with Fortes, he plainly stated that 'Nuer lineages are not corporate, localized, communities' and 'clans and their lineages are not distinct corporate groups, but are embodied in local communities' (Evans-Pritchard 1940a: 203, 1940b: 286–87). Smith (1956: 60) thought that even though Evans-Pritchard (1940a: 264) said that Nuer clans 'and even their lineages have no corporate life', he nevertheless recognized their conceptually corporate nature, but I cannot find the evidence on which Smith bases this conclusion.

It is true that he did say (1951: 5) that 'the lineages of Nuerland are dispersed groups, though in a certain sense they may be regarded as corporate groups in the form they take as political segments in fusion with other elements', but this statement is not a fundamental revision of his view that the lineages are not corporations. Thus, they lack a leader, for example. Oddly Holy (1996: 88–89) accused Evans-Pritchard of seeing Nuer lineages as corporations and listed among his errors 'ascribing corporateness to what are empirically ... only categories of people'. As evidence that these were Evans-Pritchard's views, he cited only Fortes.

Goody (1961: 5) surveys a series of criteria which might be used to define corporate groups, namely the presence of a leader (in a hierarchical system of authority), ownership and transmission of property, physical proximity, and periodic assembly. Goody chooses to regard unilineal descent groups as corporate if they are vested with rights in material property which is inherited. This criterion poses an immediate problem because it may well be that the only property that such a group owns is rights over a specific ritual or myth. Or perhaps not even that: Turton (1980: 73) states that Mursi descent groups only exist by virtue of claims on the distribution of bridewealth. Goody defines descent as concerning eligibility for membership in kin groups. He also requires that there be a general term in the language for such groups or that they be named. Whichever of these criteria is selected or whatever combination of them, each choice will produce a different set of societies with and without corporate descent groups. Goody (1961: 10) noted that:

> When we include within the category 'double descent' all those systems which have some kind of descent group, however minimal its functions, based upon both lines of descent, then the societies brought together under this head have little or nothing in common but this fact alone

His wish to limit 'double descent' to systems in which 'both descent groups are corporate, that is, in which "double clanship" is accompanied by "double inheritance"', is justified by the excuse that he wishes to define analytically useful categories. Such a desire may be justified if it achieves a specific, clearly stated purpose, but it is difficult to see why this or a similar definition would be analytically useful generally for comparative studies (cf. Barnes 1980: 116). The question must arise of what becomes of the systems defined out of relevance? What is their analytic status? Goody concludes by providing a classification of societies which have previously been deemed to have double descent according to whether they fit his definition or deviate from it in certain specific ways. To that extent the classification is convenient and useful, although possibly it would not serve much purpose to extend it. However, its analytic contribution could have been achieved without insisting on any specific general definition.

Dumont (1971: 83) observed that Fortes argued that in the last analysis all unilineal groups are corporations and characterized Talensi lineages as corporations on the simple fact of their observed segmentary opposition, in contrast to Evans-Pritchard. The issue Dumont said was whether society is made up of groups or relations, that is whether anthropology is to be substantialist, as he saw was the predominant trend of British anthropology of his day, or structuralist. The problem was not in recognizing that groups act in unity when and if they do, but in characterizing groups as moral persons (corporations) which never do. Although he recognized

Goody as significantly deviating from the tradition leading from Rivers to Fortes by insisting on simply the transmission of property within groups, he saw them as representing two steps in the same movement toward a view of the group independent of its ties to the exterior, a triumph of the Hegelian individual, as he put it (Dumont 1971: 83–85).

The illustrious set of anthropologists that *Current Anthropology* invited to comment on Goody's article showed no sign of accepting Goody's definitions as their own or of agreeing among themselves. Fischer (1961: 14), for example, wanted to distinguish between double descent systems with and those without corporate groups, and Bulmer (1961: 13) refused to accept the criterion of corporateness based on property-holding and commented, 'does not this criterion suggest, for example, that since the Nuer lineage is not corporate it is not particularly important?' De Josselin de Jong (1961: 14), in keeping with the tradition of the Leiden School, wished to employ a definition of double descent that did not even require the presence of groups, corporate or otherwise. I tried to respond to Leach's suggestion that 'we think again about the relationship between "corporateness" and "descent"' (Leach 1957: 54, 1961: 122), by examining the considerable variety of descent arrangements in a region of eastern Indonesia (Barnes 1980). I concluded, at least for the sample I looked at, that there was no clear comparative tie between functions and the principles that constituted groups and that it was not clear why descent groups needed to maintain exclusive corporate boundaries (1980: 117). Perhaps we can echo a point Leach made about another institution and say that all universal definitions of descent groups are vain.

Davenport (1959: 558) suggested that we adopt the view that 'A rule of descent will be considered unilinear when ascription through a specified kin relationship approaches a frequency of 100 percent and when the norms of society do not under normal conditions provide alternatives'. This definition might be spoken of as analogue rather than digital in the jargon of computer science. It is a more specific version of Radcliffe-Brown's statement (1952: 39) that 'Where the rights and duties derived through the father preponderate in social importance over those derived through the mother we have what it is usual to call a patrilineal system'. It is notable that the definition makes no explicit reference to indigenous interpretations or norms, although Davenport did include the caveat, 'when the norms of the society do not under normal conditions provide alternatives'. Moreover it leaves us with no clear way of determining what frequency is sufficient to judge whether it approaches 100 per cent. For comparative purposes it is of not much use. Various

authors have questioned whether we can estimate relative strength
of descent groups for comparison (e.g. Buchler 1966: 40; McKinley
1971: 238–39; Needham 1971: 8).

A late convert to Fortesian views, Scheffler has introduced a
new set of definitional criteria. He agrees with Fortes in regarding
a rule of descent as not the relation of filiation between parent
and child, but a relation to antecedents prior to the parent in
question – a point which has not provoked much disagreement in
the English-speaking world. Furthermore, he accepts the tradition,
of which Fortes is a representative, which sees the term 'descent
group' as appropriately applied only to groups constituted by a
unilineal rule, which of course has been controversial. He also
distinguishes three forms of filiation, depending on whether the
filiation is necessary and sufficient, necessary but not sufficient,
or sufficient but not necessary. In addition, there are three further
possibilities depending upon whether descent is without regard to
sex of the parent, patrifiliation or matrifiliation. Multiplying the
two sets of possibilities reveals nine logical possibilities. He makes
the further reasonable observation that the different possibilities
have systematically different implications for the groups they may
constitute and that 'any attempt to generalize across the board
about such groups as equally patrilineal descent groups is bound to
prove unproductive'. Thus, and again I am in agreement, various
attempts to apply beyond Africa the model of segmentary descent
that is deemed to derive from Africa have been misconceived from
the beginning because there never was such a model (Scheffler
2001: x-xii). However, Scheffler still thinks that there are correct
definitions of descent and descent groups. What I cannot discern is
what problem he thinks is best addressed by using his definitions.
Without an achievable explanatory goal and procedure, we are
left with a squabble of competing definitions. Scheffler (2001: 55)
observes that 'There are many different kinds of jural collectivity'.
In fact there are actually many different kinds of collectivity. Why
one type, say corporate descent groups, is more important for
understanding than another lacks any convincing explanation.

There is after all no 'true' definition of descent. None of the
empirical examples we know of is any less true or interesting
than any other. Most definitions of descent that have been offered
can be buttressed with known examples. The problem is not that
anthropologists have not known about the variety. Most have taken
it as a starting point in their deliberations. But most seem not to have
accepted that the variety is in fact the message.[1] My view here of
course is closest to that of Leach (1961: 4) and Needham (1971:
8–13). We have no evidence to conclude that societies with corporate

descent groups as defined by Goody or anyone else represents either a stage toward which all other societies are tending or one from which they are changing. A century and a half of evolutionary speculation has produced no confidence in any evolutionary scheme for the development of systems of descent. It is true that evolutionary thought reappears in surprising places (Needham 1967: 44–48; Lévi-Strauss 1949: 275–77). Plausible arguments are not the same thing as certain ones.

Even Leach (1962: 130–31) subscribed to the view that we should follow Rivers (1924: 86) and restrict the phrase 'descent groups' to unilineal institutions where membership is 'determined permanently and without option by the circumstances of birth'. Where 'descent does not in itself specify who is or who is not a member of any particular group, it is ... misleading to describe the operative corporations as "descent groups"'. The same view was endorsed by Louis Dumont (1961: 25), who wished 'to restrict "descent" to what is in fact its most frequent use, i.e., membership in an exogamous group'. His purpose, however, was not specifically comparative but to facilitate dialogue between 'descent theorists' and 'alliance theorists', i.e. to bridge a disagreement within British anthropology at the time. Leach's argument was that such a definition ensures that an individual has no option about membership and that groups are discrete and non-overlapping. Both Forde (1963: 12–13) and Firth (1963) showed, however, that the aim of establishing discrete corporations may be achieved by allowing descent to operate in combination with other factors. In this respect Southwold's comment is instructive that Ganda 'Clans, it might be said, recruit mainly by birth, but also by conversion' (Southwold 1971: 38).[2] If we had a secure evolutionary explanation of descent groups, we might be able to argue that discrete groups as defined by Leach offer an evolutionary advantage. In a survey of eastern Indonesian cultures (Barnes 1980: 98), I found that 'Some cultures ... allow a variety of ways to ensure perpetuation, and in some cases they result in alternative forms of social organization within the same society'. Maine's generalization that corporations never die reveals itself in eastern Indonesia as an aspiration which can too easily fail, as I have been able to document in respect of several named descent groups which have disappeared. From this circumstance I concluded that Maine's view might be inverted and that we might instead recognize that corporations are always concerned with the risk of dying. Hence societies which restrict themselves to exclusive unilineal institutions may be the most difficult to explain, that is to say the most in need of explanation. It is not clear in fact why descent groups should maintain exclusive corporate boundaries; and yet in some societies they do.

We do not even have a clear idea of what societies cannot do in respect of applying rules of descent. Certainly we have nothing like a proven set of causal connections which lead to one outcome rather than another. It is almost certain that anything that can be shown to have been achieved by an arrangement of exclusive descent groups in Rivers's sense and that of Leach can be and has been achieved by other non-exclusive arrangements. When Needham (1971: 8–13) suggested that we look away from substantive concentration on complexes of rights and look instead at the logically possible rules of descent, he was shifting away from the tradition which associates descent firmly with group membership. Descent in his usage simply means rules of transmission, regardless of application. He is well to note that this approach is without regard to social feasibility or known realization, since two of the possibilities have been shown, at least on the evidence available to date, not to be empirically exemplified, at least in respect of descent group formation. Indeed two more formal rules have been proposed, equally without exemplification for the formation of descent groups (Barnes 2006: 333–36).

The Omaha of Nebraska have often been taken as an instructive case for exploring the relationship between descent groups and social classification, indeed one of the classic instances. Godelier (2004: 198) notes that there are some anthropologists who refuse to recognize Crow-Omaha systems as a separate type, and he is right about that. Needham (1971: 14) commented that nothing of any real elucidatory value has come out of the comparative attention to the 'Omaha' type: 'The reason is simply that a variety of terminologies all posses this supposedly definitive feature [the equation of mother's brother with mother's brother's son] but differ from each other in practically everything else'; 'Intensive analyses of individual "Omaha terminologies" have repeatedly confirmed the invalidity of the type'. I have tried to show that the terminology of the Omaha of Nebraska differs in significant respects from the terminology of the Samo of Upper Volta, which is now famous as an 'Omaha' terminology, and that the differences parallel significant differences in marriage rules (Barnes 1982: 116; see Héritier 1981). Since Héritier's work on the Samo, following Lévi-Strauss's speculations, has made 'Omaha' alliance a famous type in anthropology and since the Omaha do not have 'Omaha' alliance or anything like it, perhaps it is useful to repeat here the similarities and differences in marriage rules that I displayed in that earlier very obscurely placed publication.

Table 7.1. Samo – Omaha comparison.

SAMO	OMAHA
1. F's lineage (prohibited)	F's clan (prohibited)
2. M's lineage (prohibited)	M's clan (prohibited)
3. FM's lineage (prohibited)	FM's sub-clan (prohibited)
4. MM's lineage (prohibited)	MM's sub-clan (prohibited)
5. Any lineage from which a classificatory F has taken a wife (prohibited)	Doubtful, but to judge by unpublished information not practically true for the Omaha
6. FMM's lineage (permitted)	FMM's sub-clan (prohibited)
7. MMM's lineage (permitted)	MMM's sub-clan (prohibited)
8. Any lineage from which a classificatory B has taken a wife (prohibited)	Any sub-clan from which a classificatory B has taken a wife (permitted)
9. W's lineage (prohibited)	W's sub-clan (permitted and preferred)
10. WM's lineage (prohibited)	WM's sub-clan (permitted)
11. WFM's lineage (prohibited)	WFM's sub-clan (permitted)
12. WMM's lineage (prohibited)	WMM's sub-clan (permitted)

Thus except for the first four rules, the Samo differ in every one of the rules indicated in that table. There is a further Omaha series of prohibitions for which there is no Samo counterpart, involving lines traced through ego's junior relatives and children.

Godelier's discussion of terminologies begins with reference to a classic paper by A.L. Kroeber (1909) and proceeds via another important paper by Lowie (1928, 1948: 63) to expand a summary presentation by Murdock (1949: 223–24), who by the way leaves out 'Dravidian'. Kroeber wanted to undermine Morgan's distinction between classificatory and descriptive terminologies and provided a list of features by which terminologies are ordered (Morgan 1870: 12). We might paraphrase Kroeber by saying that all relationship terminologies are classificatory from someone's perspective and may also contain some descriptive terms, that the principles which order a given terminology are several and will therefore, given a limited number of terms, be to some degree in competition for expression in the terminology, that European terminologies express a smaller number of his list of features than do those of American Indian languages, and that sociological inferences from relationship terminologies must be subjected to extreme caution (Kroeber 1909: 83–84). Lowie (1928: 265) concluded from Kroeber that 'kinship terminologies are not so many coherent "systems" but are each founded on a variety of disparate principles, all of which must be enumerated for a complete definition' (see also Lowie 1917: 122). 'We shall ... do well to amend our phraseology and to speak rather of kinship categories, features, or principles of classification than of types of kinship systems' (Lowie 1917: 105, see Needham 1971: 17).

Godelier (2004: 213) follows Murdock in naming different 'types' after specific ethnic groups or regions. Hence we find the ancient Romans blessed with a 'Sudanese' terminology. His primary classification, including the horrendous jargon, is derived from Lowie. Where each kind of relative in the first ascending genealogical level is accorded a separate term the category is 'bifurcate collateral'. Where, for example, father's brother and father are called by the same term, but mother's brother is not (and similar arrangements for the other relatives), the category is 'bifurcate merging'. This form of arrangement is compatible, if carried through in lower levels, with a rule of lineage exogamy and is termed by Needham as 'lineal'. Where, as in English, father is called by a separate term, while father's brother and mother's brother are called by the same term (and similarly for mother, father's sister and mother's sister), the category is 'lineal', thus a completely different usage from Needham's. Where all relatives at that level and of the same sex are called by the same term, the category is 'generational'. The type of bifurcate collateral (as in ancient Rome) is 'Sudanese'. The type of lineal is 'Eskimo'. The type of generational is 'Hawaiian'. With bifurcate merging we encounter a difference suggesting there may be a problem in the classificatory works, for Godelier lists four types for this category, namely 'Australian', 'Dravidian', 'Iroquois' and 'Crow-Omaha'.

There is a great deal of academic history behind these categories and types, and Godelier did not invent them. But there are problems in the detail. The term 'Dravidian' is appropriate to the Tamil-speaking peoples of south Indian, to which Trautmann (1981) has given considerable attention. Its fame rests on the fact that it fits well with a marriage rule with the bilateral cross-cousin (the category which includes the mother's brother's son and father's sister's son for a woman or father's sister's daughter and the mother's brother's daughter for a man). Now Godelier ranges under this type those societies like the Kachin of Burma, who prohibit the father's sister's daughter for a man (mother's brother's son for a woman), but prescribe marriage to the category including the mother's brother's daughter (father's sister's son) and whose terminology fits this arrangement. For those who are concerned about the differences between these forms of terminology (and marriage alliance), the confusion is just as disturbing as the muddle, also present in the literature, between the latter form of terminology (asymmetric prescriptive as opposed to symmetric prescriptive) and the Omaha terminology (which has no marriage prescription) for no better reason than that many asymmetric terminologies, like the Omaha terminology, have equations that might be deemed appropriate for patrilineal descent (Barnes 1982: 116).

There is a terminological confusion in Godelier's *Métamorphoses de la parenté* concerning terminologies of asymmetric prescriptive marriage alliance, such as those of the Kachin of highland Burma, the Gilyak of Siberia, the Toba Batak of Sumatra, and others. Godelier classifies them not only as (1) asymmetric prescriptive, but also (2) Dravidian, (3) asymmetric Dravidian, (4) Kachin, and (5) Jingpaw (a language of one of the Kachin groups). The last two are merely ethnic or linguistic descriptions and require no comment. The third reveals the implicit assumption in Godelier's interpretation, namely that Dravidian terminologies prescribe marriage and that they come in two varieties, symmetric and asymmetric. Historically, however, the term 'Dravidian' has been reserved for the symmetric prescriptive terminologies of South India, and it is most unusual to say that asymmetric prescriptive terminologies are Dravidian. No such relationship terminology has been reported for Dravidian peoples.

Kryukov (1998: 308), on whom Godelier partly relies, says that Kachin terminology is normally considered to be of the Omaha type.[3] The true situation is the following. In both terminological features and in marriage rules the Kachin differ systematically in absolutely essential ways from the Omaha of Nebraska, who in both respects differ systematically from the Samo of Burkina-Faso, whom Godelier (2004: 191), following Héritier, speaks of as having a terminology of the Omaha type.[4] This terminological mess is only permitted by insisting on using the equations and distinctions of a single genealogical level or segment of the terminology for the classification of terminologies used throughout Godelier's book, instead of looking at the complete relationship terminologies and giving full consideration to the other social institutions that accompany them.[5]

Godelier (2004: 537) then refers in passing to speculation by Guermonprez (1993) that the asymmetric prescriptive terminologies of some eastern Indonesian peoples had been imposed on previous cognatic systems, thus in contradiction of Needham's evolutionary speculations mentioned above. Needham does not hold the field alone, and Guermonprez was preceded by Fox (1984–1985). However, having introduced the matter, Godelier might have given it more attention, because it is contrary to his own views on the direction of transformation of Dravidian systems. Fox does not postulate a prior cognatic system, as does Guermonprez, but argues instead that the resources of Austronesian languages, including a clear and consistent demarcation of generations, prominent use of gender in classification, and the use of age (elder versus younger as well as birth order), permit the development within a particular region of a great variety of systems from lineal to cognatic and prescriptive to non-prescriptive.

Godelier returns to relationship terminologies and declares that their transformations are irreversible and do not advance in the same direction (2004: 533). The idea is similar to a position taken by Needham (1967: 43–46) in an article to which Godelier alludes only indirectly. Godelier (2004: 533; 2007: 222–23) tells us that we know today that ancient China had a Dravidian terminology, although to judge by the information available to his two sources, that conclusion is far from being fully demonstrated and is undoubtedly unprovable. The principal evidence was adduced by Kryukov (1998: 297) and attributed by him to Granet (1930: 157), namely that the Chinese term *sheng* applied to FZS, MBS, WB, ZH.[6] The equations effected by this term are of course compatible with a system of bilateral cross-cousin marriage such as is found among people speaking Dravidian languages. However, such equations are also found in the absence of such a marriage rule. In the absence of further equations pointing in the same direction, as well as definite information about marriage regulations of the relevant period, we can only say that we do not know for sure that ancient China had such a marriage system. It remains only a speculative possibility. Godelier (2004: 534 n1) does as least acknowledge that Kryukov's speculation that the Latin terminology was also originally Dravidian suffers from the fact that there is absolutely no evidence that would either prove or disprove it (Kryukov 1998: 298).

Whatever the case may have been in the past, these views underline the fact that we lack clear and incontrovertible evidence that systems of descent or alliance follow a single sequence of development over time. Wherever we look our types are merely steps within a range of variation, and the closer we look the more detailed is the variation. The more willing we are to recognize the effects of human imagination, the less certain we must be that social institutions are the products of invariable social laws or that the true explanations are to be found in those variations which come closest to substantialist preconceptions of some trains of thought within the history of anthropology. Godelier (2007: 531) writes that a relationship terminology tells us nothing about the political, religious and economic relationships in a given society. Since, he claims, relationship terminologies do not change by themselves and do not evolve without reason, it is necessary at all costs to discover the forces and interests which lead members of a society to modify the rules that organize marriage and matrimonial alliances, that is to say the principles which organize descent, inheritance and transmission. Would that we could, but we usually lack the relevant historical knowledge which would reveal these forces. That these changes do take place, we know without any doubt. We also know, as indicated above by Godelier, that a given form of relationship terminology may be found in association with rather different political and economic arrangements. Godelier has done much to substantiate his claim that religion is among the strongest forces driving changes in terminology, marriage and descent. Even so, the history of evolutionary speculation in anthropology has never produced anything like certainty in our understanding of how and why such patterns change.

Notes

1. Needham (1971: 8) traced a tradition recommending a concentration on varieties of function rather than rule of descent from Fison in 1879 via Wake in 1889 to Lewis in 1965.
2. It must be added that Southwold also said that 'Ganda clans are not even putative descent groups'. From this statement we can form an idea of how he would define 'descent groups'.
3. See, for example, the table of types according to the presence or absence of specific terms for affines (Godelier 2004: 543) in which Dravidian appears in the absent column, while Crow-Omaha appears in the present column. This table is, at least, not compatible with Kryukov's usage.
4. See Barnes (1982: 115). Godelier (2004: 193, see also 188 and 539 n2) ranges the Omaha together with the Samo as practicing sister exchange. In fact the Omaha prohibit marriage with ZHZ, which precludes sister exchange, and in the Omaha genealogies recorded by Dorsey there are no examples of the exchange of sisters (Barnes 1982: 117).
5. My name appears in association with an article that employs the classification in question (Trautmann and Barnes 1993).
6. In fact Granet does not mention *sheng* in the place cited, nor have I found it elsewhere in the book (Granet 1929, 1930). Godelier (2004: 533 n3) attributes it to another publication by Granet (1939), but I have not located it there either. According to Kryukov, the term belongs to a vocabulary of the Erya dating to the first millenium BC, but in a vocabulary of the second century AD it had very different applications.

Bibliography

Aberle, David F. 1961. 'Matrilineal Descent in Cross-Cultural Perspective', in D.M. Schneider and K. Gough (eds), *Matrilineal Kinship*. Berkeley: University of California Press, p.655–730.

Barnes, R.H. 1980. 'Marriage, Exchange and the Meaning of Corporations in Eastern Indonesia', in J.L. Comaroff (ed.), *The Meaning of Marriage Payments*. London: Academic Press, p.93–124.

———— 1982. 'Kinship Exercises', *Culture* 2(2): 113–17.

———— 2006. 'Maurice Godelier and the Metamorphosis of Kinship: A Review Essay', *Comparative Studies in Society and History* 48(2): 326–58.

Buchler, I.R. 1966. 'Measuring the Development of Kinship Terminologies: Scalogram and Transformational Accounts of Omaha-type Systems', *Bijdragen tot de Taal-, Land- en Volkenkunde* 122(1): 36–63.

Bulmer, R. 1961. 'Comment', *Current Anthropology* 2(1): 13.

Davenport, W. 1959. 'Nonunilinear Descent and Descent Groups', *American Anthropologist* 61(4): 557–72.

Dumont, L. 1961. 'Descent, Filiation and Affinity', *Man* 61(11): 24–25.

——— 1971. *Introduction à deux théories d'anthropologie sociale: Groupes de filiation et alliance de marriage.* Paris, La Haye: Mouton.

Evans-Pritchard, E.E. 1940a. *The Nuer: A Description of the Modes of Livelihood and Political Institutions of a Nilotic People.* Oxford: Clarendon Press.

——— 1940b. 'The Nuer of the Southern Sudan', in M. Fortes and E.E. Evans-Pritchard (eds), *African Political Systems.* London: International Institute of African Languages & Cultures/Oxford University Press, p.272–96.

——— 1951. *Kinship and Marriage among the Nuer.* Oxford: Clarendon Press.

Firth, R. 1957. 'A Note on Descent Groups in Polynesia', *Man* 57(2): 4–8.

——— 1963. 'Bilateral Descent Groups: An Operational Viewpoint', in I. Shapera (ed.), *Studies in Kinship and Marriage.* London: Royal Anthropological Institute (Occasional Paper No. 16).

Fischer, H. Th. 1961. 'Comment', *Current Anthropology* 2(1): 13–14.

Forde, C.D. 1963. 'On Some Further Unconsidered Aspects of Descent', *Man* 63(9): 12–13.

Fortes, M. 1953. 'The Structure of Unilineal Descent Groups', *American Anthropologist* 55(1): 17–41.

Fox, J.J. 1984–1985. 'Possible Models of Early Austronesian Social Organization', *Asian Perspectives* 26(1): 36–43.

Godelier, M. 2004. *Métamorphoses de la parenté.* Paris: Fayard.

——— 2007. *Au fondement des sociétés humaines: ce que nous apprend l'anthropologie.* Paris: Bibliothèque Albin Michel.

Goody, Jack. 1961. 'The Classification of Double Descent Systems', *Current Anthropology* 2(1): 3–26.

Granet, M. 1929. *La Civilisation chinoise: la vie publique et la vie privée.* Paris: La Renaissance du Libre.

——— 1930. *Chinese Civilization.* London: Kegan Paul, Trench, Trubner.

——— 1939. *Catégories matrimoniales et relations de proximité dans la Chine ancienne.* Paris: Annales sociologiques série B, fasc. 1–3.

Guermonprez, J.-F. 1993. 'Transformations of Kinship Systems in Eastern Indonesia', in M. Godelier, T.R. Trautmann and F.E. Tjon Sie Fat (eds), *Transformations of Kinship.* Washington: Smithsonian Institute Press, p.271–93.

Héritier, F. 1981. *L'Exercice de la parenté.* Paris: Gallimard.

Holy, L. 1996. *Anthropological Perspectives on Kinship.* London: Pluto Press.

Josselin de Jong, P.E. de. 1961. 'Comment', *Current Anthropology* 2(1): 14.

Kroeber, A.L. 1909. 'Classificatory Systems of Relationship', *Journal of the Royal Anthropological Institute of Great Britain and Ireland* 39(1): 11–22.

Kryukov, M.V. 1998. 'The Synchro-Diachronic Method and the Multi-directionality of Kinship Transformations', in M. Godelier, T.R. Trautmann and F.E. Tjon Sie Fat (eds), *Transformations of Kinship.* Washington: Smithsonian Institute Press, p.294–313.

Kuper, A. 1982. 'Lineage Theory: A Critical Retrospect', *Annual Review of Anthropology* 11: 71–95.

Leach, E.R. 1957. 'Aspects of Bridewealth and Marriage Stability among the Kachin and Lakher', *Man* 57(59): 50–55.

———— 1961. *Rethinking Anthropology*. London: Athlone Press.

———— 1962. 'On Certain Unconsidered Aspects of Double Descent Systems', *Man* 62(214): 130–34.

Lévi-Strauss, C. 1949. *Les structures élémentaires de la parenté*. Paris: Presses Universitaires de France.

Lowie, R.H. 1917. *Culture and Ethnology*. New York: McMurtrie.

———— 1928. 'A Note on Relationship Terminology', *American Anthropologist* 30(2): 263–67.

———— 1948. *Social Organization*. London: John Murray.

McKinley, R. 1971. 'A Critique of the Reflectionist Theory of Kinship Terminology: The Crow/Omaha Case', *Man* 6: 228–47.

Morgan, L.H. 1870. *Systems of Consanguinity and Affinity of the Human Family*. Washington, DC: Smithsonian Institution (Smithsonian Contributions to Knowledge no. 218).

Murdock, G.P. 1949. *Social Structure*. New York: Macmillan.

Needham, R. 1967. 'Terminology and Alliance: II. Mapuche; Conclusions', *Sociologus* 17: 39–54.

———— 1971. 'Remarks on the Analysis of Kinship and Marriage', in R. Needham (ed.), *Rethinking Kinship and Marriage*. London: Tavistock (A.S.A. Monographs 11), p.1–34.

———— 1986. 'Alliance', *Oceania* 56(3): 165–80.

Radcliffe-Brown, A.R. 1952. 'Patrilineal and Matrilineal Succession', in A.R. Radcliffe-Brown, *Structure and Function in Primitive Society: Essays and Addresses*. London: Cowen and West, p.32–48.

Rivers, W.H.R. 1924. 'On the Origin of Classificatory System of Relationships', in W.J. Perry (ed.), *Social Organization*. London: Kegan Paul, Trench, Trubner, p.175–92.

Scheffler, H.W. 2001. *Filiation and Affiliation*. Boulder, CO: Westview Press.

Smith, M.G. 1956. 'On Segmentary Lineage Systems', *Journal of the Royal Anthropological Institute* 86(2): 39–80.

Southwold, M. 1971. 'Meanings of Kinship', in R. Needham (ed.), *Rethinking Kinship and Marriage*. London: Tavistock (A.S.A. Monographs 11), p.35–56.

Trautmann, T.R. 1981. *Dravidian Kinship*. Cambridge: Cambridge University Press.

Trautmann, R.R. and R.H. Barnes. 1993. '"Dravidian", "Iroquois" and "Crow-Omaha" in North American Perspective', in M. Godelier, T.R. Trautmann and F.E. Tjon Sie Fat (eds), *Transformations of Kinship*. Washington: Smithsonian Institute Press, p.27–58.

Turton, D. 1980. 'The Economics of Mursi Bridewealth: A Comparative Perspective', in J.L. Comaroff (ed.), *The Meaning of Marriage Payments*. London: Academic Press, p.67–92.

Chapter 8

MAURICE GODELIER AND THE ASIATIC MODE

Jack Goody

Maurice Godelier has many faces. In Britain he was an inspirer of the trend, so important in the 1960s, towards a Marxist anthropology. Secondly, he was well known for his long and very detailed fieldwork among the Baruya of New Guinea, an in-depth analysis that ran somewhat against the work of much anthropology in France. In some ways this depth of analysis was more British than the British. His other outstanding feature was his long interest in kinship, the family and incest, even when these subjects had ceased to be fashionable in other parts of the world. I could discuss his contribution in each of these fields but I have recently reviewed the third and to some extent the second (Goody 2005, 2006), therefore I will concentrate on the first since that is of most immediate interest to my present work (Goody 2007).

In 1970, Godelier edited a volume, for the Centre d'Etudes Marxistes, on the Asiatic mode of production that included a translation of Marx's study of pre-capitalist socio-economic formations. That work appeared in Moscow in 1941 and was important to anthropologists in offering a Marxist analysis of 'other cultures'. Godelier's introduction to this volume was of fundamental significance in rehabilitating the notion of an Asiatic mode of production that had been declared unacceptable at the Leningrad conference in 1931. That work had been hugely important for the study of Karl Wittfogel on the hydraulic civilization of the East. At that time the idea of a distinct Asiatic mode had been set aside by Moscow because it implied the impossibility (or difficulty) for the eastern nations to achieve capitalism (and hence socialism) by the route taken in Europe and embodied in that adopted by the USSR. The great debate that took place in Chinese (and Japanese) intellectual circles has been well discussed by Blue in the work edited with Timothy Brook on modernization in China (1999). Certainly there was a strong desire for modernization in the East; to accept Marx's eurocentric account of development was to confine that part of Eurasia to a different pattern of evolution ('Asiatic exceptionalism'). Should we not allow for greater possibilities for Asia and set aside the idea of a distinct path for that continent?

The Tibilisi conference went for the second of these alternatives, thus creating a situation which was the only time a Marxist notion (of the Asiatic mode) was declared non-Marxist. It seems apparent today that the Asians were right to reject the attempt to isolate them and to claim that continent took a totally different path from the West. In the first place, Wittfogel was wrong when he envisaged oriental despotism as necessary to construct a hydraulic civilization. While the extensive water control practised from Andalusia to China may sometimes have been aided by the central government, often enough such water canals have been under local management and local law. Moreover, absolutism has not been much more in evidence in the East than in the West. The governments of both can perhaps be characterized as being 'tributary modes', perhaps somewhat more centralized in the East (Wolf 1982; Amin 1991). If this is so, then the great political distinction that was made in traditional Marxist (and European) thinking between the two parts of the Eurasian continent can be considered null and void.

How about the economic differences? Clearly the hydraulic mode did not distinguish the civilization of the Far East from that of Mesopotamia and the Near East. In Europe, rain played a more prominent part in agriculture and a plentiful water supply was important in some industrial processes. But a significant part of Chinese and Indian agriculture in the north of the country was rain-fed, with a type of agriculture broadly similar to that of Europe. In these areas there was little difference with the West, except in certain riverine villages. If we take into account the prehistorical background, both the East and the West (at least in the Eastern Mediterranean) were dominated by the Bronze Age society of a Near Eastern type associated with the Urban Revolution and the Agricultural Revolution, with the coming of the plough and of wheeled vehicles, with the development of extensive exchange (which metal technology necessarily required) and of crafts, including writing, which changed prehistory to history, as well as affecting our entire society and our daily life by introducing a new means and mode of communication. All this occurred, somewhat later in the Far East than the Near East, but earlier than Europe, throughout the Eurasian landmass from the Mediterranean to China (Goody 2009).

This unity was seen by later Europeans as being broken by a West that developed capitalism, starting with Antiquity, then Feudalism, then the Renaissance (which reinvented Antiquity), leading to capitalism. The East, which according to this account never made it to capitalism, had a different trajectory, being without Antiquity, without Feudalism (in many accounts), without the Renaissance and hence modernity, and of course without capitalism. What it had was a hydraulic civilization, or an Asiatic mode of production, of its own.

The objection of Easterners (especially communists) to this account, which excluded them from the Western path to modernity (except through 'imitation'), and made them non-progressive and unable to develop capitalism and hence to engage in the subsequent socialist revolution, is understandable. That view resulted in the categorization of the East as 'exceptional', a fate from which the notion was rescued in the West by the work of Godelier, Hobsbawm (1965), and by countless practitioners in the social sciences who insisted upon the East's special status. Nevertheless, the Orient was right in not wanting to be excluded from the line leading, via feudalism, to capitalism and then to socialism; there was for them no Asiatic exceptionalism.

Their approach was correct, since it avoids the eurocentricism implicit in Marx's sequence. That was part of a wider nineteenth-century vision of the West as leading the world. But the European vision was flawed since it assumed that the advance that continent undoubtedly held at the time went back into the past, right back to Feudalism and to Antiquity in Greece and Rome. Before that period, the Bronze Age civilizations had attained roughly the same stage of development, in all major civilizations. However, the claim was different. Antiquity was said to have seen Europe as taking the lead, especially in Athens. Politically, it was said to have 'invented democracy'; the arts too were said to have also opened up, indeed Finley thought they had been invented (Finley 1985); certainly there were developments in literacy when it developed the alphabet (with vowel signs) but this was not as significant as once thought. Much could be accomplished with the 'characters' (logographs) in Chinese, as Needham has shown with his remarkable volumes on their achievements in the sciences. Moreover the 'characters' had additional advantages, neglected by Europeans such as Diringer (1949), who like Goody and Watt (1963) regarded the alphabet as the peak of human achievement. So in a way it was, but the 'characters' had the advantage of keeping the multi-linguistic Chinese empire together since they could transcribe any language. A world script is likely to be more Chinese than English. The economy was claimed as a different 'mode', one of slave production. But that was not altogether unique, either institutionally or as a form of production. As far as the production and exchange of goods went, it differed little from other trading economies, in Phoenicia, in Egypt, in China and elsewhere.

Even though Finley has denied its status as an economy, above all as a market economy, a vigorous trade took place, not only in the Mediterranean, but with the Near East, India and even China, in fact with all the major Bronze Age economies from which Antiquity is supposed to have diverged. That exchange continued and has already been described by Braudel, one of Godelier's teachers, as 'capitalist', certainly in a mercantile sense. There had been an exchange of goods and information very early on, not only along the the Silk Route but later on by sea, between China, India, the Near East and peripherally Europe. Long-distance trade between North India and Mesopotamia goes back to the Harappan (Bronze Age), and probably before. In the sense of mercantile capitalism and long-distance commerce, it had long been present in East Asia, although the Chinese government at times forbade overseas connections for reasons of its own. It is doubtful whether these were ever very successful in south China, and in any case there was a huge internal market which was facilitated by cheap water transport and a single script. At the same time, international communication with northern tribes always contained a strong mercantile element. Although commerce may have been contrary to Confucian ideals for the literati, these bureaucrats themselves often engaged in trade and later on merchants received literati degrees. Therefore, mercantile exchange was always a strong part of Chinese life, at least since the Bronze Age; the urban cultures of that period were in an important sense built on trade, on capitalist activity of a mercantile kind, which Braudel finds widely distributed throughout Eurasia. In this respect there was for him no Asiatic exceptionalism.

But Europe was still regarded as different, according to Braudel the only place where 'true capitalism' developed. So he too saw Europe as having another trajectory. What he meant by 'true capitalism' was finance capitalism and the kind of exchange that developed in Europe, perhaps in the nineteenth century, perhaps earlier in Renaissance times, when exchange was combined with world conquest in the form of colonization. I would argue that although international exchange and internal production now differed, they differed in a temporary fashion, as we now see, only in degree and not sufficiently differentiating a 'true' from a 'proto' capitalism. China had already developed a long-distance trade to Europe in ceramics, silk, paper and other items. Some of these required mass production for an export trade, which also included the transfer of techniques, in the making of porcelain to Delft, Meissen and Staffordshire, in silk throughout Europe, in gunpowder everywhere, in paper and printing as with the compass. In all these ways the communication of goods and ideas from the East helped to ensure the 'modernization' of the West. But they also 'modernized' the East in important ways, in making possible the long-distance voyages by Chang-He, in assuming an initial superiority over northern tribes, in making possible long–distance exports which until the nineteenth century marked China out as the greatest trading nation on earth. In production too, it was ahead for many centuries in the production of books, so important in the Italian Renaissance (Eisenstein 1979) and in the whole development of science and technology (Elvin 1973). The manufacture of paper, that was intrinsic to printing, was carried out on a semi-industrial scale. So too was the manufacture of porcelain as described by Ledderose (2000) who writes of the division of labour along Adam Smithian lines. Not only was industrial production developed in conjunction with an export industry, but a degree of mechanization was also involved, especially in the textile industry, which in Europe became the motor of the Industrial Revolution. Machines for the reeling of silk which were later developed in Bologna, where silk became an important export industry, seem to have originated in China (Elvin 1973). From northern Italy the plans were smuggled into England before the mass production of cotton that was linked to the immense growth of cotton production in the south of the United States, its import by Great Britain and its export around the world as Manchester cloth. More than just the beginnings of the Industrial Revolution occurred in China.

It is certain that at times Europe has gained the advantage in 'modernization' and that was not confined to the economic. But earlier still China had an advantage in the economy and in culture more generally, and apparently may do so again as far as the modern economy and 'true capitalism' are concerned. In other words, there was nothing in the earlier way of life that prevented China (and certainly its neighbour, Japan) from catching up in this way, nothing that deemed Asia 'exceptional' in this regard: different, yes, but hardly different in the kind of interaction and exchange that had taken place in Bronze Age societies throughout the Eurasian continent. Even the Renaissance, as I have argued recently, was not unique to Europe, since 'looking back' to an earlier (and indeed more 'pagan') culture could and did take place in other literate societies, like the Song, which has rightly been called the Chinese Renaissance (Goody 2010). While Maurice Godelier did a good service in recognizing the differences within 'pre-capitalist' modes of production, he perhaps erred on the side of ethnocentricism in respect of the Asiatic mode.

Bibliography

Amin, S. 1991. *Capitalism in the Age of Globalisation: The Management of Contemporary Society*. London: Zed Books.

Blue, G. 1999. 'China and Western Social Thought in the Modern Period', in G. Blue and P. Brook (eds), *China and Historical Capitalism: Genealogies of Sinological Knowledge*. Cambridge: Cambridge University Press, p.57–109.

Braudel, F. 1984 [1979]. *Civilization and Capitalism, 15th–18th Century*, Vol. 2. 'The Wheels of Commerce'. London: Phoenix Press.

Diringer, D. 1949. *The Alphabet: A Key to the History of Mankind*. London: Hutchinson's Scientific and Technical Publications.

Eisenstein, E.L. 1979. *The Printing Press as an Agent of Change: Communication and Cultural Transformations in Early Modern Europe*. Cambridge: Cambridge University Press.

Elvin, M. 1973. *Patterns of the Chinese Past*. London: Eyre and Methuen.

Finley, M. 1985. *Democracy: Ancient and Modern*. London: Hogarth.

Godelier, M. 1970 *Sur les sociétés précapitalistes: textes choisis de Marx, Engels, Lénine*. Paris: Editions Sociales.

Goody, J. 2005. 'The Labyrinth of Kinship', *New Left Review* 36: 127–39.

———— 2006. 'Gordon Childe, the Urban Revolution and the Haute Cuisine: An Anthropo-archaeological View of Modern History', *Comparative Studies in Society and History* 48: 503–19.

———— 2007 *The Theft of History*. Cambridge: Cambridge University Press.

———— 2009. *The Eurasian Miracle*. Cambridge: Polity Press.

———— and I. Watt. 1963. 'The Consequences of Literacy', *Comparative Studies in Society and History* 5: 304–45.

———— 2010. *Rennaissances: The One or the Many?* Cambridge: Cambridge University Press.

Hobsbawm, E. 1965. *Precapitalist Economic Formations*. New York: International Publishing.

Ledderose, L. 2000. *Ten Thousand Things: Module and Mass Production in Chinese Art*. Princeton: Princeton University Press.

Wittvogel, K. 1957. *Oriental Despotism*. New Haven: York University Press.

Wolf, E.R. 1982. *Europe and the People without History*. Berkeley, CA: University of California.

Chapter 9

THE DIALECTIC OF COSMOPOLITANIZATION AND INDIGENIZATION IN THE CONTEMPORARY WORLD SYSTEM: CONTRADICTORY CONFIGURATIONS OF CLASS AND CULTURE

Jonathan Friedman

Introduction

I first met Maurice Godelier in the late 1960s when as a student I had the good luck to attend a quite fantastic summer seminar which was informally held at the Collège de France and in which the participants were Claude Meillassoux, P.P. Rey, E. Terray, Maurice Godelier and a number doctoral students. It was an exciting occasion to say the least. Whatever the disagreements, and there were plenty at a theoretical level, this was a period just before things became more tribalized, not only on the left, of course. This was also the tail end of an intellectual period in which debate was, no matter how vicious, not linked to embodied intellectual identities. There were long sessions with some quite ferocious debates, a long lunch at a local couscous restaurant with plenty of wine, and then a return to business for a few more hours in the afternoon. The emergence of a synthesis between Marxism and structuralism implied a shift in perspective, one that was implicit in Maurice Godelier's work, while the more Althusserian influenced researchers had a tendency to fall back on the kind of functionalism that was characteristic of cultural materialism and cultural ecology in the United States. Here it took the form of 'determination in the last instance' where no matter what seemed to be organizing a material reproductive process it was, in the last analysis, a mere substitute or extension of the forces of production. Thus if political relations were understood as dominant in feudalism they were interpreted as a functional response to a material base in which there is a disjuncture between possession and property, making it necessary for political intervention in the very organization of the economy. The fact that what had begun in open debate had ended in ideological retrenchment became clear to me when I tried to publish an article on fetishism in La Pensée that was rejected on the grounds that I had the audacity to suggest that the latter was an autonomous social operator rather than a function of the infrastructure (later published in Critique of Anthropology 1 in 1974).

The Marxist model that I have grown up with, one very much inspired by my encounter with the juncture of structuralism and Marxism, is based on certain minimal characteristics and principles. A social order is a system in the sense that it is ordered by systemic properties that are discoverable via a process of hypothesis and falsification, not by mere observation. This order is a contradictory order insofar as it consists of a set of tendencies that are relatively autonomous with respect to their internal properties but nevertheless joined together in the process of social reproduction. The notion of relative autonomy in this approach referred to the fact that particular sets of relations contained their own intentionality, not deducible from that of the larger whole. The fundamental totality in this approach is social reproduction rather than 'society' as such or some form of technological causality. Reproduction implies a temporal dimension as well as a necessary historical dynamic. And it provides a perspective on the social that embraces the contradictory nature of the latter, and the transformational nature of all social orders. This general approach works just as well for the study of kinship as for capitalist based worlds even if the specific logics involved are radically different. In an era pervaded by a postmodernist effort to fragment rather than grasp unifying logics, where globalization is understood as a new evolutionary era, 'millennial capitalism', neoliberalism, all of which can only be described in terms of contingent, fragile 'assemblages', it is useful to attempt more systemic alternatives. The following is one such attempt.

Class Structure, Elite Formation and Social Polarization as Cultural Process

The study of class became a very unpopular subject in the 1980s and 1990s in many quarters of anthropology and other social sciences. This was an era in which culture became a dominant mode of understanding the world even though in principle there is absolutely nothing contradictory about considering the two together. For many, class has been associated with other vulgarities such as exploitation and a whole array of material things which are not considered sufficiently sophisticated for the culturally oriented social scientist. Some of the critique of class analysis is well taken. There was, in many approaches, a tendency to reduce the basic structures of social life to relations of exploitation, to 'relations of production' understood as technological organization. The notion that there were general cultural features of modern capitalist society, for example, that were not class based, was rejected by Marxists and other social determinists. According to this perspective, culture was the reflection of class position and as such had to be entirely dependent upon such a position. Commercial mentalities, cultural distinctions related to life-style, such as housing, interior decorating, clothing and all forms of 'taste' (Bourdieu 1979), were understood as direct products of social position (i.e. including sub-class differentiation). It should be noted that there was a serious critique of such models even by those who were very much focused on the issue of class. Distinctions were indeed being made all the time, but there was no clear way to determine their content. And, of course, statistical results of the correlation between class position and cultural form were not convincing. Another failure of explanation is a better expression of the decline of class analysis. The Birmingham school, which began its career by examining the relation between popular cultural forms and class, punks, mods and skinheads, discovered that the class relation did not really work and that popular culture was not firmly based on social position. The development of this school away from class analysis to the study of cultural forms in themselves, the movement from class to 'the politics of pleasure' (Harris 1992) and the dispersal of its members to the United States, from Yale and Harvard to Hollywood, is indicative of the changes that occurred in the 1980s.

The shift away from issues of class cannot, of course, be reduced to the failure of models of distinction and style. On the contrary, it is related to a broader reconfiguration of identity and power in Western societies. An excellent attempt to diagnose the shift can be found in much of the sociological work on the advent of the information society, globalization, new social movements etc. The shift is one of the cornerstones of the writings of Alain Touraine over the past few decades. The argument, oversimplified, is that capitalist modernity was based on a class polarization of society that pitted capital against labour in a political struggle for control over the historical direction of society. Since the 1980s that modernity, or at least the opposition on which it was founded, has disintegrated. The power of labour has decreased, the working class has fragmented, and as a result the working class movements have been replaced by more locally or simply more generalized issues such as environment, feminism etc.; all of this announces the advent of movements based on cultural identity rather than class.

Within anthropology there has been a parallel shift of interests since the late 1970s towards issues of culture and cultural identity. This is clearly the case in the United States but even in Europe there have been similar tendencies. The use of the term culture, which was quite uncommon, became increasingly popular in the 1980s. In France, where the notion of culture was peripheral at least in the social sciences, as there were an array of notions, from collective representations, to symbolic structures which covered much of the same ground, the same shift can be clearly observed in the emergence of such terms as 'idéologiques' and 'mentalités' in France and semantic anthropology in England. The latter emerged from a period characterized by a more materialist and social determinist anthropology, as the role of culture became increasingly dominant, reflected in the trajectory of Marshall Sahlins. I have suggested that this change in perspective might be related to the decline of modernism, understood here as the decline in an orientation to the future, to abstract rationalism and a development 'away' from the 'traditional'. It is a period characterized by the decline of some of modernism's primary vehicles – Marxism, developmentalism, rationalism, followed by an intensifying critique of science and of universalism that are typical of an emergent 'post-modernism'.

Much of the discourse produced in the past couple of decades of cultural studies and even anthropology has been based on this former turn to culture. One well-known anthropologist of globalization, echoing in perverted fashion, Franz Fanon, is said to have remarked, 'when I hear the word *class* I go for my gun'.

It is clearly the case that class is not an adequate term when analysing many of the social forms that anthropologists have dealt with, but since the absence of class was assimilated to a more general culturalism its more recent application to the world of the modern global system poses a serious hindrance to an adequate understanding of reality.

The purpose of this contribution is to suggest a set of relevant links among phenomena that are quite salient today but which are not often connected. It requires a rethinking of what has often been referred to as globalization without serious analysis, especially in the human sciences. I feel that it is impossible to dissociate questions about the structure of state societies from those of class and cultural identity and from the larger context within which states are constituted and reproduced. This is not to argue that there is a higher order of determination, the global, above all the rest. On the contrary, it is to argue that the global is simply the emergent properties of the articulation of numerous local processes. There may well be hierarchies of control, but these are part of the nature of formal organizations themselves. UNESCO and the IMF should not be confused with global social processes. They may well have as their objective the regulation of international and interstate relations, but they are constituted in the same social reality and they are, in social terms, small worlds of their own, even where they span large geographical distances. Our purpose then is to work toward an understanding of class formation in what has come to be known as the 'era of globalization'. This requires a reassessment of the usage of the term globalization itself (Friedman 2007).

Globalization has become a pop term in the media, since its original introduction in business economics. It has made the tour through economic geography, cultural sociology and sociology, and is increasingly to be found in postcolonial studies and anthropology. I shall not go into detail here, but shall instead briefly summarize some major tendencies in this discourse and its underlying assumptions. There is, of course, a literature on the issues that has emerged in political economy informed works in economic geography, critical economics, and sociology. Much of this work is quantitative and is argued in empirical terms. It documents a number of changing realities: the rapid increase since the 1970s of capital export in the form of foreign direct investment, the asymmetric distribution of these flows toward East Asia and to a lesser degree to countries like India and Brazil, the increasing salience of multinational companies (sometimes called transnational to stress what is in fact a false notion of deterritorialization), the enormous increase in financial and speculative transactions relative to total production, the development of new speculative markets such as derivatives which are greater than the entire world economy measured in terms of goods and service transactions.

This development has often been interpreted in technological terms, as the product of the computer and internet revolutions that have totally transformed productive activity as well as speeding up transaction times. Such accounts are not new of course (Bell 1973) and it is interesting for an anthropologist who has been through the long critique of technological determinist evolutionism to encounter it yet again. It should, of course, be taken seriously, but for most of these otherwise empirically based researchers, the technological connection is simply assumed. Castells (2000), one of the most recent advocates of this kind of evolutionism, has been cautious in his use of the arguments, but in the second edition of his *Network Society* he is at pains to account for the argument proposed by one of the US's major economists and specialists on productivity, who has painstakingly argued that productivity has not changed significantly since the advent of the 'new economy' (Gordon 2000). It is only in the actual production of microchips that we can speak of a real revolutionary increase in productivity, but this sector is minute in relation to the rest of the economy and has not offset the general downward trend since the 1970s. The answer is, 'Wait! Things will change'. This is similar to an answer supplied by one neo-evolutionary anthropologist to another in a seminar when questioned why the enormous demographic densities in Highland New Guinea had not led to the development of stratified societies, according to the then popular demographic determinist theory. 'Wait!' he said. Well, we are all still waiting, and the IT sector is not in terribly good shape. Of course all kinds of things can change in the future, but it is not clear that this kind of evolutionism is capable of accounting for the desired results. And desire seems to be an essential component in this discussion. Many want to believe that we have entered a new world, whether good or bad, and the tendency is to think of it as basically good, which is progress after all. The advent of the network society is part of a complex of terms that includes globalization, as if the latter were simply another expression of this colossal transformation of human society. I am not, it should be noted, arguing against the reality of globalization, but of its world historical status, and while clearly it might well be argued that there is something new happening here, it is important to be able to challenge what appears to many as self-evident. In fact it is the self-evidence itself that should make us wary. While the globalization literature among those dealing with empirical realities is certainly important and exciting, if sometimes informed by ideologically based desires that have found their way into anthropology, it remains grounded in the analysis of processes of capital export, outsourcing, as part of the decentralization of capital accumulation (Dicken 1998).

Models of Global Systems

The difference between globalization and global systemic perspectives in anthropology is worth reviewing here, since the results of the two approaches are quite divergent. I have suggested that globalization, especially its anthropological variant, has been proposed as a stage of world history and that it is very much based on an experience or a fantasy of a world on the move. In anthropological terms this takes the form of the transition from roots to routes and a struggle against localism contained within the celebration of movement itself. As I have dwelt upon this issue in several other publications, I shall only indicate some of the most general characteristics of the argument here. These are reducible to three. Firstly, is the necessary movement from smaller to larger units and from simpler to more complex organizations. Secondly, and following the first, there exists the notion that globalization is about the global era that we are now entering, an era fraught with conflicts perhaps, but one which harbours a new diasporic way of life which ultimately promises to supersede the nation state (Appadurai 1993). The latter is understood as the source of most of the evils of modernity, especially essentialism and its offspring, nationalism and racism. Thirdly, the new world is a world of border crossing, hybridity, experimental identification, but also (for some) of hypercapitalism, the network society, and increasing exploitation, at least in its initial stages. The latter is sometimes referred to as millennial capitalism (Comaroff and Comaroff 1999). Much of the discourse produced in the cultural globalization literature, of which the former partakes, is saturated with a terminology of the trans-x and post-x sort. Such terms concern the transcendence of existing borders. They may be borders of the body and I have suggested that the root metaphor for much of this discourse can be found in the post-feminism of writers such as Judith Butler. A feeling of wanting to escape from all forms of fixed or grounded identity and a profound desire to belong to something higher, more expansive, are common characteristics of this discourse, one that finds cosmopolitans in the most dubious places and is want to trash indigenes as redneck enemies of the world society to come (Malkki 1992; Kelly 1995). One might ask: What is the problem? Why is it necessary to take sides on such issues? I have suggested that this is the product of a cosmopolitan agenda, one that harbours a moral classification of the world into dangerous classes/locals and liberal/progressive world citizens. This popular and proliferating discourse is not, I suggest, an internal theoretical development within any particular social science. On the contrary, it is the spontaneous self-understanding that is generated in a certain position within the contemporary world system in transformation. This is why I have referred to the way in which people talk on the intranet in certain multinational consultancies, in much of the media and among top officials in diplomatic, international political and economic arenas, and the way in which the managerial

New Age conceives of the New World (Barnum 1992), as some of the true sources of contemporary imaginations of globalization in more sophisticated circles. In sum, my assessment of globalization is that it is the expression of a positional identity within the global system rather than a description of or theoretical perspective on the contemporary world. The conversion of the former into the latter consists in a practice of labelling the world rather than attempting to comprehend it.

The global systemic perspective is vastly different, not least with respect to the notion of globalization itself. The latter is seen not as a world historical stage, but as a phase phenomenon in the cyclical development of hegemonic expansion and contraction. Globalization, in the Braudelian perspective, is the expression of hegemonic decline in which a decentralization of capital accumulation creates chaos as well as a shift in investment from old to new centres or potential hegemons. Arrighi argues on the basis of historical research that massive financial expansions have accompanied all the major hegemonic declines in the history of the European world system:

> To borrow an expression from Fernand Braudel (1984: 246) – the inspirer of the idea of systemic cycles of accumulation – these periods of intensifying competition, financial expansion and structural instability are nothing but the 'autumn' of a major capitalist development. It is the time when the leader of the preceding expansion of world trade reaps the fruits of its leadership by virtue of its commanding position over world-scale processes of capital accumulation. But it is also the time when that same leader is gradually displaced at the commanding heights of world capitalism by an emerging new leadership. (Arrighi 1997: 2)

This kind of approach has been fully developed in the work of Arrighi (2003) but is also present in much of the literature on world systems. Our own work led to the suggestion, as early as the 1970s, that civilizations were all examples of such expansion and contraction processes and that modern 'world' systems were simply a continuation of much older processes. The similarities in this process can be expressed graphically as a set of cycles that tend toward a limit. The individual cycles express shifting hegemony within a larger systemic arena while the larger cycle expresses the ultimate limits of expansion of the system as a whole. Globalization, in this kind of a systemic process, corresponds to periods of crisis and hegemonic transition. Globalization as a phenomenon of transition has been well documented for the major shifts in hegemony in the Western dominated world system. The hegemonic shift from Italy to the Iberian peninsula and from there to Holland and then Britain is accompanied by major changes in investment flows from old to new potential hegemons.

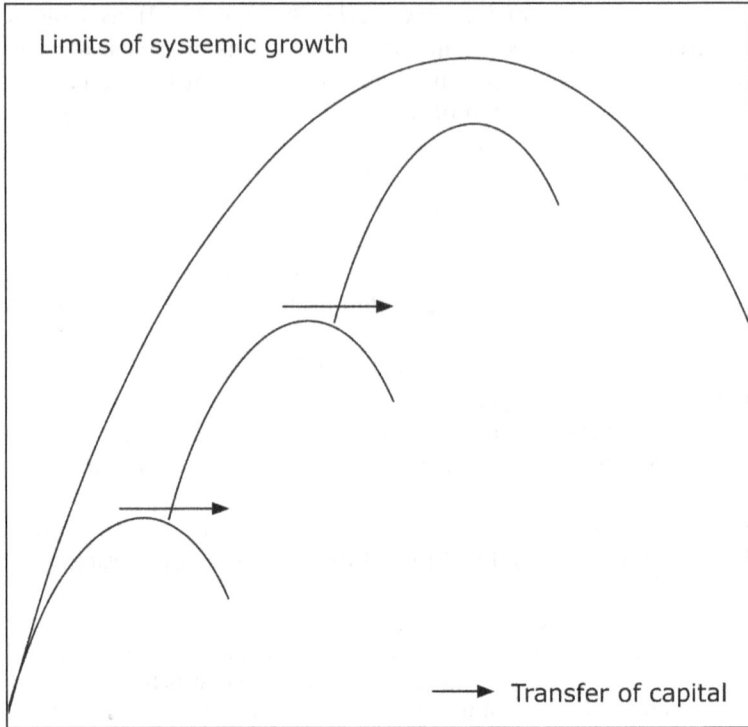

Figure 9.1. Local cycles and system cycle.

The most recent such shift was at the end of the nineteenth century. The major themes of this period are similar enough to the present to warrant investigation. There was massive globalization of capital, on a scale easily comparable to the present. Foreign direct investment, which was a minor phenomenon relevant to portfolio investment, reached nine per cent of world output in 1913, a proportion that was not surpassed until the early 1990s (Bairoch and Kozul-Wright 1996: 10). Openness to foreign trade in 1993 was not markedly different to that in 1913 (Briggs and Snowman 1996). There were massive British investments in the United States, and Germany was rapidly becoming an industrial giant. Britain was no longer the world's workshop: its share of world manufacturing declined from close to fifty per cent to fourteen per cent in 1913 as the United States increased its relative industrial dominance. The decline of hegemonic Britain occurred in a situation of increasing competition and crises of overproduction and recurrent depressions at the end of the nineteenth century. There was also mass migration in this period. Expanding trade occurred in parallel with large-scale migration. In a recent comparison of the end of this century and the last, the *Economist* stated the following:

As in the late 20th Century, trade was booming, driven upwards by falling transport costs and by a flood of overseas investment. There was also migration on a vast scale from the Old World to the New.

Indeed, in some respects the world economy was more integrated n the late 19th Century than it is today. The most important force in the convergence of the 19th Century economies was mass migration mainly to America. In the 1890s, which in fact was not the busiest decade, emigration rates from Ireland, Italy, Spain and Scandinavia were all above 40 per thousand. The flow of people out of Europe, 300,000 people a year in mid-century, reached 1 million a year after 1900. On top of that, many people moved within Europe. True, there are large migrations today, but not on this scale. (*Economist*, 20 December-2 -January: 73 2001)

Many of the current debates concerning immigration and 'multiculturalism' were already prevalent in this period. This was also an age of technological revolution. Stock markets were connected by cable and investment could flow between continents at revolutionary new speeds (Hirst and Thompson 1996: 3). There was an enormous celebration of new technologies: electric lighting, telephones, automobiles and even airplanes and x-rays. This was a period that witnessed the rise of contradictory ideologies that are prevalent today. At one extreme there was the Futurist religion of technology and, at the other, cults of tradition, *Gemeinschaft* and the local.

Even more important is the fact that this phase of globalization came to an end in the 1920s and was followed by a long period of de-globalization that lasted until the 1950s and involved a major world war. It is only in the 1950s that globalization began again and intensified from the 1970s until the present.

This does not imply that nothing has happened in world history, but simply that some properties of historical processes have remained invariant if not identical. Even in recent times, the similarities between the current end of millennium crisis and that which occurred in the period from 1870 to 1920 does not vitiate the equally important fact that there are crucial differences in structure as well. The previous globalized era was characterized by stronger national states and by a much lower ratio of direct foreign investment to portfolio investment. While there were equivalents to today's multinationals, they were fewer in number and not nearly as complex. Much of this difference has to do with technological developments that have made the internationalization of productive processes a more profitable possibility.

It is often argued that today's global financial economy is a new phenomenon, but here as well, there are clear precedents. The very notion of Finance Capital in such well-known works as that of Hilferding (1910) dealt with what appeared to be a massive expansion and control of the financial sector with respect to industrial production. This is a crucial issue, because it is a structural rather than an historical phenomenon. The relation between the accumulation of money capital and the accumulation of productive capital, i.e. the capacity to produce commodities and productive services, is a fundamental contradictory relation in capitalist reproduction. This is simple in situations where capital shifts from productive to non-productive activities, a shift that usually occurs simultaneously with capital export (globalization). The latter process is simply the expression of the uneven distribution of profitability in the world arena. The fact that a rapidly increasing percentage of direct investment in the late 1990s consisted in mergers and acquisitions is a product of a situation in which such activity is more rational than investment in new production. An important aspect of the cycle of expansion and contraction described graphically above is the increasing divergence of 'fictitious' versus real accumulation as production becomes increasingly unproductive in relation to other activities.

Of course Figure 9.2 is an oversimplification of a complex process but the tendencies to which it points are important. It implies that in hegemonic declines there is not only a tendency to the massive export of capital in the form of globalization, but also to a shift from productive to non-productive forms of investment, to real estate, stock market speculation, derivative markets, a process that increases the commodification of the world as the pressure on accumulation

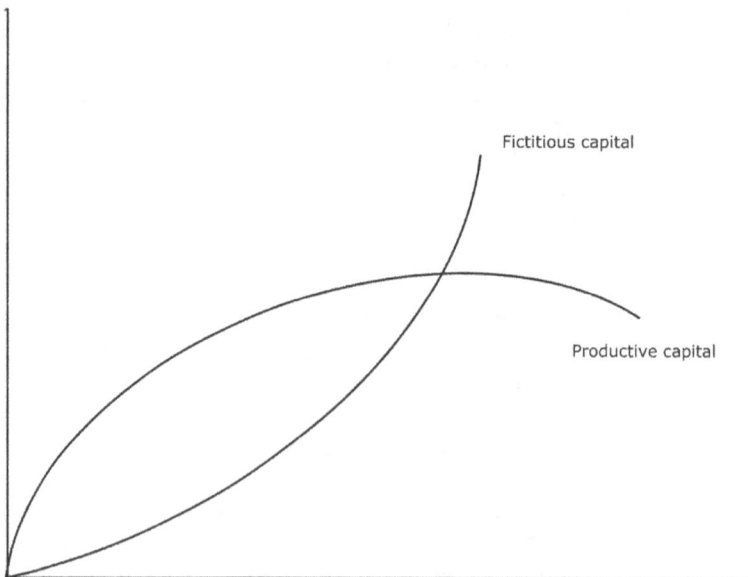

Figure 9.2. The relation between fictitious and real accumulation.

accelerates. Commodification consists in the fragmentation of reality into clusters of property rights that can be sold on the market. The creation of private titles is a practice of capitalization that creates wealth out of named categories. And for those Marxists who interpret *Capital* and the theory of value as a reduction of the latter to labour time or even to the cost of reproduction of labour, it should be noted that Volume III of that work deals primarily with the divergence between real value and fictitious value as the primary contradiction of accumulation. It is in periods of globalization that international capitalist classes become most salient, according to this model. This is not to say that they emerge only in such periods. On the contrary, we argue below that they are permanent features of capitalist civilization. What might be said to be specific to such periods is the rapid elaboration of such elites and of the discourses that they produce or that are produced around them. The reason for this is in part the availability of funds to support such populations, populations who represent and struggle for a particular perspective on the world, one that can be summarized as cosmopolitan.

Structures of the Long Run

Categories such as globalization, cosmopolitan elites, national elites, social classes, immigrant minorities, regional minorities and indigenous populations are not restricted to a particular historical era. They are basic structural features of the capitalist state system, and more specifically the nation state system. Their salience may vary over time, but they exist, at least potentially, throughout the history of the system. It might be argued that the nation form is a product of capitalist state organization. This is, however, a mere potential that depends upon a number of different processes, some of which are strongly connected to the commodification of social relations within the state. The process by which local sodalities and institutions are dissolved by the joint action of the state and commerce and by which the individual is liberated from dependency on lower order social relations to become dependent upon the wage relation, whether high or low, is a process that gradually empties the social space between the self and the state. This is a variable process that only approximates an ideal type in social democratic states which in the contemporary period have sought to sever all bonds that are not themselves state organized. Thus the family may be replaced by a string of socializing agencies, from day care to university, at the same time as the wage labour-tax nexus becomes generalized to such an extent that the individual becomes totally independent, economically, on former social networks. This is a process that has been described in terms of individualization and is a principle characteristic of 'modernity'. It is in a highly atomized social field that identification with the state can replace other collective identities, if national socialization is practiced. The space is then filled with propositions about reality, about relations to nature, to destiny, to history. This, of course, can occur without the dissolution of lower-level structures as has been proven throughout the nineteenth and twentieth centuries. The nation state form is not merely a relation between individualized subjects and a larger collectivity. It is also an organization that both envelops and cuts across class relations. This is a complex affair with plenty of variation of course, but it is crucial to understanding the dynamics of interstate relations as well as the transformation that we have come to know as the welfare state. As this is not an essay in history but in structure, I do not intend to delve into the variations of national identity within modern states. I shall focus on a single phenomenon, the relation of a self-defined people and the state as the focal point for a practice of self-identification, in either positive or negative terms, depending on the particular social position from which actors practice their identifications. Thus the fusion of state and people in Sweden earlier in this century can be contrasted with what appears to be a radical opposition between nation and state in Australia (Kapferer 1988). It has been argued that class struggle has been organized in terms of a We, a self-identified people, against capital, with or without the support of the state. The state has been 'captured' by certain working class movements, at least ideologically, transforming the former into an extension of peoplehood. Sweden is certainly a prime example of this, but it is to be noted that the fusion thus imposed has a strange past. The notion of 'people's home' (in Swedish *folkhemmet*), a society equivalent to a family, is not an invention of the left but of the conservatives, a not uncommon constituent of their paternalistic ideology, known in other areas as a characteristic of the 'company town'. This was assimilated into social democratic ideology and has played a crucial role in national politics, allowing elites to impose a total restructuring of working class lives, from racial hygiene to housing, in the name of a union of a national population under the aegis of a single social project. It is not then so extraordinary that the word 'society' commonly substitutes for state in political and even everyday discourse. While the Swedish case is extreme, the same parameters can be found in most nation states. They relate to the role of the state as an instrument of the people and to the need to pronounce broadly social goals that indicate the self-evident responsibility of the state with regard to the people's welfare. This ideology concerns the rights of the working class as well as the responsibility of capitalists. While there are clearly liberal interpretations of the nation state in which the market is said to ensure the welfare of all, it is necessary that the welfare of all is stressed, i.e. that the capitalists also wish the best for their workers. The 'good' in this model is welfare itself, the wellbeing, well financed, of ordinary people. The taming of social elites is part of the process of welfare development, the submission of all to a common project. The logic of this process of consolidation, in which people and state become joined if not fused, generates the category of the 'we', a 'we the people'. And this occurs under the umbrella of the territorial state itself. It is bounded and tends toward the assimilation or at least integration of differences within a larger core of a project. It is also riven with contradictions in the real interests of those involved. These account, for example, for what is called the neo-liberal project as an attempt to re-establish the dominance of capital and capitalists (Duménil and Lévy 2004; Harvey 2005).

It might well be argued that the nation state as such is not a constant in the history of the modern world, but that a certain tendency in class formation has been more of a structure of longue durée. Here I would like to suggest something along these lines, but the structure to which I refer is not a particular set of class categories. Instead it is a tendency to the distribution of positions with respect to local populations and the larger regional, or global, arena. This is a structure which distributes a number of categories with respect to one another, from interstate or cosmopolitan elite relations to localized relations to limited territories. It is similar to the notion of an elementary structure as in the 'atom of kinship'[1] insofar as it entails that the state order is defined at its summit as an external relation to other states that in this way constitute one another in the larger relation. I have previously represented the structure as in Figure 9.3 which portrays the contemporary order of the nation state, one that is historically specific with respect to the valences of the categories. Thus the culturally cosmopolitan category in that graphic would have been something more akin to modernist internationalism a hundred years ago, rather than the hybrid cosmopolitanism of today. Similarly migration would not be maintained in the form of diasporas but integrated into the body of the nation state as territorial minorities at least and assimilated at most.

The graphic representation in Figure 9.3 applies to a global arena organized into nation states, but the categories are similar in fundamental ways even in previous state formations. In earlier eras, for example, the state elites were at the same time cosmopolitan elites, aristocrats that participated in an interstate realm in which royalties and aristocracies were joined in marriage and political alliances, in which they sent handicraft specialists, architects and artists from

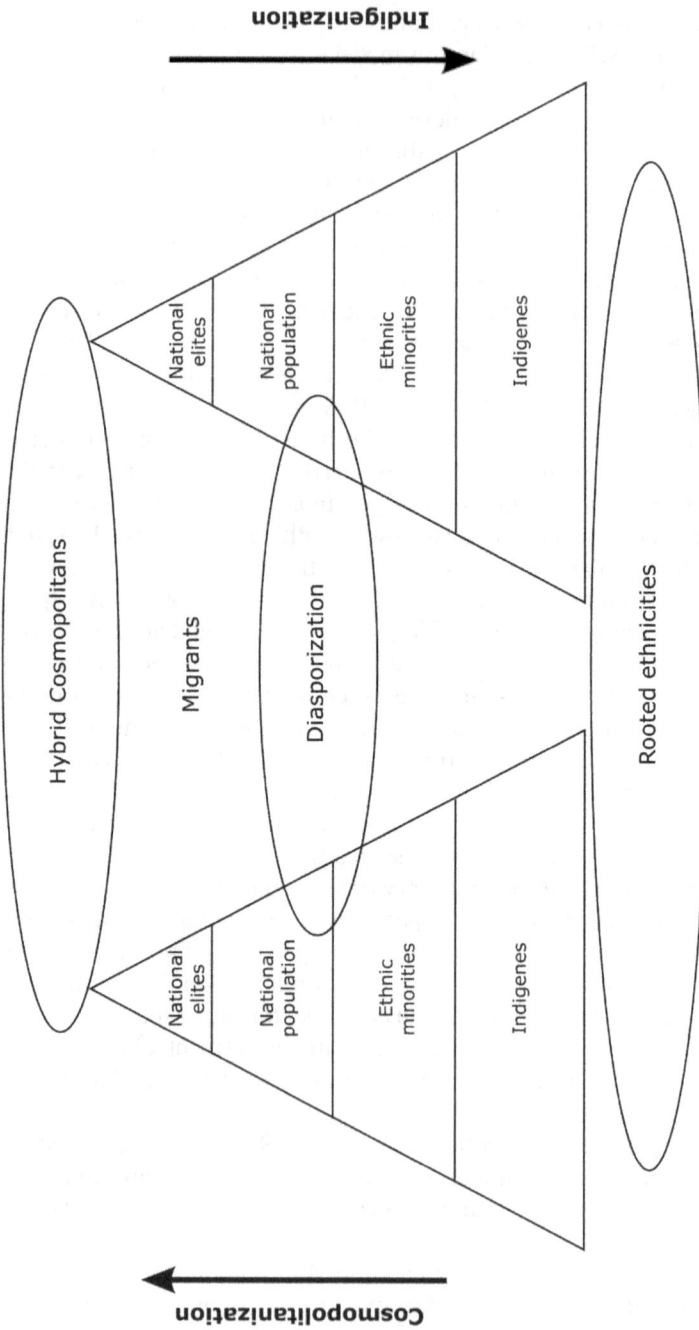

Figure 9.3. The dialectic of cosmopolitanization and indigenization.

court to court in generous gestures. The variant of this structure at the turn of the eighteenth century could have been depicted as in Figure 9.4.

These states were not nation states in any sense. They were aristocratic/royal domains linked by marriage and political alliances as well as by conflict and warfare. Territorial populations were not integrated into the larger territory as a mass of individuals. Instead there were numerous regional and local political structures. Migration was certainly an integral part of the dynamics of such states, the product of royal policies and demands for specialized labour. But insofar as ordinary people were subjects rather than citizens, they were essentially pawns in a larger set of strategies. National or ethnic identity was limited primarily to local groups and regions or to diasporic populations. There was clearly identification with larger units on the part of warriors and those who could gain advantage by becoming attached to royal courts. What is important for this discussion is the continuum from the local to the interstate level and the potential oppositions that developed among the levels. However, it should be clearly noted that the very praxis of the absolutist state created a social field of national identity. Long before the French Revolution there were letters of 'naturalization' offered to foreigners who came to live in the country. This was a hotly debated issue surrounding the imposition of taxes on foreigners in 1697. There was a great deal of migration and aristocratic tourism following the war against the Augsburg coalition. As one contemporary described it:

> After peace had been established, there had been such a great number of arrivals of foreigners in Paris that one could count fifteen to sixteen thousand of them in the suburb of Saint-Germain alone... at the beginning of the following year, one found out that there were thirty-six thousand of them in the same suburb alone. (Annales de la Cour de la Ville, 1697–1698, in Dubost and Sahlins 1999: 15)[12]

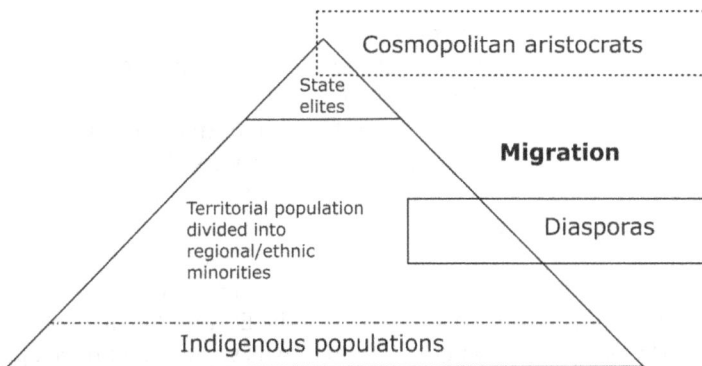

Figure 9.4. Categories of the absolutist state.

And the word 'nation' is used to identify individuals throughout the period, such as Anne Sauvage, 'anglaise de nation' described as 'not married in France, not following the customs of Paris and not naturalized'.[23] Or Jacques Lieurard, a protestant convert from the North of France wrongly taxed as 'son of a foreigner native of Holland',[34] or again the use of the expression 'Français imparfaits' (Dubost and Sahlins 1999: 378–80).

Immigrant status was also inherited for three generations for those arriving after 1600, that is, it was defined in terms of descent from specific national origins. The author Fénélon expresses in his *Aventures de Télémaque* a clear opposition to what he associates with the urban, commercial, foreign merchants and the international realm from a position that can be interpreted as Christian and agrarian (idem: 391). There is a twofold set of representations generated in this division between the peasant and the urban sectors of the larger territory. The latter is implicated in the royal strategy of the state elites to increase the base of their wealth, demographically and especially in terms of capital, the former identify with an increasingly salient notion of a national population, sedentary and exploited by the latter. It might be suggested that this growing opposition is the foundation for the French Revolution in which 'peoplehood' is established as a sovereign body within the confines of the territorial state, already the foundation of the nation state. As the Abbé de Sieyès stated the case, it is the sovereign people and not the king that incarnates the nation. The 'Third Estate' is a 'Corps d'associés vivant sous une loi commune et représentés par le même législateur' (Sieyès 1789, in Noiriel 2001: 89).

It is also noteworthy that there is a clear notion of a larger interstate world in opposition to the local and the parochial that also has a historical continuity. This is more clearly expressed in the elite sector than in the popular sector. It accounts for the early appearance of religious doctrines that are global in scope. In the early seventeeth century there are fairly clear expressions of a notion of a single humanity, of the need for the establishment of a world order, not in fact, foreign to the Catholic Church's interpretation. The Rosicrucians published a pamphlet in 1614 entitled *Fama*, in which it is proposed that all learned men throughout the world should join forces towards the establishment of a synthesis of science. Behind this effort stood, allegedly, an *illuminated* brotherhood – the children of light, who had been initiated in the mysteries of the Grand Order. This 'Brüderschaft der Theosophen' was said to have been founded by Christian Rosencreutz (1378–1484), who had become an initiate during his travels in the Middle East in the fifteenth century. He founded a brotherhood which was supposed to have operated in secret ever since.

Now it is somewhat less clear to what extent there were indigenizing or nationalizing tendencies in the early history of Europe, but it is widely accepted that the nation state was very much the project of state oriented elites with the caveat that the latter produced an opposing project rooted in the exploited classes to capture the state and make it an instrument in the service of its own needs. The various regional and local resistances that proliferated within emerging absolutist states are evidence that there were and are numerous sub-state identities of varying strength right up until the present. It is necessary to find the resonance bases for the different collective identifications that characterize our history in order to avoid falling into the trap of envisioning such identities as mere intellectual constructs that people have somehow been seduced into accepting.

The cosmopolitanism of certain elites is apparently a well-established European habitus or even tradition. This is clearly evident in the history of the Freemasonry. The latter, after being taken over by aristocrats and then wealthy financial capitalists, expressed a set of values that are equally visible in today's world. Thus the New Age managerialism that is so common in the contemporary world of elites has its more aristocratic forerunners in the Freemasonry of the past. These themes can be outlined as follows:

1. An opposition to organized religion in its Western form.
2. An attraction to Oriental religious philosophy, not least its holism.
3. An interest in primitive and ancient religions.
4. The individual as the centre of spirituality and a direct link to the sacred or godhead, understood in pantheistic terms.
5. The superiority of the elect who can attain this relation to the sacred.
6. In political terms, an orientation to the world as a whole, to Mankind
   A. this implies opposition to the nation state or any other subnational units except as sources of spirituality
   B. the internal differentiation between leaders and followers, or the elect and the rest.
7. In class terms this is the formation in ideological terms and identity terms of an international elite.
8. A millennaristic view of the future – the New Age which is to come.

The latter incorporate notions of holism and of being chosen by higher powers. The elite is the 'chosen few', chosen to lead all of humanity to the promised land. It implies distance from rather than identity with the populations that are under its rule and this provides a link to the pluralism that is so prevalent in older and newer versions of multiculturalism.

> The cosmopolitan bourgeoisie in the eighteenth century came to adopt a perspective own society as if it were a foreign one a target for 'colonial' exploitation. Freemasonry provided a cover for developing the new identity on which the exploitation of members of one's own community is premised. By entering the masonic lodges, merchants and those otherwise involved in the long-distance money economy such as lawyers and accountants, realised the primordial alientation from the community which is the precondition for market relations, exploitation of wage labour, and abstract citizenship. (Ravenstock-Huessy 1961: 364 in Van der Pijl 1998: 99

Another aspect of this particular global position is its association with finance rather than industrial production, so that finance is associated with the cosmopolitan as opposed to industry which is understood as vulgarly localized:

> By being expressly non-manual, divorced from actual labour, British masonry reproduced the aristocratic preference for arms-length control over direct entrepreneurial involvement. The English gentleman preferred to sit above the commercial fray, pulling levers, dangling rewards and applying sanctions. (Hampden-Turner and Trompenaars 1994: 321)

This is an important logic, one that connects finance with the cosmopolitan, and in turn with a sense of a higher power and even of a mission. The values of the humanism that emerged in the enlightenment are very much woven together with this particular version of cosmopolitanism.

The Small Worlds of Cosmopolitanism

One of the outcomes of the continuity of the category – cosmopolitan elite – as a constant category of the modern state is the production of social worlds that are more or less bounded socially even if unbounded with respect to the territorial unit. Cosmopolitan identity commonly represents itself as world encompassing as opposed to the smaller worlds of national and other more localized populations. This is a significant misrepresentation of reality, one that confuses geographical with social closure. It has led to absurd assertions that, for example, diasporas are instances of cosmopolitan openness, a notion that flies in the face of practically all that is known of such transnational groups where boundaries must absolutely be maintained if the diaspora is to survive, implying high levels of endosocial relations including endogamy and, consequentially, strict control over children. It is, in this respect, enlightening to investigate the life of transnational elites, which display some of the characteristics of diasporas. An interesting study of what has been called l'immigration dorée in France (Wagner 1999) reveals a number of interesting properties of the social life that has developed in such transnational *elites*. Focusing on foreign elite communities via their relation to international schools and other associations, she depicts a two-layered structure, one newer, the product of the recent emergence of a transnational managerial class, and the other the old more aristocratic cosmopolitan elites. Although Wagner has concentrated on a relatively limited time period, it appears that almost a third of all transnationals in her sample marry other transnationals, though not necessarily of the same nationality. They send their children to a limited number of schools where education consists in learning to be international. The students play at representing the world, at being a United Nations devoted to a celebration of cultural difference and they often have official connections with these international organizations. But, there is more than culture here as they also identify themselves in the idiom of blood, even where it is mixed:

> I have expatriat blood ... I am an American expatriate, in passport and nationality, but my family and that of my wife as well have numerous branches in many countries, which means that we always have had one foot in the United States and another abroad. (Wagner 1999: 116)
> My father was something of a vagabond, and we had it in our veins. My brothers, it's the same: I have a brother in Austria, one in Finland, a sister in Spain. My father moved a lot, and I must have gotten it from him. (idem: 116)[5]

The very expression 'ex-patriot blood' expresses a combination of roots and routes of the kind announced in much of the post-colonial cultural studies literature. The transnational is concretized in biological terms. The self-definition of a cosmopolitan ethos, which is common to both aristocratic and managerial groups, is an essential part of their self-understanding. The idiom of blood translates cultural difference into a common denominator, one that is sometimes referred to as 'blue blood', no matter what the nationality. Thus the cosmopolitan world is an ethnic world as well, one that crosses national borders, but which is distinctive and thus quite closed and bounded. However, it expresses itself in terms of the transcendence of national borders rather than in the creation of new, class-based borders: 'La curiosité, l'ouverture, la tolérance sont des termes souvent employés pour désigner ces qualités' (idem: 142).

This is the ethos of the world traveller – always open to new adventures, to new kinds of experience and different kinds of people. But it should be noted that the actual social arenas of these

232 Jonathan Friedman

cosmopolitans is limited to a number of associations, clubs, schools where they constantly meet and are able to identify one another by their common interests, tastes, but also differences regarding national origins and cultures.

The ethnic-class aspect of this identity is also the expression of the opposition between themselves and the more terrestrial ordinary nationals. They are even referred to as terrestrials in some comments.

> So, the terrestrial is someone who has a limited space. His activity concentrates on the land that he owns. If someone else comes into his land, he won't accept it. He is linked to his family; to his children he wants to keep around him, since it his family that farms the land ... (idem: 204)[6]

And there is the opposition including the usual classification of the local 'other':

> I believe that the popular class is attached to its origins. English people in France rather belong to the middle classes. In England, popular classes are more nationalist than other classes, they are less open. (idem: 189)[7]

If the cosmopolitan is a constant structure in the modern territorial and nation state, it becomes increasingly salient in periods of globalization. One may even speak of an unstable opposition between the local, national and the international in which ideological dominance shifts markedly over time.

At the very top of the social hierarchy are the families that have been designated the *grandes fortunes*. This group keeps its distance from the others, with its own clubs and associations, listed and ranked in journals like *Le petit mondain*, and in terms of their places of residence (Pinçon and Pinçon-Charlot 1996: 120).

> Cosmopolitanism of relationships, multiterritoriality extended to foreign countries, these are the two essential components of high society. (idem: 120)[8]

Wagner presents the example of the comte de Châtel. His genealogy is mixed due to marriages among the elites from Italy, England, Belgium and Argentina. The family's capital is directly linked to the family's international segmentary structure. M. de Châtel is never an ex-patriot when he travels. He is always on his own property somewhere in the world. But he is also a professional chameleon in cultural if not class terms.

> Yes, people believed I was English in England, just as they believe I am an Argentinean in Argentina. This is one of the sole gifts that God has provided me with. I imitate accents with great facility (he imitates the

accent of Marseilles). It isn't of much use, but nevertheless! (Wagner 1999: 122)[9]

The differentiation between the upper crust and the managers, beside being socially marked in very clear terms, is also a difference between a cosmopolitan identity in which an aristocratic world tends to be homogeneous, and a more multinational world in which cultures are compared and ranked. This may be more of a variation than a true difference since there is a strong overlap in perspectives. But Wagner's findings suggest a difference in the two spheres:

> The two relationships with the foreign remain nevertheless distinct. The international defines itself in opposition to the cosmopolitan. *Cosmopolitism* rests on the cohesion of a small elite aristocracy, and does not really engage relationships between different cultures. Quite the opposite, the international culture of managers rests precisely on the valorization of the diversity of national cultures. (idem: 212)[10]

This is related to the degree to which the ethnicization of the elite overrides its transcendence of national borders, but in both groups there is a tendency toward a distancing from the local and the national and identification with the international or transnational:

> The capacity to be at home, in the material as well as the social and symbolic sense, in several countries, the incorporation of a cosmopolitan identity that produces effects on all dimensions of the person, define the model towards which the international culture of executives is driven. (idem: 212)[11]

Cosmopolitanization and Globalization

In the graphics above I suggest that there is a tendency toward the cosmopolitanization of elites in periods of strong globalization such as we have today. This can be understood as a product of the convergence of social and spatial mobility, one that situates its adherents above the world where they can encompass the diversity that lies below without being part of it, except in the sense of being able to consume it in the form of products. This distinction creates an opposition to the local as something which is decidedly lower in status and conflates immobility with cultural poverty. It is a mistake, however, to assume that the encompassing self-representation of the cosmopolitan implies a real engagement with the world. Geographical mobility, yes, but this is within a narrow sphere of class in which relations established are bounded and often highly segregated, in which identity is strong and homogenous with respect to status and position.

The recent generalization of cosmopolitanism to all transnational domains appears in this light to express a kind of struggle for ideological hegemony. This generalization is what tends to equate cosmopolitanism with globalization itself and to argue for the evolution from local to global referred to above. Locals are not merely at the bottom of this process, they are also represented as precursors to the present. They are in this sense primitive, but in a way that conflates the Freudian primitivity, libidinous and inhabiting all of us with a temporal sense of being backward, and the two are of course strongly associated.[12] It is this which, ultimately, makes the local dangerous, as in the expression 'classes dangereuses'. 'Primitive' culture, of course, is perfectly wonderful, but it needs to be extracted from its lived context and transformed into objects that can be consumed without danger. The museological understanding of culture that has become increasingly popular in recent years expresses this sublimation or even displacement of the libinous of otherness into objects of consumption/contemplation and celebration. It is this transformation that enables diversity to be collected and displayed in the salons of the elites. This is also essential to the identification of such elites with diversity and multiculturalism. The strength of this ideology depends on the balance of forces within which it is produced.

Cosmopolitanism tends to emerge simultaneously with and in dialectical relation to localizing ideologies, with nationalism, indigenism and regional identities. This is happening today just as it occurred in the most recent previous period of globalization between 1870 and 1920. It is interesting to compare the two periods in this respect. The British Empire contained a core of cosmopolitanism that is quite central to developments later in the century. The strategy of Cecil Rhodes and his *Society of the Elect* was to set the agenda for the continued success of the Empire. The League of Nations, one of the strong international developments of this period, may well have been conceived by this group as was the Union of South Africa and the Commonwealth. One of the members of the group expresses the flexibility of this particular elite:

> Milner was not really a conservative at all. Milner had an idea – the idea that he obtained from Toynbee and that he found also in Rhodes and in all the members of his Group. This idea had two parts: that the extension and integration of the Empire and the development of social welfare was essential to the continued existence of the British way of life, and that this British way of life was an instrument which unfolded all the best and the highest capabilities of mankind. (Quigley 1981: 29)

But the group was perfectly capable of forsaking internationalism for reasons of expediency and, after 1931, it embraced the model of national economic regulation (idem: 248). While this all sounds like the extension of empire, it must be understood as part of hegemonic decline. The turn of the century witnessed the fragmentation of empire, not least of a formal empire, the Habsburgs. That empire was understood as traditionalist, religiously orthodox, rigid and yet its ranks were swelled by a new liberal class of cosmopolitans, many of whom were Jews and who were protected by the imperial court. Thus what is today considered progressive could easily be associated with the past, with absolutism, while nationalism was understood as the way of the future. While the situation was obviously more complicated than this, since there were other powerful cosmopolitanisms in Europe, the emerging conflict in the world system was spurred on by national competition, all of which led to the Great War. The configuration of the period is brilliantly captured in Gellner (1998):

> Hence the deep irony of the situation: an authoritarian Empire, based on a medieval dynasty and tied to the heavily dogmatic ideology of the Counter-Reformation, in the end, under the stimulus of ethnic, chauvinistic, centrifugal agitation, found its most eager defenders amongst individualist liberals, recruited in considerable part from an erstwhile pariah group and standing *outside* the faith with which the state was once so deeply identified. (Gellner 1998: 12)

This was an arena that plunged into a war and strengthened existing nation states as well creating new such entities, and which also established the League of Nations. It was riddled with all of the contradictions referred to above. In the end, however, the cosmopolitan was by and large defeated. In the current situation there are clearly similar tendencies, but political organization seems to have a stronger tendency towards empire formation, however fragile. Thus it might appear that cosmopolitan tendencies are on the rise.

Cosmopolitanism as Ideology

International organizations, such as the United Nations, UNESCO, the World Bank and the World Economic Forum, have all converged on a similar set of representations of the world. And there is also the heritage of the Rhodes group style as hegemony shifted to the United States, one that is visible in the post-Second World War clubs such as the Bilderberg, the Trilateral Commission and the Mount Pelerin society where overlapping membership is pervasive and which goes public with Davos and the World Eeconomic Council. Global media such as CNN also partake in this ideology which is significant given the force of repetitive imaging and moral framing in the creation of everyday reality, however virtual. It is also significant that a large number of intellectual elites, academics and politicians have been socialized into this worldview. I have tried to detail the way in which academic anthropology has been influenced by this trend (Friedman 1997, 1999, 2000), partaking in the 'postcolonial aura' that celebrates movement in itself as 'the good' along with an array of trans-x identities, the transnational, translocal, transsexual, bordercrossing etc. as opposed to the dangerous redneck locals who are associated with nationalism, racism, roots and that greatest of all evils, essentialism. This has even become a critique of what is assumed to be the general anthropological perspective, and can be summed up in expressions such as the following:

> ...anthropologists' obsession with boundedness is parallelled by the ways in which the people they study try to deal with seemingly open-ended global flows. (Meyer and Geschiere 1999: 3)

What a pity that the people we study have got it just as wrong as ourselves. We are obviously all in need of re-education.

It should be noted that cosmopolitanism is not equivalent to internationalism. This is an important distinction that even attracted the attention of Marcel Mauss who discussed it as 'deux sortes d'attitudes morales bien distinctes' (Mauss 1920 [1969]: 629). He chose to define cosmopolitanism as a set of ideas and tendencies oriented to the destruction of the nation, while internationalism was merely against nationalism as such but not opposed to the nation state. Thus the socialist international struggled with these two concepts and eventually chose the international rather than the cosmopolitan. But there is another difference as well. The cosmopolitanism of the turn of the last century was largely modernist in the legacy of Kant. It identified itself with universal, moral, rational and scientific values. Contemporary cosmopolitanism is the descendent of aristocratic transnationalism discussed above. It is a self identified status position and one which is quite the contrary of Kantian universalism in that it celebrates and encompasses difference rather than opposing it. This is why the notion of hybridity is a logical consequence of the formation of such identities. The cosmopolitan today is not rationalist-universalist but primarily an expression of the fusion of all cultures and peoples, expressed in the song title 'We are the world'.

Empire, Globalization and Academic Discourse

The large volume by Hardt and Negri is an interesting example of the continuing reinforcement of a particular ideology of the global. This can be found in some of the authors' major pronouncements. For them, there is no question that we are entering a post-imperialist world, one revealed by the end of the Vietnam War, by the disappearance of the Wall and by the globalization of the world economy. They understand all of this in evolutionary terms even if they are aware of the previous existence of empires and that such structures are themselves fragile in the long run. The main changes that they signal are:

1. There is a rhizomatic transformation in the sense of the development of networks of power and economic relations replacing state and other vertical forms, including fordist economic organization.
2. There is a foucauldian totalization of power which emerges as everywhere and nowhere, therefore not in any one hegemonic place such as the US or in a governmental institution.
3. Openness is extended to the extreme so that there is no longer any 'outside'.
4. The nomadic emerges as dominant figure, at least in discourse.
5. The 'multitude' formation begins to replace the proletariat.

The United States is the forerunner in this development. Europe is still based on territorially strong national sovereignty while the US has transcended all that. In the US model we already have a tendency towards Empire. Unfortunately the Indians had to go as they could never really be inside, but the project remains an open one, the frontier that has always to be confronted and transcended and therefore incorporated. This is the self-representation of American pluralism and is therefore positive for very many both right and left who vote for the immigrant nation which is the basic identity of the United States. Empire is also an inevitable evolutionary trend, which explains the largely felicitous attack on Arrighi's theory of cycles. More consistent with current globalizing ideology is the treatment of the nomadic as the wave of the future. The latter is defined as revolutionary whereas the local is relegated to the backward, even harbouring fascist potential. Here is the strongest argument for the globalists. Not only do they represent the good and progressive, but their very existence is enough to perform their historical task and pave the way for the final revolution of the multitude. Where Hardt and Negri place themselves in all of this is unclear, but the totalizing and prophetic style of the presentation is clearly something that produces resonance. The book in its sixth printing and has been hailed from many quarters. It is an extraordinary text, praised by reviewers in such disparate publications as *Foreign Affairs* and the *New York Times*, lauded by authors close to journals such as *Public Culture*. The text has a ring of radical chic, perhaps, transcending a number of former perspectives. No longer is there a class issue. The latter is fast becoming a 'multitude' whose principle characteristic is its lack of a single unifying identity or strategic goal. The resistance to emergent Empire is simply the essence of all multitude activities since they express projects that are not the dictates of higher powers. The world to come is one that is totalized under the sign of Empire in the same sense as globalization is assumed to make the world into a single place. For both, there is no longer an outside. The empire is defined as all-encompassing, without boundaries, and the multitudes are characterized as migrant/nomadic, not because they are forced to be so, but because they are the essence of global desire, the desire to be on the move, to deterritorialize. It is this which makes movement in itself, geographical movement, which is progressive while immobility is reactionary. The same underlying perspective can be found among anthropological adepts of globalization, who see a future in a diasporic world of transnationals (Appadurai, Kelly) who express a higher stage and higher status than the apparently potential rednecked homebodies who make up, unfortunately for these authors, more than ninety-eight per cent of the world's population. Both globalization discourse and *Empire* represent the same set of basic themes. The major difference between the two is that *Empire* includes a more holistic, political image of the future than can be found in most of the globalization literature, since the latter is almost entirely focused on lateral relations of transmission and movement. Hardt and Negri take on the state and they also reformulate the issue of class relations within their vision. But their totalizing perspective, the holism referred to above, is of the same order. This is why Foucault is so important in characterizing power, which is no longer a verticalized relation, but a generalized structure of total control. If the multitude threatens this structure, it is because it expresses in essence the same properties – openness, nomadism and multiculturism. So perhaps the revolution has already occurred? If the projects of the multitude are an extension of those of empire then it is basically all the same.

There are interesting points of similarity and overlap here between this supposedly radical thinking and cosmopolitan ideology. They are products of a real ideological shift or inversion that can be summarized in the following terms:

Table 9.1. Ideological shifts in cosmopolitan ideology.

1968	1998
The national	The post-national
The local	The global
Collective	Individual
Social(ist)	Liberal
Homogeneous	Heterogeneous
Monocultural	Multicultural
Equality (sameness)	Hierarchy (difference)

These terms are meant to capture the transition of self-identified progressive thinking over a period of thirty years. These terms form sets of dualist oppositions and they are of course somewhat oversimplified, but not enough to miss the nature of the shift. The post-national is today seen as the royal road to the future of mankind whereas the national is a horrible leftover from a nationalist past, including essentialist and therefore racist tendencies. In both types of texts there is an expression of this new nomadic desire to transcend the prison of locality. Individualism has increasingly replaced the former collectivist ideology and has managed to associate the latter with Foucauldian totalistic control. Similarly the liberal has successively cannibalized the socialist from the inside, producing a great deal of confusion of the kind expressed in ideologies such as New Labour and contemporary social democracy in general. The heterogeneous has become a goal in itself, a generalized cultural pluralism of different identities – ethnic, religious, territorial, gender – and of political projects (all based on such cultural identities). This is a paradox in conditions where the advocates of such a position are also liberal individualists since the cultural identities in question are collective. The multicultural quandary is an expression of the same shift toward heterogeneity. The only consistent way out of the contradictions of this position is in the transformation of culture from a structure of existence to a mere role set, so that the individual can practice culture by choice, by elective affinity, like joining the golf club instead of the Wahabists, at least on Monday. In the process of this transition, equality is increasingly replaced by hierarchy via an emphasis on difference. This is the key to pluralism as a political form, one in which elite rule is essential. Difference becomes the dominant value while equality is seen as an ugly result of totalitarian rule.

It is significant that a work like *Empire* that is so clearly marked by the radical politics of at least one of its authors can become a Harvard University Press bestseller in the United States, and enthusiastically welcomed in the pages of *Foreign Affairs* as by authors connected to *Public Culture*. This book provides a kind of political framework in two ways. It enables the cosmopolitans to reinforce their progressive identities by mere association (e.g. to Negri), eliminating the relevance of class and pointing the way towards a structure of global power in which the nomadic is defined as the prophetic call of the future revolution.

Finale: The Transformation of Governance?

Empire is a fine piece of ideological fusion, one that provides a kind of *raison d'être* for the hegemony of the new cosmopolitan elites. If there is a tendency or at least a conscious effort at establishing global governance, it is one that is also borne within cosmopolitanism as indicated above. It is one that places an elite above the masses rather than being imprisoned as their representatives. This disjuncture is one that may indeed be worth analysing today as its salience increases. In political terms the transition captures a process of hierarchization-centralization that is evident in the recent political evolution in Europe where a former left/right opposition was partly replaced by what is referred to as the 'Third Way' or perhaps more revealing, the German *Neue Mitte*, in which there is a fusion of social democracy and neo-liberal politics, in which social democracy is the shell and neo-liberalism the core. Similar tendencies were evident in American 'New Democracy' (Jacobs and Shapiro 2000). The hierarchic and encompassing theme is also expressed in the discourses of international organizations such as UNESCO, to say nothing of the already mentioned World Economic Forum. *Empire* is an almost uncanny expression of many of these tendencies in globalizing discourse and its ambivalent reference to Foucouldian global governance, without a physical centre, yet all encompassing, is an excellent concentration of what seems to be 'in the air' among certain globalizers. The popularity of the book among certain elites might well be due to the resonance of its message for those who are already tuned in. The existence of 'empire' or of a 'global elite' might be said to generate the conceptual transformation of the working classes into a 'multitude', a process that is clear in the emergence of elite multiculturalism as expressed in many countries in Europe. The relation between globalization, the reconfiguration of class relations and the production of hegemonic representations is both a viable and important subject to which an anthropology endowed with a clear sense of structural transformation should be able to contribute.

In discussions back in the 1970s on the nature of the 'Asiatic' state, to which Maurice Godelier (Godelier 1964; Friedman 1994) made

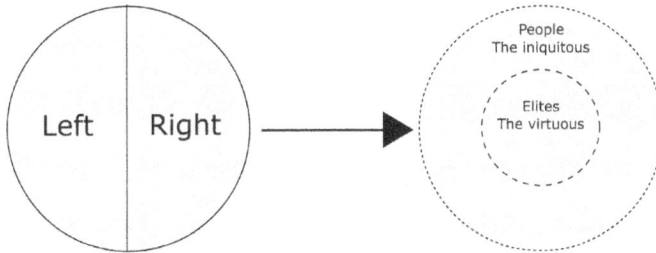

Figure 9.5. Diametric to concentric dualism in European political space.

such important contributions, some of the same issues were taken up. What is the nature of theocratic rule? On what grounds can one discuss the transition from a situation where a chief performs rituals for the community with respect to the gods, to one where he is himself the god, in other words where the relation of representation of the people to the gods becomes a relation of representation of the gods to the people? This is no mere symbolic game or ritual text, a magnificent drama. Rather, it is the very form taken by the material existence of political power. A similar inversion would return popular sovereignty to the state in the above discussion, this time by transforming the (sovereign) people into peoples, a multitude or what was once referred to as *les classes dangereuses* and the state into a cosmopolitan absolute ruler, a representative of pure virtue and even of 'democracy', now incorporated into the bodies of the rulers themselves. It is interesting to consider the way in which this representation can be mapped in structuralist terms as a transition from diametric to concentric dualism. If this kind of analysis can be applied to contemporary political change, it reinforces the need to combine structural analysis with an account of material process, a synthesis that has been the core of Maurice Godelier's research.

Notes

1. Lévi-Strauss' article on the "atom of kinship" argued that the local kinship group was dependent for its very definition and existence on a wife-giving unit, represented by the Mother's Brother,thus defining the external relation of determination with respect to group formation (1945, 1958 in *Anthropologie structural I*). This was opposed to Radcliffe-Brown and other functionalist definitions of the lineage group and the foundation of his *Elementary Structures of Kinship* (1969, 1949).
2. 'Depuis que la paix était faite, il y avait eu dans Paris un si grand abord d'étrangers que l'on en comptait quinze à seize mille dans le faubourg Saint-Germain

seulement... au commencement de l'année suivante, on trouva qu'il y en avait trente-six mille dans ce seul faubourg.'

3. 'pas mariée en France, qu'elle ne suit pas la coutume de Paris et qu'elle n'est pas naturalisée'.

4. 'fils d'un étranger originaire de Hollande'.

5. '"j'ai le sang ex-patrié"... Je suis américain, de passeport et de nationalité mais ma famille et celle de ma femme aussi, ont un grand nombre de ramifications dans beaucoup de pays, ce qui fait qu'on a toujours eu un pied aux Etats-Unis un pied à l'étranger'. 'Mon père était un peu vagabond, et on avait ça dans les veines. Mes frères, c'est pareil: j'ai un frère en Autriche, un en Finlande, une soeur en Espagne. Mon père se déplacait beaucoup, et j'ai dû prendre ça'.

6. 'Alors le terrien, c'est quelqu'un qui a un espace limité. Son activité se concentre sur la terre qu'il possède. Si l'autre va sur sa terre, il ne l'acceptera pas. Il est attaché à sa famille, à ses enfants, qu'il veut garder chez lui, parce que sa famille cultive sa terre... L'Allemand est industriel et commercial. Pour lui, le monde est grand...'

7. 'Je crois que la classe populaire est plus attachée à ses origines. Les Anglais en France sont plutôt des gens des classes moyennes. En Angleterre les classes populaires sont plus nationalistes que les autres, moins ouvertes.'

8. 'Cosmopolitisme des relations, muliterritorialité étendue aux pays étrangers, ce sont là deux composantes essentielles de la haute société.'

9. 'Oui on me prenait pour un Anglais en Angleterre, comme en Argentine on me prend pour un Argentin. C'est un des seuls dons que m'ait donné le bon Dieu. J'imite les accents avec énormément de facilités (*il imite l'accent marseillais*). Ca ne sert pas a grand-chose, mais bon!'

10. 'Les deux formes de rapports à l'étranger restent néamoins bien distincts. *L'international* se définit aussi par opposition au *cosmopolite*. Le cosmopolitisme repose sur la cohésion d'une petite élite aristocratique, et ne met pas reellement en jeu des relations entre des cultures différentes. A l'inverse, la culture internationale des cadres repose justement sur la valorisation de la diversité des culture nationales.'

11. 'La capacité d'être chez soi, au sens à la fois matériel, social et symbolique dans plusieurs pays, l'incorporation d'une identité cosmopolite qui produit ses effets sur toutes les dimensions de la personne définissent bien le modèle vers lequel tend la culture internationale des cadres.'

12. Thus being primitive in the temporal sense as in the sense of the human life cycle and primitive in the geographical sense of being out there are joined. Being before and being out there are thus logically linked to a concentric understanding of the self and society. The libidinous refers to the lack of control over basic desires that Freud interprets as paramount for the infantile situation.

Bibliography

Abbé Sieyès, E.-J. 1789. Qu'est-ce que le tiers état?

Appadurai, A. 1993. 'Patriotism and Its Futures', *Public Culture* 5: 415–40.

Arrighi, G. 1997. 'Globalisation, State Sovereignty, and the "Endless" Accumulation of Capital', revised version of a paper presented at the Conference on 'States and Sovereignty in the World Economy', University of California, Irvine, 21–23 February 1997.

———— 2003. 'The Political Economy of Global Turbulence', *New Left Review* 50: 1–67.

Bairoch, P. and R. Kozul-Wright. 1996. 'Globalization Myths: Some Historical Reflections on Integration, Industrialization and Growth in the World Economy', *UNCTAD Discussion Paper* no.113.

Barnum, C. 1992. 'Effective Membership in the Global Business Community', in J. Renesch (ed.), *New Traditions in Business. Spirit and Leadership in the 21st Century*. San Francisco: Berrett-Koehler, p.141–59.

Bell, D. 1973. *The Coming of Post-industrial Society: A Venture in Social Forecasting*. New York: Basic Books.

Bourdieu, P. 1979. *Distinction*. Paris: Minuit.

Braudel, F. 1984. *The Perspective of the World*. New York: Harper and Row.

Briggs, A. and D. Snowman. 1996. *Fins de Siecle: How Centuries End, 1400–2000*. New Haven: Yale University Press.

Butler, J. 1993. *Bodies that Matter: On the Discursive Limits of Sex*. New York: Routledge.

Castells, M. 2000. *The Rise of Network Society*. Oxford: Blackwell.

Comaroff, J. and J. Comaroff. 1999. 'Occult Economies and the Violence of Abstraction: Notes from the South African Postcolony', *American Ethnologist* 26(2): 279–303.

Dicken, P. 1998. *Global Shift: Transforming the World Economy*. New York: Guilford Press.

Dubost, J.-F. and P. Sahlins. 1999. *Et si on faisait payer les étrangers*. Paris: Flammarion.

Duménil, G. and D. Lévy. 2004. *Capital Resurgent: Roots of the Neoliberal Revolution*. Cambridge: Harvard University Press.

Fanon, F. 1971. *Peau noir, masques blancs*. Paris: Seuil.

Fénélon, F. de Salignac de la Mothe. 1920. *Les Aventures de Télémaque*. Paris: Hachette.

Friedman, J. 1974. 'The Place of Fetishism and the Problem of Materialist Interpretations', *Critique of Anthropology* 1(1): 26–62.

———— 1994 [1979]. *System, Structure and Contradiction in the Evolution of 'Asiatic' Social Formations*. Republication of 1979 book with a new introduction and appendix. Walnut Creek: Altamira-Sage.

———— 1997. 'Global Crises, the Struggle for Cultural Identity and Intellectual Pork-barreling: Cosmopolitans, Nationals and Locals in an Era of De-hegemonization', in P. Werbner (ed.), *Debating Cultural Hybridity*. London: Zed Press, p.79–89.

———— 1999. 'The Hybridization of Roots and the Abhorrence of the Bush', in M. Featherstone and S. Lash (eds), *Spaces of Culture: City, Nation, World*. London: Sage, p.230–56.

———— 2000. 'Des Racines et (Dé)routes', *L'Homme* 157: 187–206.

———— 2002. 'From Roots to Routes: Tropes for Trekkers', *Anthropological Theory* 2(2): 21–36.

———— 2007. 'Globalization, Global Systems and Anthropological Theory', in I. Rossi (ed.), *Frontiers of Globalization Research*. New York: Springer, p.109–32.

Gellner, E. 1998. *Language and Solitude: Wittgenstein, Malinowski, and the Habsburg Dilemma.* Cambridge, New York: Cambridge University Press.

Godelier, M. 1964. *La notion de 'mode de production asiatique' et les schémas marxistes d'évolution des sociétés.* Paris: Centre d'études et de Recherches marxistes.

Gordon, R.A. 2000. 'Does the "New Economy" Measure up to the Inventions of the Past', *National Bureau of Economic Research Working paper 7833,* Cambridge, MA 02138 http://www.nber.org/papers/w7833.

Hardt, M. and A. Negri. 2000. Empire. Cambridge: Harvard University Press.

Harris, D. 1992. *From Class Struggle to the Politics of Pleasure: The Effects of Gramscianism on Cultural Studies.* London, New York: Routledge.

Harvey, D. 2005. *A Brief History of Neoliberalism.* Oxford, New York: Oxford University Press.

Hilferding, R. 1910. *Das Finanzkapital; eine Studie über die jüngste Entwicklung des Kapitalismus.* Vienna: I. Brand.

Hirst, P.Q. and G. Thompson. 1996. *Globalization in Question: The International Economy and the Possibilities of Governance.* Cambridge, UK, Oxford, UK, Cambridge, MA: Polity Press and Blackwell Publishers.

Jacobs, L.R. and R.Y. Shapiro. 2000. *Politicians Don't Pander: Political Manipulation and the Loss of Democratic Responsiveness.* Chicago: University of Chicago Press.

Kapferer, B. 1988. *Legends of People, Myths of State.* Washington, DC: Smithsonian Institution.

Kelly, J. 1995. 'Diaspora and World War, Blood and Nation in Fiji and Hawaii', *Public Culture* 7(3): 475–97.

Malkki, L. 1992. 'National Geographic: The Rooting of Peoples and the Territorialization of National Identity among Scholars and Refugees', *Cultural Anthropology* 7(1): 24–44.

Mauss, M. 1920. 'La nation et l'internationalisme', Conference communication in French. 'The Problem of Nationality'. London: Proceedings of the Aristotelien Society, p.242–51. (Reproduced in M. Mauss. 1969. *Oeuvres.* 3. Cohésion sociale et division de la sociologie. Paris: Les Editions de Minuit, p.626–34).

Meyer, B. and P. Geschiere. 1999. 'A Time and the Global: Against the Homogeneous, Empty Communities in Contemporary Social Theory', in B. Meyer and P. Geschiere (eds), *Globalization and Identity: Dialectics of Flow and Closure.* Oxford: Blackwell, p.1–16.

Noiriel, G. 2001. *Etat, nation et immigration: vers une histoire du pouvoir.* Paris: Belin.

Pijl, K. van der. 1996. *Transnational Classes and International Relations.* London: Routledge.

Pinçon, M. and M. Pinçon-Charlot. 1996. *Les grandes fortunes.* Paris: Payot.

Quigley, C. 1981. *The Anglo-American Establishment: From Rhodes to Cliveden.* New York: Books in Focus.

Ravenstock-Huessy, E. 1961 [1931]. *Die europaischen Revolutionen und der Character der Nationen.* Stuttgart: Kohlhammer.

Sieyès, E.J. 1999 and 2007. *Des Manuscrits de Sieyès.* 1773–1799, Tome I et II, publiés par Christine Fauré, Jacques Guilhaumou, Jacques Vallier et Françoise Weil, Paris: Champion.

Touraine, A. 1992. *Critique de la modernité.* Paris: Fayard.

Turner, C.H. and A. Trompenaars. 1994. *The Seven Cultures of Capitalism. Value Systems for Creating Wealth in the United States, Britain, Japan, Germany France, Sweden and the Netherlands.* London: Pinkus.

Wagner, A.C. 1999. *Les nouvelles élites de la mondialisation: une immigration dorée en France.* Paris: Presses Universitaires de France.

PUBLICATIONS BY MAURICE GODELIER

Books, Edited Volumes and Book Translations

1966. *Rationalité et irrationalité en économie*. Paris: Maspéro. (Translations: English, New Left Books; Italian, Feltrinelli; Spanish, Siglo XXI; German, Zuhrkampf).

1970. *Antropologia, storia, marxismo*. Parma: Guanda.

1970. *Sur les sociétés précapitalistes* (editor). Paris: Editions Sociales. (Translations: Italian, Feltrinelli; Spanish, Siglo XXI and Editorial Estela).

1971. with J. Copans, S. Tornay and C. Backès-Clément (editors). *L'Anthropologie, science des sociétés primitives?* Paris: Denoël.

1973. *Horizon, trajets marxistes en anthropologie*. Paris: Maspéro. (Translations: English, Spanush, Italian, Portugese and Japanese).

1974. *Un Domaine contesté, l'anthropologie économique* (editor). Paris: Mouton.

1975. *Rapporti di produzione, miti, societa*. Rome: Feltrinelli.

1976. with R. Cresswell (editors). *Outils d'enquête et analyse anthropologique*. Paris: Maspéro (Bibliothèque d'Anthropologie).

1982. *La Production des Grands Hommes. Pouvoir et domination masculine chez les Baruya de Nouvelle-Guinée*. Paris: Fayard. This book received the prize of the French Academy in 1982. (Translations: English, Cambridge University Press; German, Campus; Spanish, Akal, Madrid).

1982. *Les sciences de l'homme et de la société en France. Analyse et propositions pour une politique nouvelle*. Report produced for Jean-Pierre Chevènement, Minister of State, Ministry for Research and Industry. Collection of official reports. La Documentation Française, 2 volumes.

1984. *L'Idéel et le Matériel: pensée, économie, sociétés*. Paris: Fayard. (Translations: English, Verso; Italian, Riuniti; Spanish, Taurus; German). New edition in 1992, Paris: Biblio-essais.

1991. with M. Strathern (editors). *Big Men, Great Men, Personifications of Power in Melanesia*. Cambridge, C.U.P. (new edition in 2008).

1991. *Wird der Westen das universelle Modell der Menschkeit?* Vortrag im Wiener Rathaus, 13 Juni, 1990. Vienna: Picus Verlag, Wiener Vorlesungen im Rathaus, Bd. 5.

1991. *Transitions et subordinations au capitalisme* (editor). Paris: Editions de la Maison des Sciences de l'Homme.

1991. with F. Héritier-Augé et al. *Les Musées de l'Education Nationale*, Mission d'Etude et de Réflexion, Paris, La Documentation Française. Report for the Minister of State, Ministry for National Education.

1996. with J. Hassoun (editors). *Meurtre du Père, Sacrifice de la sexualité. Approches anthropologiques et psychanalytiques*. Paris: Arcanes, 'Les Cahiers d'Arcanes'.

1996. *L'Enigme du Don*. Paris: Fayard (English and Russian translations).

1998. with M. Panoff (editors). *La production du corps*. Paris: Archives Contemporaines (new edition in one volume in 2009: *Le Corps Humain. Conçu, Supplicié, Possédé, Cannibalisé*. Paris: CNRS).

1998. with M. Panoff (editors). *Le corps humain, Supplicié, Possédé, Cannibalisé*. Paris, Archives Contemporaines (new edition in one volume in 2009: *Le Corps Humain. Conçu, Supplicié, Possédé, Cannibalisé*. Paris: CNRS).

1998. with T. Trautmann and F.E. Tjon Sie Fat (editors). *Transformations of Kinship*. Washington, London: Smithsonian Institution Press.

2002. *L'état des Sciences de l'Homme et de la Société en France et leur rôle dans la construction de l'Espace Européen de la Recherche. Etat des lieux et propositions*. Report for the Prime Minister.

2004. *Métamorphoses de la Parenté*. Paris: Fayard.

2005. with F. Jullien and J. Maïla. *Le grand âge de la vie*. Paris: PUF - Fondation d'Entreprise EISAI.

2007. *Au Fondement des sociétés humaines. Ce que nous apprend l'anthropologie*. Paris: Albin Michel.

2009. *Communauté, Société, Culture. Trois clefs pour comprendre les identités en conflits*. Paris: CNRS éditions. (Publication of the Huxley Memorial Lecture of 2008).

2009. with M. Panoff (editors). New editions of *Le Corps Humain. Conçu, Supplicié, possédé, cannibalisé*. Paris: Editions du CNRS.

Articles, Chapters and Published Interviews

1960

'Les structures de la méthode du *Capital*' I. *Economie et Politique* 70: 35–52.

'Les structures de la méthode du *Capital*' II. *Economie et politique* 71: 15–36.

1961

'Les structures de la méthode du *Capital*' III. *Economie et politique* 80: 49–63.

1963

'Economie politique et philosophie', *La Pensée* 111: 98–112.

1964

'Economie politique et anthropologie économique' (review of R.E. Salisbury, *From Stone to Steel*), *L'Homme* IV (3): 118–32.

'La notion de mode de production asiatique et les schémas marxistes d'évolution des sociétés', *Les Cahiers du CERM*, Editions Sociales. 53 pages.

'Théorie marginaliste et théorie marxiste de la valeur et des prix', *Cahiers de Planification* 3 (Publication de l'Ecole Pratique des Hautes Etudes), republished in *La Pensée* 120, 77–90.
'La Mesure de la valeur: problème de gestion optimale', *Cahiers de Planification* 3.
'Les écrits de Marx et Engels sur le mode de production asiatique', *La Pensée* 114, 56–73.
'Structures agraires et terroirs africains', *Annales*, 3: 621–24.

1965

'La notion de mode de production asiatique', *Les Temps Modernes* XX (228): 2002–2027.
'Objet et méthode de l'anthropologie économique', *L'Homme* V (2): 32–91.
'Théorie marginaliste et théorie marxiste de la valeur et des prix', *La Pensée* 120: 77–90.
'Discussions et débats sur le mode de production asiatique', *La Pensée* 122: 60–62.

1966

'Système, structure et contradiction dans *le Capital*', *Les Temps Modernes* 246: 841–64.
'Economie politique et anthropologie économique (à propos des Siane de la Nouvelle-Guinée)', *L'Homme* VIII (3): 118–32.
'Remarques sur les concepts de structure et de contradiction', *Aletheia* May issue.

1967

Deluz, A.; M. Godelier. 'A propos de deux textes d'anthropologie économique', *L'Homme* VII (3): 78–91.
'Science de l'histoire et théorie des systèmes; response to B. Besnier', *Aletheia* 6, April Issue: 224–31.
'System, Structure and Contradiction in *The Capital*', in R. Miliband and J. Saville (eds), *The Socialist Register*. London: Merlin.

1968

'Les Méthodes de simulation en économie', *The Social Sciences, Problems and Orientations*. Unesco/Mouton, p.409–21.

1969

'Land Tenure among the Baruya of New Guinea', *Journal of the Papua New Guinea Society* 3: 17–23.
'La pensée de Marx et d'Engels aujourd'hui et les recherches de demain', *La Pensée* 143: 92–120.
'Economique (Anthropologie)', in *Encyclopedia Universalis*, p.935–38.

1970

'La monnaie de sel des Baruya de Nouvelle-Guinée', *L'Homme* IX (2): 5–37.
'Economie marchande, fétichisme, magie et science selon Marx dans *le Capital*', *La Nouvelle Revue de Psychanalyse* II: 197–213.
'Logique dialectique et analyse des structures. Response to Lucien Sève, *La Pensée* 149: 3–28.

1971

'Mythe et histoire: réflexion sur les fondements de la pensée sauvage', *Annales* 3–4: 541–68.

'Définition et champ de l'anthropologie économique', in J. Copans, S. Tornay, M. Godelier (eds), *L'anthropologie, Science des Sociétés Primitives*. Paris: Editions E.P., p.177–243.

'Lewis H. Morgan' in *Encyclopedia Universalis*, p.323–25.

'Qu'est-ce que définir une formation économique et sociale? L'exemple des Incas', *La Pensée* 159: 99–106.

with C.D. Ollier and D.P. Prover: 'Soil Knowledge amongst the Baruya of Wonenara, New Guinea', *Oceania* 42(1): 33–41.

'Marxisme, anthropologie et religion', *Raison Présente* 18: 45–65.

1972

'Le visible et l'invisible chez les Baruya de Nouvelle-Guinée', in J. Thomas and L. Bernot (eds), *Langues et techniques*, papers in homage to André-Georges Haudricourt, Nature et société. Paris, Klincksieck, volume 2: 263–69.

'Functionalism, Structuralism and Marxism'. Foreword to the English Edition, in *Rationality and Irrationality in Economics*, by M. Godelier. New York and London, Monthly Review Press.

1973

'Le Concept de tribu. Crise d'un concept ou crise des fondements empiriques de l'anthropologie?, *Diogène* 81: 3–28.

'Parures papoues, un art entre deux mondes', *Atlas*. February issue: 73–92.

with J. Garanger. 'Outils de pierre, outils d'acier chez les Baruya de Nouvelle-Guinée', *L'Homme* XIII(3): 187–220.

'Modes de production, rapports de parenté et structures démographiques', *La Pensée* 172: 7–31.

'L'Oeuvre de Karl Polanyi', preface to K. *Polanyi, les systèmes économiques dans l'histoire et dans la théorie*. Paris, Larousse Université (Sciences Humaines et Sociales, série Anthropologie), p.9–30.

'Tribu', in *Encyclopedia Universalis*, vol. 18, Paris, p.313–19.

'Remarques épistémologiques sur la comparaison entre modes de production et organisation sociale'. Report presented at the *IXe Congrès International des Sciences Anthropologiques*. Chicago, September 1973.

'Anthropologie économique', in R. Cresswell (ed.), *Manuel d'anthropologie*, Paris: Armand Colin.

1974

'Vers une théorie marxiste des faits religieux', *Lumière et Vie. Revue de formation et de réflexions théologiques* 117–118: 85–94.

'Considérations théoriques et critiques sur le problème des rapports entre l'homme et son environnement', *Information sur les Sciences Sociales* XIII(6): 31–60.

'Anthropologie et biologie: vers une coopération nouvelle', *Revue Internationale des Sciences Sociales* XXVI(4): 666–90.

'La Notion de réciprocité chez Karl Polanyi', Special issue: 'Pour une histoire anthropologique', *Annales E.S.C.* 26(6): 1371–74.

'Une anthropologie économique est-elle possible?' in E. Morin and M. Piatelli (eds), *Unité de l'Homme, pour une anthropologie fondamentale*. Paris: Le Seuil, p.175–201, preceded (141–47) and followed (202–12) by discussions. Papers presented at the Royaumont Conference in 1972.

'Une remarque sur la notion de délire', in E. Morin, M. Piatelli (eds), *Unité de l'Homme, invariants biologiques et unversaux culturels*. Paris: Le Seuil. Paper presented at the Royaumont Conference in 1972.

'Salt Currency and the Circulation of Commodities among the Baruya of New Guinea', in G. Dalton (ed.), *Studies in Economic Anthropology*. Washington: American Anthropological Studies 7: 52–73.

1975

'L'Anthropologie des Dieux', *L'Homme* XV(1): 99–102.

'Economie', in R. Cresswell (ed.), *Elements d'Anthropologie*, vol. 2, Paris: Armand Colin, p.80–131.

'Heurs et malheurs du métier d'ethnologue', *Les Temps Modernes* 344: 1217–24.

'Toward a Marxist Anthropology of Religion', *Dialectical Anthropology* 1(1): 81–85.

'Raison, mythe et société dans la Grèce antique. Interview with J.P.Vernant and M. Caveing', *Raison Présente* 35: 7–30.

'Anthropologie, histoire, idéologie', interview with C. Lévi-Strauss and M. Augé, *L'Homme* XV(3–4): 177–88. (English translation in *Critique of Anthropology* 2(6): 44–55).

'Modes of Production, Kinship, and Demographic Structures', ASA Studies, vol. 2, p.3–27. Reprinted in M. Bloch (ed.), *Marxist Analyses and Social Anthropology*. London: Malaby, p.3–27.

'Perspectives ethnologiques et questions actuelles sur le travail', *Lumière et Vie* XXIV(124): 35–58.

1976

'Le Marxisme dans les sciences humaines', *Raison Présente* 37: 65–79.

'Terroir', in *Outils d'enquête et d'analyse anthropologiques*: Paris: François Maspéro, p.140–51.

'Perspectives ethnologiques et questions actuelles sur le travail', *Lumière et Vie* 24: 35–58.

'Le Sexe comme fondement ultime de l'ordre social et cosmique chez les Baruya de Nouvelle-Guinée: mythe et réalité', in A. Verdiglione (ed.), *Sexualité et pouvoir*. Paris: Payot, p.268–306.

'Rapporti di produzione, miti, societa', Serie *Oposcoli marxisti* 11. Milano: Feltrinelli, 67 pages.

'Economy and Religion: An Evolutionary Optical Illusion', *Research Seminar on Archaelogy and Related Subjects*, University of London. Published in *The Evolution of Social System*, Pittsburgh: University of Pittsburgh, 1978, p.3–11.

'Sur la notion de civilisation. Interview with Maurice Godelier', *Revue Française d'Etudes Américaines* 3, April issue: 11–25.

1977

'Sur la notion de civilisation', interview with M. Godelier, *Revue des Etudes Américaines* 3: 11–25.

'Infrastructures, sociétés, histoire', *Dialectiques* 22: 41–53.

'Politics as "Infrastructure": An Anthropological Thought on the Example of Classical Greece and the Notions of Relations of Production and Economic Determination', in J. Friedman and M.J. Rowlands (eds), *The Evolution of Social System*, London: Duckworth, p.13–28.

'Economy and Religion: An Evolutionary Optical Illusion', in J. Friedman and M.J. Rowlands (eds), *The Evolution of Social System*, London: Duckworth, p.3–12.

1978

'L'Appropriation de la nature: territoire et propriété dans quelques formes de sociétés précapitalistes', La Pensée, 1981 March issue: 7–50. English translation: 1979. 'The appropriation of nature', Critique of Anthropology 4(13–14): 17–27.

'L'anthropologie économique', in *L'anthropologie en France. Situation actuelle et avenir*, Paris: Editions du CNRS, p.47–79.

'The Object and Method of Economic Anthropology', in D. Seddon (ed.), *Relations of Production: Marxist Approaches to Economic Anthropology*, London-Totowa, NJ: Frank Cass and cie, p.49–126.

'The Concept of "Asiatic Mode of Production" and Marxist Model of Social Evolution', in D. Seddon (ed.), *Relations of Production: Marxist Approaches to Economic Anthropology*. London-Totowa, NJ: Frank Cass and cie, p.209–57.

'Territory and Property in Primitive Society', *Social Sciences Information* XVII(3): 399–426.

'Travail et travailleur: perspectives anthropologiques et historiques, problèmes actuels', Société Française de Psychologie, *Que va devenir le travail?* Paris: Entreprise moderne d'édition, p.28–40.

'Pouvoir et langage. Réflexions sur les paradigmes et les paradoxes de la "légitimité" des rapports de domination et d'oppression', *Communications* 28: 21–27.

'Economia', in *Enciclopedia Einaudi*, Torino: Einaudi, p.197–223.

'La Part idéelle du réel: essai sur l'idéologique', *L'Homme* XVIII(3–4): 155–88.

'Infrastructures, Societies and History', *Current Anthropology* XIX(4): 763–71.

'La part "idéelle" du réel et le problème des fondements de la dominance des structures non économiques', *L'Arc* 72, special issue by Georges Duby, p. 49–56.

'Le pouvoir masculin', *Le Groupe Familial* 78, special issue 'l'Homme au masculin', p.2–11.

'Reproduction des ecosystèmes et transformation des systèmes sociaux', *Economie Rurale* 124(2):10–15.

'Ethnologie et fait religieux: table ronde', *Revue Française de Sociologie* XIX(4): 571–84.

1979

'Les rapports hommes/femmes: le problème de la domination masculine', in CERM (ed.), *La Condition féminine*. Paris: Editions Sociales, p.23–44.

'EpistemologicalCommentsontheProblemof ComparingModesof Production and Societies', in S. Diamond (ed.), *Toward a Marxist Anthropology: Problems and Perspectives*. La Haye: Mouton, p.71–92.

'Formazione economico-sociale', in *Enciclopedia Einaudi*. Torino: Einaudi, p.342–73.

'Anthropologie et économie', in *L'Anthropologie en France, situation actuelle et avenir*, Paris 18–22 avril 1977. Paris: Editions du C.N.R.S. (Colloques Internationaux du C.N.R.S.), 573: 47–79.

'On Infrastructures, Societies and History; Reply', *Current Anthropology* XX(1): 108–11.

'Lavoro', in *Enciclopedia Einaudi*. Torino: Einaudi, p.31–81.

'Stone Tools and Steel Tools among the Baruya of New Guinea. Some Ethnographic and Quantitative Data', *Social Sciences Information* 18(4–5): 633–78.

1980

'Memorandum pour une enquête sur le travail et ses représentations', translated and published as 'Aide-mémoire for a Survey of Work and Its Representations', *Current Anthropology* XXI(6): 831–85.

'Economic Institutions', in I Rossi (ed.), *People in Culture: A Survey of Cultural Anthropology*. New York: J.F. Bergin Publ. & Praeger, p.255–312.

'Una Antropologia de la Sociedad Capitalista', *I Congresso Espanol de Antropologia* 1, Universidad de Barcelona, departamento Antropologia Cultural: 15–22.

'The Emergence and Development of Marxism in Anthropology in France', in E. Gellner (ed.), *Soviet and Western Anthropology*. London: Duckworth, p.3–17.

'Economique (Anthropologie)', *Encyclopedia Universalis*, vol. 5. Paris: France S.A., p.935–38.

'Economie et Religion. Eléments d'analyse marxiste d'une pratique symbolique', in S. Latouche (ed.), *Pratique économique et pratique symbolique*, Paris: Anthropos, p.361–72.

'Language and History. Work and its Representation: A Research Proposal', *History Workshop Journal* 10: 164–74.

'Modo di Produzione', in *Enciclopedia Einaudi*. Torino: Einaudi, p.423–67.

'Primitivo', in *Enciclopedia Einaudi*. Torino: Einaudi, p.1130–45.

'Proprieta', in *Enciclopedia Einaudi*. Torino: Einaudi, p.367–84.

'Hiérarchies sociales chez les Baruya de Nouvelle-Guinée', *Journal de la Société des Océanistes* XXXVI(69): 239–59.

'L'Etat: les processus de sa formation, la diversité de ses formes et de ses bases', *Revue Internationale des Sciences Sociales* XXXII(4): 657–71.

'Le marxisme dans les sciences humaines', *Raison Présente* 55: 105–18.

'Il lavoro: realtà e concezioni. Intervista a Maurice Godelier', *La Ricerca Folkorica* ('Il lavoro et le sue rappresentazioni') 9: 11–19.

'Work and Its Representations: A Research Proposal', *History Workshop Journal* 10(1): 164–74.

1981

'Riproduzione', in *Enciclopedia Einaudi*. Torino: Einaudi, p.87–111.

'Transizione', in *Enciclopedia Einaudi*. Torino: Einaudi, p.460–94.
'D'un mode de production à l'autre: théorie de la transition', *Recherches Sociologiques* 2: 161–93.
Preface to B. Doray, *Le taylorisme, une folie rationnelle?*, Paris: Dunod.
'Temps mythique, temps historique, temps quotidien chez les Baruya de Nouvelle-Guinée', *Temps Libre* 4: 7–15.
'Het ideële als element van het reële. Essay over het ideologische', *Mens en maatschappij*. Deventer, the Netherlands, 55: 65–102.
'The Asiatic Mode of Production', in P. Kegan (ed.), *The Asiatic Mode of Production*. London: Routledge, p.264–77.
'Charivari chez les Baruya de Nouvelle-Guinée', in J. Le Goff and J.C. Schmitt (eds), *Le Charivari*. Paris: Ecole des Hautes Etudes en Sciences Sociales / Mouton (Civilisations et sociétés), p.347–51.
'Economic Anthropology and History, the Work of Karl Polanyi', *Research in Economic Anthropology* 4: 65–69.

1982

'Social Hierarchies among the Baruya of New Guinea', in A. Strathern (ed.), *Inequality in New Guinea Highlands Societies*. Cambridge: C.U.P., p.3–34.
'Myths, Infrastructures and History in Levi-Strauss', in I Rossi (ed.), *The Logic of Culture*. New York: J.-F. Bergin Publisher Inc., p.232–61.
'Un mariage très catholique', *Magazine Littéraire* 189: 34–36.
'Réponse de Maurice Godelier sur la recherche en sciences sociales', *Le Débat* 22: 23–29.
'Les sciences de l'homme ont-elles un avenir en France?', *La Recherche* 13(135): 896–99.
'Un haut lieu de l'anthropologie', *Spirales* 15: 22–24.

1983

'Malthus and Ethnography', in J. Dupâquier, A. Fauve-Chamoux and E. Grebenik (eds), *Malthus Past and Present*. London: Academic Press, p.125–50.
'A Teoria da Transicao em Marx', *Ler Historia* 2: 99–142.
'Formation économique et sociale', in G. Labica (ed.), *Dictionnaire du marxisme*. Paris: PUF, p.377–80.
'Pour une politique pluridisciplinaire', *Mex* 5: 8–9.
'Transition', in G. Labica (ed.), *Dictionnaire du marxisme*. Paris: PUF, p.377–80.
Preface to Marie-Elizabeth Handman, *La violence et la ruse. Hommes et femmes dans un village grec*, Aix-en-Provence: EdiSud, CNRS.

1984

'Marx et la domination masculine', in G. Halimi (ed), *Fini le Féminisme? Perdre plus que nos Chaînes*. Paris: Gallimard, p.84–98 (Presented originally at the conference 'Féminisme et socialismes', Palais de l'UNESCO in Paris).
'Malthus et les sociétés de son temps. Les sources ethnographiques de la pensée de Malthus', in J. Dupâquier, A. Fauve-Chamoux and E. Grebenik (eds), *Malthus Hier et Aujourd'hui*. Paris: éd. du CNRS.
'To Be a Marxist in Anthropology', in J. Maquet and N. Daniels (eds), *On Marxian Perspectives in Anthropology*, Essays in honor of Harry Hoijer.

Malibu: Undena Publications for the UCLA Dept. of Anthropology, p.35–57.

1985

'Le Progrès des sciences et des techniques: l'évolution des savoirs et des qualifications', communication at the *Colloque La Société française et son école*. Paris, 8–9 juin 1985.

'Ethnie, tribu, nation chez les Baruya de Nouvelle-Guinée', *Journal de la Société des Océanistes* XLI(81): 159–68.

'Le processus de formation de l'Etat', in A. Kazancigil (ed.), *L'Etat au Pluriel*, Paris: UNESCO-Economica, p.21–37.

'The Worst of Architect is Better than the Best of Bees. A Debate between Eric Wolf and Maurice Godelier', *Critique of Anthropology* 5(2): 5–19.

Interview in *Entretiens avec Le Monde* 6. Paris: La Découverte/Le Monde, p.147–56.

1986

'Allocution', in M. Gast and M. Panoff (eds), *L'Accès au terrain en pays étranger et d'outre-mer.* Paris: L'Harmattan, p.12–25.

1987

'Analyse des processus de transition', *Revue Internationale des Sciences Sociales* 114, UNESCO: 447–57.

'Analyse des processus de transition', *Information sur les sciences sociales* 26(2): 265–83.

'Mode de production', in *Marxistisches Wörterbuch*. Berlin: F.U.

'Produktionsweise als Theoretische Kategorie', *Das Argument* 29(165): 635–50.

'Mode de production asiatique', in *Lexicon der Ethnologie*. Francfort: Campus Verlag.

'Georges Bataille: l'endroit d'où il nous parle', introduction to *Textes d'ailleurs. Georges Bataille et les ethnologues,* papers collated by Dominique Lecoq and Jean-Luc Lory. Paris: Editions de la Maison des sciences de l'homme, p.1–6.

'L'Histoire marche comme les crabes, à l'oblique', Interview with Guitta Pasternak for *Le Monde*, 26 August: 11–12.

1988

'Trahir le secret des Hommes. Les Baruya, une société segmentaire de Nouvelle-Guinée', *Le Genre Humain* 16–17: 243–65.

'Interdiction de l'inceste et naissance de la société humaine', *Le Journal des Psychologues* 60: 14–18.

'La Prohibition de l'inceste ou le débordement de la parenté', *Journal des Psychologues*, special issue 'Cultures et personnalité', p.25–32.

'Ne plus sous-estimer l'identité sociale et culturelle', interview with Yves Sintomer and Isabelle Etienne, $E = MC2$ 23: 36–41.

'Structuralism and Marxism', in Tom Bottomore (ed.), *Interpretations of Marx*. Oxford: Basil Blackwell Ltd, p.72–80.

1989

'Betrayal: A Key Moment in the Dynamic of Segmentary Tribal Societies. The Case of the New Guinea Baruya', *Oceania* 59(3): 165–80.

'Mélanésie-Nouvelle Guinée: quelques chemins depuis l'indépendance', *Hérodote* 52: 132–45.

'L'étrange éducation des Baruya de Nouvelle- Guinée', *Le Monde de l'éducation* 158: 50–53.

'Sexualité, parenté et pouvoir', *La Recherche* 20(213): 1141–55.

'Private Politics – A Multidisciplinary Approach to Big Man Systems', *American Anthropologist* 91(2): 474–75.

'Kinship and the Evolution of Society', in A. Gingrich, S. Haas, S. Haas and G. Paleczek (eds), *Kinship, Social Change, and Evolution*. Proceedings of a Symposium held in Honour of Walter Dostal. Vienna: Wiener Beiträge zur Ethnologie und Anthropologie, vol 5.

'Incest Taboo and the Evolution of Society', Herbert Spencer Lecture 1986. Published in A. Grafen (ed.), *Evolution and its Influence*. Oxford: Clarendon Press, p.63–92.

'La constitution de l'anthropologie sociale comme discipline scientifique et objet d'enseignement', Roundtable 'Didactique et Histoire'. *Actes du Colloque Université: idéologie et culture*. Athens, p.641–49.

1990

'L'oeuvre de Marx', *Actuel Marx* 7 ('Le marxisme analytique anglo-saxon'): 139–63.

'Inceste, parenté, pouvoir', *Psychanalystes* 36: 33–51.

'La théorie de la transition chez Marx', *Sociologie et sociétés* XXII(1): 53–81.

'Transformation de la nature et rapports sociaux', in *Les rapports sociaux et leurs enjeux;* seminaire du Centre de Sociologie Urbaine, 1986–1988: 2.

'Avant-propos', in P. Lemonnier, *Guerres et Festins: Paix, Echanges et Compétitions dans les Highlands de Nouvelle-Guinée*. Paris: éditions de la MSH.

'Sociétés à Big Men, sociétés à Grands Hommes: figures du pouvoir en Nouvelle-Guinée', *Journal de la Société des Océanistes* 91(2): 75–94.

1991

'Les contextes illusoires de la transition au socialisme', in J. Bidet and J. Texier (eds), *Fin du communisme? Actualité du marxisme?* Paris: P.U.F. Collection Actuel Marx Confrontation.

'Ordres, classes, Etat chez Marx', *Actuel Marx* 9 ('Le monde est-il un marché?'): 123–42.

'Le couple infernal de l'économie et du pouvoir', interview in *Les Cahiers Marxistes* 178: 27–37.

'L'Occident est-il le modèle universel de l'humanité? Les Baruya de Nouvelle-Guinée entre la transformation et la décomposition', *Revue Internationale des Sciences Sociales* 128: 411–23.

'Dimensions idéelles, matérielles et sociales de l'activité technique dans les sociétés primitives', *Culture technique* 22: 134–43.

Preface to Jacques Perrin (ed.), *Construire une science des techniques*. Maison d'Edition l'Inter disciplinaire, Limonest.

'Le mode de production asiatique: un concept stimulant, mais qui reste d'une portée analytique limitée', *Actuel Marx* 10 ('Ethique et Politique'): 181–99.

'Les Baruya de Nouvelle-Guinée. Un exemple récent de subordination économique, politique et culturelle d'une société "primitive" à l'Occident', in M. Godelier (ed.), *Transitions et subordinations au capitalisme*. Paris: Editions de la Maison des Sciences de l'Homme, p.379–99.

1992

'Corps, parenté, pouvoir(s) chez les Baruya de Nouvelle-Guinée', *Journal de la Société des Océanistes* 94: 3–24.

'L'Ouest et les Autres', Interview for *Kultura*, 31 juillet 1992, p.3.

'Baruya, les guerriers assagis', *Sciences et Avenir* 90 (Hors série: 'Les derniers sauvages'): 36–41.

'Cuerpo, Parentesco y Poderes entre los Baruya de Nueva Guinea', *Cuicuilco, Revista de la Escuela Nacional de Antropologia e Historia* 32: 73–92.

1993

'De la philosophie à l'anthropologie', Interview with Maurice Godelier. *Société Française* 44: 59–64.

'Comment défendre les sciences de l'homme', Le débat 73:77–80.

'Remarques sur la notion d'idéel et sur quelques-uns de ses usages possibles', in M. Amiot, I. Billiard and L. Brams (eds), Système et paradoxe. Autour de la pensée d'Yves Barel. Paris: Seuil, p.184–94.

'Zahlungsmittel und Reichtum in verschiedenen Gesellschaftstypen und ihre Begegnung am Rande des Kapitalismus', in T. Fillitz, A. Gingrich and G. Rasuly-Paleczek (eds), Kultur, Identität une Macht. Ethnologische Beiträge zu einem Dialog der Kulturen der Welt. Frankfurt am Main: IKO Verlag für Interkulturelle Kommunikation, p.49–70.

'L'anthropologie sociale: quelques perspectives', Annales de la Fondation Fyssen 7: 9–16.

'Lévi-Strauss, Marx and after? A Reappraisal of Structuralist and Marxist Tools for Analyzing Social Logics', Poznan Studies in the Philosophy of the Sciences and the Humanities 33: 105–40.

'O Ocidente, Espelho Partido. Uma avaliaçao parcial da antropologia social, acompanhada de algumas perspectivas', Revista Brasileira de Sciencias Sociais 21(8): 5–21.

'A propos de l'incidence du sexe dans la pratique de terrain' (interview), Journal des Anthropologues 52: 63–75.

'Les femmes et le pouvoir politique. Point de vue d'un anthropologue', in G. Duby and M. Perrot (eds), Femmes et Histoire. Paris: Plon, p.101–12.

'Anthropologie et Sociologie: quel genre de science pratiquons-nous?', Raison Présente 8 ('Les sciences humaines en débat, I): 1–44.

'L'Occident, miroir brisé. Une évaluation partielle de l'anthropologie sociale assortie de quelques perspectives', *Annales E.S.C.* 5: 1183–1207.

'Mirror, Mirror on the Wall...The Once and Future Role of Anthropology: A Tentative Assessment', in R. Borofsky (ed.), *Assessing Cultural Anthropology*. New York: McGraw-Hill, p.97–112.

'L'Ouest et les Autres', Conversation with Rossen Roussev, Deyan Deyanov and Liliana Deyanova, *Kritika e Humanism* 4: 53–57.

'Le Sentiment Entravé', interview with Guitta Pessis-Pasternak, in *Dérives Savantes, ou les paradoxes de la vérité*. Paris: Cerf (coll. Passages), p.71–74. (Initially published in *Le Monde*, 28 August 1983).

'Ordres, classes, Etat chez Marx', in *Visions sur le développement des Etats Européens. Théories et historiographies de l'Etat moderne*, Collection de l'Ecole Française de Rome 171, p.117–35.

'El tiempo en que vivimos', entrevista con M. Godelier. Manola Sepulveda Garza, ENAH, Mexico, 8 p.

'Monnaies et richesses dans divers types de société et leur rencontre à la périphérie du capitalisme', *Les Cahiers du CREA-Ecole Polytechnique* 16: 203–27.

'Is the West the Model for Humankind? The Baruya of New Guinea between Change and Decay', in T. Otto (ed.), *Pacific Islands Trajectories. Five Personal Views*. Canberra, Nijmege: Department of Anthropology, Research School of Pacific Studies, The Australian National University, and The Centre for Pacific Studies, University of Nijmegen, p.56–82.

1994

'L'Ouest et les Autres' (follow up), conversation with Rossen Roussev, Deyan Deyanov and Liliana Deyanova, in *Kritika e Humanism* 5.

'Monnaies et richesses dans divers types de société et leur rencontre à la périphérie du capitalisme', *Actuel Marx* 15: 77–97.

'Deconstruct to Reconstruct: An Interview with Maurice Godelier', *The Journal of the International Institute* 1(2): 4–7.

Preface to P.P. Chamorro and J.H. Ramirez, *Poner Monachil en el Mapa*. Madrid: Eudema.

'Interview de Manola Sepulveda Garza avec Maurice Godelier ', *Concordia, Internationale Zeitschrift für Philosophie* 26: 114–19.

1995

'L'anthropologie sociale est-elle indissolublement liée à l'Occident, sa terre natale?', *Revue Internationale des Sciences Sociales* 143, UNESCO: 141–58. Published in English as 'Is Social Anthropology Indissolubly Linked to the West, its Birthplace?, *International Social Science Journal* 143: 141–58. Published in Spanish as 'Esta la antropologia social indisolublemente atada al Occidente, su tierra natal?', *Revista Internacional de Sciencias Sociales* 143.

'L'Enigme du Don – 1ère partie', *Social Anthropology* 3(1): 15–47.

'L'Enigme du Don – 2ème partie', *Social Anthropology* 3(2): 95–114.

'Qu'est-ce qu'un acte sexuel?', *Revue internationale de psychopathologie* 19: 351–82.

'Machine ventriloque: les Enigmes du Masculin', interview with M. Godelier, *Barca* 4: 197–218.

'Sexualité et société. Propos d'un anthropologue', in N. Bajos, M. Bozon et al. (eds), *Sexualité et Sida, Recherches en sciences sofciales*. Paris: ANRS, Collection Sciences Sociales et Sida, p.117–21.

'El Occidente, espejo roto. Una evaluacion parcial de la antropologia social combinada con algunas perspectivas', *Cuicuilco* 1(3): 59–86.

Prologue to Pablo Palenzuela Chamorro y Javier Hernandez Ramirez, *Estudio antropologico de un proceso de transformacion cultural. Poner Monachil en el mapa*. Universidad de Granada.

1996

'Sexualité et société', in J. Cournut, P. Denis, M. Godelier et al. (eds), *Psychanalyse et sexualité. Questions aux sciences humaines*. Paris: Dunod, p.27–40.

'Sexualité et société', *Journal des Anthropologues* 64–65: 49–63.

'Meurtre du Père ou Sacrifice de la Sexualité?', in M. Godelier and J. Hassoun (eds), *Meurtre du Père, Sacrifice de la sexualité. Approches anthropologiques et psychanalytiques*. Paris: Arcanes 'Les Cahiers d'Arcanes', p.21–52.

'Assassinio del padre. Una riflessione antropologica e comparativa sulla teoria freudiana della cultura e della societa', *Prometeo* 14(53): 14–29.

'L'éducation des Grands Hommes' (interview), in A. Hocquard (ed.), *Eduquer, à quoi bon? Ce qu'en disent philosophes, anthropologues et pedagogues*. Paris: Presses Universitaires de France, p.137–53.

'Is the West the Mirror or the Mirage of the Evolution of Humankind?', in L Arizpe (ed.), *The Cultural Dimensions of Global Change: An Anthropological Approach*. UNESCO Publishing, Culture and Development Series, p.63–75.

'Inceste: "l'interdit original"', in *Le social et les paradoxes du chaos. Entretiens avec Guitta Pessis-Pasternak*. Paris: Desclée de Brouwer.

Commentary to 'Etudes Américanistes et Anthropologie', in S. Gruzinski and N. Wachtel (eds), *Le Nouveau Monde, Mondes Nouveaux. L'expérience américaine*. Paris: Editions Recherche sur les Civilisations, Editions de l'EHESS.

'Servir, vendre ou donner?' Interview by Marie Rebeyrolle, *Les Cahiers de l'ENSPTT* 2: 71–77.

'Anthropologie sociale et histoire locale', *Gradhiva* 20: 83–94 (Spanish translation in *Sociologica* 1, 1996).

1997

'Can Marx Survive the Collapse of Communism or "Real Socialism"?', in Faleh A. Jabar (ed.), *Post-Marxism and the Middle East*. Beirut, London: Saqi Books.

'American Anthropology as Seen from France', *Anthropology Today* 13(1): 3–5.

'Liens de parenté, tabou de l'inceste et polygamie', *Sciences et Avenir*, special issue 'Sexe et Société', avril: 90–93.

'Du passé faut-il faire table-rase?' *L'Homme* 143: 101–16.

with M. Panoff, 'La Production du corps', *La Pensée* 312: 63–75.

Interview with Maurice Godelier, I. *Info Crea* 4 (Centre de Recherches et d'Etudes Anthropologiques, Fac. d'Anthropologie et de Sociologie, Université Lumière Lyon 2): 31–37.

'Simbologica del cuerpo, orden social y logica del poder', Interview with Maurice Godelier by Marie-Odile Marion, in Marie-Odile Marion (ed.), *Simbologicas*. Mexico: Plaza y Valdes Editores, Conacyt, Consejo Nacional para la Ciencia y la Tecnologia.

'Sexualité et société', *Sciences et Avenir* 'Le Sexe' 110.

'Interview de Maurice Godelier sur "L'Enigme du Don"', *Anthoepotes* I(2): 20–24.

1998

'Parenté et famille, réflexions d'un anthropologue', Questions to Maurice Godelier by Jean-Paul Thomas, *Raison Présente* 125: 17–34.

Interview of Maurice Godelier by Nicolas Journet, *Sciences Humaines* 23, 'Un musée pour les Cultures': 19–20.

Interview of Maurice Godelier, II. *Info Crea* 5 (Centre de Recherches et d'Etudes Anthropologiques, Fac. d'Anthropologie et de Sociologie, Université Lumière Lyon 2): 26–32.

'Funciones, formas y figuras del poder politico', *Actas del Congreso Internacional Estructuras de poder en la sociedad Iberica*. Barcelona: Centre Cultural de la Fundacion 'La Caixa', p.13–21.

'Sur le "Don"'. Un interview avec Tetsuji Yamamoto et Nobuko Miyoshi, in Tetsuji Yamamoto (ed.), *Philosophical Designs for a Socio-Cultural Transformation. Beyond Violence and the Modern Era*. Ginza, Boulder CO: EHESC/Rowman & Littlefield Publishers, p.233–47.

'Things You Give or Sell and Things You Don't Give or Sell but Keep Yourselves', *Suomen Antropologi, Journal of the Finnish Anthropological Society* 23(4): 16–28.

'Deconstructions, Changing Perspectives and Progress in Understanding Social Phenomena: An Anthropologist's Point of View', *Folk* 40: 5–22.

1999

'Chefferies et Etats, une approche anthropologique', in P. Ruby (ed.), Les Princes de la Protohistoire et l'émergence de l'Etat, Actes de la table ronde internationale de Naples (1994). Naples, p.19–30.

'Sciences Humaines et Sociales. Des Disciplines de plus en plus Analytiquement Efficaces', *Le journal du CNRS* 119/120: 20–21.

'Introspection, rétrospection, projections', a conversation with Hosham Dawod, *Gradhiva* 26: 1–24.

'Créer de nouveaux musées des arts et civilisations à l'aube du IIIe millénaire', in E. Vaillant and G. Viatte (eds.), *Le musée et les cultures du monde*. Paris, Ecole Nationale du Patrimoine, Les Cahiers de l'Ecole Nationale du Patrimoine n° 5, p.299–304.

'Insights into an Itinerary. An Interview with Maurice Godelier' by Hosham Dawod, *Folk* 41: 5–44.

'Quelles cultures pour quels primates? Définition faible ou définition forte de la culture?', in A. Ducros, F. Joulian and J. Ducros (eds), *La Culture est-elle naturelle?* Paris: Espérance, Collection des Hesperides.

2000

'Le métier de chercheur', *Sciences de l'Homme et de la Société, Lettre du Département CNRS* 58: 12–18.

'Postface', in *Le paradoxe de l'acceptation et du refus*. Paris: Fayard, p.565–70.

'L'anthropologie économique', *Socio-anthropologie* 7(1): 33–49.

'Is Anthropology Still Worth the While? Some Responses to Voices from America', *Ethnos* 65(3): 301–16.

'L'art naît dans le passage de l'imaginaire au symbolique', Interview, *La Recherche*, Hors série 4: 102–104.

'Acerca de las cosas que se dan, de las cosas que se venden y de las que no hay que vender ni dar sino qua hay que guardar. Una reevaluacion critica del Ensayo sobre el Don de Marcel Mauss', *Hispania* LX/1(204): 11–26.

'Things You Don't Give or Sell but Which You Keep: Valuable and Social Objects', in L.-A. Varet, S.-C. Kolm, and J. Mercier Ythier (eds), *The Economics of Reciprocity, Giving and Altruism*. London: MacMillan and New York: St. Martin's Press.

'L'anthropologue et le musée. Entretien avec Maurice Godelier', *Le Débat* January-February: 85–95.

'Introduction', *La nouvelle revue du pacifique. The New Pacific Review* 1(1): 16–18.

'Unir art et savoir', in *Les Arts Premiers au Louvre, Connaissance des Arts* Hors Série 149: 55–62.

'The Disappearance of the "Socialist System": Failure or Confirmation of Marx's Views on the Transition from One Form of Production and Society to Another?', in W. Bonefeld and K. Psychopedis (eds), *The Politics of Change. Globalization, Ideology and Critique*. Hampshire and New York: Palgrave Macmillan, p.149–72.

Godelier, M. and J. Kerchache. *Chefs-d'œuvre et civilisations: Afrique, Asie, Océanie, Amériques (les Arts premiers au Louvre)*. CDRom. Paris: Réunion des Musées Nationaux.

2001

'Pratiques sexuelles et ordre social', *La Recherche* Hors Série 6: 98–102.

'Formes et fonctions du pouvoir politique. A propos des concepts de tribu, ethnie et Etat', *La Pensée* 325: 9–19.

'Les sciences humaines et sociales en France', *La Revue Parlementaire* October 2001: 14–15.

'A propos d'éthique et d'entreprise', *Le MAG* (le Magazine du Groupe Pinault-Printemps-Redoute) 44(2): 28–31.

2002

'L'imaginaire, le symbolique et le réel', Interview with Maurice Godelier, *Sciences Humaines* 35: 20–22.

'Surrogates for Humans and for Gods', in M. Jeudy-Ballini and B. Juillerat (eds), *People and Things. Social Mediations in Oceania*. Durham, North Carolina: Carolina Academic Press, p.79–102.

'Briser le miroir du soi', in C. Ghasarian (ed.), *De l'ethnographie à l'anthropologie réflexive. Nouveaux terrains, nouvelles pratiques, nouveaux enjeux*. Paris: Colin, p.193–212.

'Maurice Godelier, des Papous dans la tête', *La recherche* 352: 21–22.

2003

'Plaidoyer pour les sciences de l'Homme et de la Société', in *Quel avenir pour la recherche? Cinquante savants s'engagent*. Paris: Flammarion, p.80–84.

'Un homme et une femme ne suffisent pas pour faire un enfant: analyse comparative de quelques théories culturelles de la procréation et de la conception', *Ethnologies Comparées, Revue électronique semestrielle* (6): http://alor.univ-montp3.fr/cerce/revue.htm

'Anthropologie et recherches féministes. Perspectives et rétrospectives', in J. Laufer, C. Marry and M. Maruani (eds), *Le travail du genre. Les sciences sociales du travail à l'épreuve des différences de sexe.* Paris: La Découverte/ MAGE, p.23–34.

'Objects and Societies. Combining the Pleasures of Art and Knowledge for the Museum Publics', in M. Godelier, *Is Social Anthropology Indissolubly Linked to the West, its Birthplace? A Series of Special Lectures of Distinguised Scholars.* Edited by KARK & DWF, Korea.

2004

'Some Remarks on the Hard Core of Soft Sciences', in *Knowledge and the World: Challenges beyond the Science Wars.* Berlin, Heidelberg, New York: Springer Verlag and Universität Bielefeld.

'An Anthropologist among the Macaques', in B. Thierry, M. Singh and W. Kaumanns (eds), Macaque Societies: A Model for the Study of Social Organization. Cambridge: Cambridge University Press.

'Quelques remarques sur les noyaux durs des sciences molles. Un exemple pris dans l'anthropologie', Natures, Sciences, Sociétés 12: 179–83. (Online at http://www.edpsciences.org/articles/nss/pdf/2004/02/nss4206.pdf)

2005

'Aspects Internationaux des Sciences Humaines et Sociales', Introduction to M.-C. Hoock-Demarle, *La Galaxie Diderot. Les lettres et sciences humaines à Paris 7–Denis Diderot.* Paris: Editions Syllepse.

'Représentations de la famille: le point de vue d'un anthropologue', *La Lettre de la Fondation pour l'Innovation Politique* 9: 2–3.

'Il faut toujours plus qu'un homme et une femme pour faire un enfant', *Médecine Sciences* 21: 99–101.

'Femmes, sexe ou genre?', in M. Maruani (ed.), *Femmes, genre et sociétés. L'état des savoirs.* Paris: La Découverte.

'De la vieillesse magnifiée à la vieillesse marginalisée et même expulsée du monde des vivants', in M. Godelier, F. Jullien and J. Maïla, *Le grand âge de la vie.* Paris: PUF and Fondation Eisai, p.13–47.

'Une femme et un homme ne suffisent pas à faire un enfant', *Sciences de l'Homme et Sociétés* 81: 11–17.

'Un homme et une femme ne suffisent pas à faire un enfant', interview with Maurce Godelier, *La Lettre de l'Enfance et de l'Adolescence* 59: 15–24.

'Controverse. Autour du livre de Maurice Godelier "Métamorphoses de la Parenté"', *Travail Genre et Sociétés* 14: 149–96.

'Aspects and Stages of the Westernization of a Tribal Society', in S. Tcherkézoff and F. Douaire-Marsaudon (eds), *The Changing South Pacific. Identities and Transformations.* Canberra: Pandanus Books.

'La parenté et l'histoire. Entretien avec Maurice Godelier', *Afrique & Histoire* 4: 247–81.

'Parenté, familles, interdits sexuels', http://www.canal-u.tv/

2006

'Die Vision: Einheit von Kunst und Wissenschaft im Musée du Quai Branly', in C. Grewe (ed.), *Die Schau des Fremden: Ausstellungskonzepte zwischen Kunst, Kommerz und Wissenschaft*. Stuttgart: Franz Steiner Verlag, p.215–30.

'Mythes et légitimations idéologiques de la domination masculine', in C. Vidal (ed.), *Féminin, Masculin, mythes et idéologies*. Paris: Belin.

'Actualité de la Parenté. Dans une perspective anthropologique', *Informations Sociales* 131: 22–28.

'Les domaines des Sciences Humaines et Sociales', *Magazine Parlementaires de France* 9: 35–36.

'L'imaginaire et le symbolique n'épuisent pas le réel', Interview of Maurice Godelier by Marie Rose Moro and Lucie Truffaut, *L'Autre: Cliniques, cultures et sociétés* 7(2): 185–92.

'Une expérience africaine. Entretien avec Maurice Godelier par Philippe Geslin', *Ethnographiques.org* 10 (online).

'Was Mauss nicht gesagt hat: Dinge, die man verschenkt, Dinge, die man verkauft, une solche, die man weder verkauft noch verschenkt, sondern für sich behält', in M. Rosenberger and F. Reisinger (eds), *Geschenkt – umsonst gegeben? Gabe une Tausch in Ethik, Gesellschaft une Religion*. Frankfurt am Main: Peter Lang, p.191–218.

'Préface' to the second French edition of S. Price, *Arts Primitifs, Regards Civilisés. Paris: Ecole Nationale Supérieure des Beaux-Arts*, p.9–16.

'Nous avons plus que jamais besoin des sciences sociales', interview of M. Godelier by T. Hazebroucq and J. Lojkine, *Nouvelles Fondations* 2: 20–27.

'Qu'est-ce qui fait une société?', *Sciences Humaines* 5: 66–70.

'Trois commentaires', in P. Brunel, C. Attias-Donfut, J. Morval and Jacques Lévy, *Penser l'espace pour lire la vieillesse*. Paris: PUF.

2007

'Entretien avec Maurice Godelier', by Jean-François Bert, *Le Portique* 19: 107–17.

'Entretien avec Maurice Godelier dans le cadre du débat "La Loi doit-elle tout autoriser?"', *Le Pèlerin* 6487: 10–12.

'Familles: qui transmet quoi?', *La Gazelle* 7: 1.

'Enregistrement audio de la présentation de Maurice Godelier lors de la journée d'hommage à Charles Bettelheim', http://cemi.ehess.fr/document. php?id=1085.

'Débat: Pouvoir et sociétés sans écrit: quelles sources?' Discussion between Patrice Brun and Maurice Godelier, *Archéopages* 19: 54–59.

'Reflexiones sobre el poder, las jerarquias y la teoria social', Interview of M. Godelier by G. Gil. *Ava*, revista de antropologia (Posadas, Misiones, Argentine), 10.

'Carte blanche à Maurice Godelier', *Sciences Mag* 2: 11.

'The Asian Production Method: Stimulating Concepts with Limited Analytic Meaning', *Terra Humana* 1: 3–18 (in Russian).

'Face à la rétraction des possibles', *Quand est-ce que je vieillis?* Paris: Edition de la Fondation EISAI, P.U.F.: 71–83.

'La famille est au fondement des individus, pas des sociétés', interview of M. Godelier, *Carnets de santé* article 137. http://www.carnetsdesante.fr/spip. php?article137.

'Au fondement des sociétés humaines: entretien avec Maurice Godelier', by Thomas Perrot. http://www.nonfiction.fr/.

2008

'Death of a Few Celebrated Truths and Others that Are Worth Restating' (Inaugural Raymond Firth Lecture), *Journal de la Société des Océanistes* 125(2): 181–92.

'Maurice Godelier', in A. Dhoquois (ed.), *Comment je suis devenu Ethnologue*. Paris: Editions Le Cavalier Bleu, p.111–31.

'Entretien avec Silvain Sismondi', *Paris Notre Dame, Journal du Diocèse de Paris* 28 February 2008.

'Qui suis-je?', *extract of the Conférence de Carême, La Vie* 28 février 2008: 18–19.

'Au coeur des rapports sociaux: l'imaginaire dont les archéologues ne perçoivent que les restes symboliques', *Archéopages*, Hors Série "ConstructionS de l'archéologie": 81–83.

'Préface', in N. Bajos et M. Bozon (eds), *La Sexualité en France. Pratiques, Genre et Santé*. Paris: La Découverte, p.9–16.

'L'anthropologie, par Maurice Godelier', *Qui dites-vous que je suis?* Paris: Editions Parole et Silence, p.75–86.

'Freud et l'anthropologie: inspiration ou prétexte?', *L'Autre (Cliniques, Cultures et Sociétés)* 9(2): 255–70.

'Préface' to *Enquête sur la Sexualité en France. Pratiques, Genre et Santé*. Paris: INSERM, INED, ANRS and Ed. La Découverte.

'Pratiquer l'anthropologie, c'est se soumettre à l'ascèse', *Sciences et Avenir* July 2008: 46–49.

'Des rites d'initiation de Nouvelle-Guinée aux attentats des Twin Towers. L'anthropologie à la recherche des fondements des sociétés concrètes', in *Pensées pour le Nouveau Siècle*. Paris: Fayard, p.131–56.

'La référence à qui? A quoi? Comment? en anthropologie', *Les Cahiers du Musée des Confluences* 1: 9–18.

2009

'What Are the Social Relations that Make a Set of Human Groups and Individuals a *Society?*', *Suomen Antropologi, Journal of the Finnish Anthropological Society* 34(1): 5–18.

'From Imaginary Realities to Social Realities; A Conversation with Maurice Godelier', *Suomen Antropologi, Journal of the Finnish Anthropological Society* 34(1): 62–69.

'Comprendre l'altérité sociale et existentielle d'autrui', *Journal des Anthropologues* 116–17: 35–54.

NOTES ON CONTRIBUTORS

John Barker is Professor and Department Head of Anthropology at the University of British Columbia. Over the past three decades, he has published extensively on Christian missions and contemporary Christianity amongst indigenous peoples in Oceania and British Columbia, with forays into Christian creationism, the history of anthropological fieldwork, and Melanesian art. His edited works include *Christianity in Oceania* (University Press of America, 1990), *Regional Histories in Oceania* (with Dan Jorgensen, special issue of Oceania, 1996), *At Home with the Bella Coola Indians* (with Douglas Cole, UBC Press, 2003), and *The Anthropology of Morality in Melanesia and Beyond* (Ashgate, 2007). His recent research has focused upon the impact of the international environmental movement on Oceanic societies on the subject of *Ancestral Lines: The Maisin of Papua New Guinea and the Fate of the Rainforest* (University of Toronto Press, 2008).

Robert H. Barnes is Professor of Social Anthropology at the University of Oxford and Faculty Fellow of St Antony's College. He specializes in Indonesia and has long experience in eastern Indonesia, but he has also published on native American peoples. His principal publications are: *Kédang: a study of the collective thought of an eastern Indonesian people*, with a foreword by Rodney Needham (Oxford: The Clarendon Press, 1974); *Two Crows denies it: a history of controversy in Omaha sociology* (Lincoln, Nebraska: University of Nebraska Press, 1984 and 2005); (with Andrew Gray and Benedict Kingsbury) *Indigenous Peoples of Asia*, Monographs and Occasional Paper Series, Number 48 (Ann Arbor, Michigan: Association for Asian Studies); and *Sea Hunters of Indonesia: Fishers and Weavers of Lamalera* (Oxford: Clarendon Press, 1996).

Laurent Dousset is Associate Professor (Maître de Conférences) at the EHESS (School for Advanced Studies in Social Sciences) and is director of the CREDO (Centre for Research and Documentation on Oceania, Marseilles). His has carried out research in Aboriginal Australia, in particular in the Western Desert area, investigating kinship, social organization, discourses about first contact situations, social transformations as well as working in the domain of legal anthropology. He has also developed several IT knowledge systems for the social sciences. Among his publications are *Kinship and Change in Aboriginal Australia* (an edited issue of Anthropological Forum, with McConvell and Powell, 2002), *Assimilating Identities: Social Networks and the Diffusion of Sections* (Oceania Monographs, 2005) and *Mythes, missiles et cannibales. Le récit d'un premier contact en Autralie* (Société des Océanistes, 2011). He is currently preparing the biography of an Aboriginal woman.

Jonathan Friedman is Directeur d'études EHESS and Distinguished Professor Department of Anthropology at the University of California San Diego. He has undertaken research on Upland Southeast Asia, the Pacific and to a lesser extent Central Africa. He has contributed to the establishment of what is today called global systemic anthropology as well as making earlier contributions to the debates on Marxist and Materialist anthropology in the 1970s. The research on global systems led to multidisciplinary cooperation in research projects and to a number of publications together with political scientists, economists, sociologists and archaeologists. Among his published books are *System, Structure and Contradiction in the Evolution of 'Asiatic' Social Formations* (Altamira-Sage, 1998, originally 1979), *Cultural Identity and Global Process* (Sage, 1994), *Modernity and identity* (with S. Lash, Blackwell, 1992), *Melanesian Modernities* (with J. Carrier, Lund University Press, 1996), *Worlds on the move: Globalization, migration and cultural security* (with S. Randeira, Tauris, 2004), *World System History: The Science of long term change* (with R. Denemark, B. Gills and G. Modelski, Routledge, 2000); *Globalization, the state and violence* (Altamira, 2002), *La Quotidianità del Systema Globale* (Bruno Mondadori, 2005) and *Hegemonic Declines: Past and Present* (with C. Chase-Dunn, Paradigm Press, 2005).

Jack (John) Rankine Goody, born in 1919, was educated at St John's College, Cambridge. During the Second World War he served in the near East, Italy and Germany. After the war he spent five years in Ghana during which he carried out anthropological fieldwork, and later worked in India (Gujarat) and China. He has written extensively on literacy, the family, the Bagre myth of the LoDagaa, and on cuisine and the culture of flowers. His most recent books include *Ghana Observed, Africa Reconsidered* (Institute of African Studies, Legon, Ghana, 2007), *The Theft of History* (Cambridge University Press, 2007), *Renaissances: The One or the Many?* (Cambridge University Press, forthcoming), *The Eurasian Miracle* (Polity Press, forthcoming), and *Myth, Ritual and Orality* (forthcoming).

Gilbert Herdt is Professor and Founder of the Department of Sexuality Studies at San Francisco State University, and also Founder and Director Emeritus of the National Sexuality Resource Center (NSRC). Previously he has taught at Stanford University (1979–1985) and the University of Chicago (1985–1998). Gil has conducted major fieldwork in Papua New Guinea (1974–1993), and Chicago (1986–1989). Dr Herdt has been a pre-doctoral Fulbright scholar to Australia (1974–1977), Individual Postdoc NIMH Fellow (1977–1980), and Guggenheim Fellow (1997–1998), and has received grants from the NIH, NEH, Spencer Foundation, Wenner-Gren Foundation, Ford Foundation, etc. Herdt has published 35 scientific books, anthologies and monographs, and more than 110 scientific peer-reviewed journal articles, and chapters, beginning with *Guardians of the Flutes*, 1981, his best known book.

Margaret Jolly is an Australian Research Council Laureate Fellow and Professor in Anthropology, Gender and Cultural Studies and Pacific Studies in the School of Culture, History and Language in the College of Asia and the Pacific. She is an historical anthropologist who has written extensively on gender in the Pacific, exploratory voyages and travel writing, missions and contemporary Christianity, maternity and sexuality, cinema and art. Her books include *Women of the Place, Kastom, Colonialism and Gender in Vanuatu* (Chur: Harwood Academic Publishers, 1994); *Sites of Desire, Economies of Pleasure: Sexualities in Asia and the Pacific*, edited with Lenore Manderson (Chicago: University of Chicago Press, 1997); *Maternities and Modernities: Colonial and Postcolonial Experiences in Asia and the Pacific*, edited with Kalpana Ram (Cambridge: Cambridge University Press, 1998); *Borders of Being: Citizenship, Fertility and Sexuality in Asia and the Pacific*, edited with Kalpana Ram (Ann Arbor: University of Michigan Press, 2001); *Oceanic Encounters: Exchange, Desire, Violence*, edited with Serge Tcherkézoff and Darrell Tryon (Canberra: ANU E-Press, 2009).

Mark S. Mosko is Professor of Anthropology in the Research School of Pacific and Asian Studies at the Australian National University and a Fellow of the Academy of Social Sciences in Australia. On the basis of four years of ethnographic fieldwork among the North Mekeo peoples of Papua New Guinea, he has authored *Quadripartite Structures* (Cambridge University Press 1985) and *Gifts that Change* (Berghahn Books, forthcoming) as well as some fifty scholarly articles and book chapters which address indigenous social organization, personhood, agency, myth, ritual, chieftainship, gender, exchange theory, Christianity, and social change. He also co-edited *Transformations of Hierarchy* (with Margaret Jolly, *History and Anthropology* vol.7, 1994) and *On the Order of Chaos* (with Fred Damon, Berghahn Books, 2005).

He is currently conducting ethnographic research at Omarakana in the Trobriand Islands, the site of Malinowski's path-breaking research. His recent article, 'Partible Penitents: Dividual Personhood and Christian Practice in Melanesia and the West', was awarded the 2008 Curl Prize for Best Essay by the Royal Anthropological Institute of Great Britain and Ireland.

Joel Robbins is Professor and Chair of Anthropology at the University of California, San Diego. His work focuses on cultural change, the anthropology of Christianity, the globalization of Pentecostalism, and the study of language, exchange, and ritual. Along with a number of articles on these topics, he is the author of the book *Becoming Sinners: Christianity and Moral Torment in a Papua New Guinea Society* (2004) and is co-editor of the journal *Anthropological Theory*.

Serge Tcherkézoff is Professor of Anthropology (directeur d'études) at the School for Advanced Studies in Social Sciences (EHESS) in Paris-Marseille. He has founded, with Maurice Godlier and Pierre Lemonnier, the CREDO (Centre for Research and Documentation on Oceania), and is a research unit member of CNRS, EHESS, and the University of Provence. He is also associated to the Australian National University and to Canterbury University. After working in the 1970s on African ethnography, he has been engaged in fieldwork in Polynesia since the early 1980s. Besides his publications on the theory of anthropology and holism since the early 1980s, and on the transformations of the Samoan society in the 1980–1990s, his more recent books bring together the results of his field studies and an ethnohistorical critique of European narratives about early encounters in Polynesia (mainly Tahiti and Samoa). He is currently working on two books: the study of Maussian holistic models of the gift applied to the Samoan case, and a critical reading of Louis Dumont's models.

Polly Wiessner is Professor of Anthropology at the University of Utah and received her PhD in Anthropology and Archaeology from the University of Michigan in 1977. She has conducted research among the !Kung (Ju/'hoansi) Bushmen of the Kalahari Desert over the past thirty-five years on subsistence, reciprocity, social security systems to reduce risk, and style and social information in material culture. For the past twenty-five years she has also carried ethnohistorical studies among the Enga of highland New Guinea, tracing developments in warfare, ritual, and exchange that occurred from the time from the introduction of the sweet potato some three hundred years ago until the present. She is currently working on contemporary issues in Enga: the breakdown of traditional marriage, warfare with high-powered weapons and how people are updating customary law to confront the problems of a rapidly changing world. She has published numerous books and articles including *Food and the Status Quest* (with W. Schiefenhoevel, 1997), *Historical Vines: Enga Networks of Exchange, Ritual and Warfare in Papua New Guinea* (with Akii Tumu, 1998).

INDEX

King, C. 56, 64n5
Kinsey, A. 88, 89
Kinsey, A. *et al.* 88, 100
kinship 191–203
  alliance 191–2, 202–3
  ascription through kin relationships
    195–6
  asymmetric prescriptive
    terminologies 200, 201
  Austronesian languages 201
  bifurcation 200
  categories and types 199–201
  China, relationship terminologies in
    202
  classificatory works 199–201
  cognatic categories 192, 201
  collectivity 196
  corporate groups 193–4
  corporate organization 193
  corporateness and descent, relation
    between 195
  corporations, systems of 191, 192
  Crow-Omaha descent systems 198
  definitional criteria 193–6
  definitions 191–2
  descent 191
    definitions of 196–7
  descent groups 191, 192, 193,
    195–6
    double descent group systems
      194–5
    restriction to unilineal
  institutions 197
  descent rules 195–6
    application of 198
  Dravidian terminologies 199, 200,
    201–2, 203
  Gilyak of Siberia 201
  group membership 194
  Indonesia, descent groups in 193,
    197, 201
  Kachin of Burma 200, 201
  kinship movement, gender and 133–
    4
  leadership, authority and corporate
    groups 193–4
  Leiden School 195
  marriage and 27, 33, 36–8, 191–2,
    202–3
  matrifiliation 196
  matrilinear groups 192
  matrimonial alliances 191–2, 202–
    3
  metamorphoses of, Godelier's study
    of 191–2
  Mursi descent groups 194
  Nuer lineages 193, 195
  Omaha of Nebraska 198–9, 201
  patrifiliation 196

  patrilinear groups 192, 193, 195,
    196
  perpetuation 197
  property transmission within groups
    194–5
  recruitment 197
  relations (Enga of Papua New
    Guinea) 11–12, 18, 67, 68, 70,
    74, 82, 83
  relationship terminologies 198–201,
    202
  Samo of Burkina-Faso 201
  Samo-Omaha descent comparisons
    198–9
  segmentary decent 196
  structures 225
  Talensi lineages 194–5
  Tamils of South India 200
  terminologies and systems 198–201
  Toba Batak of Sumatra 201
  unilineal descent groups 193
  unilineal institutions 192, 197
  World Ethnographic Sample 192
Kirch, P. 161
Kolsus, T. 147n21
Kon, I. 97
Kroeber, A.L. 199
Kryukov, M.V. 201, 202, 203n3, 203n6
Kulick, D. and Wilson, M. 89, 99
Kuper, A. 193
kwaimatnie (sacred objects of the
  Baruya) 35, 158
Kyakas, A. and Wiessner, P. 69, 70, 75,
  76, 84n3
Kyalae, L. 84, 84n2

Lacey, R. 68
Lang, S. 99
Langness, L.L. 91
language ideologies
  exchange in Melanesian societies
    and 26, 27, 29–30, 31, 32, 34,
    35, 39–41
  in West and in Melanesia, keeping
    and giving in 30–33, 39, 40–41
  language as ideology 9
Layard, J. 91, 110, 113, 118, 120, 132,
  138, 139
Leach, E.R. 4, 185n5, 195, 196, 197
leaders *(kamongo)* 69, 72
leadership
  authority and corporate groups
    193–4
  link between the inalienable and the
    alienable 16–17
  modes of 162
  modes of exchange and 155
  new great men and 58–61
  Oceanic leadership 47
  types of 61

Rumsey, A. and Robbins, J. 32, 40
Russian Geographical Society 112
Rutherford, D. 63

Sabu of Papua New Guinea *see* Kawo
    and Sabu
sacred objects
    the inalienable and destruction of
        12–13, 69, 73
    societal guidance from the
        inalienable and 67–8
    society and 38–9, 40–41
Sahlins, M. 10, 47, 54, 159, 161, 162,
    185n1, 185n2
salt-makers *(tsaimaye)* 158
Sambia Anga-speaking society 90–91,
    92
Samo of Burkina-Faso 201
Samo-Omaha descent comparisons
    198–9
Samoa, chiefly succession in 159–60
Saussure, F. de 28, 29, 30
Sauvage, A. 227
Scaglion, R. 158, 159, 161, 185n1
Scheffler, H.W. 196
Schieffelin, B. 30, 31
Schieffelin, B., Woolard, K.A. and
    Kroskrity, P.V. 29
Schwimmer, E. 47, 56
scientific positivism 90
Searle, J.R. 31
secrecy
    epistemology of 26
    exchange and, among Urapmin of
        Papua New Guinea 33–8
    Godelier and
        cosmological importance of 33
        social relations and 38–9
    problem of 25–6
    social life and 27, 32–3
segmentary decent 196
segregated dwelling patterns, suspension
    of 119–20
self-identification 224
Seligmann, C. 160, 163, 164, 165
Selwyn, G. 116, 117
semantic anthropology 215
sex
    relocation of meanings and practices
        of 103–4
    role of 14
    sex role temperament 88–9
sex for money *(pasinja meri)*, exchange
    of 76, 79–80
sexology 87
    contemporary sexuality and,
        historical view 88–90
    origins of 103

sexology studies 14
sexual cultures
    distinctiveness of 101
    possibility of homogeneity in 98
sexual diversity, work on 99
sexual lifeways 101
Sexual Nature, Sexual Culture (Abramson,
    P. and Pinkerton, S.) 92–4
sexual revolution of 1960s 89–90
sexual science 87
sexuality
    material and immaterial relations in
        Vanuatu and 128
    in society, Godelier's work on 86–7
sexuality studies 86–104
    AIDS/HIV work 87, 96, 98, 99
    'Americanization' of 89
    biological essentialism 87
    biopsychological/developmental
        perspective 101–2
    convergence, sexual cultures and
        sexual lifeways 100–102
    cultural constructionism 87
    cultural genitals 92
    democratization of sexuality 97–8
    early history 86–7
    European sexology 89
    feminist psychoanalytic perspectives
        91
    future of, past in relation to 97–100,
        102–4
    gender, concept of 88–9
    hermaphrodite bodies 92
    human rights, rhetoric of sexuality
        as 99
    identity 102
    instrumental changes 89–90
    interdisciplinarity 87
    *Male and Female: A Study of the Sexes
        in a Changing World* (Mead, M.) 90
    man's house, social institution of
        91–2
    medical orientation 86–7
    migrations, impact of 99
    New Guinea anthropology, historic
        place of 90–91
    nineteenth-century perspective
        86–7
    personality and culture studies 91
    repression among the Sambia 90–91
    reproductive technologies 99
    Sambia Anga-speaking society 90–
        91, 92
    scientific positivism 90
    sex
        relocation of meanings and
            practices of 103–4
        role of 14

www.ingramcontent.com/pod-product-compliance
Lightning Source LLC
Chambersburg PA
CBHW060029030426
42334CB00019B/2240